Crisis Patient Prioritisation and the Law: The Pandemic Experience

Crisis Patient Prioritisation and the Law: The Pandemic Experience

Massimo Foglia
Tomáš Holčapek
Martin Šolc
Petr Šustek
(eds)

Wolters Kluwer

Citation:

Massimo Foglia, Tomáš Holčapek, Martin Šolc, Petr Šustek (eds) *Crisis Patient Prioritisation and the Law: The Pandemic Experience* (Kluwer Law International 2024)

Published by:
Kluwer Law International B.V.
PO Box 316
2400 AH Alphen aan den Rijn
The Netherlands
E-mail: lrs-sales@wolterskluwer.com
Website: www.wolterskluwer.com/en/solutions/kluwerlawinternational

Sold and distributed by:
Wolters Kluwer Legal & Regulatory U.S.
920 Links Avenue
Landisville, PA 17538
United States of America
E-mail: customer.service@wolterskluwer.com

ISBN 9789403529486
MI# 10121552-0001
Web PDF ISBN 9789403529684
MI# Web PDF 10121568-0001
e-ISBN 9789403529585
MI# e-Pub 10121560-0001

This book was written with support from the state budget by the Technology Agency of the Czech Republic under the ETA Programme for Applied Research, Experimental Development and Innovation in Social Sciences and Humanities.

TABLE OF CONTENTS

List of Authors VII
Introduction VIII
National Report Form (Questionnaire) X

LEGAL-ETHICAL GROUNDS OF CRISIS PATIENT PRIORITISATION 1
Martin Šolc

AUSTRIA 17
Karl Stöger

BRAZIL 41
Flávia Cambraia and Marcelo Chiavassa de Mello Paula Lima

CZECH REPUBLIC 57
Tomáš Holčapek

FRANCE 75
Maxime Lassalle

ITALY 91
Roberto Pucella and Massimo Foglia

PORTUGAL 105
Carla Barbosa

SERBIA 129
Marija Karanikić Mirić

SOUTH AFRICA 155
Bernard Wessels

SPAIN 173
Albert Ruda

SWITZERLAND 197
Dr. Inesa Fausch

UNITED STATES 217
Lance Gable and Marie Carp and Allison Tuohy

CONCLUDING REMARKS 247
Petr Šustek

Index 256

LIST OF AUTHORS

Carla Barbosa (Portugal; University of Coimbra)

Flávia Cambraia (Brazil; Mackenzie Presbyterian University)

Marie Carp (USA; Wayne State University)

Marcelo Chiavassa de Mello Paula Lima (Brazil; Mackenzie Presbyterian University)

Inesa Fausch (Switzerland; Swiss Institute of Comparative Law)

Massimo Foglia (Italy; University of Bergamo)

Lance Gable (USA; Wayne State University)

Tomáš Holčapek (Czech Republic; Charles University)

Marija Karanikić Mirić (Serbia; University of Belgrade)

Maxime Lassalle (France; University of Burgundy)

Roberto Pucella (Italy; University of Bergamo)

Albert Ruda (Spain; University of Girona)

Martin Šolc (Czech Republic; Charles University)

Karl Stöger (Austria; University of Vienna)

Petr Šustek (Czech Republic; Charles University)

Allison Tuohy (USA; Wayne State University)

Bernard Wessels (South Africa; Stellenbosch University)

INTRODUCTION

On April 15, 2021, the Centre for Medical Law at the Charles University (Faculty of Law) in Prague, and the Department of Law of the University of Bergamo organized an international conference on “Legal Liability for Allocation of Scarce Resources in Health Care in the Covid-19 Pandemic”.

Both old and charming medieval cities have sadly also something tragic in common: they have witnessed one of the deadliest waves of Covid-19 in today’s pandemic. In Italy, Bergamo became a symbol of the suffering and resistance of Italian people in early Spring 2020. The Czech Republic managed to contain the virus very successfully at first, only to become one of the world’s worst hit countries since Autumn of the same year.

The need to prioritise patients for the use of scarce resources such as medical devices or intensive care beds was similar in some hospitals in both countries. However, as we discussed the options provided by the law, we found out that they differ significantly not only between Italy and the Czech Republic, but among many countries which fight the pandemic. That prompted us to organise an international conference where experts from all around the world will share their experience and ideas on this matter.

In many countries, there is however, a pressing need to clarify what health professionals and hospitals can and cannot do. While the law takes various approaches in different countries, legal uncertainty is an all-too-common feature. If we learnt from each other and moved forward towards solving the unsolvable questions of patient triage, this conference would fulfil its aim. We trust this post-conference publication is another step in accomplishing this common purpose.

Prioritisation of patients in the situation of scarce resources, especially concerning intensive care, has been a crucial issue in many countries during the Covid-19 pandemic. The conference participants did exchange their countries’ experiences and approaches, promoting the understanding of the complex problem and finding new ways of its solution. The research aims were to provide a rich and detailed description of existing systems of liability for allocation of scarce resources in selected countries, to investigate the interactions between those systems, and to make a comparison of their solutions. The project also sought to explore the political choice to be made by national lawmakers for addressing identical legal and social problems.

National reporters were asked to answer specific and crucial questions, such as:

1. What are the criteria for the allocation of scarce health care resources in your country?
2. What values are the allocation criteria based on?

3. In what type(s) of document(s) are the allocation criteria set? Is it in binding or non-binding guidelines, in the law, or in another type of document?
4. Are providers of health care obliged by the law to provide (urgent) care to all patients? If the answer is yes, are there any legally recognised exceptions from this duty?
5. On what legal basis is it possible to apply the allocation criteria in practice?
6. What level of legal certainty do the health professionals and the health care providers have when applying the allocation criteria?
7. What are the civil and criminal liability implications of allocation of scarce health care resources? Have there already been any related legal suits and/or criminal proceedings?

The results of the research comprise eleven *country reports* (Austria, Brazil, Czech Republic, France, Italy, Portugal, Serbia, South Africa, Spain, Switzerland, USA), which are based on a common set of headings (see Annex below), and a concluding set of *case studies.* The choice of countries was designed to allow the comparison of the different major legal traditions in Europe and spread of countries from elsewhere in the world, the latter through the inclusion in the study of USA, Australia, Brazil and South Africa. The selection also reflected the need to ensure different approaches to allocation criteria and liability issues were adequately represented.

Massimo Foglia, Tomáš Holčapek, Petr Šustek, Martin Šolc

NATIONAL REPORT FORM (QUESTIONNAIRE)

A. Questionnaire

1. What are the criteria for the allocation of scarce health care resources in your country?
2. What values are the allocation criteria based on?
3. In what type(s) of document(s) are the allocation criteria set? Is it in binding or non-binding guidelines, in the law, or in another type of document?
4. Are providers of health care obliged by the law to provide (urgent) care to all patients? If the answer is yes, are there any legally recognised exceptions from this duty?
5. On what legal basis is it possible to apply the allocation criteria in practice?
6. What level of legal certainty do the health professionals and the health care providers have when applying the allocation criteria?
7. What are the civil and criminal liability implications of allocation of scarce health care resources? Have there already been any related legal suits and/or criminal proceedings?

B. Case studies

Case 1

As a result of a rapid worsening of the epidemiological situation, the material and personal capacities have been drastically overloaded in all the hospitals in the country. Within just a few minutes, ambulances transport ten patients to one particular hospital's emergency unit. The patients all need admission to the hospital, preferably to the intensive care unit (ICU). However, only two beds are available there. Other hospitals are overwhelmed too, so it is not possible to transport patients to any of them. All of the ten newly coming patients suffer from COVID-19; they have breathing difficulties, fast-rising fever, and decreasing oxygen saturation. Nevertheless, they differ in age, comorbidities, clinical fragility, and other factors.

Theoretically, the eight patients who cannot be admitted to beds can be placed in improvised settings in the hospital corridors, laying on gurneys or mattresses on the floor. Nevertheless, it will be impossible to provide them with the care they need.

Evaluation of the case

- What criteria can be used to choose the patients who will be admitted to the beds (i.e. what are the possible allocation criteria)?
- What legal consequences can this decision have for the health professionals and the hospital? How strong is their legal certainty that there will be no adverse legal consequences if they follow the above-mentioned criteria?
- What legal defences could the health professionals and the hospital use against a civil lawsuit and/or criminal prosecution for the allocation decision?

Additional questions

- Would it be legally permissible to lower the standard of care provided to all patients in order to provide at least basic decent care to the newly admitted patients who are placed in the hospital corridors? To what extent?

Case 2

Two patients in an ICU are suffering from COVID-19. After admission to the hospital, they were provided with the high-flow nasal oxygen therapy (HFNO). During one night, the condition of both patients starts to worsen rapidly. At dawn, it is clear that neither of them will survive without artificial ventilation. However, there is just one ventilator available.

Evaluation of the case

- What criteria can be used to choose which of the two patients will be provided with artificial ventilation and which one will be left without it, possibly to die?
- What legal consequences can this decision have for the health professionals and the hospital? How strong is their legal certainty that there will be no adverse legal consequences if they follow the above-mentioned criteria?
- What legal defences could the health professionals and the hospital use against a civil lawsuit and/or criminal prosecution for the allocation decision?

Additional question

- If the allocation criteria specified in your answer to the first question to this case consisted of the patients' clinicical features (such as their age, clinical fragility, etc.), please identify what criteria could be used for the allocation decision if all the relevant clinical features of both patients were practically the same?

Case 3

There is a single extracorporeal membrane oxygenation (ECMO) device in the hospital. It is currently being used for an 84-year-old patient suffering from COVID-19, with diabetes as an underlying disease, clinical frailty score (CFS) 6–7 (moderate to severe frailty). It is possible that the patient will survive and will be discharged from the hospital if the ECMO treatment is continued. However, a younger COVID-19 patient is admitted to the hospital. This new patient is 51 years old, otherwise healthy, but her health condition has been rapidly deteriorating. Soon she will most likely need ECMO to survive.

Evaluation of the case

- Can it be legally permissible for the hospital staff to discontinue the ECMO treatment of the older patient and provide palliative care to her in order to save the younger and healthier patient's life? Please keep in mind that the older patient could survive if the treatment continued, but her chances may be lower than those of the younger patient.
- If the answer to the first question is positive, what specific criteria can be used in clinical decision-making regarding replacing one patient with another with respect to a particular treatment unavailable for all?
- What legal consequences can this decision have for the health professionals and the hospital? How strong is their legal certainty that there will be no adverse legal consequences if they follow the above-mentioned criteria?
- What legal defences could the health professionals and the hospital use against a civil lawsuit and/or criminal prosecution for the allocation decision?

Additional question

- Suppose there are two different scenarios: a) the older patient was admitted to the hospital and provided with the ECMO treatment, and only later, after several days, the younger patient was admitted, and b) the younger patient was admitted before the older patient, however, the older patient required ECMO treatment soon after admission while the younger patient's health condition deteriorated only after a longer time when the ECMO was already occupied (i. e. at the time when the younger patient was admitted to the hospital, she did not yet need it). Would there be any difference in the allocation decision making between these two scenarios?

The list of abbreviations

Bibliography

LEGAL-ETHICAL GROUNDS OF CRISIS PATIENT PRIORITISATION

Martin Šolc[1]

It has been one and a half centuries since an Austrian legal theorist Georg Jellinek wrote his famous remark about the relationship between the two fundamental normative systems: *the law is the minimum of morality*.[2] This formulation, brief and striking enough to be remembered as well as disputed,[3] contributed to the concept of law as an ethical minimum.[4] From this perspective, the law is seen as an instrument to enforce the minimum standards of moral behaviour that are vital for society.[5] The set of moral norms, on the other hand, is much wider and also encompasses the rules that are either less important or can only be carried out by an especially moral person (a "saint" in the broadest sense of the word).

In the outlined way, ethics contributes to the law in at least three ways. First, it defines the fundamental principles of morality, i.e., the criteria by which we can determine whether a certain action is moral or immoral. Since different ethical theories come to various conclusions in this respect, the development of legal regulation throughout the centuries has reflected the changes in predominant ethical approaches in the society. Second, ethics establishes fundamental norms of behaviour that are also protected and enforced by the law. Third, it gives rise to many other norms that are not directly included in the law but contribute to the social context in which the law operates.

Crisis patient prioritisation is a very sensitive activity both from the perspective of ethics and law. Many particular issues arise there that need to be addressed: how exactly the indication to intensive care should be evaluated, what are the

---

1 Researcher at the Centre for Medical Law and assistant at the Department of Civil Law, Charles University Faculty of Law. Email: solcma@prf.cuni.cz.

2 In original: *"Das Recht ist nichts Anderes, als das ethische Minimum."* — literally meaning: *"The law is nothing but the minimum of morality."* Georg Jellinek, *Die Socialethische Bedeutung von Recht, Unrecht und Strafe* (Alfred Hölder 1878) 42.

3 For example, it has been claimed that Jellinek's definition is wrong since many legal norms are morally indifferent, and the content of some legal norms might be even incompatible with moral norms. See Viktor Knapp, *Teorie práva [Theory of Law]* (C. H. Beck 1995) 85–86.

4 See for example Joseph Shatin, 'The Notion of a Minimum Content of Natural Law' (1974) 4 Archiv für Rechts- und Sozialphilosophie 547.

5 See for example Edmond Cahn, *The Sense of Injustice: An Anthropocentric View of Law* (New York University Press 1949) 38–46.

contraindications and how strict or flexible should they be, how to define impermissible discrimination in this context, etc. The answers to these issues form ethical rules that are either directly encompassed in the law, or are given legal relevance by being used to evaluate the compliance with the standard of care and the potential breach of professional duty.

All these particular problems can only be meaningfully addressed by identifying and applying principles of a certain ethical theory (or their combination). Otherwise, the proposed solutions will likely be incoherent, superficial, and unreasonable. We believe that this is precisely what ethics has to offer to the very practical and pressing problems of law: the deeper unifying source of individual norms that can ensure they are not contradictory or arbitrary.

To provide the broader legal context, this chapter starts with the introduction of the very fundamental human rights grounds of patient prioritisation. Then, it looks into the ethical grounds by presenting the most important ethical theories and analysing their (potential and actual) influence on the legal regulation of patient prioritisation.

1. Human rights grounds

The right to protection of health is acknowledged as a human right by international law documents as well as by many national constitutions all around the globe. For example, according to Article 25(1) of the United Nations Universal Declaration of Human Rights, everyone has the right to a standard of living adequate for the health and well-being of himself and of his family, including, among others, medical care. The International Covenant on Economic, Social and Cultural Rights of 1966 obligates the States Parties to recognise the right of everyone to the enjoyment of the highest attainable standard of physical and mental health (Article 12). The demonstrative list of steps the States Parties shall take to achieve the full realisation of this right includes the prevention, treatment and control of epidemic diseases and the creation of conditions which would assure to all medical service and medical attention in the event of sickness.

Similar provisions are encompassed in several regional human rights treaties. As important examples, we might mention the African Charter of Human and People's Rights (Article 16) or the Additional Protocol to the American Convention on Human Rights in the Area of Economic, Social and Cultural Rights (Article 10). In Europe, the right to health care is embodied in the Charter of Fundamental Rights of the European Union (Article 35) as well as in several Council of Europe documents. The European Social Charter explicitly guarantees the right to protection of health in Article 11. The Convention on Human Rights and Biomedicine[6] addresses

[6] The Convention for the Protection of Human Rights and Dignity of the Human Being with regard to the Application of Biology and Medicine (also known as the Oviedo Convention) of 1997.

several aspects of such right, including the right to equitable access to health care in Article 3 or the right to the provision of health care in accordance with relevant professional standards in Article 4. The European Convention on Human Rights[7] does not explicitly address the right to protection of health. Nevertheless, the most serious failures to enable the access to health care attributable to the Member States might represent violations of the right to life (Article 2) or the right to respect for private and family life (Article 8).[8]

According to the European Court of Human Rights (hereinafter the "ECtHR"), the right to life does not only oblige the Member States to refrain from depriving persons of their lives but also *"to take appropriate steps to safeguard the lives of those within its jurisdiction"*[9]. *While it was made clear in several ECtHR decisions*[10] that the inaccessibility of health care might infringe the right to life, the Strasbourg court only rarely finds such violation. There are two types of situations when it might occur:

- When the patient's life was *"knowingly put in danger by denial of access to life-saving emergency treatment"*.[11]

  An incorrect or delayed treatment is not sufficient to be a basis for this type of violation.[12] An example might be found in a Turkish case in which a pregnant woman was, with a delay, diagnosed with spontaneous abortion and indicated for a life-saving emergency operation. The medical facility that could perform the surgery, however, required the deposit to its operating found, which the patient's family did not have enough money to pay. For this reason, the hospital declined to hospitalise the patient. She died during the transfer to another hospital in a private ambulance where no medical personnel was present.[13]

  In relation to the pandemic rationing, this type of fundamental right violation might occur if the patients were denied the life-saving treatment even though there still were available resources to provide such care: for example, if they were not admitted to intensive care simply to leave some beds available for more perspective patients, or if their exclusion from the provision of care was based on impermissible discriminatory criteria.

---

7 Convention for the Protection of Human Rights and Fundamental Freedoms of 1950.

8 The paragraphs below containing an overview of the ECtHR case law regarding violations of Article 2 and Article 8 of the European Convention on Human Rights by failing to ensure the access to health care is based on an apt analysis in Petr Šustek, 'Non-Compliant Patients and the Restrictions of their Exercise of Right to Health' in: Pavel Šturma, Milan Lipovský (eds) *70th Anniversary of the Universal Declaration of Human Rights* (rw&w Science & New Media 2019) 136–138.
Martin Šolc, 'The Pandemic and the Law: Challenges of Covid-19 to the Ethical and Legal Paradigm of Health Care' in: Pavel Šturma (ed) *Czech Yearbook of Public & Private International Law. Česká ročenka mezinárodního práva veřejného a soukromého. Vol. 12* (Česká společnost pro mezinárodní právo 2021) 378.

9 See *L. C. B. v. the United Kingdom* App no 23413/94 (ECtHR, 9 June 1998) § 36.

10 See for example *Nitecki v. Poland* App no 65653/01 (ECtHR, 21 March 2002), or *Pentiacova and Others v. Moldova* App no 14462/03 (ECtHR, 4 January 2005).

11 *Lopes de Sousa Fernandes v. Portugal* App no 56080/13 (ECtHR, 19 December 2017) § 191.

12 See ibid § 191.

13 See *Mehmet Şentürk and Bekir Şentürk v. Turkey* App no 13423/09 (ECtHR, 9 April 2013).

– A *"systemic or structural dysfunction in hospital services"* that resulted in the deprivation of access to life-saving emergency treatment.[14]
  Such a violation is attributable to the respective Member State if *"the authorities knew about or ought to have known about that risk and failed to undertake the necessary measures to prevent that risk from materialising, thus putting the patients' lives, including the life of the particular patient concerned, in danger"*[15].
  It might be illustrated with another case from Turkey. A premature infant was born in a hospital that had no neonatal unit. She was transferred to another facility which nevertheless lacked available space and equipment. The baby passed away even though she could have been saved, was she provided with necessary medical care in time.[16]
  In the context of the pandemic rationing, the second type of violation of the right to life is conceivable if there were no scarce resources available at the time when the patient needed them, but the lack of such resources was the result of the State's wrong policies leading to the systemic failures that made the health system especially vulnerable to the consequences of public health crises.

In both types of situations, four criteria must be cumulatively fulfilled so the Member State will be held responsible for breaching the right to life:[17]

1) A provider of health care denied a patient emergency medical treatment despite being fully aware that it puts the patient's life at risk; such an act or omission goes beyond a mere error or medical negligence.
2) The dysfunction at issue is objectively and genuinely identifiable as systemic or structural; individual instances of dysfunction do not qualify as sufficient to be attributable to the state authorities in this context.
3) There is a causal link between the dysfunction and the harm sustained by the patient.
4) The dysfunction at issue has resulted from the failure of the State to meet its obligation to provide a regulatory framework in the broader sense.

If the lack of access to health care does not threaten the patient's life but interferes with their private and family life (for example, by preventing them from improving their quality of life), Article 8 of the European Convention on Human Rights might be breached. Nevertheless, these cases have only been identified by the ECtHR very rarely.[18]

---

14 See *Lopes de Sousa Fernandes v. Portugal* App no 56080/13 (ECtHR, 19 December 2017) § 192.

15 ibid § 192.

16 See *Aydoğdu v. Turkey App no 40448/06 (ECtHR, 30 August 2016).*

17 See *Lopes de Sousa Fernandes v. Portugal* App no 56080/13 (ECtHR, 19 December 2017) §§ 191–196.

18 See Petr Šustek, 'Non-Compliant Patients and the Restrictions of their Exercise of Right to Health' in: Pavel Šturma, Milan Lipovský (eds) *70th Anniversary of the Universal Declaration of Human Rights* (rw&w Science & New Media 2019) 137.

Even in light of the ECtHR case law, the right to protection of health remains rather vague to interpret and apply, especially in very specific situations such as the pandemic. It is the aim of this book to summarise and analyse how selected jurisdictions approach the difficult dilemmas that arise from this uncertainty.

2. Ethical grounds

Normative ethics has traditionally been divided into three major theories: deontology, consequentialism (mainly in the form of utilitarianism), and virtue ethics.[19] In this chapter, we will briefly introduce the fundamentals of these basic normative theories and outline their possible practical consequences for crisis patient prioritisation. We will also briefly address several newer approaches — principlism and case-based moral reasoning.

2.1. Deontology: inherent morality of an action

Deontology (from the Greek *deon* = duty) is a traditional approach to moral reasoning which attributes moral significance to the inherent character of an action. In other words, moral goodness or badness is an inherent property of an action and does not depend on its consequences. A central figure of contemporary deontological ethics is the Enlightenment Prussian philosopher Immanuel Kant.[20]

According to Kant's moral philosophy, agents act based on maxims, i.e., practical rules usable in real life. A maxim might be "always help others in need", but also "lie anytime it suits your interests", etc. Triage rules could arguably also be defined as maxims (such as "always treat those who come for your help first", or "prioritise those with higher chances of survival"). It is clear that we can define mutually exclusive maxims, which means that some of them are morally good while others are wrong. The test is rather straightforward: a particular maxim is good if it fits all the four formulations of the so-called categorical imperative.[21]

For patient prioritisation, the following two formulations of the categorical imperative might be considered especially relevant:

- *"[A]ct as if the maxim of your action were to become by your will a universal law of nature"*[22]

[19] See 'Virtue Ethics' (*Stanford Encyclopedia of Philosophy,* 8 December 2016) <https://plato.stanford.edu/entries/ethics-virtue/> accessed 4 May 2022.

[20] For an introduction to deontology, see 'Deontological Ethics' (*Stanford Encyclopedia of Philosophy,* 30 October 2020) <https://plato.stanford.edu/entries/ethics-deontological/> accessed 23 May 2022.

[21] See Immanuel Kant, *Groundwork of the Metaphysics of Morals* (Cambridge University Press 1997) 31, par. 4:421.

[22] See ibid 31, par. 4:421.

– *"So act that you use humanity, whether in your person or in the person of any other, always at the same time as an end, never merely as a means"*[23]

Based on the former formulation, a maxim is only good if it could be a universal law. There can be no situational exceptions from general rules. Therefore, the principles of patient prioritisations should be the same regardless of the severity of the crisis and must not be sacrificed for the perceived greater good.[24]

According to the latter above-cited formulation of the categorical imperative, it is impermissible to sacrifice the life or health of another. By doing so, the agent would use the humanity in another merely as a means to help the third person. In the Kantian understanding of morality, the abandoned person would be stripped of their dignity.

At this point, it might be important to mention that Kant distinguishes between perfect and imperfect duties. Perfect are duties *not to act* according to maxims that are not even conceivable as a universal law since they would lead to a contradiction — for example, if there was a universal law that everyone should lie, nobody would believe anything and lying would become useless. Imperfect duties, in turn, regard maxims that could theoretically make a universal law, but we cannot rationally will it (e.g., a maxim that no one should help others in need).[25] The fulfilment of perfect duties deserves no special praise, but their breach is blameworthy. On the other hand, the failure to act on imperfect duties does not deserve blame, but their fulfilment is praiseworthy.

In an admittedly simplifying manner, this dichotomy resembles the above-outlined understanding of law as the minimum of morality. Legal obligations are similar to perfect duties in the sense that compliance with them is not particularly praiseworthy, but their violation should be sanctioned. Less crucial moral obligations that are not enforced by the law might be understood as close to imperfect duties.

What does it mean for patient prioritisation? We might, for example, imagine health professionals who undergo extreme personal risks to care for the sick, or a patient who refuses life-saving treatment so it can be provided to someone younger. Such heroic acts should rather be considered imperfect duties. Voluntary self-sacrifice may be, in some cases, highly moral and admirable. As a rule, though, sacrificing one's life or health for the sake of others is not required by the law (while this should not be confused with the obligation to bear a reasonable risk).

On the contrary, not sacrificing others is considered a perfect duty. Nobody is praised for not destroying others for the greater good, while any attempt to do so would be morally impermissible and most likely illegal. That is why the

23 See ibid 38, par. 4:429.

24 See Petr Šustek, Martin Šolc, 'Prioritizace pacientů v intenzivní péči: etika a právní odpovědnost v době pandemie [Patient Prioritisation in Intensive Care: Ethics and Legal Liability at the Time of Pandemic]' (2022) 3 Jurisprudence 6.

25 See Immanuel Kant, *Groundwork of the Metaphysics of Morals* (Cambridge University Press 1997) 31–33, pars. 4:422-4:424.

deontological ethical approach tends to be restrictive and supports a rather passive position towards the external risks. If the risk materialises, it might be very bad for the affected person, but at least nobody bears the moral guilt.

In the context of crisis patient prioritisation, this means that health professionals cannot sacrifice the patient for the sake of others. It is, however, not trivial to understand what such a "sacrifice" means. Arguably, it is not necessarily defined according to the active-passive behaviour distinction (which raises many questions such as whether withdrawal of life support is rather an action or cessation of action[26]). From the Kantian perspective, the crucial issue is whether the patient is solely used as a means to achieve the goals that are external to them. If the life-sustaining treatment that might still be beneficial for the patient is withheld or withdrawn from them because it is deemed potentially more beneficial to another person, the patient is used as a means to free the scarce resources. They are not being dealt with as an end in themselves. For this reason, it can be argued that health professionals are not allowed to withhold or withdraw life-sustaining treatment from the patient for the sake of other patients.[27]

On the other hand, deontology puts stress on a dignified approach to others, which can be interpreted as a reason for strong support for quality palliative care. Prolonging suffering without a real benefit to the patient — the so-called dysthanasia — can sometimes be understood as the use of the patient to achieve external goals, especially if it is motivated by a mere habit, insensitivity, or even financial interests. It might be considered a categorical duty to terminate life-sustaining treatment when it puts a heavy burden on the patient that is disproportionate to its potential benefits. Knowing when to transfer the patient to full palliative care can be the best the doctors can do for them. In this perspective, the benefit for other patients who may now use a scarce resource (such as a ventilator) is just a lucky side-effect.

2.2. Consequentialism: morality lies in the consequences

While deontology understands morality as an inherent property of an action, consequentialist ethical approaches[28] judge actions as moral or immoral based on their consequences. As a result, it cannot be said that some action is always good or wrong — circumstances and context always co-determine their moral value. There

[26] See for example Tomáš Holčapek, 'Rozhodnutí soudu jako zdroj oprávnění zásahu do integrity [Judicial Decision as a Source of Right to Interfere with Integrity]' (2018) 3 Časopis zdravotnického práva a bioetiky 3–6.

[27] See Petr Šustek, Martin Šolc, 'Prioritizace pacientů v intenzivní péči: etika a právní odpovědnost v době pandemie [Patient Prioritisation in Intensive Care: Ethics and Legal Liability at the Time of Pandemic]' (2022) 3 Jurisprudence 7.

[28] See 'Consequentialism' (*Stanford Encyclopedia of Philosophy,* 3 June 2019) <https://plato.stanford.edu/entries/consequentialism/> accessed 4 May 2022.

are many possible ways to apply consequentialism in ethical considerations. The especially influential one is utilitarianism.

2.2.1. Utilitarianism: the greatest good for the greatest number

Classical utilitarianism is built upon four basic principles.[29] The first one is the principle of consequentialism, that answers the question of how to morally evaluate actions with the above-outlined answer: every action is as good or wrong as its consequences. Nevertheless, we need to ask for a criterion based on which we can judge whether the consequences are good or not. According to utilitarianism, this criterion lies in the principle of utility: the consequence is good if and only if it is useful for something that is good in itself. According to the principle of hedonism, the good in itself is found in happiness, that is, in pleasant experiences. Since probably everything is mixed with a certain discomfort, the principle of hedonism requires utilitarian calculus. If the calculus of the amounts of pleasures and pain is positive (there is more pleasure than pain), then the consequence is good; but if there was another option with a greater surplus of pleasure over pain, such an option would be even better.

At this point, utilitarianism might seem disturbingly egotistical. Nevertheless, it also encompasses the social principle, according to which it is the social utility that matters. In other words, the agent should act not to maximise their own pleasure, but to achieve the highest possible surplus of pleasure over pain overall, for all people affected.

These principles are often summarised in the rule that the utilitarians should aim at achieving *"the greatest amount of good for the greatest number"*. More precisely, utilitarianism strives for maximising the net good in the world (the highest positive calculus of pleasure and pain possible).[30]

It is easy to see why utilitarianism has been so influential since the second half of the twentieth century. In the contemporary political, economic, and social discourse, the calculus of costs and benefits (monetary or other) is often crucial. However, even utilitarianism has several serious problems. Perhaps most importantly, it makes it very difficult to explain why a minority should not be sacrificed if it fits the majority's interests.[31] The possible consequences of unlimited utilitarian policies might include a total lack of care for certain minorities or even their active oppression or destruction, which is often perceived as inhumane, probably suggesting

29 See Arno Anzenbacher, *Úvod do etiky [Introduction to Ethics]* (Zvon 1994) 32–34.

30 See 'Consequentialism' (*Stanford Encyclopedia of Philosophy,* 3 June 2019) <https://plato.stanford.edu/entries/consequentialism/> accessed 4 May 2022.

31 See Martin Šolc, 'The Pandemic and the Law: Challenges of Covid-19 to the Ethical and Legal Paradigm of Health Care' in: Pavel Šturma (ed) *Czech Yearbook of Public & Private International Law. Česká ročenka mezinárodního práva veřejného a soukromého. Vol. 12* (Česká společnost pro mezinárodní právo 2021) 374.

a certain strong deontological root of our moral intuitions. While some modifications of utilitarianism were proposed in order to solve this problem (such as the rule utilitarianism that applies the above-described principles to rules rather than individual actions),[32] it remains utilitarianism's crucial weakness.

When applied to patient prioritisation, utilitarianism will put stress on the calculus of overall pleasure and pain resulting from each decision (or each triage rule). It will typically compare not only chances of survival, but also the quality of life of the respective patients should they not die, along with their remaining life expectancy. The prioritisation of the younger over the older, as well as of the healthy over those with chronic health conditions, is a very likely by-effect.

A purely utilitarian approach to triage might also encompass considerations for the patient's broader social utility. It would not represent any kind of reward or tribute to such a person, since utilitarianism always calculates the amount of pleasure or pain regardless of who perceives it — in this regard, all persons are equal.[33] Nevertheless, those who are believed to be of higher social utility might be given precedence since their survival would probably lead to the maximisation of the total net good in society (for example, by saving other lives, sustaining the economy, etc.). Similar grounds for prioritisation, however, are considered impermissible discrimination and therefore are illegal in most countries.

Nevertheless, in the very nature of the concept of triage, there is a utilitarian aspect that cannot be overlooked. After all, its aim is the maximisation of the lives saved, even at the cost of abandoning other patients who would possibly profit from medical attention under less strenuous circumstances. Throughout this book, we can see how different countries impose various deontological limitations on this utilitarian basis of patient prioritisation.

2.3. Virtue ethics: what would a virtuous doctor do?

Arguably the oldest of the ethical approaches we outline in this chapter is virtue ethics. Unlike both deontology and consequentialism, virtue ethics focuses on the agent rather than the action. The goal of ethical life is to become a virtuous person. Therefore, an action is good if it helps the agent to become virtuous.[34]

According to Aristotle, each action pushes the acting person in a certain way, either towards a virtue or a vice. In this classical view, virtues are understood as a moderate position between two extremes which are vices. For example, fortitude is a virtue between cowardice on the one side of the spectre and carelessness on the

32 See 'Consequentialism' (*Stanford Encyclopedia of Philosophy*, 3 June 2019) <https://plato.stanford.edu/entries/consequentialism/> accessed 4 May 2022.

33 See ibid.

34 For a closer introduction to virtue ethics, see 'Virtue Ethics' (*Stanford Encyclopedia of Philosophy*, 8 December 2016) <https://plato.stanford.edu/entries/ethics-virtue/> accessed 4 May 2022.

other side.[35] For a health professional, traditional virtues of prudence (which can be roughly translated to rationality), justice, fortitude, and temperance may be as important as for anyone else.

In the clinical context, prudence might be understood as a knowledgeable use of evidence-based medicine with regard to the patient's individual condition and needs. Fortitude may be found in the area between the frivolous tendency to take unnecessary risks and the practice of defensive medicine. We can also further elaborate the basic virtues into a number of particular moral and technical virtues such as empathy (as a virtue between the vices of insensitivity and hypersensitivity), good communication, clinical skilfulness, or responsibility (between irresponsibility and an obsessive fear of mistakes).

Virtues are not determined once and for all: every time a person acts virtuously, they become more virtuous, and every time they act oppositely, they lean towards a vice. In the beginning, carrying out virtuous acts is usually difficult, but it becomes ever easier as the person grows in the relevant virtue. In this manner, virtues are trained.[36] For example, it might be very hard to act bravely when a person is not used to it, but only by acting bravely the person becomes brave, and every new brave act is gradually easier for them. In the same way, a doctor might need to intentionally focus on good bedside manners at first, but if they are consistent in this approach, they start to develop empathy and communication skills with ever less effort. A virtue can become a moral habit. Nevertheless, the same applies to any vice.

When using virtue ethics in any clinical situation, the crucial question is: what would a good doctor do? Or, in other words, what action will make the acting person a more virtuous doctor?[37]

In the context of crisis prioritisation, some issues are probably not ambivalent from the perspective of virtue ethics. There can be little doubt that a virtuous physician will carefully assess the benefits a particular patient might have from a life-sustaining treatment, or that they will adequately communicate with the patient (if possible) and their loved ones. However, the prioritisation decision-making itself is far less clear. We can imagine a situation when a physician withdraws the ventilation support from an 80-year-old person who has rather small (but not negligible) chances of survival in order to try to save a 45-year-old mother of three children. Does this decision make the doctor insensitive, or even more empathetic? Most prioritisation decisions are connected with a certain level of legal uncertainty, as is all too evident from the national reports collected in this book. Does taking such a legal risk strengthen the virtue of fortitude, or rather the vice of recklessness?

---

35 See Aristotle, *Nicomachean Ethics* (2nd edn, Hackett Publishing 1999) 20.

36 See ibid 18–20.

37 Several authors have analysed medical ethics from the perspective of physician's virtue. See for example Edmund D. Pellegrino, David C. Thomasma, *The Virtues in Medical Practice* (Oxford University Press 1993), or James F. Drane, *Becoming a Good Doctor: The Place of Virtue and Character in Medical Ethics* (2nd edn, Sheed & Ward 1995).

It is arguably impossible to answer these and other similar questions solely on the basis of virtue ethics. It seems to be crucial to first know how to evaluate individual actions in order to judge what impact (positive or negative) they are going to have on the agent. For example, it is probably not feasible to decide on the permissibility of withdrawal of life support without deciding first whether we will judge the action based on its inner quality or consequences. While virtue ethics can be used as an interesting framework for decision-making, it probably needs further concretisation that may be provided by a different, action-centred ethical approach.

2.4. Principlism: four principles as a practical guidance

In 1979, American philosophers Tom L. Beauchamp and James F. Childress published the first edition of their book *Principles of Biomedical Ethics* in which they proposed a special normative ethical framework for health care. Their ethical approach, often called *principlism*, became highly influential for its practical usability and intelligibility.

The framework is based on the four prima facie principles: beneficence (doing good), nonmaleficence (not doing harm), justice (securing just access to health care), and autonomy (of the patient's will).[38] Their rather broad definitions require a careful interpretation for each situation in real life. The principles can often become contradictory in practice: for example, trying to help a patient always entails a certain level of risk. As the principles are not hierarchical, their collisions must be resolved based on (usually *ad hoc*) proportional judgment.[39]

In their crucial book, Beauchamp and Childress directly address triage in a very brief manner. They mention that it is based on a utilitarian rationale of achieving maximum effectiveness and efficiency of the use of medical resources, which are allocated according to individual patients' needs and prospects. Triage decisions are, therefore, usually based on medical utility. However, certain aspects of patients' narrow social utility — comparative social worth — are deemed by the two authors not only acceptable but inescapable in certain situations.[40] They have even foreseen a potential pandemic situation when they wrote:

"For example, in an earthquake disaster in which some injured survivors are medical personnel who suffer only minor injuries, they can justifiably receive priority for treatments if they are needed to help others. Similarly, in an outbreak of pandemic influenza, it is justifiable to inoculate physicians and nurses first to enable them to care for others. Under such conditions, a person may receive priority for treatment on grounds of narrow social utility if and only if his or her contribution

---

[38] See Tom L. Beauchamp, James F. Childress, *Principles of Biomedical Ethics* (7th edn, Oxford University Press 2013).

[39] See ibid ix.

[40] See ibid 291–292.

is indispensable to attaining a major social goal. As in analogous lifeboat cases, we should limit judgments of comparative social value to the specific qualities and skills that are essential to the community's immediate protection, without assessing the general social worth of persons."[41]

Prioritisation of certain professional groups is, therefore, not understood as a reward or acknowledgment of their past contributions. Physicians, nurses, and other essential workers might be prioritised only for their instrumental value, only and if only it is necessary to enable them to keep working for the benefit of others. This has certain ramifications that might be controversial but are very rational from the utilitarian perspective: for example, a doctor who has very little chance to go back to the workforce should not be prioritised, but their colleague who is more likely to resume their work can reasonably be given priority.

The more general application of principlism to crisis patient prioritisation is possible and meaningful. It requires a creative interpretation of the principles and their collisions in various specific contexts. It is worth mentioning that Beauchamp and Childress mention pandemic influenza as one of the situations when the public needs to be engaged in setting the allocation criteria. Public health crises cannot be efficiently addressed without the trust and cooperation of the public.[42] As difficult as it is, the cultivation of public discourse on prioritisation criteria seems to be an important task. It is also the main goal this book hopes to contribute to.

2.5. Case-based moral reasoning: moral precedents instead of universal rules

While all the above-outlined normative frameworks are based on universal moral principles, some ethical theories are sceptical towards such universal rules. According to these approaches, decision-making is in fact informed by moral intuitions and experiences with similar cases. Ethics should not deny this but rather reflect it by basing moral rationing on the families of relevant cases that have already been resolved in the past.[43]

Casuistry has been mostly abandoned in ethics for several centuries. Its partial revival at the turn of the millennium can be attributed to two important observations. First, principle-based approaches have been perceived as contextually insensitive by some authors. Second, there is the experience with the debates on highly controversial matters such as abortion that only seem to lead to both sides of the discussion being entrenched in their principles they believe to be universally valid.[44]

[41] ibid 292.

[42] See ibid 292.

[43] See ibid 397–410.

[44] See Jaromír Matějek, *Etické poradenství: jak řešit etické problémy každodenní medicíny [Ethics Consultation: How to Solve the Ethical Problems of Everyday Medicine]* (Triton 2021) 210-211.

Casuistry, on the other hand, aims at solving concrete problems with regard to their unique circumstances, while it understands the solutions as only presumably correct and not a logical necessity.[45]

Casuistic ethical reasoning might be, for example, carried out as follows: there are identified 1) the ethical questions relevant to the case as well as 2) the principles involved, and 3) the conclusions of analogous previous cases are applied to the case. In the third step, the relevant previous cases are found that are well-analysed and their solutions are generally accepted. Then, there are compared the similarities and differences between these (so-called paradigmatic) cases and the disputed case that is being solved.[46]

For addressing the problem of pandemic patient prioritisation, we would need to identify similar cases of health care rationing carried out in the context of a crisis that have a solution that seems to be broadly accepted, if not self-evident. In modern societies in peacetime, a certain form of triage typically occurs following mass accidents. However, in this context, it is usually possible to distribute patients among several health facilities so everyone can be treated according to their medical needs (even though a time delay resulting from the patient's transfer might be important for the outcomes of care). On the other hand, the greatest fear regarding patient prioritisation in the context of the Covid-19 pandemic was that there might simply not be enough scarce medical resources for all the patients in a particular health system. This consideration might lead us to look for paradigmatic cases in rather extreme contexts, most likely triage at the times of war. The problem is that war triage and pandemic triage, while similar in certain aspects, are still very different in other important features. Therefore, it seems to be rather difficult to identify relevant paradigmatic cases for the purpose of pandemic prioritisation.

Even if we found such reliable cases that can form the basis for casuistic reasoning, it would still be arguably necessary to choose an ethical theory that will be used in analysing the relationship between the general principles and particular circumstances.[47] While it is possible to try to use the casuistic approach without reference to any fundamental ethical theory, it might lead to overly subjective, intuitional, and situational conclusions.

2.6. Ethical eclecticism

Many ethical frameworks might possibly be applied to any moral problem, including patient prioritisation. Some of them are general in their nature (such as deontology, utilitarianism, and virtue ethics) while others are specialised to a certain area of application (perhaps most importantly, principlism). As we have outlined above,

[45] See ibid 213.
[46] See ibid 215–219.
[47] See ibid 220.

special approaches usually require further concretisation of their rules or principles provided by the general theories. Moreover, these general ethical systems, however contradictory they may be in pure theory, might in practice complement each other in a meaningful way. Modern medical ethics often understands normative theories as different perspectives, each of which has its advantages and weak spots. Instead of picking one theory as the foundation for all decision-making, contemporary ethics often combines their various aspects in order to address the needs of real life in a flexible, practical, and yet comprehensive and well-argued manner.[48]

Prioritisation guidelines issued during the Covid-19 pandemic have sometimes been criticised for being too ambiguous. One of the harshest criticisms came from Jonathan Lewis and Udo Schuklenk, who pointed out that such guidelines typically refer to ethical principles that are nice-sounding, but conflicting, disparate, and too vague for practical application. As a result of the insufficient guidelines, Lewis and Schuklenk believe that prioritisation decision-making was in fact left to health professionals, resembling the times before the emergence of modern autonomy-based bioethics.[49]

However, this view might be too one-sided. Even ethical theories that seem contradictory at first sight might be synthesised into a coherent and functioning system. Most Covid-19-related triage guidelines are based on the utilitarian notion of maximising effectiveness and saving as many patients as possible. At the same time, they also usually contain strict deontological limitations such as the impermissibility of discrimination on the grounds of sex, social position, or sole age, the obligation to provide palliative care in all cases, the prohibition of withdrawing life support for the sake of other patients, or similar rules.

This combination of utilitarian foundation and categorical limitations is far from new in medical ethics. Medical research might provide a good example. Any research on human beings brings about a certain risk to its participants, simply because the medicines, devices, or procedures that are being tested are still in the research phase. The fact that such a risk is considered permissible is arguably based on consequentialist calculus that takes into account the potential benefits of the research, even though it might be argued that the participation in research is also good from the deontological perspective based on the good intentions of the persons involved. There are many categorical limitations to conducting research, however, including the fact that its ethical permissibility is defined by its design and no potential benefits may justify a research project that would be too risky or harmful for the participants.[50]

---

48 See Tom L. Beauchamp, James F. Childress, *Principles of Biomedical Ethics* (7th edn, Oxford University Press 2013) 383–385, or Martin Šolc, 'The Pandemic and the Law: Challenges of Covid-19 to the Ethical and Legal Paradigm of Health Care' in: Pavel Šturma (ed) *Czech Yearbook of Public & Private International Law. Česká ročenka mezinárodního práva veřejného a soukromého. Vol. 12* (Česká společnost pro mezinárodní právo 2021) 378.

49 See Jonathan Lewis, Udo Schuklenk, 'Bioethics met its COVID-19 Waterloo: The doctor knows best again' (2021) 1 Bioethics 3–5 doi: https://doi.org/10.1111/bioe.12840.

50 See Munzarová, Marta, *Lékařský výzkum a etika [Medical Research and Ethics]* (Grada 2005) 48. See also various legal regulations of medical research including Chapter V of the Convention on Human Rights and Biomedicine.

Conclusion

The very nature of patient prioritisation consists in careful search for the balance of competing interests under circumstances where the consequences of each action are uncertain. On the one hand, there are the rights and interests of the patient in issue; on the other hand, there are other patients whose lives are at stake, needing scarce health resources. However, the need for finding a proper balance is also crucial on the individual level of each patient. There might occur two unfortunate outcomes. There is a risk of what is sometimes called misthanasia: the premature death hastened by the lack of access to needed health care. However, the overly intensive care might lead to dysthanasia, prolonging the patient's suffering rather than life with any meaningful quality. While the legal ramifications are as a rule more serious in the former cases, the latter should also be avoided, at least from the ethical perspective. Both situations might represent a violation of patient's rights and arguably interfere with their dignity.[51]

Ethical and legal discussion on patient prioritisation aims at navigating these dilemmas. Different normative ethical theories may come to distinct solutions. Utilitarianist approaches will be more open to scarce resources rationing even at the cost of sacrificing the lives of some patients, especially those with worse prognosis. Such an instrumental use of patients for the sake of others is unthinkable for deontological theories which focus on the inner moral quality of each action. Traditional virtue ethics endorses choices that make the decision-maker a more virtuous physician; for example, that teach them to be more skilful, empathetic, or responsible.

Modern medical ethics is often navigated by the four principles of beneficence, nonmaleficence, justice, and autonomy. While these principles have many times proven useful in guiding clinical dilemmas, it requires a creative interpretation of all the principles and their mutual relations. Importantly, the authors of principlism emphasize the importance of the public debate in a pandemic situation, strengthening the public trust and cooperation. Another ethical approach that is popular nowadays is casuistry. However, it might be difficult to find relevant paradigmatic cases that could serve as a basis for ethical discussion on pandemic rationing. Moreover, casuistry arguably cannot work without the inputs of one of the fundamental normative theories.

Today's ethics is often based on an eclectic approach. Various normative theories are often seen not as mutually exclusive, but rather as complements that can enable us to understand problems in their complexity. Ethical and legal approaches to pandemic rationing are also, as a rule, eclectic. Their very basis is the utilitarian notion of maximisation of good for the greatest numbers (while there is often

[51] See Adriano Marteleto Godinho, 'Coronavírus e mistanásia: a morte indigna dos excluídos e a responsabilidade civil do estado' in: *Carlos Edison do* Rêgo *Monteiro Filho, Nelson Rosenvald, Roberta Densa (eds) Coronavírus e responsabilidade civil: impactos contractuais e extracontractuais (Editora Foco 2021) 451–457.*

a vivid discussion on what the pursued good should be: the lives saved, the number of life-years, the quality-adjusted life years, etc.). This approach is strictly limited by several deontological maxims, such as the prohibition of impermissible discrimination on the grounds of social position, sole age, etc.

Most ethical guidelines as well as legal regulations of crisis patient prioritisation reflect such a combination of consequentialist and deontological fundaments with the application of particular norms stemming from principlism or other theories. In this book, we collected several national reports analysing such legal responses throughout the world. It is up to the reader to make their own judgment as to whether and to what extent the particular legal approaches manage to navigate coherently and practically among the many ethical problems.

AUSTRIA

Karl Stöger[52]
University of Vienna

A. Questionnaire

1. What are the criteria for the allocation of scarce health care resources in your country?

Preliminary remark[53]: As the comparative project analyses allocation decisions in the context of COVID-19, this national report focuses on inpatient (hospital) care as it is in this context that scarcity of resources (especially ICU resources) played a central role for COVID-19 patients and other patients with serious health issues.

There is no explicit codification of allocation criteria (in the context of triage decisions) in Austrian health law (neither by legislative nor administrative acts). However, Art. 16 para. 1 lit. d. of the Federal Hospital Act[54] (*Kranken- und Kuranstaltengesetz; KAKuG)* states that in non-profit hospitals, the extent and quality of "medical treatment must only depend on the state of health of the patient". In this context, "state of health" means the **condition of the patient in relation to the required treatment. The question is therefore how urgently a patient needs a particular treatment.** This obligation is of particular importance during a pandemic as non-profit hospitals are under a statutory obligation to admit patients for treatment (see question 4 below). Art. 16 makes clear that any allocation of scarce resources in hospitals must be based exclusively on an individual assessment of the **state of health** (as defined above: urgency of required treatment) of the patient in question.

52 Professor of Medical Law at the Department of Constitutional and Administrative Law at University of Vienna (karl.stoeger@univie.ac.at, ORCID-ID 0000-0002-0294-2910).

53 This text was finalised at the end of April 2021 and updated before being printed in summer 2023. However, the relevant legal framework in Austria did not change during this period. For comments on the first draft, the author is very much indebted to Professor Alexander Tipold. For valuable assistance in preparing the manuscript, I am grateful to Patrizia Pompe and Manja Seebacher. The usual disclaimer applies.

54 Due to a specific feature of the Austrian Constitution with regard to the attribution of legislative competencies, the Federal Hospital Act adresses provincial parliaments and obliges them to enact provincial legislation on hospital matters (*Landeskrankenanstaltengesetze*) within the framework delimited by the Federal Act. For the purpose of this national report, it is possible to refer exclusively to the Federal Hospital Act.

Factors like race, gender, age or pre-existing conditions can only be taken into account if they have an **impact** on the state of health of the patient. Furthermore, Art. 8 para 2 of the Federal Hospital Act requires that all hospitals treat their patients "in accordance with the principles and recognised methods of medical science". This means that hospital personnel[55] must adhere to these standards when performing an assessment of a patient's health status as to the urgency of required treatment.

Consequently, (only) the individual state of health must be taken into account when prioritising patients in the context of elective care like planned surgery. The more urgent a patient requires surgery, the sooner he or she is to be admitted to the hospital. In this respect, Arts. 8 para. 2 and Art. 16 para. 1 lit. d. of the Federal Hospital Act also embody the State's "obligation to protect" the life and health of hospital patients (as stated by the ECtHR's case-law[56] on Arts. 2 and 8 ECHR[57]) and its obligation to make sure that publicly-financed hospital care (as delivered by non-profit hospitals in Austria) must be available without dicrimination.[58] Accordingly, the hospital authorities, which are directly bound by fundamental rights, would have to step in if patients in hospitals were subjugated to allocation criteria which are not based on the above-mentioned individual assessment of their state of health according to medical standards.[59]

As patients have to be treated according to medical standards only, this can also result in patients not being admitted to ICU care if there is no (longer) any medical indication to do so due to their poor condition (so that palliative measures are medically more appropriate than ICU treatment). Furthermore, it is obvious that the rules of informed consent must be respected: If a patient does not wish to receive ICU treatment, he or she has to be treated according to the "second best" medical standard. In both cases, adherence to medical standards will include palliative care.

In **"triage" situations**, the starting point for a legal assessment is different[60]: If a given number of patients requires, according to their state of health and the applicable medical standards, a certain treatment (e.g. ICU care) but there are not sufficient resources available, the hospital cannot meet its obligation to provide all patients with the standard of care that their state of health demands. This failure

55 For details on the question which medical professions are allowed to determine the urgency of treatment, see note 81 below.

56 *Calvelli and Ciglio v Italy* ECHR 2002–I 25 can still be regarded as the leading case in this context.

57 In Austria, the European Convention of Human Rights (*Europäische Menschenrechtskonvention; EMRK*) is part of the national constitional framework, which means that its provisions are directly applicable as fundamental rights and can be invoked before national courts.

58 Cf. Walter Berka, 'Die Verantwortung des Staates für die medizinische Versorgung' (2019) 5a RdM 227, 233; Benjamin Kneihs, 'Art. 2 EMRK' in Benjamin Kneihs and Georg Lienbacher (eds), *Rill-Schäffer-Kommentar Bundesverfassungsrecht* (Verlag Österreich 2020) para 20.

59 Cf. Christian Kopetzki, 'Art. 2 EMRK' in Karl Korinek and Michael Holoubek (eds), *Kommentar zum österreichischen Bundesverfassungsrecht* (Verlag Springer 2002) para 76; Karl Stöger, 'Darf die Art der Beschaffung die medizinische Therapie beeinflussen?' (2019) 5 RdM-ÖG 15, 16.

60 Cf. Stefan Huster, 'Wer hat Angst vor der Triage' in Tatjana Hörnle et al (eds), *Triage in der Pandemie* (Mohr Siebeck 2021) 90ff: *"Triage als Sonderfall"* ("Triage as an exceptional situation") as compared to other allocation decisions in medicine.

can be the result of "faulty" planning of hospital capacities: In principle, hospital capacities are carefully planned according to average needs (including some spare capacities for emergency situations). If these capacities are, especially in a medical emergency, not available in a hospital as planned (e.g. due to lack of personnel), the Austrian Supreme Court has repeatedly ruled that the hospital or state-funded social insurance agencies are obliged to make sure that the patient is transferred to another hospital (including a hospital abroad) without having to bear the additional costs.[61] These rulings can be explained by the court's point of view that the patient must not bear negative (financial and physical) consequences if duly planned capacities are not available. However, in case of a global pandemic in which duly planned capacities are exhausted and patients cannot or only to a very limited extent be transferred domestically or even abroad, the logic behind the Supreme Court's decision cannot apply. In this situation, the scarcity of capacities cannot be attributed to insufficient planning or be regarded as an "individual bottleneck". On the contrary, if hospital operators were obliged to permanently keep available resources for the event of a global pandemic, this would place a disproportionate burden not only on them, but on the whole publicly-funded health care system and would therefore in itself constitute a misallocation of resources. Accordingly, in the situation of a global pandemic (or e.g. a major disaster which goes beyond the scope that is normally planned for) the scarcity of resources does not indicate a violation of capacity planning obligations. **Nevertheless, in such a situation hospitals cannot meet their obligation to treat all patients according to medical standards.** In other words: If a decision has to be made who will receive necessary treatment and who will not, this decision cannot be regarded as part of a treatment "according to medical standards" as defined by Art. 8 para. 2 (according to these standards, every patient would have to be cared for according to his or her medical needs).

In this case, the Austrian legal order **does not provide any "positive" allocation criteria** for a triage situation. In somewhat stark contrast to Germany,[62] so far

---

[61] The first case concerned additional costs of treatment after a patient had to be transferred to a hospital abroad due to the closure of a hospital department due to a bottleneck in staff capacities (Austrian Supreme Court 4 June 2004, 2 Ob 27/03i), while in the second case all neonatological emergency capacities in the western part of Austria were occupied while a Swiss hospital still had sufficient capacities, but charged more than the Austrian tariff (Austrian Supreme Court, 29 March 2001, 2 Ob 60/01i).

[62] In Germany, a vast amount of scholarly literature with highly diverging views is available: cf. from the first phase of the pandemic (with further reference) Jochen Taupitz, 'Verteilung medizinischer Ressourcen in der Corona-Krise: Wer darf überleben?' (2020) 38 MedR 440; Alexander Brade, Maxi Müller, 'Corona-Triage: Untätigkeit des Gesetzgebers als Schutzpflichtverletzung' (2020) 24 Neue Zeitschrift für Verwaltungsrecht 1792; in particular, the first three contributions (by Steffen Augsberg, Ralf Poscher and Stefan Huster) of the book *'Triage in der Pandemie'* (Triage in times of pandemic; eds Tatjana Hörnle et al) are dedicated to the question *"Darf oder muss der Gesetzgeber Triage regeln?"* ("May or must triage by regulated by the legislator?").
The German Constitutional Court finally decided in a much discussed ruling that the German legislator was under an obligation to enact legislation on triage criteria in case of an epidemic-driven scarcity of treatment resources (Bundesverfassungsgericht 16 December 2021, 1 BvR 1541/20).

there has been no call for the legislator to enact specific legislation. Instead, a group of lawyers and doctors explicitly rejected (while referring to the German discussion) any legislative proposal in this regard claiming that triage decisions could always be based on medical criteria for each individual case.[63] Another legal expert also called for a broad consensus among medical societies and not necessarily for the legislator to take action.[64] In fact, this happened in Austria: **There are, since March 2020, medical recommendations by a Medical Society and by the Austrian Bioethics Commission on how to handle triage sitations, later followed by more recommendations which are comparable in content** (see question 3 for details). In Austria, cases of ICU triage remained a very rare exception due to slightly over-average ICU capacities (which proved to be a stroke of luck during the pandemic). However, there were reports by doctors of some cases of ICU triage in several hospitals, in particular in the province (Land) of Upper Austria, during the second wave in November 2021. This, from a statistical point of view, minor dimension of the problem (though, of course, the challenges for patients, medical personnel and families should not be underestimated) and the absence of investigations by the public prosecutors to date probably contributed to this rather pragmatic approach.[65] Nevertheless, five aspects should not be overlooked:

(1) While triage on a systematic scale did (according to the knowledge of the reporter) not occur in Austrian hospitals during COVID-19, priorisations decisions were of course taken, resulting in the postponement of medical examinations and surgeries, thereby leading to "collateral" medical damage. It was also reported in the media that triage decisions were only narrowly avoided during the "third wave" in March/April 2021 by the establishment of additional ICU capacities. However, it seems that a few ICU triage decisions which met the criteria of triage decisions as understood by this comparative project, took place in November 2021, in particular in the province (Land) of Upper Austria ("fourth wave"; see above).

(2) It is true that doctors, especially in anaestesia and intensive care, are in principle in a position to handle triage situation from a medical point of view. However,

As a result, Art. 5c of the German Infection Protection Act was enacted. It is only applicable in the context of infectious diseases and focusses on the short-time probability of survival. For an analysis of this piece of legislation from an Austrian perspective, cf. Tipold A, 'Triage und § 5c deutsches Infektionsschutzgesetz' (2023) 1 ZfG 7. In Austria, as mentioned above, no specific or general legislation on the matter has been passed to date.

63 Alois Birklbauer, Markus Grimm, Wolfgang Kröll and Oliver Neuper, 'Triage – Der Nicht-Ärzte liebstes Kind' (2020) 24 JMG 125.

64 Benedikt Kommenda, 'Damoklesschwert über Ärzteschaft' *Die Presse* (Vienna, 20 July 2020) (Interview with Richard Soyer, Professor of Criminal Law, University of Linz, and Attorney at Soyer Kier Stufer in Vienna).

65 This impression is somewhat confirmed by an article by Georg Streit, 'Gesundheitsversorgung in der Pandemie: Triage – oder kommen alle dran?' (2020) 3 JMG 141, 142 who expresses his hope *"that sufficient resources will be sufficient to avoid traige decisions — and corresponding judgments by a criminal court"*.

when a triage decision concerns two or more persons with a comparable condition from a medical point of view as to the urgency of required treatment ("state of health"), this decision is not medico-scientific: While it is true that the chances of survival can be evaluated through the application of medical criteria, the decision whether to refer to the chances of survival, to follow the principle of priority of arrival[66] (e.g. if three ambulances arrived within ten minutes) or to draw lots, is not a medical one, but a (professional) decision based on ethical standards and moral convictions — which can vary considerably and do not have the same democratic underpinning as a decision by parliament.[67] This is exactly why calling for the democratically elected legislator to resolve this situation is quite understandable. If, however, the legislator does not enact relevant provisions, the decision is left do the doctors whose behaviour in this situation will be evaluated ex post by courts and public prosecutors. In the absence of clear legal rules, there is no legal certainty as to the outcome of this evaluation. As will be shown in questions 5 and 6, there is indeed considerable legal uncertainty in particular as far as "ex-post-triage" (transfer of resources from one patient who already used them to another one who has better perspectives of survival) is concerned. This is why clear legal rules on triage decisions would also be an advantage from the point of view of doctors and hospital operators.

(3) At the same time, it is far from certain that legally binding guidelines enacted by Parliament would provide more guidance than once again referring to recommendations by medical societies.[68] The most probable scenario is that they would explicitly rule out the application of certain criteria.[69] However, such "negative" criteria can already today be deduced from existing legislation (see next bullet-point below). Still, these rules would allow doctors and hospital operators to claim that the law explicitly allows to follow medical recommendations on triage decisions, thereby offering them more legal certainty and a clear defence in case of criminal or civil procedures.

(4) Even in the absence of specific legislation on triage decisions, the above-mentioned general provisions on medical treatment in hospitals apply. This means that doctors are only "free" to decide between different patients once their

66 Explicitly in favor of this principle (against the recommendations by medical societies) in German scholarly literature e.g. Josef Franz Lindner, 'Die ‚Triage' im Lichte der Drittwirkung der Grundrechte' (2020) 38 MedR 723, 727.

67 For this opinion among German scholars, cf. Jochen Taupitz, 'Verteilung medizinischer Ressourcen in der Corona-Krise: Wer darf überleben?' (2020) 38 MedR 440, 442; very detailled considerations (in particular on the relation between law and ethics) can be found in the contribution by Bijan Fateh-Moghadam and Thomas Gutmann, 'Gleichheit vor der Triage. Rechtliche Rahmenbedingungen der Priorisierung von COVID-19-Patienten in der Intensivmedizin' in Tatjana Hörnle et al (eds), *Triage in der Pandemie* (Mohr Siebeck 2021) 312ff.

68 Cf. Stefan Huster, 'Wer hat Angst vor der Triage' in Tatjana Hörnle et al (eds), *Triage in der Pandemie* (Mohr Siebeck 2021) 107.

69 Cf. Steffen Augsberg, 'Regelbildung für existentielle Auswahlentscheidungen' in Tatjana Hörnle et al (eds), *Triage in der Pandemie* (Mohr Siebeck 2021) 22ff.

condition (state of health) as to the urgency of the required treatment is comparable from a medical point of view, eg two patients requiring ICU care. When assessing this question of comparability, doctors are obliged to perform an individual assessment of the state of health of the patient according to medical standards, from which any non-medical aspects have to be excluded. Only after this individual assessment has been completed, the actual "triage decision" (e.g. who receives the ventilator or ECMO unit) can be made. Under its obligation to protect (in this case, under Art. 2 ECHR), the state would immediately have to intervene if doctors discriminated patients by giving priority to those who require treatment less urgently than others.[70]

(5) If the triage decision is based on the individual perspective of survival of a patient (as recommended by medical societies in Austria, see questions 2 and 3 below), medical criteria have to be applied nevertheless. Once a hospital applies medical criteria, it is still bound by Art. 8 para. 2 of the Federal Hospital Acts which requires its staff to treat patients "in accordance with the principles and recognised methods of medical science". This also means that criteria that must not be applied when regularly prioritising patients must not be used in triage situations either: e.g. gender, race, age etc., unless they are linked to the medical perspective.

2. What values are the allocation criteria based on?

The currently existing allocation documents (see question 3) are based on the (moderately utilitarian) concept to save as many lives as possible while refraining from rating the "value" of an individual human life. The Austrian Bioethics Commission, a scientific advisory board to the Federal Chancellor, **summarized and endorsed** the recommendations of Austrian,[71] German[72] and Swiss[73] medical societies as quoted (official translation; emphasis added by the reporter): *"The approach arising from this aims to* ***save as many people as possible*** *with the extremely scarce resources that are available in a triage situation. The* ***short-term probability of survival*** *becomes a decisive point of reference in this situation: in terms of starting (or withholding) and continuing (or withdrawing) intensive care treatment, the prognosis should be based as far as possible on whether the individual concerned will be*

---

70 Cf. Again Christian Kopetzki, 'Art. 2 EMRK' in Karl Korinek and Michael Holoubek (eds), *Kommentar zum österreichischen Bundesverfassungsrecht* (Verlag Springer 2002) para 76, explicity adressing the scarcity of ICU beds in note 338.

71 Namely the recommendation by the Austrian Society for anesthesiology, resuscitation and intensive medicine (Österreichische Gesellschaft für Anästhesiologie, Reanimation und Intensivmedizin – ÖGARI); see below question 3.

72 Georg Markmann, Gerald Neitzke, Jan Schildmann et al, 'Decisions on the allocation of intensive care resources in the context of the COVID-19 pandemic' [2020] DIVI 477.

73 Daniel Scheidegger et al, 'COVID-19 pandemic: triage for intensive-care treatment under resource scarcity' [2020] Swiss Medical Weekly.

able to ***survive the intensive care treatment****. Of equivalent value to the objective of life support and survival, the issue of* ***avoiding chronic critical illness*** *must also be used to justify the indication. The term 'chronic critical illness' describes a state of surviving a life-threatening situation with resulting permanent and irreversible dependence on intensive care measures."*

As a result, the currently recommended criteria are based on the approach to give priority to those with the most promising probability of survival (without permanent reliance on intensive care), therefore saving as many lives as possible in the context of the pandemic. The **long-term perspective** (e.g. remaining life expectation after recovery) is **not** taken into account, nor are **non-medical** criteria (e.g. profession of the patient).

These allocation criteria do, in the reporter's opinion, not contradict the binding "negative" legal criteria outlined in question 1. However, their assessment from the point of view of criminal (and civil) law leaves some questions open (see questions 4 and 5 below).

3. In what type(s) of document(s) are the allocation criteria set? Is it in binding or non-binding guidelines, in the law, or in another type of document?

As described in the answer to question 1) above, there are neither specific legislation nor any administrative acts regulating allocation criteria in a triage situation. Specific criteria were published by the **Austrian Society for Anesthesiology, Resuscitation and Intensive Medicine (Österreichische Gesellschaft für Anästhesiologie, Reanimation und Intensivmedizin — ÖGARI)** in late March 2020[74] in a recommendation that was signed by about 20 members of the society (in other words: only doctors). The document recommends the use of different medical scores (activity of daily life, frailty, POSPOM [PreOperative Score to predict PostOperative Mortality], SOFA [Sequential Organ Failure Assessment]) to determine which patient has the highest short-time probability of survival. ÖGARI's recommendation proposes to include all patients requiring the same level of (ICU) care into the group subjected to the triage decision, not only patients affected by COVID-19. It is important to note that the recommendation explicitly refers not only to **"ex-ante triage"** (triage between several persons before the beginning of ICU care), but also to **"ex-post triage"** (transfer of resources from one patient who already uses them to another one who has better perspectives of survival). They recommend the same procedure for both situations, namely a medical evaluation of the question which

---

74 ÖGARI – Österreichische Gesellschaft für Anästhesiologie, Reanimation und Intensivmedizin, 'ICU – Triage im Falle von Ressourcen-Mangel, Empfehlungen aus Anlass der SARS-CoV-2-Pandemie' (*ÖGARI*, 26 March 2020) <www.oegari.at/web_files/cms_daten/gari_sop_triage_covid-19_arge_ethik_final_26.3.2020.pdf> accessed 25 July 2023.

patient has the highest short-time probability of survival (without permanent reliance on intensive care). These recommendations are **non-binding medical guidelines**. However, there has been so far no objection to them by other medical societies, state authorities or civil society, on the contrary, their existence has repeatedly been acknowleged by other scientists. The Austrian Bioethics Commission also endorsed them (see immediately below). As long as they remain more or less undisputed, they provide, from a legal point of view, some guidance for doctors. When a triage decision is evaluated ex post (by the public prosecutor, a court or the hospital authorities), it is very likely that the professional conduct of doctors who followed the recommendations by ÖGARI (or other medical societies) will be qualified as being in accordance with the medical "state of the art", thereby opening a way for their actions to be regarded as either justified or at least excusable from a legal point of view (see questions 5 to 7).

The **Austrian Bioethics Commission** published an opinion entitled "Management of scarce resources in healthcare in the context of the COVID-19 pandemic" (see already question 2 above) at the end of March 2020 which referred, amongst others, to the ÖGARI recommendations. The Bioethics Commission is an interdisciplinary advisory board to the Federal Chancellor, not a medical society. Due to its interdisciplinary composition (including lawyers), its opinion goes beyond the medical scope and is not limited to triage questions. However, one entire section of the opinion is dedicated to triage and discusses ex-ante as well as ex-post triage. It refers to several medical recommendations (including the ÖGARI recommendations), before explicitly addressing the legal perspective as well (official translation)[75]: *"Nevertheless, triage remains a dilemma in each scenario because the decision to withhold or withdraw indicated life-saving treatment in favour of another person cannot be justified in the context of legalo-ethical values and legal norms, particularly as one life cannot be weighed up against another life according to its quality. For those doctors who have to make such decisions in a catastrophic situation such as a pandemic (the decision to start or to continue intensive care treatment is also such a decision), the exculpatory circumstance provided by the state of emergency is recognised by society and the legal community in view of this dilemma, as expressed e.g. in section 10 of the Austrian Criminal Code (Strafgesetzbuch; StGB)."* Thereby the recommendation only refers to exculpation/excusability, not justification (on this, see question 5 below). The Bioethics Commission's opinion can be regarded twofold from a legal point of view: On the one hand, it is an information document that in principle endorses recommendations by medical societies, but places them into the bigger picture, including ethical and legal aspects. On the other hand, it can also serve as a documentation of the "state of the art" in triage questions,

[75] Bioethics Commission, 'Management of scarce resources in healthcare in the context of the COVID-19 pandemic' (*Federal Chancellery, Republic of Austria*, 31 March 2020) <www.bundeskanzleramt.gv.at/en/topics/bioethics-commission/publications-bioethics.html> or <https://rm.coe.int/management-scarce-resources/16809e40f1> accessed 25 July 2023.

thereby — though not a merely medical recommendation — having a (non-binding) value as an expert opinion comparable to that of a medical society. Still, as the Bioethics Commission is an independent advisory board, it does not have the value of a binding decision by a state authority.

In November 2020, the **Federation of Austrian Societies of Intensive Care Medicine (FASIM — Verband der Intensivmedizinischen Gesellschaften Österreichs)** published a "consensus paper" entitled „Ethical Guidance on allocatory questions concerning the use of scarce ressources in ICU care"[76] which is based on the ÖGARI recommendations and the Bioethics Commission's opinion, but — in contrast to the former — also includes some ethico-legal remarks. It also proposes to apply the same decision criteria to ex-ante triage and ex-post triage. Its legal value is comparable to that of ÖGARI's recommendation (non-binding expert opinion), however, its factual (medical) authority might be regarded as superior as it has been jointly published by several medical societies.

4. Are providers of health care obliged by the law to provide (urgent) care to all patients? If the answer is yes, are there any legally recognised exceptions from this duty?

In principle, three different obligations of hospital providers have to be distinguished:

(1) Art. 22 of the Federal Hospital Act obliges non-profit hospitals (which form the backbone of the inpatient care system) to admit for treatment all patients that are either "in need of hospitalization" or that wish to undergo surgery (without need of hospitalization, e.g. cosmetic surgery). However, it is in principle admissible to prioritise the admission of these patients according to their state of health, in other words: the use of waiting lists for planned treatments and/or surgery is admissible.[77]

(2) However, Art. 22 para. 4 of the Federal Hospital Act requires non-profit hospitals to admit certain patients without delay, namely those *"whose mental or physical condition requires immediate inpatient treatment due to danger to their life or danger of otherwise unavoidable serious damage to their health"* (the same applies to women about to give birth). These persons have to be admitted even if the regular capacities of a hospital are exhausted and a transfer

[76] FASIM – Federation of Austrian Societies of Intensive Care Medicine / Verband der Intensivmedizinischen Gesellschaften Österreichs, 'Allokationsethische Orientierungshilfe für den Einsatz knapper intensivmedizinischer Ressourcen' (*ÖGARI*, 11 November 2020) https://www.oegari.at/web_files/cms_daten/konsensus_fasim_allokation_intensiv_finale_fassung_text_11.11.2020_korr_neu_fin.pdf accessed 25 July 2023.

[77] The admissibility of waiting lists is clearly confirmed by Art. 5a para. 2 Federal Hospital Act which obliges hospital operators to make data on waiting times for certain elective treatment and surgeries publicly available by means of a "waiting list regime".

to another suitable hospital is not possible. This means that patients are — at no additional charge — to be admitted to "first class" beds (less beds in a room and additional amenities) if standard class beds are fully booked. It is common doctrinal opinion that even the occupation of all "first class" beds does not put an end to the obligation to admit patients requiring immediate care: In this case, patients have to be placed in extra beds (e.g. improvised beds in corridors).[78] However, it is also common doctrinal understanding that there is no obligation to admit additional patients if this endangers the life and health of those already admitted. This is of particular importance for infectious diseases: If it is no longer possible to isolate infected patients from other patients, leading to the risk of other patients being infected, the hospital can refuse the admission of patients beyond its maximum capacity.[79] In this case, several Austrian provinces (*Länder*) have included provisions on "emergency hospitals" in their hospital statutes, which would at least offer minimum care (though not the standard of care usually prescribed for hospitals).[80]

(3) Art. 23 of the Federal Hospital Act requires that all hospitals — including profit-orientated ones — offer essential first aid to anyone. However, this obligation does not go beyond immediate help which is necessary to stabilize a patient until it is possible to transfer her or him to a hospital which is obliged to admit him or her for treatment. Treatment of COVID-19-patients goes beyond first aid as described by this provision.

According to Art. 24 of the Federal Hospital Act, patients may only be discharged from hospital care if they no longer require it. This means that it is inadmissible to discharge patients once they have been admitted and still require hospital care. In contrast to this, it is admissible to postpone planned treatments/surgeries for the benefit of patients who require hospital care more urgently (which would also allow to discharge patients shortly before treatment/surgery).

In the context of COVID-19, this means that patients have to be admitted to non-profit hospitals not only as long as planned capacities are available but also (if capacities in other hospitals are exhausted) beyond that point as long as their admission does not endanger health or life of other patients. However, if it is not possible to treat all these patients according to the state of the art (e.g. due to lack of ventilators or ECMO devices), triage decision will have to be made.

78 Cf. (including further references) Christian Kopetzki, 'Krankenanstaltenrecht' in Michael Holoubek and Michael Potacs (eds), *Öffentliches Wirtschaftsrecht* (4th edn, Verlag Österreich 2019) 548.

79 Cf. (including further references) Karl Stöger, *Krankenanstaltenrecht* (Manz Verlag 2008) 633ff.

80 Cf. Karl Stöger, *Krankenanstaltenrecht* (Manz Verlag 2008) 250ff, 634.

5. On what legal basis is it possible to apply the allocation criteria in practice?

As mentioned above, there ist no specific legal provision addressing triage and triage criteria. Acccordingly, triage decisions have to be made by doctors (if need be, with the assistance of medical professions)[81]. Their decision will then be evaluated ex post on the basis of criminal and civil law. In this respect, it is necessary to differentiate between ex-ante triage (triage between several persons before the beginning of ICU care) and ex-post triage (transfer of resources from one patient who already uses them to another one who has better perspectives of survival).

Ex-ante triage: As explained in questions 2 and 3 above, all currently recommended allocation criteria for COVID-related ex-ante triage due to limited resources are based on the approach to give priority to those with the most promising short-time probability of survival (without permanent reliance on intensive care). Nevertheless, the doctors involved in such a decision cannot meet their obligation to treat all patients according to medical standards and can therefore be liable under criminal and civil law for injury or death of the non-prioritised patient. However, several legal scholars understand this situation as one of a **conflict of duties** of the doctors in charge, resulting in their actions being justified (and not merely excused).[82] In contrast to this opinion, other scholars as well as the Austrian Bioethics Commission regard doctors as merely excused due to a **state of necessity** (Art. 10 Austrian Criminal Code).[83] In any case, the Austrian criminal law doctrine would deny criminal liability of the doctors involved. The same would apply from the point of view of civil law: In principle, the hospital operator has breached its contract with the patient to treat him or her according to medical standards, while the doctors involved have violated his or her physical integrity. However, from the point of view of contractual liability or tort law the hospital operator and the

[81] According to the Austrian Supreme Court, the assessment and decision which type of treatment a patient requires is reserved for doctors and must not be performed by other medical professions (Austrian Supreme Court , 11 May 2010, 4 Ob 36/10p). However, it is admissable that nursing staff determines the potential waiting time until a patient is seen by a doctor in accordance with "standard" triage systems like the Manchester Triage System (Circular Letter of the Ministry of Health, 'Manchester Triage System of July 4, 2013, 92250/0028-II/A/2/2013' (2013) 6 ÖZPR 169; this circular letter is a non-binding interpretation of the law by the Ministry of Health). As to triage in the context of limited resources, it is obvious that this decision goes beyond the professional scope of nursing staff and must be made by a doctor (with the potential assistance of nursing staff if certain scores refer to questions which require expertise in nursing matters).

[82] Cf. Helmut Fuchs and Ingeborg Zerbes, *Strafrecht Allgemeiner Teil I* (11th edn, Manz Verlag 2021) ch 18, para 7; Karin Bruckmüller and Stefan Schumann, 'Priorisierung und Rationierung medizinischer Leistungen' in Michael Kierein, Paula Lanske, Sandra Wenda (eds), *Jahrbuch Gesundheitsrecht* (NWV Verlag 2009) 134ff: the doctor *"acts in conformity with the law as long as (s)he cares about at least one of the patients"*.

[83] Peter Lewisch, 'Nach § 3' in Frank Höpfel and Eckart Ratz (eds), *WK StGB* (2nd edn, RDB 2020) para 146ff, para 149; Alexander Tipold, '§ 3' in Otto Leukauf and Herbert Steininger (eds), *StGB* (4th edn, Linde 2019) para 48.

doctors would again be regarded as justified or at least excused.[84] In this situation, it is nevertheless conceivable that, as all non-profit hospital are required to have sufficient insurance cover, damages could be awarded to the patient or the heirs for reasons of equity due to the specific provision of Art. 1306a General Civil Code (*Allgemeines Bürgerliches Gesetzbuch; ABGB*). This provision allows for the award of damages if a person is harmed trough behaviour that is excused due to necessity[85] (most scholars regard it as applicable in case of justified behaviour as well[86]).

In the national reporter's opinion, ex-ante triage should be regarded as a justified conflict of duties. If only one patient can be treated according to medical standards due to a (justified) lack of resources, it would be hard to see why doctors could be regarded as acting unlawfully in such a situation. This also has an important implication: If their actions are justified and not merely excused, self-defence (e.g. by the family of a patient) is not permitted.

Ex-post triage: The legal assessment of this situation is much more uncertain than in the case of ex-ante triage. As mentioned above, the medical societies and the Austrian Bioethics Commission do not, from a medical point of view, differ between ex-ante and ex-post triage. According to their documents, the medical perspective of patients in ICU/ECMO care should be re-evaluated on a regular basis, resources can be passed on to other patients if their chances of (short-term) survival are **higher**. From a scholarly point of view, only one author so far explicitly argues that ex-post triage could be regarded as a socially adequate behaviour by the doctors involved.[87] Accordingly, their actions could be regarded as justified. However, even this author admits that a doctor who refuses to end intensive care for one patient for the benefit of another with a better medical perspective is in any case excused for not having ended the treatment.[88] At least one scholar explicitly denies the admissibility of ex-post triage even to the detriment of a person with

---

84 When discussing the concept of state of necessity, civil law scholars on a regular basis refer to the criminal law provision of Art. 10 Criminal Code: e.g. Helmut Koziol, 'C/1/ Die Rechtswidrigkeit' in Helmut Koziol (eds), *Haftpflichtrecht I* (4th edn, Jan Sramek Verlag 2020) para 104; Rudolf Reischauer, '§ 1306a' in Peter Rummel (eds), *ABGB* (3rd edn, RDB 2007) para 1ff.

85 Art. 1306a (translation by Barbara C. Steininger, 'Austria (Civil Code)' in Ken Oliphant and Barbara C. Steininger (eds), *European Tort Law Basic Texts* (2nd edn, Jan Sramek Verlag 2018) 3: *"If a person, in a situation of necessity, causes damage to avert imminent danger to himself or others, the judge has to decide whether and to what extent the damage has to be compensated, thereby taking into account whether the person harmed refrained from taking defensive action out of consideration for the imminent danger to the other, the relationship between the extent of damage and the danger and lastly, the financial means of the harm-doer and of the person harmed"*.

86 Cf. Judith Schacherreiter, '§ 1306a' in Andreas Kletečka and Martin Schauer (eds), *ABGB-ON 1.09* (RDB 2023) para 1, note 3; Helmut Koziol, 'C/1/ Die Rechtswidrigkeit' in Helmut Koziol (eds), *Haftpflichtrecht I* (4th edn, Jan Sramek Verlag 2020) para 104.

87 Alois Birklbauer, 'Kapitel 16: Strafrecht' in Reinhard Resch (eds), *Corona-Handbuch* (Manz Verlag 2021) para 13.

88 Alois Birklbauer, 'Kapitel 16: Strafrecht' in Reinhard Resch (eds), *Corona-Handbuch* (Manz Verlag 2021) para 15.

a negative medical perspective. According to this opinion, such a behaviour is neither justified or excusable.[89] The Austrian Bioethics Commission and — more or less implicitly — some scholars qualify an ex-post triage decision (for the benefit of a patient with a better short-time perspective of survival) as (merely) excusable (Art. 10 Austrian Criminal Code).[90] Obviously, a mere excusable behaviour would in principle allow for self-defence by the victim or his or her family.[91] A (justifiable) conflict of duties is predominantly rejected in the case of ex-post triage as one patient would be "downgraded" from a treatment which he or she already receives.[92] Not surprisingly, an ex-post triage with the clear intention to save a (younger) patient with a longer expectancy of life to the detriment of an older patient is regarded as non-admissible[93] if these two patients have the same short-time perspective of survival. This opinion is in conformity with the general rules on hospital care as explained in question 1. Despite this legal assessment, medical societies recommend random allocation of resources in this case, referring to (completely vague) ethical considerations.[94]

---

89 Peter Lewisch, 'Nach § 3' in Frank Höpfel and Eckart Ratz (eds), *WK StGB* (2nd edn, RDB 2020) para 72. Also doubtful as to the admissibiliy of ex-post triage, however in the broader context of scarce capacities in general, Karin Bruckmüller, Stefan Schumann, 'Priorisierung und Rationierung medizinischer Leistungen' in Michael Kierein, Paula Lanske and SandraWenda (eds), *Jahrbuch Gesundheitsrecht* (NWV Verlag 2009) 135. For similar perspectives in German scholarship, cf. Bijan Fateh-Moghadam and Thomas Gutmann, 'Gleichheit vor der Triage. Rechtliche Rahmenbedingungen der Priorisierung von COVID-19-Patienten in der Intensivmedizin' in Tatjana Hörnle et al (eds), *Triage in der Pandemie* (Mohr Siebeck 2021) 329ff (in particular p. 333: "punishable act") and — from a didactic perspective — Thomas Rönnau and Kilian Wegner, 'Grundwissen – Strafrecht: Triage' (2020) 4 JuS 403ff (p. 406: "Ex-post triage is punishable").

90 Bioethics Commission, 'Management of scarce resources in healthcare in the context of the COVID-19 pandemic' (*Federal Chancellery, Republic of Austria*, 31 March 2020) <www.bundeskanzleramt.gv.at/en/topics/bioethics-commission/publications-bioethics.html> or <https://rm.coe.int/management-scarce-resources/16809e40f1> accessed 9 March 2021; Frank Höpfel, '§ 10' in Frank Höpfel and Eckart Ratz (eds), *WK2 StGB* (2nd edn, RDB 2012) para 14: "life against life"; see also Alois Birklbauer, 'Kapitel 16: Strafrecht' in Reinhard Resch (eds), *Corona-Handbuch* (Manz Verlag 2021) para 13.

91 For a critical statement in this respect Benedikt Kommenda, 'Damoklesschwert über Ärzteschaft' *Die Presse* (Vienna, 20 July 2020) (Interview with Richard Soyer, Professor of Criminal Law, University of Linz, and Attorney at Soyer Kier Stufer in Vienna).

92 Helmut Fuchs and Ingeborg Zerbes, *Strafrecht Allgemeiner Teil I* (11th edn, Manz Verlag 2021) ch 18, para 4. For details, see the comparable discussion in German literature: e.g. Tatjana Hörnle, 'Ex-post-Triage: Strafbar als Tötungsdelikt' in Tatjana Hörnle et al (eds), *Triage in der Pandemie* (Mohr Siebeck 2021) 149. This author, however, comes to the conclusion that ex-post triage could be interpreted as a conflict of duties.

93 Helmut Fuchs and Ingeborg Zerbes, *Strafrecht Allgemeiner Teil I* (11th edn, Manz Verlag 2021) ch 18, para 5.

94 FASIM — Federation of Austrian Societies of Intensive Care Medicine / Verband der Intensivmedizinischen Gesellschaften Österreichs, 'Allokationsethische Orientierungshilfe für den Einsatz knapper intensivmedizinischer Ressourcen' (*ÖGARI*, 11 November 2020) 18 www.oegari.at/web_files/cms_daten/konsensus_fasim_allokation_intensiv_finale_fassung_text_11.11.2020_korr_neu_fin.pdf accessed 9 March 2021.

From the point of view of civil liability law, the situation is comparable: It is unclear whether an ex-post triage would be regarded as justified by a majority of scholars. An excusable state of necessity would probably be accepted while it cannot be ruled out that some scholars would even deny the excusability of a relevant medical decision. It should also be noted that most civil law scholars refer to criminal law doctrine when assessing situations of necessity like triage.[95] In any case, there is a high probability that courts would award damages in this case for reasons of equity.[96]

To sum up, while the recommendations by Austrian medical societies regard ex-ante and ex-post triage as comparable from a medical perspective, this is not the case from the legal point of view. While most, if not all (criminal law) scholars seem to accept ex-ante triage as either justified or at least excusable, the picture is much more diverse in the context of ex-post triage. A minority of scholar regards it as unjustified and unexcusable (inadmissible), at least one opinion considers it to be justifiable. The majority sees, more or less implicitly, no obligation of a doctor to perform ex-post triage for the benefit of a patient with a better perspective of short-time survival, however, it seems to accept it as excusable (though not justified) if the short-term perspective of the "new" patient is clearly better than that of the "old" patient. From a civil law perspective, triage situations are not discussed on a regular basis. In any case, legal certainty is very much lacking especially in cases of ex-post triage (see question 6).

6. What level of legal certainty do the health professionals and the health care providers have when applying the allocation criteria?

Due to the lack of specific legislation and relevant case-law, the level of legal certainty for health care professionals and providers is low. While the recommendations/guidelines by medical societies are certainly helpful in practice and will also be taken into account by medical experts in an ex-post evaluation, they cannot make up for this low level of legal certainty. In most cases, it is doubtful that the admissibility of triage decisions will be assessed by a court in advance in due time (e.g. through the request for an injunction by a relative for the benefit of a patient), so in practice the decisions will be evaluated ex post through criminal law or civil law proceedings. Especially with regard to the former, healthcare professionals are exposed to considerable legal uncertainty.

While there are some reasons to believe that a court would probably follow the scholarly consensus that **ex-ante triage** does not result in criminal liability (as it is excusable, if not even justified), the situation is much more uncertain concerning

[95] See note 84 above.

[96] Helmut Koziol, 'C/1/ Die Rechtswidrigkeit' in Helmut Koziol (eds), *Haftpflichtrecht I* (4th edn, Jan Sramek Verlag 2020) para 108, note 288.

ex-post triage decisions in which punishment for murder (Art 75 Austrian Criminal Code) cannot be entirely ruled out.[97] While, as discussed in question 5, a majority of scholars seems to regard ex-post triage as (merely) excusable, some scholars even qualify it as inadmissible.

This legal uncertainty also prevails in the context of civil law liability: Even if triage decisions can be regarded as excusable, liability for reasons of equity according to Art. 1306a General Civil Code cannot be entirely ruled out (if a triage decision is regarded as justified, the probability of liability would still be lower). However, as hospitals are under an obligation to buy insurance cover, the risk of health employees to be held liable for tort (in addition to the hospital operator's contractual liability) is practically minimal.

This lack of legal certainty is a very strong argument for a legislatory answer to the challenge of life-threatening triage due to lack of resources. However, as already mentioned above, no specific or general legislation on the matter has been passed in Austria to date.

7. What are the civil and criminal liability implications of allocation of scarce health care resources? Have there already been any related legal suits and/or criminal proceedings?

So far, there is **no relevant case-law** on ex-ante or ex-post triage in Austria.

In **criminal law, ex-ante triage** to the detriment of a patient is generally regarded as a failure to act when professionally being obliged to do so (Art. 2 Austrian Criminal Code[98]). Depending on the damage caused as a result of the triage decision and the extent to which injury or death was taken into account by the health professional, it would be (unless justified or excused) punishable as bodily harm, negligent causation of death or murder. **Ex-post triage** could either be regarded as failure to continue the required treatment or as an active violation of health or life, again (unless justified or excused) punishable as bodily harm, negligent causation of death or murder.

In **civil law**, ex-ante and ex-post triage can be regarded as medical malpractice as the hospital operator does not fulfill its contractual obligation to treat the patient according to the required medical standards. Accordingly, compensation for breach of contract were (unless the triage decision is qualified as justified or excused) to be awarded for damage to health or life. Furthermore, doctors who directly participated in these decisions could personally be held liable for violation of health or life of the patient under tort law. If the conduct of the hospital or the doctors were qualified as grossly negligent or intentional, persons close to the deceased patient could claim

---

97 For a similar conclusion as to the German situation, cf. Tatjana Hörnle, 'Ex-post-Triage: Strafbar als Tötungsdelikt' in Tatjana Hörnle et al (eds), *Triage in der Pandemie* (Mohr Siebeck 2021) 184: *"A clear prognosis [of the outcome of a criminal case concerning ex-post triage] is not possible."*

98 On the specific obligation of doctors to treat their patients cf. Marianne Lehmkuhl, '§ 2' in Frank Höpfel and Eckart Ratz (eds), *WK StGB* (2nd edn, RDB 2022) para 88.

compensation for pain and suffering. If the death of the patient mentally impairs persons close to the deceased, they could also claim compensation (even in cases of light neglicence). As mentioned above in question 5, according to Art. 1306a of the General Civil Code, compensation for reasons of equity could even be conceivable if the hospital's or the doctors' behaviour is regarded as excusable (or even justified) though there is hardly any legal certainty in this respect. As mentioned above, all non-profit hospitals have to take out insurance against civil liability which would accordingly cover these damages.

B. Case studies

Case 1

As a result of a rapid worsening of the epidemiological situation, the material and personal capacities have been drastically overloaded in all the hospitals in the country. Within just a few minutes, ambulances transport ten patients to one particular hospital's emergency unit. The patients all need admission to the hospital, preferably to the intensive care unit (ICU). However, only two beds are available there. Other hospitals are overwhelmed too, so it is not possible to transport patients to any of them. All of the ten newly coming patients suffer from COVID-19; they have breathing difficulties, fast-rising fever, and decreasing oxygen saturation. Nevertheless, they differ in age, comorbidities, clinical fragility, and other factors.

Theoretically, the eight patients who cannot be admitted to beds can be placed in improvised settings in the hospital corridors, laying on gurneys or mattresses on the floor. Nevertheless, it will be impossible to provide them with the care they need.

Evaluation of the case

- What criteria can be used to choose the patients who will be admitted to the beds (i.e. what are the possible allocation criteria)?
  In this situation, all patients require medical care with the same degree of urgency (comparable "state of health" as to the necessity of treatment). However, only two of them can receive the necessary level of care. While it is clear that the hospital staff is by law obliged to allocate the two beds to two patients, there are no binding legal criteria as to the question whom they will be allocated to. In principle, different criteria could be used, like priority of arrival (even if there are only minutes between), short-time perspective of survival or drawing lots. If, however, the medical criterion of short-time perspective of survival is chosen, the relevant assessment has to be based on medical standards, which means that age, gender, race or frailty can only taken into account if they are linked to the medical perspective of survival.
  In practice, it is highly probable that hospitals staff will follow the existing recommendations by medical societies which have been issued during the

pandemic. These recommendations are based on the short-term probability of survival, including the perspective of avoiding chronic critical illness (see question 3). This is probably a "safe" option with regard to an ex post assessment of the staff's decision by a criminal or civil court.

- What legal consequences can this decision have for the health professionals and the hospital? How strong is their legal certainty that there will be no adverse legal consequences if they follow the above-mentioned criteria?
  In the worst (though improbable) case, staff could be prosecuted and tried for causing bodily harm or death through failure to act. This would also result in the hospital being obliged to pay damages for medical maltreatment. However, in the case described here (ex-ante triage) there is rather broad consensus among legal scholars that the triage decision is not punishable as it can either be justified due to conflict of duties or at least excused due to a situation of state of necessity. There is a rather high probability that public prosecutors and criminal courts would agree, although there is no existing case-law. These arguments would also, with high probability, shield hospital and staff for damage claims on the basis of contract or tort, though there is a minor risk that damages out of equity (Art. 1306a General Civil Code) would be awarded. Following medical recommendations would certainly be advisable as this would probably be judged as appropriate by prosecutors or courts in case of criminal or civil law proceedings.
- What legal defences could the health professionals and the hospital use against a civil lawsuit and/or criminal prosecution for the allocation decision?
  See immediately above.

Additional questions

- Would it be legally permissible to lower the standard of care provided to all patients in order to provide at least basic decent care to the newly admitted patients who are placed in the hospital corridors? To what extent?
  As outlined in questions 1 and 4 of this report, hospitals are under an obligation to provide care according to medical standards. Furthermore, non-profit hospitals are under an obligation to accept additional patients (even after the exhaustion of normal capacities) as long as their admission does not endanger health and life of other patients. This means that an adaptation (lowering) of the standard of care is permissible in an emergency situation as long as this is still within the bandwith of medical standards applicable in such a case. This can, for example, result in the (temporary) reduction of the number of rounds by doctors, less frequent visits by nursing staff and second-best, though medically adequate, treatment options. However, it would be against the law to admit infectious patients who cannot be sufficiently isolated from non-infected patients (in other words, infectious patients will have to be placed in the corridor of isolation wards or spatially divided entities). It would even seem permissible to discharge patients if they have been admitted for elective treatment which can be postponed without a negative impact on their state of health. However, any lowering

of standards which would negatively affect the health or even life of patients is not admissible. If this situation were to occur nevertheless, the hospital would be in violation of its (contractual) duties towards its patients. In this case, the same elements of defence (justification or excusability: collision of duties, state of necessity) as discussed above in the context of triage would be relevant.

Case 2

Two patients in an ICU are suffering from COVID-19. After admission to the hospital, they were provided with the high-flow nasal oxygen therapy (HFNO). During one night, the condition of both patients starts to worsen rapidly. At dawn, it is clear that neither of them will survive without artificial ventilation. However, there is just one ventilator available.

Evaluation of the case

- What criteria can be used to choose which of the two patients will be provided with artificial ventilation and which one will be left without it, possibly to die?
  The legal assessment of this case does not differ from Case 1. From the point of view of (criminal) law, this is still an ex-ante triage as both patients require an upgrade of the quality of their treatment which they did not receive so far. Accordingly, the situation is comparable to two newly arriving patients in a hospital with only one ICU bed available.
- What legal consequences can this decision have for the health professionals and the hospital? How strong is their legal certainty that there will be no adverse legal consequences if they follow the above-mentioned criteria?
  The legal assessment of this case does not differ from Case 1 as described above.
- What legal defences could the health professionals and the hospital use against a civil lawsuit and/or criminal prosecution for the allocation decision?
  The legal assessment of this case does not differ from Case 1 as described above.

Additional question

- If the allocation criteria specified in your answer to the first question to this case consisted of the patients' clinicical features (such as their age, clinical fragility, etc.), please identify what criteria could be used for the allocation decision if all the relevant clinical features of both patients were practically the same?
  Current recommendations on triage decisions in Austria are indeed based on clinical features (short-time perspective of survival according to medical scoring systems; see question 3 above). However, in case of a comparable medical score the consensus paper "Ethical Guidance on allocatory questions concerning the use of scarce resources in ICU" by the Federation of Austrian Societies of Intensive Care (FASIM; see list of sources) explicitly recommends *"random allocation of scarce intensive care resources [as this approach,] from an ethical perspective, most closely corresponds to the values and norms of equal opportunities for all people"*. Such an approach can be regarded as justifiable or at least

excusable from a legal point of view as it does not refer to any discriminatory criteria. As it is explicitly mentioned in a recommendation by medical societies, it is probable that it would be applied and accepted in practice.

Case 3

There is a single extracorporeal membrane oxygenation (ECMO) device in the hospital. It is currently being used for an 84-year-old patient suffering from COVID-19, with diabetes as an underlying disease, clinical frailty score (CFS) 6–7 (moderate to severe frailty). It is possible that the patient will survive and will be discharged from the hospital if the ECMO treatment is continued. However, a younger COVID-19 patient is admitted to the hospital. This new patient is 51 years old, otherwise healthy, but her health condition has been rapidly deteriorating. Soon she will most likely need ECMO to survive.

<u>Evaluation of the case</u>

- Can it be legally permissible for the hospital staff to discontinue the ECMO treatment of the older patient and provide palliative care to her in order to save the younger and healthier patient's life? Please keep in mind that the older patient could survive if the treatment continued, but her chances may be lower than those of the younger patient.
  This is a case of ex-post triage in which scarce resources are diverted from a patient who already uses them to another patient. In case that the short-time chances of survival of the younger patients are indeed higher than those of the older patient, the current medical recommendations by medical societies in Austria and the opinion of the Austrian Bioethics Commision would regard discontinuing the treatment of the older patient for the benefit of the younger patient as adequate. The Austrian Bioethics Commission would regard this decision as excusable from a legal point of view (Art. 10 Austrian Criminal Code).
  From a legal (scholarly) point of view, the admissibility of ex-post triage is much more disputed than that of ex-ante triage: While a majority of scholars — at least tacitly — seem to accept it as (merely) excusable, at least one author explicitly rejects this approach, regarding ex-post triage as absolutely inadmissible (see question 5 above).
- If the answer to the first question is positive, what specific criteria can be used in clinical decision-making regarding replacing one patient with another with respect to a particular treatment unavailable for all?
  Current recommendations by medical societies recommend to evaluate the condition of patients already treated in ICUs according to medical scoring systems (e.g. ÖGARI recommendations: activity of daily life, frailty, POSPOM [PreOperative Score to predict PostOperative Mortality], SOFA [Sequential Organ Failure Assessment]) in order to determine their short-time perspective of survival without permanent necessity of intensive care. The same scoring system should be used when determining the perspective of survival of newly arrived patients.

If the scores of the latter are clearly better, then he or she would — according to current medical recommendation — be allocated the ECMO device to the detriment of the former.

- What legal consequences can this decision have for the health professionals and the hospital? How strong is their legal certainty that there will be no adverse legal consequences if they follow the above-mentioned criteria?

An ex-post triage decision can have serious consequences from a criminal law perspective: In the worst case (for the health professional), it can be regarded as murder or intentional causation of bodily harm. As explained in more detail in question 5 above, there is no case-law, but at least one scholarly opinion that regards ex-post triage as absolutely inadmissible and consequently punishable. The hospital could be held to account under corporate criminal law. However, there are also scholarly opinions that regard ex-post triage as excusable, (only) one author even qualifies it as justifiable. From a civil law perspective, the situation is comparable: Ex-post triage can be regarded as a breach of contract resulting in damages for death and injury, although it seems conceivable that it will be regarded as excused (or even justified) by a court. Even if this were the case, it is possible that damages out of equity (Art. 1306a General Civil Code) would be awarded.

Generally spoken, legal certainty as to adverse legal consequences for staff or the hospital is much lower than in the case of ex-ante triage. If hospital staff wants to be on the "safe side", it would let the older patient keep the ICU bed. If the older and the younger patient died as a consequence, doctors would nevertheless be justified (or at least excused) for not having stopped the treatment of the older patient. Accordingly, at least for ex-post triage a clear answer by the democratically elected legislator as to its admissibility and potential criteria would be desirable.

- What legal defences could the health professionals and the hospital use against a civil lawsuit and/or criminal prosecution for the allocation decision?

The most promising defence would be to argue that the hospital and its staff was in a state of necessity and followed the recommendations of medical societies and the Bioethics Commission which regard ex-post triage as comparable to ex-ante triage. As the reallocation of ressources in this case took into account the better short-time perspective of survival of the younger patient, the ex-post triage could be defended as excusable with regard to criminal sanctions (Art 10 StGB: state of necessity) or civil liability. Alternatively, the decision could also be defended as socially adequate behaviour and, as a consequence, not only excusable, but even legitimate (=justified). This opinion is, however, still a minority opinion within legal scholarship.

Additional question

- Suppose there are two different scenarios: a) the older patient was admitted to the hospital and provided with the ECMO treatment, and only later, after several days, the younger patient was admitted, and b) the younger patient was admitted before the older patient, however, the older patient required ECMO treatment soon after admission while the younger patient's health condition deteriorated only after a longer time when the ECMO was already occupied (i. e. at the time when the younger patient was admitted to the hospital, she did not yet need it). Would there be any difference in the allocation decision making between these two scenarios?

At least from the point of view of the current recommendations by medical societies, there would be no difference between these two scenarios. From a legal point of view, the outcome is similar: In both cases, an ex-post triage would take place as an already ongoing medical treatment of a patient were "downgraded" to his or her detriment and to the benefit of another patient.

The list of abbreviations

Art.	Article
CFS	Clinical Frailty Score
ECMO	Extracorporeal membrane oxygenation
ECHR	European Convention of Human Rights
ECtHR	European Court of Human Rights
FASIM	Federation of Austrian Societies of Intensive Care Medicine
ICU	Intensive Care Unit
NFNO	High-flow nasal oxygen therapy
ÖGARI	Österreichische Gesellschaft für Anästhesiologie, Reanimation und Intensivmedizin
POSPOM	PreOperative Score to predict PostOperative Mortality
SOFA	Sequential Organ Failure Assessement

Bibliography

• Legislation

ABGB: General Civil Code (*Allgemeines Bürgerliches Gesetzbuch*); Justizgesetzsammlung No. 946/1811, as amended by Federal Gazette Part I, No. 38/2023; cited as: General Civil Code

ECHR: European Convention on Human Rights (*Europäische Menschenrechtskonvention*); Federal Gazette No. 210/1958, as amended by Federal Gazette Part III, No. 68/2021

KAKuG: Federal Act on Hospitals and Health Resorts (*Kranken- und Kuranstaltengesetz*); Federal Gazette No. 1/1957, as amended by Federal Gazette Part I, No. 79/2022; cited as: Federal Hospital Act

StGB: Criminal Code *(Strafgesetzbuch),* Federal Gazette No. 60/1974, as amended by Federal Gazette Part I, No. 100/2023; cited as: Criminal Code

- **Case law**

Austrian Supreme Court (Oberster Gerichtshof; OGH) 11 May 2010, 4 Ob 36/10p
Austrian Supreme Court (Oberster Gerichtshof; OGH) 4 June 2004, 2 Ob 27/03i
Austrian Supreme Court (Oberster Gerichtshof; OGH) 29 March 2001, 2 Ob 60/01i
Calvelli and Ciglio v Italy ECHR 2002-I 25

- **Books**

Augsberg S, 'Regelbildung für existentielle Auswahlentscheidungen' in Hörnle T et al (eds), *Triage in der Pandemie* (Mohr Siebeck 2021)

Birklbauer A, 'Kapitel 16: Strafrecht' in Reinhard Resch (eds), *Corona-Handbuch* (Manz Verlag 2021)

Bruckmüller K and Schumann S, 'Priorisierung und Rationierung medizinischer Leistungen' in Kierein M, Lanske P and Wenda S (eds), *Jahrbuch Gesundheitsrecht* (NWV Verlag 2009)

Fateh-Moghadam B and Gutmann T, 'Gleichheit vor der Triage. Rechtliche Rahmenbedingungen der Priorisierung von COVID-19-Patienten in der Intensivmedizin' in Hörnle T et al (eds), *Triage in der Pandemie* (Mohr Siebeck 2021)

Fuchs H and Zerbes I, *Strafrecht Allgemeiner Teil I* (11th edn, Manz Verlag 2022)

Höpfel F, '§ 10' in Höpfel F and Ratz E (eds), *WK2 StGB* (2nd edn, RDB 2012)

Hörnle T, 'Ex-post-Triage: Strafbar als Tötungsdelikt' in Hörnle T et al (eds), *Triage in der Pandemie* (Mohr Siebeck 2021)

Huster S, 'Wer hat Angst vor der Triage' in Hörnle T et al (eds), *Triage in der Pandemie* (Mohr Siebeck 2021)

Kersten F and Rixen S, *Der Verfassungsstaat in der Corona-Krise* (C.H.BECK 2020)

Kneihs B, 'Art 2 EMRK' in Kneihs BLienbacher G (eds), *Rill-Schäffer-Kommentar Bundesverfassungsrecht* (Verlag Österreich 2020)

Kopetzki C, 'Art 2 EMRK' in Korinek K and Holoubek M (eds), *Kommentar zum österreichischen Bundesverfassungsrecht* (Verlag Springer 2002)

Kopetzki C, 'Krankenanstaltenrecht' in Holoubek M and Potacs M (eds), *Öffentliches Wirtschaftsrecht* (4th edn, Verlag Österreich 2019)

Koziol H, 'C/1/ Die Rechtswidrigkeit' in Koziol H (eds), *Haftpflichtrecht I* (4th edn, Jan Sramek Verlag 2020)

Lehmkuhl M, '§ 2' in Höpfel F and Ratz E (eds), *WK StGB* (2nd edn, RDB 2021)

Lewisch P, 'Nach § 3' in Höpfel F and Ratz E (eds), *WK StGB* (2nd edn, RDB 2020)

Reischauer R, '§ 1306a' in Rummel P (eds), *ABGB* (3rd edn; RDB 2007)

Schacherreiter J, '§ 1306a' in Kletečka A and Schauer M (eds), *ABGB-ON 1.09* (RDB 2023)

Steininger B C, 'Austria (Civil Code)' in Oliphant K and Steininger B C (eds), *European Tort Law. Basic Texts* (2nd edn, Jan Sramek Verlag 2018)

Stöger K, *Krankenanstaltenrecht* (Manz Verlag 2008)

Tipold A, '§ 3' in Leukauf O and Steininger H (eds), *StGB* (4th edn, Linde 2019)

• Articles

Berka W, 'Die Verantwortung des Staates für die medizinische Versorgung' (2019) 5a RdM 227
Birklbauer A, Grimm M, Kröll W and Neuper O, 'Triage – Der Nicht-Ärzte liebstes Kind' (2020) 3 JMG 125
Brade A and Müller M, 'Corona-Triage: Untätigkeit des Gesetzgebers als Schutzpflichtverletzung' (2020) 24 Neue Zeitschrift für Verwaltungsrecht 1792
Kommenda B, 'Damoklesschwert über Ärzteschaft' *Die Presse* (Vienna, 20 July 2020)
Kröll W, 'Das Damoklesschwert der Triage über der Ärzteschaft' (2020) 3 JMG 151
Lindner J F, 'Die ‚Triage' im Lichte der Drittwirkung der Grundrechte' (2020) 38 MedR 723
Markmann F, Neitzke G, Schildmann J et al, 'Decisions on the allocation of intensive care resources in the context of the COVID-19 pandemic' [2020] DIVI 477
Rönnau T and Wegner K, 'Grundwissen – Strafrecht: Triage' (2020) 4 JuS 403
Scheidegger D et al, 'COVID-19 pandemic: triage for intensive-care treatment under resource scarcity' [2020] Swiss Medical Weekly
Stöger K, 'Darf die Art der Beschaffung die medizinische Therapie beeinflussen?' (2019) 5 RdM-ÖG 15
Streit G, 'Gesundheitsversorgung in der Pandemie: Triage – oder kommen alle dran?' (2020) 3 JMG 141
Taupitz J, 'Verteilung medizinischer Ressourcen in der Corona-Krise: Wer darf überleben?' (2020) 38 MedR 440
Tipold A, 'Triage und deutsches Infektionsschutzgesetz' (2023) 1 ZfG 7

• Other secondary sources

Bioethics Commission, 'Zum Umgang mit knappen Ressourcen in der Gesundheitsversorgung im Kontext der Covid-19-Pandemie' (*Federal Chancellery, Republic of Austria*, 31 March 2020) <https://www.bundeskanzleramt.gv.at/dam/jcr:772d37b0-3db9-4c8b-b4fe-e6dca7b1b8d3/200402_Covid_Bioethik.pdf> accesssed 25 July 2023
Bioethics Commission, 'Management of scarce resources in healthcare in the context of the COVID-19 pandemic' (*Federal Chancellery, Republic of Austria*, 31 March 2020) <www.bundeskanzleramt.gv.at/en/topics/bioethics-commission/publications-bioethics.html> or <https://rm.coe.int/management-scarce-resources/16809e40f1> accesssed 25 July 2023
Circular Letter of the Ministry of Health, 'Manchester Triage System of July 4, 2013, 92250/0028-II/A/2/2013' (2013) 6 ÖZPR 169
ÖGARI – Österreichische Gesellschaft für Anästhesiologie, Reanimation und Intensivmedizin, 'Checkliste: ICU – Triage im Falle von Ressourcen-Mangel' (*ÖGARI*, 26 March 2020) <www.oegari.at/web_files/cms_daten/gari_checkliste_triage_icu_final_26.3.2020.pdf> accesssed 25 July 2023
ÖGARI – Österreichische Gesellschaft für Anästhesiologie, Reanimation und Intensivmedizin, 'ICU – Triage im Falle von Ressourcen-Mangel, Empfehlungen aus Anlass der SARS-CoV-2-Pandemie' (*ÖGARI*, 26 March 2020) <www.oegari.at/web_files/cms_daten/gari_sop_triage_covid-19_arge_ethik_final_26.3.2020.pdf> accesssed 25 July 2023
FASIM – Federation of Austrian Societies of Intensive Care Medicine / Verband der Intensivmedizinischen Gesellschaften Österreichs, 'Allokationsethische Orientierungshilfe

für den Einsatz knapper intensivmedizinischer Ressourcen' (*ÖGARI*, 11 November 2020) <www.oegari.at/web_files/cms_daten/konsensus_fasim_allokation_intensiv_finale_fassung_text_11.11.2020_korr_neu_fin.pdf> accesssed 25 July 2023

BRAZIL

Flávia Cambraia[99] and Marcelo Chiavassa de Mello Paula Lima[100]

Mackenzie Presbyterian University

Introduction

To provide a better understanding on the right to health in Brazil, it's important to highlight that the Brazilian Federal Constitution (1988) establishes, in article 24, XII, the existence of concurrent jurisdiction to legislate on the right to health. This means that all federal entities (the Union, the States, the Federal District, and the Municipalities) are competent to legislate on themes related to health remedies.

The Union is competent to create general rules regarding health remedies, while the states and the municipalities legislate upon complementary rules (§§ 1° and 2° of art. 24 of the CF[101]). In the absence of a Federal rule on the issue, all federal entities will have full capacity to legislate (§ 3° of art. 24 of the CF).

In this context, Federal entities can adopt measures regarding problems related to the COVID-19 pandemic, such as measures to contain the spread of the virus, strategies and major allocations of scarce resources, since the measure respects the supremacy of the Union to legislate upon the theme.

Furthermore, during the COVID-19 pandemic, in the decision of April of 2020,[102] the Federal Supreme Court restated its position expressly stating the concurrent jurisdiction among federal entities to legislate on the matter. It examined the Provisional Presidential Decree, edited by President Jair Bolsonaro (which regulated the proceeding to use of funds to purchase assets, services, and inputs destinated to face the challenges imposed by the pandemic). The decision also aimed to make it clear that, although the Union legislate on certain measures and proceedings related

[99] PhD in Criminal Law (UFMG-Brazil), with research period in Germany (Universität Augsburg and Humboldt Universität zu Berlin). Professor of Criminal Law at Mackenzie Presbyterian University.

[100] PhD in Private Law (Universidade de São Paulo – USP – Brazil). Professor of Private Law and Digital Law at Mackenzie Presbyterian University.

[101] Constituição da República Federativa do Brasil de 1988 <www.planalto.gov.br/ccivil_03/constituicao/constituicao.htm> accessed 8 April 2021.

[102] STF, 'STF reconhece competência concorrente de estados, DF, municípios e União no combate à Covid-19' (STF notícias, 15 April 2020) <http://portal.stf.jus.br/noticias/verNoticiaDetalhe.asp?idConteudo=441447&ori=1> accessed 11 April 2021.

to health, due to the COVID-19 it must preserve the autonomy of the States, the Federal District and Municipalities once they all have the competence to adopt legislative and administrative measures to face the pandemic.

Therefore, the Federal Government must respect the measures and decisions adopted in the States and Municipalities, by its governors and mayors. The idea is to allow that each region of the country has the autonomy to deal with the challenges posed by the pandemic, regarding the specific necessities and its own characteristics.

Lastly, Brazil has the "Sistema Único de Saúde — SUS" (the Brazilian Universal Healthcare Program), which constitutes the larger system of public health in the world. The access is universal, equal, and free, in other words all Brazilian citizens can use it, without any kind of distinction between people, including resident alien or any person that needs medical assistance while in the country.[103] SUS is present in article 196 of the Federal Constitution and on the Federal Regulation number 8.080/1990.[104] It is the State duty to provide measures related to health, this is a right to all citizens.

Thus, aiming to guarantee the access of all citizens affected by the COVID-19 virus, the Act 13.979 of February of 2020[105] provides measures to face the public health emergency, of international relevancy, due to the coronavirus, responsible for the 2019 outbreak and establishes in article 3, § 2°, II the universal right to receive free medical care.

A. Questionnaire

1. What are the criteria for the allocation of scarce health care resources in your country?

In Brazil, the rules on the allocation of scarce resources does not has specific Regulation. The Office of the President's Chief of Staff proposed some recommendations, as well as Medical Associations and class representatives, but without binding effects. Among them, it is important to highlight:

(i) Guidance on the patient's treatment with COVID-19, prepared by Ministry of Health;[106]

---

103 SUS, 'Sistema único de saúde' (*Secretaria de Estado de Saúde*) <www.saude.mg.gov.br/sus> accessed 11 April 2021.

104 Lei n° 8.080, de 19 de setembro de 1990. Dispõe sobre as condições para a promoção, proteção e recuperação da saúde, a organização e o funcionamento dos serviços correspondentes e dá outras providências <www.planalto.gov.br/ccivil_03/leis/l8080.htm> accessed 11 April 2021.

105 Lei n° 13.979, de 6 de fevereiro de 2020. Dispõe sobre as medidas para enfrentamento da emergência de saúde pública de importância internacional decorrente do coronavírus responsável pelo surto de 2019 <www.planalto.gov.br/ccivil_03/_ato2019-2022/2020/lei/l13979.htm> accessed 7 April 2021.

106 Ministério da Saúde, 'Orientações Para Manejo De Pacientes Com Covid-19' (*Portal de Boas Práticas*, June 2020) <https://portaldeboaspraticas.iff.fiocruz.br/wp-content/uploads/2020/06/Covid19-Orienta-esManejoPacientes.pdf> accessed 16 August 2021.

(ii) Handling Coronavirus (COVID-19), prepared by the Service of Control of Hospital Infections of the Sociedade Beneficente Israelita Albert Einstein;[107]
(iii) Resolution number 13, of June 5th of 2020, prepared by the Medical Council of Rio Grande do Sul, on the Allocation of Resources in Intensive Care Unities during the pandemic;[108]
(iv) Guidance on confronting the COVID-19 pandemic in the Healthcare network on Health, prepared by the Ministry of Health;[109]
(v) Guidance on COVID-19 by the Brazilian Medical Association;[110]
(vi) Institutional Protocol of Service to patient suspected of infection or confirmed with COVID-19, prepared by the Hospital do Coração (HCOR);[111]
(vii) Protocol on the Allocation of Resource in depletion during the COVID-19 pandemic, prepared by the Brazilian Intensive Care Medicine Association;[112]
(viii) Recommendation number 05/2020, prepared by the Medical Council of Pernambuco (CREMEPE);[113]

Due to the pandemic, especially during critical times, almost all medical professionals and equipment acted in the front of the crisis. The measures included: the suspension of elective surgeries (non-essential) for undetermined period; the use of medical students in the frontline of the pandemic; the creation of new temporary hospital beds as well as providing Ventilatory Support in hospital beds for the exclusive support of COVID-19 patients, in exceptional nature (Regulation number 1521/2020, Ministry of Health).[114]

---

107 Serviço De Controle De Infecção Hospitalar Da Sociedade Beneficente Israelita Albert Einstein, 'Manejo Coronavírus (COVID-19)' <https://medicalsuite.einstein.br/pratica-medica/Documentos%20Doencas%20Epidemicas/Manejo-de-casos-suspeitos-de-sindrome-respiratoria-pelo-COVID-19.pdf> accessed 16 August 2021.

108 Resolução CRM-RS nº 13, de 5 de junho de 2020. Estabelece os critérios sobre Alocação de Recursos em Unidades de Terapia Intensiva durante a pandemia <www.in.gov.br/web/dou/-/resolucao-n-13-de-5-de-junho-de-2020-261274042> accessed 16 August 2021.

109 SUS, 'Guia Orientador para o enfrentamento da pandemia COVID-19 na Rede de Atenção à Saúde' (*Conselho Nacional de Secretarias municipais de Saúde*, March 2021) <www.conasems.org.br/wp-content/uploads/2021/04/Covid-19_guia_orientador_4ed.pdf> accessed 16 August 2021.

110 AMB, 'Diretrizes Covid-19' (*Associação Médica Brasileira*, 1 April 2020) <https://amb.org.br/wp-content/uploads/2020/04/DIRETRIZES-AMB-COVID-19-01.04.2020.pdf> accessed 16 August 2021.

111 HCOR, 'Protocolo Institucional de Atendimento ao paciente com suspeita ou confirmação de COVID-19' (*Hospital do Coração*, March 2020) <www.hcor.com.br/area-medica/wp-content/uploads/sites/3/2020/11/protocolo_atendimento_coronavirus_v14.pdf> accessed 16 August 2021.

112 AMIB, 'Protocolo AMIB de alocação de recursos em esgotamento durante a pandemia por COVID-19' (*Associação de Medicina Intensiva Brasileira*, 24 April 2020) <www.amib.org.br/fileadmin/user_upload/amib/2020/abril/24/Protocolo_AMIB_de_alocacao_de_recursos_em_esgotamento_durante_a_pandemia_por_COVID-19.pdf> accessed 16 August 2021.

113 Recomendação nº 05/2020 do Conselho Regional de Medicina de Pernambuco <www.cremepe.org.br/wp-content/uploads/2020/04/RECOMENDA%c3%87%c3%83O-CREMEPE-N%c2%ba-05_v.final_.pdf> accessed 16 August 2021.

114 Portaria nº 1.521, de 15 de junho de 2020. Autoriza a habilitação de leitos de suporte ventilatório pulmonar para atendimento exclusivo dos pacientes da COVID-19 <www.in.gov.br/web/dou/-/portaria-n-1.521-de-15-de-junho-de-2020-261697745> accessed 8 April 2021.

Still, there is no Federal Act in the country to dictate upon general rules on the support to patients and use of hospital resources. Due to the absence of regulation on the matter, the competent actors made decisions based on clinical and ethical criteria,[115] regarding the philosophical utilitarianism (to save more people as possible). In most cases, the decision-makers used three criteria: (i) higher probability of survival; (ii) equality; (iii) equity.[116]

In this sense, in the scenario of only one ventilatory support, by the protocol its destination will be for the patient that presents higher chance of survival, instead of someone with few chances to resist, regardless age, ethnicity, social position, professional qualification, political preference, or who was first at the hospital. If there are patients in similar conditions, the choice will be through raffle.[117]

In addition, the Brazilian Intensive Care Medicine Association stablished the following criteria to triage, which several hospitals in the country used:

Even if exists different recommendation that shows significant differences among themselves, the consensus is that the stronger principle is of prioritize patients with better chances of benefit and with higher expectations of survival. Equalize the opportunity of individuals to face different cycles of life is also a recommended criteria by some guidelines and recommendations. The emphasis on the maximization of benefits can be translated through the objectives: i) save a higher number of lives (survival in short-term); ii) save the higher number of years of live (survival in long-term), and iii) equalize the opportunity of individuals to face different cycles of life.[118]

Summing up, the first criteria is to save the higher number of lives (utilitarianism). Among those lives, the younger will have priority over the older (to save the higher number of years of life and to allow that a higher amount of people can finish the cycles of life — childhood, adult life, and old age — again, utilitarianism).

The debate by several medical councils in Brazil concern to the adoption of these criteria, but the absence of a national plan that could serve as a guideline resulted in different priorities around the country, depending about each council. However, it is possible to say that the criteria included those ethical principles.[119]

---

115 Erika Satomi et al, 'Alocação justa de recursos de saúde escassos diante da pandemia de COVID-19: considerações éticas' (2020) 18 Einstein (São Paulo) <www.scielo.br/scielo.php?script=sci_arttext&pid=S1679-45082020000100903&lng=en&nrm=iso> accessed 6 de April 2021.

116 Marcelo José dos Santos et al, 'Covid-19: instruments for the allocation of mechanical ventilators — a narrative review' (2020) 582 Critical Care 24 <https://ccforum.biomedcentral.com/articles/10.1186/s13054-020-03298-3> accessed 6 April 2021.

117 Fernando Rister de Sousa Lima et al (eds), *Covid-19 e os impactos no direito: mercado, estado, trabalho, família, contratos e cidadania* (Grupo Almedina 2020).

118 AMIB, 'Protocolo AMIB de alocação de recursos em esgotamento durante a pandemia por COVID-19' (*Associação de Medicina Intensiva Brasileira*, 24 April 2020) <www.amib.org.br/fileadmin/user_upload/amib/2020/abril/24/Protocolo_AMIB_de_alocacao_de_recursos_em_esgotamento_durante_a_pandemia_por_COVID-19.pdf> accessed 7 April 2021.

119 Marcelo José dos Santos et al, 'Covid-19: instruments for the allocation of mechanical ventilators — a narrative review' (2020) 582 Critical Care 24 <https://ccforum.biomedcentral.com/articles/10.1186/s13054-020-03298-3> accessed 6 April 2021.

2. What values are the allocation criteria based on?

In the absence of a Federal Act, there are three criteria that have been used to the allocation of scarce resources, also based on clinical and ethical criteria:[120] (i) clinical criteria; (ii) non-clinical criteria; and (iii) tie-breaker criteria.

In the first one — clinical criteria — the motto is to "save more lives". To achieve this result, there were used some factors as the (in)existence of comorbidities, the severity rate of the patient, and the who is most likely to die. Thus, solely based on clinical criteria, the resource is allocated to the patient with higher chances to survive.

The second criteria — nonclinical —, is related to equality. Seeks to give priority to allocate the resources based upon the idea that all patients should have the same opportunity to live the "same" number of years and experience the same cycle of live. In this hypothesis, if the case is dealing with two patients with the same comorbidities, respiratory failure and diagnosed with COVID-19 (with the same chances of survival), the allocation of the resource will be to the younger patient.

In the third criteria — tie-braker criteria — the guideline will be the "equity". When patients dispute scarce resource and present the same chances, including the cycle of live, it must take in account the equity principle. Therefore, the decision is adopted by luck, and this decision should be communicated in a fair and transparent way to the parties in the relation,[121] including the communication to the family and patient (when conscious enough).

3. In what type(s) of document(s) are the allocation criteria set? Is it in binding or non-binding guidelines, in the law, or in another type of document?

As already explained in the previous questions, there is no Law or Act in Brazil regarding the allocation of scarce resources. Thus, most guidelines come from the Federal Medical Council (CFM), through resolutions. Among them, there is the CFM Resolution n° 2.156/2016, on the criteria for admission to intensive care units (ICU), which, although not designed for a pandemic and in the case of complete saturation of the health system, has rules on allocation of scarce resources.

---

[120] AMIB, 'Protocolo AMIB de alocação de recursos em esgotamento durante a pandemia por COVID-19' (*Associação de Medicina Intensiva Brasileira*, 24 April 2020) <www.amib.org.br/fileadmin/user_upload/amib/2020/abril/24/Protocolo_AMIB_de_alocacao_de_recursos_em_esgotamento_durante_a_pandemia_por_COVID-19.pdf> accessed 7 April 2021.

[121] Marcelo José dos Santos et al, 'Covid-19: instruments for the allocation of mechanical ventilators — a narrative review' (2020) 582 Critical Care 24 <https://ccforum.biomedcentral.com/articles/10.1186/s13054-020-03298-3> accessed 6 April 2021; AMB, 'Recomendações para triagem de pacientes em UTIs no atual momento da pandemia' (*Associação Médica Brasileira*, 1 April 2021) <https://amb.org.br/wp-content/uploads/2021/04/recomendacoes-triagem-paciente-uti.pdf> accessed 11 April 2021.

In addition to the Resolutions of the Federal Medical Council, the pandemic gave rise to the need for specialized medical boards to take on the responsibility of establishing criteria for the treatment and allocation of scarce resources. Among them, the guidelines mentioned in the answer to the first question stand out due to the importance of the institutions that issued them.

4. Are providers of health care obliged by the law to provide (urgent) care to all patients? If the answer is yes, are there any legally recognised exceptions from this duty?

Under the terms of the Brazilian Federal Constitution,[122] the right to health is a universal and free right. In this sense, under normal conditions, the public health service cannot exempt itself from providing emergency treatment.

The pandemic, however, is not a normal situation, so this rule needs to be analyzed considering the resources available at the location, or, if possible, the transfer of the patient to another location that has the necessary resources.

5. On what legal basis is it possible to apply the allocation criteria in practice?

There are no legal norms with binding effects in relation to this topic. In this way, the rules dictated by the Ministry of Health (enabling Lung Ventilatory Support beds for exclusive care of COVID-19 patients, on an exceptional basis),[123] by the Federal Council of Medicine and/or by specialized medical boards may be subject to inspection by Organs competent bodies and even considered illegal (for example, discriminatory against older patients).

If this happens, medical decisions made based on these rules may be questioned and health professionals may be liable in civil or criminal basis for their actions (both who created them and who applied them).

122 Constituição da República Federativa do Brasil de 1988 <www.planalto.gov.br/ccivil_03/constituicao/constituicao.htm> accessed 8 April 2021.

123 Portaria nº 1.521, de 15 de junho de 2020. Autoriza a habilitação de leitos de suporte ventilatório pulmonar para atendimento exclusivo dos pacientes da COVID-19 <www.in.gov.br/web/dou/-/portaria-n-1.521-de-15-de-junho-de-2020-261697745> accessed 8 April 2021.

6. What level of legal certainty do the health professionals and the health care providers have when applying the allocation criteria?

These professionals would only have adequate legal certainty if the resource allocation criteria were available in Law. As they are not, they act with considerable degrees of uncertainty that cannot be ignored.

The rules issued by the CFM or by specialized medical boards do not serve to exempt them from eventual civil and/or criminal liability for their acts. However, they help in the judge's decision-making, mainly because they result from rules issued by professional associations and which, ultimately, aim at the best interests of patients.

Given the nature of the activity performed by physicians, and the risks arising from the profession, especially in the scenario of the covid-19 pandemic, the Brazilian legal system has protective rules for physicians in the exercise of their activities.

From a civil point of view, the physician's responsibility is always subjective (article 951 of the Civil Code and article 14, § 4 of the Consumer Protection Code), whether in his individual role or in a hospital institution. In both cases, the doctor is only liable, in tort, for the damage caused, when it is proven that the harmful result resulted from negligence, imprudence or malpractice — liability arising from fault, as well as willful acts. On this, in fact, it is worth bringing the definition of medical error embodied in the Code of Medical Ethics of the Federal Council of Medicine (Resolution No. 2217, of September 27, 2018[124]): *Art. 1°: Cause damage to the patient, by action or omission, characterized as malpractice, imprudence or negligence.*

In the criminal sphere, the physician's responsibility is only intentional (for example, he intentionally decided not to treat a certain patient).

In the context of COVID-19 and aiming to bring greater legal security to public agents in general (especially in the health area), a Provisional Measure was issued which sought to relativize the accountability of public agents during the pandemic. This is MP 966/2020,[125] which determined that the agent would only be held liable (in the scenario in question, the physician's liability) when the existence of intent or gross error is proven.[126] The Supreme Court, called upon to analyze the constitutionality of this Provisional Measure (which brings some immunity to public agents), defined that the concept of gross error is one that:

---

124 Resolução n° 2.217, de 27 de setembro de 2018. Aprova o Código de Ética Médica <www.in.gov.br/materia/-/asset_publisher/Kujrw0TZC2Mb/content/id/48226289/do1-2018-11-01-resolucao-n-2-217-de-27-de-setembro-de-2018-48226042> accessed 6 April 2021.

125 Medida provisória n° 966, de 13 de maio de 2020. Dispõe sobre a responsabilização de agentes públicos por ação e omissão em atos relacionados com a pandemia da covid-19 <www.planalto.gov.br/ccivil_03/_ato2019-2022/2020/mpv/mpv966.htm> accessed 8 April 2021.

126 Eugênio Fachini Neto, 'Responsabilidade médica em tempos de pandemia: precisamos de novas normas?' (2020) 3 Revista IBERC 93.

"1. An administrative act that entails a violation of the right to life, health or the environment balanced by non-compliance is considered a gross error:

(i) scientific and technical standards and criteria;

(ii) the constitutional principles of precaution and prevention.

2. The authority responsible for deciding must require that the technical opinions on which it will base its decision expressly address:

(i) scientific and technical standards and criteria applicable to the matter, as established by internationally and nationally recognized organizations; and

(ii) observance of the constitutional principles of precaution and prevention, under penalty of becoming co-responsible for any violations of rights."[127]

Separate discussions, in September 2020, the aforementioned Provisional Measure lost its legal effectiveness as it was not converted into Law by the National Congress, thus reestablishing the general rule of responsibility of public agents.

In this sense, the basic rule of civil/criminal liability of health professionals is to try to save the patient's life, using all available resources and doing everything in their power. The doctor will not be held responsible for the lack of resources and/or materials, nor for the failure to save the patient's life (unless there is an intentional/culprit attributable act).[128]

It is possible, however, that it responds for the adoption of criteria for allocation of resources derived from professional bodies and specialized medical boards, especially when the Judiciary Branch understands that these documents violate legal rules and precepts.

7. What are the civil and criminal liability implications of allocation of scarce health care resources? Have there already been any related legal suits and/or criminal proceedings?

Brazilian law provides for the civil and/or criminal liability of the physician in cases of proof of intent or guilt. So far, there is no news of lawsuits against doctors for fraud in the allocation of scarce resources; nor were there any reports of negligence, recklessness or malpractice (which would result in liability for fault) in the management of scarce resources during the treatment of patients with COVID-19.

As a general rule, if the criteria for resource allocation are considered illegal, doctors could be prosecuted, in the criminal sphere, for failure to help (Article 135 of the Penal Code) and even intentional and/or wrongful murder (Article 121, § 3 and 4 of the Penal Code).

In the civil sphere, they would be prosecuted for not trying to save the patient's life (even if to the detriment of another patient), and could respond guiltily *ex*

[127] ADIs nº 6421, 6422, 6424, 6425, 6427, 6428 e 6431. Relatoria do Ministro Luís Roberto Barroso.

[128] Ruy Rosado de Aguiar Júnior, 'Responsabilidade civil do médico' in Sálvio de Figueiredo Teixeira (eds), *Direito e Medicina: aspectos jurídicos da medicina* (Del Rey 2000).

vi articles 186 and 951, both of the Civil Code and article 14, § 4 of the Consumer Protection Code. In these cases, the indemnity would cover moral and property damages (emerging damages and loss of profits, pursuant to articles 948/950 of the Civil Code), including the possible obligation to pay maintenance to the deceased's family and funeral expenses.

B. Case studies

Case 1

As a result of a rapid worsening of the epidemiological situation, the material and personal capacities have been drastically overloaded in all the hospitals in the country. Within just a few minutes, ambulances transport ten patients to one particular hospital's emergency unit. The patients all need admission to the hospital, preferably to the intensive care unit (ICU). However, only two beds are available there. Other hospitals are overwhelmed too, so it is not possible to transport patients to any of them. All of the ten newly coming patients suffer from COVID-19; they have breathing difficulties, fast-rising fever, and decreasing oxygen saturation. Nevertheless, they differ in age, comorbidities, clinical fragility, and other factors.

Theoretically, the eight patients who cannot be admitted to beds can be placed in improvised settings in the hospital corridors, laying on gurneys or mattresses on the floor. Nevertheless, it will be impossible to provide them with the care they need.

Evaluation of the case

- What criteria can be used to choose the patients who will be admitted to the beds (i.e. what are the possible allocation criteria)?
  The decision of the two patients who will be allocated to the beds should take into account the clinical, non-clinical and tie-breaking criteria adopted in the country. All are based on ethical values, namely — the patient most likely to survive, equality and equity. In this scenario, it should be analyzed which of the patients have the worst prognosis (worst clinical picture obtained in the screening), then the age of the patients is analyzed in order to know which, in addition to the smaller probability of survival, is the youngest, leading the "life cycle" is taken into account in order to guarantee the value of equality. Finally, if the result is not found between 2 patients out of 10, the decision criterion is equity, which will be decided at random, and the decision must be transparent and justified by the professionals responsible for the decision made.[129]

[129] AMIB, 'Protocolo AMIB de alocação de recursos em esgotamento durante a pandemia por COVID-19' (*Associação de Medicina Intensiva Brasileira*, 24 April 2020) <www.amib.org.br/fileadmin/user_upload/amib/2020/abril/24/Protocolo_AMIB_de_alocacao_de_recursos_em_esgotamento_durante_a_pandemia_por_COVID-19.pdf> accessed 7 April 2021; AMB, 'Recomendações para triagem de pacientes em UTIs no atual momento da pandemia' (*Associação Médica*

- What legal consequences can this decision have for the health professionals and the hospital? How strong is their legal certainty that there will be no adverse legal consequences if they follow the above-mentioned criteria?
  In this situation, doctors must always act within the limits of resources available to them, to perform all possible procedures to ensure that everyone has access to the resources necessary for the treatment of COVID-19. Since these are not resource allocation criteria established by law, there is the possibility that, in the face of a judicial prognosis, such criteria may be considered unlawful, in which case hospitals and doctors may be held responsible in both the civil and criminal spheres for the resource allocation criteria adopted.[130]
  As a rule, the civil responsibility of doctors is subjective (articles 186 and 951 of the Civil Code and article 14, § 4 of the Consumer Protection Code), while the criminal responsibility of doctors will only be intentional, always observing the possibility of acting differently in the concrete case and the state of necessity.
  From the point of view of the hospital and/or nursing home, civil liability is, as a rule, objective (in the terms of article 927, Sole Paragraph, of the Civil Code and article 14, caput of the Consumer Protection Code), whether due to its own act (the decision to adopt a certain criteria for resource allocation, for example), or due to damages caused by its medical professionals working there (article 932, item III cumulated with article 933, both of the Civil Code). The jurisprudence of the Superior Court of Justice, however, seems to follow the path of not recognizing objective liability for harmful acts by health professionals, and the fault or malice of these professionals must be proven.
- What legal defences could the health professionals and the hospital use against a private lawsuit and/or criminal prosecution for the allocation decision?
  Given the pandemic scenario that has collapsed the global health system, the defense for health professionals who find themselves in the situation of having to choose who will have access to resources and who will not, often this decision translating into who will live and who will not, the defense offered by the legal system for these professionals (and hospitals) is the exclusion of illegality referring to the state of necessity, as provided in article 23, item I and article 24 of the Penal Code.[131] The fact that the country is in a completely atypical state, resulting from the epidemiological situation, is a safeguard for doctors and health professionals who exercise their activities ethically and legally.
  From the civil responsibility point of view, the defense in relation to the adoption of a certain resource allocation criteria must be based on the practices

Brasileira, 1 April 2021) <https://amb.org.br/wp-content/uploads/2021/04/recomendacoes-triagem-paciente-uti.pdf> accessed 11 April 2021.

130 Marcelo José dos Santos et al, 'Covid-19: instruments for the allocation of mechanical ventilators — a narrative review' (2020) 582 Critical Care 24 <https://ccforum.biomedcentral.com/articles/10.1186/s13054-020-03298-3> accessed 6 April 2021.

131 Decreto-Lei nº 2.848, de 7 de dezembro de 1940. Código Penal <www.planalto.gov.br/ccivil_03/decreto-lei/del2848compilado.htm> accessed 7 April 2021.

recommended by the Federal Council of Medicine and the specialized medical boards, showing, as far as possible, that the uniformity of the criteria makes it clear that these are the best solutions to react to the difficulties imposed by the pandemic.

Additional questions

- Would it be legally permissible to lower the standard of care provided to all patients in order to provide at least basic decent care to the newly admitted patients who are placed in the hospital corridors? To what extent?
  The response needs to be divided into two distinct approaches. If treatment has already been started, then it cannot be modified, or the patient's chances of survival will be diminished. Once started, it must be finished. The principles of the legal system do not seem to be consistent with purposefully diminishing the chances of survival.
  On the other hand, if this is a criterion adopted for future hospitalizations, it will be necessary to analyze whether there is a medical basis for this decision. If this practice aims only to provide better minimum conditions for everyone, without implying better chances of survival, then the answer must be negative. If, from a medical point of view, this increases the possibility of medical survival, then it seems to us that it meets the objective of protecting life and safeguarding health, guaranteed as fundamental rights in the Brazilian Federal Constitution.

Case 2

Two patients in an ICU are suffering from COVID-19. After admission to the hospital, they were provided with the high-flow nasal oxygen therapy (NFNO). During one night, the condition of both patients starts to worsen rapidly. At dawn, it is clear that neither of them will survive without artificial ventilation. However, there is just one ventilator available.

Evaluation of the case

- What criteria can be used to choose which of the two patients will be provided with artificial ventilation and which one will be left without it, possibly to die?
  Although there is no law on the subject, medical associations and specialized medical boards have established premises for dealing with the pandemic, as explained above. These premises are based on three distinct criteria: (i) clinical; (ii) non-clinical and (iii) tie-breaker. As both patients present the same clinical picture (and the same criticality), the clinical criterion in which analyzes the comorbidities, severity and probability of death is not enough to decide who will receive the resource. In this case, the criterion to be adopted should be the non-clinical one, with values based on equality, where the age criterion should be analyzed. In other words, the ventilator should be managed for the younger patient, using the life cycle criterion. In the event that both are in the same age group, the analysis must be established from the tie-breaker criterion, where the

decision will be made by lottery, through clear and transparent information to the patient and family members.[132]

- What legal consequences can this decision have for the health professionals and the hospital? How strong is their legal certainty that there will be no adverse legal consequences if they follow the above-mentioned criteria?
  As a general rule, if the resource allocation criteria adopted are considered unlawful, physicians could be prosecuted, in the criminal sphere, for failure to provide assistance (article 135 of the Penal Code), and even for malicious and/or culpable homicide (article 121, § 3° and 4° of the Penal Code).
  In the civil sphere, they would be sued for not trying to save the patient's life (even if to the detriment of another patient) and could be culpably held accountable *ex vi* articles 186 and 951, both of the Civil Code and article 14, §4 of the Consumer Protection Code.
  The same consequences could apply to hospital managers who adopted these resource allocation criteria.
- What legal defences could the health professionals and the hospital use against a private lawsuit and/or criminal prosecution for the allocation decision?
  Given the pandemic scenario that has collapsed the global health system, the defense for health professionals who find themselves in the situation of having to choose who will have access to resources and who will not, often this decision translating into who will live and who will not, the defense offered by the legal system for these professionals (and hospitals) is the exclusion of illegality referring to the state of necessity, as provided in article 23, item I and article 24 of the Penal Code. The fact that the country is in a completely atypical state, resulting from the epidemiological situation, is a safeguard for doctors and health professionals who exercise their activities ethically and legally.

Additional question

- If the allocation criteria specified in your answer to the first question to this case consisted of the patients' clinical features (such as their age, clinical fragility, etc.), please identify what criteria could be used for the allocation decision if all the relevant clinical features of both patients were practically the same?
  In situations where all patient characteristics are identical or very similar, the criterion adopted is a tie-breaker criterion, based on the value of equity, in which decisions about the management of scarce resources are based on chance, and decisions must be presented in a fair and transparent way to the parties.[133]

[132] Marcelo José dos Santos et al, 'Covid-19: instruments for the allocation of mechanical ventilators — a narrative review' (2020) 582 Critical Care 24 <https://ccforum.biomedcentral.com/articles/10.1186/s13054-020-03298-3> accessed 6 April 2021.

[133] Marcelo José dos Santos et al, 'Covid-19: instruments for the allocation of mechanical ventilators — a narrative review' (2020) 582 Critical Care 24 <https://ccforum.biomedcentral.com/articles/10.1186/s13054-020-03298-3> accessed 6 April 2021.

Case 3

There is a single extracorporeal membrane oxygenation (ECMO) device in the hospital. It is currently being used for an 84-year-old patient suffering from COVID-19, with diabetes as an underlying disease, clinical frailty score (CFS) 6–7 (moderate to severe frailty). It is possible that the patient will survive and will be discharged from the hospital if the ECMO treatment is continued. However, a younger COVID-19 patient is admitted to the hospital. This new patient is 51 years old, otherwise healthy, but her health condition has been rapidly deteriorating. Soon she will most likely need ECMO to survive.

Evaluation of the case

- Can it be legally permissible for the hospital staff to discontinue the ECMO treatment of the older patient and provide palliative care to her in order to save the younger and healthier patient's life? Please keep in mind that the older patient could survive if the treatment continued, but her chances may be lower than those of the younger patient.
  If treatment has already been started, then it cannot be changed, otherwise the patient's chances of survival may be diminished. Once started, it must be finished, unless there are medical reasons for stopping it. Not even the high probability of death can be used as a reason for interruption. Furthermore, the principles of the legal system do not seem to be compatible with purposefully diminishing the chances of survival.
  Furthermore, based on the resource allocation rules that have been adopted in the country, even if there is an age difference (non-clinical criterion), the resource should be kept with the first patient because, besides the fact that the treatment has already started, the probability of survival is high, and this is the first criterion analyzed (clinical criterion) during the triage for allocation of scarce resources.[134]
- If the answer to the first question is positive, what specific criteria can be used in clinical decision-making regarding replacing one patient with another with respect to a particular treatment unavailable for all?
  The answer to the previous question was negative.
- What legal consequences can this decision have for the health professionals and the hospital? How strong is their legal certainty that there will be no adverse legal consequences if they follow the above-mentioned criteria?
  The answer to the previous question was negative.
- What legal defenses could the health professionals and the hospital use against a private lawsuit and/or criminal prosecution for the allocation decision?
  The answer to the previous question was negative.

---

134 AMIB, 'Protocolo AMIB de alocação de recursos em esgotamento durante a pandemia por COVID-19' (*Associação de Medicina Intensiva Brasileira*, 24 April 2020 <www.amib.org.br/fileadmin/user_upload/amib/2020/abril/24/Protocolo_AMIB_de_alocacao_de_recursos_em_esgotamento_durante_a_pandemia_por_COVID-19.pdf> accessed 7 April 2021.

Additional question

- Suppose there are two different scenarios: a) the older patient was admitted to the hospital and provided with the ECMO treatment, and only later, after several days, the younger patient was admitted, and b) the younger patient was admitted before the older patient, however, the older patient required ECMO treatment soon after admission while the younger patient's health condition deteriorated only after a longer time when the ECMO was already occupied (i. e. at the time when the younger patient was admitted to the hospital, she did not yet need it). Would there be any difference in the allocation decision making between these two scenarios?

  There would be no difference in the decision about who would receive the resource, since the criterion that determines who will receive the treatment is not in relation to the time of admission to the hospital, but to their prognosis. If at the time the older patient presented a worsening condition, the younger one remained in a less serious condition, the criterion that should be analyzed is the clinical one (comorbidities, severity and need for treatment, given the possibility of survival). The supervening worsening of the younger patient has no influence on the previous decision that had to be taken by the doctors.

The list of abbreviations

CC	Civil Code
CF	Brazilian Federal Constitution
CFM	Federal Medical Council
CP	Penal Code
UTI	Intensive Care Unit

Bibliography

• Legislation

Constituição da República Federativa do Brasil de 1988 <www.planalto.gov.br/ccivil_03/constituicao/constituicao.htm> accessed 8 April 2021

Decreto-Lei nº 2.848, de 7 de dezembro de 1940. Código Penal <www.planalto.gov.br/ccivil_03/decreto-lei/del2848compilado.htm> accessed 7 April 2021

Lei nº 8.080, de 19 de setembro de 1990. Dispõe sobre as condições para a promoção, proteção e recuperação da saúde, a organização e o funcionamento dos serviços correspondentes e dá outras providências <www.planalto.gov.br/ccivil_03/leis/l8080.htm> accessed 11 April 2021

Lei nº 13.979, de 6 de fevereiro de 2020. Dispõe sobre as medidas para enfrentamento da emergência de saúde pública de importância internacional decorrente do coronavírus responsável pelo surto de 2019 <www.planalto.gov.br/ccivil_03/_ato2019-2022/2020/lei/l13979.htm> accessed 7 April 2021

Medida provisória nº 966, de 13 de maio de 2020. Dispõe sobre a responsabilização de agentes públicos por ação e omissão em atos relacionados com a pandemia da covid-19 <www.planalto.gov.br/ccivil_03/_ato2019-2022/2020/mpv/mpv966.htm> accessed 8 April 2021

Portaria nº 1.521, de 15 de junho de 2020. Autoriza a habilitação de leitos de suporte ventilatório pulmonar para atendimento exclusivo dos pacientes da COVID-19 <www.in.gov.br/web/dou/-/portaria-n-1.521-de-15-de-junho-de-2020-261697745> accessed 8 April 2021

Recomendação nº 05/2020 do Conselho Regional de Medicina de Pernambuco <www.cremepe.org.br/wp-content/uploads/2020/04/RECOMENDA%c3%87%c3%83O-CREMEPE-N%c2%ba-05_v.final_.pdf> accessed 16 August 2021

Resolução CFM nº 2.156/2016. Estabelece os critérios de admissão e alta em unidade de terapia intensiva <https://sistemas.cfm.org.br/normas/visualizar/resolucoes/BR/2016/2156> accessed 6 April 2021

Resolução CRM-RS nº 13, de 5 de junho de 2020. Estabelece os critérios sobre Alocação de Recursos em Unidades de Terapia Intensiva durante a pandemia <www.in.gov.br/web/dou/-/resolucao-n-13-de-5-de-junho-de-2020-261274042> accessed 16 August 2021

Resolução nº 2.217, de 27 de setembro de 2018. Aprova o Código de Ética Médica <www.in-.gov.br/materia/-/asset_publisher/Kujrw0TZC2Mb/content/id/48226289/do1-2018-11-01-resolucao-n-2-217-de-27-de-setembro-de-2018-48226042> accessed 6 April 2021

• Books

Aguiar Júnior R R de, 'Responsabilidade civil do médico' in Sálvio de Figueiredo Teixeira (eds), *Direito e Medicina: aspectos jurídicos da medicina* (Del Rey 2000)

França G V de, *Direito médico* (16th edn, Forense 2019)

Lima F R de S et al (ed), *Covid-19 e os impactos no direito: mercado, estado, trabalho, família, contratos e cidadania* (Grupo Almedina 2020)

• Articles

Facchini Neto E, 'Responsabilidade médica em tempos de pandemia: precisamos de novas normas?' (2020) 3 Revista IBERC 93

Santos M J dos et al, 'Covid-19: instruments for the allocation of mechanical ventilators — a narrative review' (2020) 582 Critical Care 24 <https://ccforum.biomedcentral.com/articles/10.1186/s13054-020-03298-3> accessed 6 April 2021

Satomi E et al, 'Alocação justa de recursos de saúde escassos diante da pandemia de COVID-19: considerações éticas' (2020) 18 Einstein (São Paulo) <www.scielo.br/scielo.php?script=sci_arttext&pid=S1679-45082020000100903&lng=en&nrm=iso> accessed 6 April 2021

• Other secondary sources

AMB, 'Recomendações para triagem de pacientes em UTIs no atual momento da pandemia' (*Associação Médica Brasileira*, 1 April 2021) <https://amb.org.br/wp-content/uploads/2021/04/recomendacoes-triagem-paciente-uti.pdf> accessed 11 April 2021

AMB, 'Diretrizes Covid-19' (*Associação Médica Brasileira*, 1 April 2020) <https://amb.org.br/wp-content/uploads/2020/04/DIRETRIZES-AMB-COVID-19-01.04.2020.pdf> accessed 16 August 2021

AMIB, 'Protocolo AMIB de alocação de recursos em esgotamento durante a pandemia por COVID-19' (*Associação de Medicina Intensiva Brasileira*, 24 April 2020) <www.amib.org.br/fileadmin/user_upload/amib/2020/abril/24/Protocolo_AMIB_de_alocacao_de_recursos_em_esgotamento_durante_a_pandemia_por_COVID-19.pdf> accessed 7 April 2021

HCOR, 'Protocolo Institucional de Atendimento ao paciente com suspeita ou confirmação de COVID-19' (*Hospital do Coração*, March 2020) <www.hcor.com.br/area-medica/wp-content/uploads/sites/3/2020/11/protocolo_atendimento_coronavirus_v14.pdf> accessed 16 August 2021

IBSP, 'Pandemia de COVID-19 – Protocolo de Alocação de Recursos em Esgotamento' (*Instituto Brasileiro para Segurança do Paciente*, 25 March 2021) <www.segurancadopaciente.com.br/seguranca-e-gestao/pandemia-de-covid-19-protocolo-de-alocacao-de-recursos-em-esgotamento/> accessed 5 April 2021

Ministério da Saúde, 'Orientações Para Manejo De Pacientes Com Covid-19' (*Portal de Boas Práticas*, June 2020) <https://portaldeboaspraticas.iff.fiocruz.br/wp-content/uploads/2020/06/Covid19-Orienta-esManejoPacientes.pdf> accessed 16 August 2021.

Nelson Rosenvald, 'Por uma isenção de responsabilidade dos profissionais de saúde por simples negligência em tempos de pandemia' (*Migalhas*, 5 May 2020) <www.migalhas.com.br/depeso/326088/por-uma-isencao-de-responsabilidade-dos-profissionais-desaude-por-simples-negligencia-em-tempos-de-pandemia> accessed 5 April 2021

Serviço De Controle De Infecção Hospitalar Da Sociedade Beneficente Israelita Albert Einstein, 'Manejo Coronavírus (COVID-19)' <https://medicalsuite.einstein.br/pratica-medica/Documentos%20Doencas%20Epidemicas/Manejo-de-casos-suspeitos-de-sindrome-respiratoria-pelo-COVID-19.pdf> accessed 16 August 2021

STF, 'STF reconhece competência concorrente de estados, DF, municípios e União no combate à Covid-19' (*STF notícias*, 15 April 2020) <http://portal.stf.jus.br/noticias/verNoticiaDetalhe.asp?idConteudo=441447&ori=1> accessed 11 April 2021

SUS, 'Sistema único de saúde' (*Secretaria de Estado de Saúde*) <www.saude.mg.gov.br/sus> accessed 11 April 2021

SUS, 'Guia Orientador para o enfrentamento da pandemia COVID-19 na Rede de Atenção à Saúde' (*Conselho Nacional de Secretarias municipais de Saúde*, March 2021) <www.conasems.org.br/wp-content/uploads/2021/04/Covid-19_guia_orientador_4ed.pdf> accessed 16 August 2021

CZECH REPUBLIC

Tomáš Holčapek
Charles University

A. Questionnaire

1. What are the criteria for the allocation of scarce health care resources in your country?

From autumn 2020 to spring 2021, the Czech Republic was undergoing one of the worst waves of Covid-19 epidemic in the world. It came as a surprise of sorts. In spring 2020, the country was very successful at containing the virus. The number of cases, and especially the mortality rate, were lower than in most other European countries. That is why the country opened almost fully during summer 2020. This may be one of the most important reasons for its subsequent calamity.[135]

The country's health care system is based on universal mandatory health insurance.[136] The robust net of health facilities enabled the country to face the dramatic increase in hospitalisations with comparably good results. In spite of a very high Covid-19 incidence in the worst months of the pandemic, Czech health system never collapsed. Major hospitals in big cities such as university hospitals in Prague functioned without essential limitations of intensive care (even though planned care was often practically halted). However, the situation was different in many other facilities, especially in smaller regional hospitals. After the first weeks of 2021, some doctors openly admitted to practice patient triage on the basis of legally questionable criteria such as age. The situation desperately called for clarification of legal framework for these clinical decisions, a clarification that never came in any official or consensually-approved form.

Patient prioritisation, in the meaning we use in this book, denotes selection of patients who will be denied certain care (e.g. intensive care) even though they would have received it in normal conditions. Such allocation decisions might typically affect admission to an intensive care unit or the use of a particular medical

135 Cf. Dalibor Glück, 'A year into Covid-19 pandemic, Czech 'success story' becomes cautionary tale' (*Radio Prague International,* 3 January 2021) <https://english.radio.cz/a-year-covid-19-pandemic-czech-success-story-becomes-cautionary-tale-8710743> accessed 29 June 2023.

136 Cf. Petr Šustek and Karel Hlaváček, 'Veřejné zdravotní pojištění [Public Health Insurance]' in Petr Šustek, Tomáš Holčapek et al., *Zdravotnické právo [Health Law]* (Wolters Kluwer 2016) 579–646.

device (such as a ventilator or an ECMO machine). Prioritisation needs to be based on medical evaluation, i.e. on the assessment of severity and urgency of the patient's medical condition and their prognosis.

Strong contraindication criteria (such as particular values of physiological parameters that always lead to the patient's exclusion from intensive care) are not recommended, and are not typical for the Czech practice. After all, one of the main aspects of the legal definition of standard of care is respect for the individuality of the patient.[137] If possible, each patient must be assessed as an individual with their own medical and personal history and specifics.

Furthermore, it would not be legally safe to compare the patient with other patients according to criteria that are not directly related to the question of who is medically indicated for a particular treatment. A comparison based on social status, race, nationality and similar factors would represent impermissible discrimination. For the same reason, prioritisation based solely on the patient's age would also be illegal, putting the doctor and the provider of health services in a risky position. Age can only be used as one of the criteria for the assessment of the patient's health status and prognosis, but it should not be a sole or absolute factor.

Withholding a scarce resource from a patient needs to be justified by the lack of benefit for the particular patient. In other words, the relevant health service must be considered futile or inappropriate and this justification should be documented in the patient's medical records.

2. What values are the allocation criteria based on?

The values providing the fundament for rationing criteria have never been concisely and explicitly declared by the law, by any official statement, or in either of the main legal-ethical documents on prioritisation (see below). Nevertheless, utilitarianism seems to be the most important philosophical basis for any such criteria, as suggested by the preference for maximisation of benefits[138] or for the use of available resources for the greatest number of patients with the greatest effect of the treatment.[139] The major legal-ethical documents refer to principlism (beneficence,

137 Section 4(5) of Act No. 372/2011 Coll., on Health Services.

138 Cf. David Černý, Adam Doležal, Tomáš Doležal, 'Etická a právní východiska pro tvorbu doporučení k rozhodování o alokaci vzácných zdrojů při poskytování zdravotních služeb v rámci pandemie COVID-19 [Ethical and Legal Framework for the Creation of Guidelines for the Decisions Regarding Scarce Resources Allocation in the Provision of Health Services in the COVID-19 Pandemic]' (2nd edn, Kabinet zdravotnického práva a bioetiky Ústavu státu a práva AV ČR, October 2020) 9 <https://zdravotnickepravo.info/wp-content/uploads/2020/10/Eticka-a-pravni-vychodiska-pro-tvorbu-doporuceni-v-ramci-COVID-19_podzim-2020.pdf> accessed 29 June 2023.

139 Cf. Renata Černá Pařízková, Petr Šustek, Lukáš Prudil, Jolana Kopsa Těšinová, Martin Šolc, Karel Cvachovec, Ondřej Dostál, Tomáš Holčapek, Marek Vácha, Pavel Ševčík, Vladimír Černý, 'Stanovisko výboru ČSARIM 13/2020: Rozhodování u pacientů v intenzivní péči v situaci nedostatku vzácných zdrojů [Statement of the Committee of the Czech Society for Anaesthesiology,

nonmaleficence, justice, and autonomy as basic principles of medical ethics) as one of the ethical foundations (see below).[140]

In a way similar to the approach taken by other countries, utilitarian perspective is highly limited by a set of boundaries.[141] Perhaps most important of these limitations is the prohibition of discrimination based on any other than medical criteria, such as social inequality, race, sex, disability, or arguably also mere age of the patient.[142] In principle, allocation criteria reflect the overall values behind the health care regulation in general: utilitarian focus on effectiveness combined with the framework of solidarity and non-discrimination.

Resuscitation and Intensive Medicine no. 13/2020: Decision-Making Regarding Patients In Intensive Care in a Situation of a Lack of Scarce Resources]' (2020) 5 *Anesteziologie a intenzivní medicína* 250.

140 David Černý, Adam Doležal, Tomáš Doležal, 'Etická a právní východiska pro tvorbu doporučení k rozhodování o alokaci vzácných zdrojů při poskytování zdravotních služeb v rámci pandemie COVID-19 [Ethical and Legal Framework for the Creation of Guidelines for the Decisions Regarding Scarce Resources Allocation in the Provision of Health Services in the COVID-19 Pandemic]' (2nd edn, Kabinet zdravotnického práva a bioetiky Ústavu státu a práva AV ČR, October 2020) 7 <https://zdravotnickepravo.info/wp-content/uploads/2020/10/Eticka-a-pravni-vychodiska-pro-tvorbu-doporuceni-v-ramci-COVID-19_podzim-2020.pdf> accessed 29 June 2023, Renata Černá Pařízková, Petr Šustek, Lukáš Prudil, Jolana Kopsa Těšinová, Martin Šolc, Karel Cvachovec, Ondřej Dostál, Tomáš Holčapek, Marek Vácha, Pavel Ševčík, Vladimír Černý, 'Stanovisko výboru ČSARIM 13/2020: Rozhodování u pacientů v intenzivní péči v situaci nedostatku vzácných zdrojů [Statement of the Committee of the Czech Society for Anaesthesiology, Resuscitation and Intensive Medicine no. 13/2020: Decision-Making Regarding Patients In Intensive Care in a Situation of a Lack of Scarce Resources]' (2020) 5 *Anesteziologie a intenzivní medicína* 250.

141 Cf. Martin Šolc, 'Legal-Ethical Grounds of Crisis Patient Prioritisation' in this book, or Martin Šolc, 'The Pandemic and the Law: Challenges of Covid-19 to the Ethical and Legal Paradigm of Health Care' in Pavel Šturma (ed), *Czech Yearbook of Public & Private International Law. Česká ročenka mezinárodního práva veřejného a soukromého. Vol. 12* (Česká společnost pro mezinárodní právo 2021) 371–380.

142 Cf. Renata Černá Pařízková, Petr Šustek, Lukáš Prudil, Jolana Kopsa Těšinová, Martin Šolc, Karel Cvachovec, Ondřej Dostál, Tomáš Holčapek, Marek Vácha, Pavel Ševčík, Vladimír Černý, 'Stanovisko výboru ČSARIM 13/2020: Rozhodování u pacientů v intenzivní péči v situaci nedostatku vzácných zdrojů [Statement of the Committee of the Czech Society for Anaesthesiology, Resuscitation and Intensive Medicine no. 13/2020: Decision-Making Regarding Patients In Intensive Care in a Situation of a Lack of Scarce Resources]' (2020) 5 *Anesteziologie a intenzivní medicína* 250, David Černý, Adam Doležal, Tomáš Doležal, 'Etická a právní východiska pro tvorbu doporučení k rozhodování o alokaci vzácných zdrojů při poskytování zdravotních služeb v rámci pandemie COVID-19 [Ethical and Legal Framework for the Creation of Guidelines for the Decisions Regarding Scarce Resources Allocation in the Provision of Health Services in the COVID-19 Pandemic]' (2nd edn, Kabinet zdravotnického práva a bioetiky Ústavu státu a práva AV ČR, October 2020) 23 <https://zdravotnickepravo.info/wp-content/uploads/2020/10/Eticka-a-pravni-vychodiska-pro-tvorbu-doporuceni-v-ramci-COVID-19_podzim-2020.pdf> accessed 29 June 2023.

3. In what type(s) of document(s) are the allocation criteria set? Is it in binding or non-binding guidelines, in the law, or in another type of document?

Prioritisation is usually guided by internal documents of the hospitals. They often use scoring systems such as the clinical frailty scale (CFS).[143] The quality of such internal documents varies. Some of them are very detailed and coherent, manifestly more so than any available Czech document with purported general applicability. However, scoring systems must only be used as one of the factors in the decision-making process. Allocation decision-making cannot be reduced to mechanical application of algorithmic criteria. The overall assessment of the patient's health condition and prognosis needs to remain paramount.

Furthermore, the obvious downside of the application of internal documents is the risk of what can be called implicit rationing.[144] In that case, prioritisation is based on non-transparent and arbitrary criteria. In the worst scenarios, rules that would never be permissible if openly declared (including clearly discriminatory criteria) might be applied in secret under the disguise of medical discretion.

Two main relevant documents on allocation criteria with the ambition to inspire the practice in the whole country have been published. They are non-binding, and while they sparked certain discussion, they have admittedly not been universally accepted in clinical practice.

The first of them was the *Ethical and Legal Framework for the Creation of Guidelines for the Decisions Regarding Scarce Resources Allocation in the Provision of Health Services in the COVID-19 Pandemic* (hereinafter "Framework") published by the Czech Academy of Science' Research Unit for Medical Law and Bioethics in March 2020, with a revised version published in October of the same year.[145] The Framework provides a relatively detailed set of criteria combined with

---

143 Cf. Kenneth Rockwood and Olga Theou, 'Using the Clinical Frailty Scale in Allocating Scarce Health Care Resources' (2020) 3 *Canadian Geriatrics Journal* 254–259 doi: https://doi.org/10.5770/cgj.23.463.

144 Cf. Petr Šustek, 'Czech Expert Statements on Patient Prioritisation in the Covid-19 Pandemic in International Comparison' in Pavel Šturma (ed), *Czech Yearbook of Public & Private International Law. Česká ročenka mezinárodního práva veřejného a soukromého. Vol. 12* (Česká společnost pro mezinárodní právo 2021) 358.

145 Cf. David Černý, Adam Doležal, Tomáš Doležal, 'Etická a právní východiska pro tvorbu doporučení k rozhodování o alokaci vzácných zdrojů při poskytování zdravotních služeb v rámci pandemie COVID-19 [Ethical and Legal Framework for the Creation of Guidelines for the Decisions Regarding Scarce Resources Allocation in the Provision of Health Services in the COVID-19 Pandemic]' (2nd edn, Kabinet zdravotnického práva a bioetiky Ústavu státu a práva AV ČR, October 2020) <https://zdravotnickepravo.info/wp-content/uploads/2020/10/Eticka-a-pravni-vychodiska-pro-tvorbu-doporuceni-v-ramci-COVID-19_podzim-2020.pdf> accessed 29 June 2023. Cf. also Petr Šustek, 'Czech Expert Statements on Patient Prioritisation in the Covid-19 Pandemic in International Comparison' in Pavel Šturma (ed), *Czech Yearbook of Public & Private International Law. Česká ročenka mezinárodního práva veřejného a soukromého. Vol. 12* (Česká společnost pro mezinárodní právo 2021) 350-352.

several decision-making algorithms. As a result of cooperation between lawyers specializing in medical law and a philosopher, the document builds upon the theory of principlism (beneficence, nonmaleficence, justice, and autonomy as basic principles of medical ethics)[146] and provides the proposal of four special ethical principles for the times of crisis: maximisation of benefits, fairness, support for those who help others, and prioritisation of patients with the worst state of health.[147] In cases of indication for scarce resources (e.g. for an admission to an ICU), the Framework distinguishes three groups of patients depending on the likelihood of positive outcome of the therapy. Patients who have the lowest chance to survive would only be provided with palliative care. Among those with a higher chance of survival, the Framework advises to prioritise workers essential for managing the pandemic (such as health professionals, important workers in nuclear plants etc.). The rest of patients should be prioritised on the basis of drawing of lots (in the absence of other distinguishing criteria) or age (based on the assumption that death is worse for a younger person who loses more lifetime than an older one).[148]

Another major document was issued in November 2020 under the title *Decision-Making Regarding Patients In Intensive Care in a Situation of a Lack of Scarce Resources* in the form of a statement of the Committee of the Czech Society for Anaesthesiology, Resuscitation and Intensive Medicine (ČSARIM) of the Czech Medical Society of J. E. Purkyně (hereinafter "Statement").[149] A legal analysis written by medical law experts was attached to the Statement as its appendix.[150] While the Framework analysed ethical and legal options for finding and justifying practical allocation criteria, the Statement clearly aimed at providing health professionals and health service providers with some legal certainty in highly uncertain times. For that

---

146 David Černý, Adam Doležal, Tomáš Doležal, 'Etická a právní východiska pro tvorbu doporučení k rozhodování o alokaci vzácných zdrojů při poskytování zdravotních služeb v rámci pandemie COVID-19 [Ethical and Legal Framework for the Creation of Guidelines for the Decisions Regarding Scarce Resources Allocation in the Provision of Health Services in the COVID-19 Pandemic]' (2nd edn, Kabinet zdravotnického práva a bioetiky Ústavu státu a práva AV ČR, October 2020) 7 <https://zdravotnickepravo.info/wp-content/uploads/2020/10/Eticka-a-pravni-vychodiska-pro-tvorbu-doporuceni-v-ramci-COVID-19_podzim-2020.pdf> accessed 29 June 2023.

147 ibid 8.

148 ibid 12–14.

149 Cf. Renata Černá Pařízková, Petr Šustek, Lukáš Prudil, Jolana Kopsa Těšinová, Martin Šolc, Karel Cvachovec, Ondřej Dostál, Tomáš Holčapek, Marek Vácha, Pavel Ševčík, Vladimír Černý, 'Stanovisko výboru ČSARIM 13/2020: Rozhodování u pacientů v intenzivní péči v situaci nedostatku vzácných zdrojů [Statement of the Committee of the Czech Society for Anaesthesiology, Resuscitation and Intensive Medicine no. 13/2020: Decision-Making Regarding Patients In Intensive Care in a Situation of a Lack of Scarce Resources]' (2020) 5 *Anesteziologie a intenzivní medicína* 249–251. Cf. also a brief review in English in Petr Šustek, 'Czech Expert Statements on Patient Prioritisation in the Covid-19 Pandemic in International Comparison' in Pavel Šturma (ed), *Czech Yearbook of Public & Private International Law. Česká ročenka mezinárodního práva veřejného a soukromého. Vol. 12* (Česká společnost pro mezinárodní právo 2021) 346–350.

150 Cf. Petr Šustek, Tomáš Holčapek, Martin Šolc, 'Příloha 1: Právní rozbor situace nedostatku vzácných zdrojů v systému zdravotní péče [Appendix 1: Legal Analysis of a Situation of a Lack of Scarce Resources in the Health System]' (2020) 5 *Anesteziologie a intenzivní medicína* 252–255.

reason, the Statement refrained from suggesting hypothetical solutions and legal defences but rather narrowed down the options to what was likely safe under current law. The most important message of the Statement is that rationing can only be based on medical indication criteria and that the already-provided intensive care can only be terminated if it is no longer indicated, not for the sake of other patients.[151] Unlike the Framework, the Statement excludes the possibility of prioritisation based on mere age,[152] and proposes the *first come, first served* principle instead of drawing lots for hypothetical cases of patients with indistinguishable medical criteria.[153]

4. Are providers of health care obliged by the law to provide (urgent) care to all patients? If the answer is yes, are there any legally recognised exceptions from this duty?

Health services are mostly provided on the basis of a contract (a specific type of contract for health care under the Act No. 89/2012 Coll., the Civil Code, hereinafter "Civil Code").[154] The providers have a statutory duty to enter into this contract with

---

151 Cf. Renata Černá Pařízková, Petr Šustek, Lukáš Prudil, Jolana Kopsa Těšinová, Martin Šolc, Karel Cvachovec, Ondřej Dostál, Tomáš Holčapek, Marek Vácha, Pavel Ševčík, Vladimír Černý, 'Stanovisko výboru ČSARIM 13/2020: Rozhodování u pacientů v intenzivní péči v situaci nedostatku vzácných zdrojů [Statement of the Committee of the Czech Society for Anaesthesiology, Resuscitation and Intensive Medicine no. 13/2020: Decision-Making Regarding Patients In Intensive Care in a Situation of a Lack of Scarce Resources]' (2020) 5 *Anesteziologie a intenzivní medicína* 251, Petr Šustek, Tomáš Holčapek, Martin Šolc, 'Příloha 1: Právní rozbor situace nedostatku vzácných zdrojů v systému zdravotní péče [Appendix 1: Legal Analysis of a Situation of a Lack of Scarce Resources in the Health System]' (2020) 5 *Anesteziologie a intenzivní medicína* 252.

152 Cf. Renata Černá Pařízková, Petr Šustek, Lukáš Prudil, Jolana Kopsa Těšinová, Martin Šolc, Karel Cvachovec, Ondřej Dostál, Tomáš Holčapek, Marek Vácha, Pavel Ševčík, Vladimír Černý, 'Stanovisko výboru ČSARIM 13/2020: Rozhodování u pacientů v intenzivní péči v situaci nedostatku vzácných zdrojů [Statement of the Committee of the Czech Society for Anaesthesiology, Resuscitation and Intensive Medicine no. 13/2020: Decision-Making Regarding Patients In Intensive Care in a Situation of a Lack of Scarce Resources]' (2020) 5 *Anesteziologie a intenzivní medicína* 250, 251, Petr Šustek, Tomáš Holčapek, Martin Šolc, 'Příloha 1: Právní rozbor situace nedostatku vzácných zdrojů v systému zdravotní péče [Appendix 1: Legal Analysis of a Situation of a Lack of Scarce Resources in the Health System]' (2020) 5 *Anesteziologie a intenzivní medicína* 253.

153 Cf. Renata Černá Pařízková, Petr Šustek, Lukáš Prudil, Jolana Kopsa Těšinová, Martin Šolc, Karel Cvachovec, Ondřej Dostál, Tomáš Holčapek, Marek Vácha, Pavel Ševčík, Vladimír Černý, 'Stanovisko výboru ČSARIM 13/2020: Rozhodování u pacientů v intenzivní péči v situaci nedostatku vzácných zdrojů [Statement of the Committee of the Czech Society for Anaesthesiology, Resuscitation and Intensive Medicine no. 13/2020: Decision-Making Regarding Patients In Intensive Care in a Situation of a Lack of Scarce Resources]' (2020) 5 *Anesteziologie a intenzivní medicína* 250, 251, Petr Šustek, Tomáš Holčapek, Martin Šolc, 'Příloha 1: Právní rozbor situace nedostatku vzácných zdrojů v systému zdravotní péče [Appendix 1: Legal Analysis of a Situation of a Lack of Scarce Resources in the Health System]' (2020) 5 *Anesteziologie a intenzivní medicína* 252, 253.

154 Sections 2936 and following of Act No. 89/2012 Coll., the Civil Code. Cf. Petr Šustek, 'Medicínské (lékařské) právo [Medical Law]' in Petr Šustek and Tomáš Holčapek (eds), *Zdravotnické právo [Health Law]* (Wolters Kluwer 2016) 38–41.

everyone who expresses their wish to do so, unless any of the exceptions exhaustively defined in the Act No. 372/2011 Coll., on Health Services (hereinafter "Act on Health Services") applies.[155] These exceptions encompass situations in which the patient lives too far away from the general practitioner, or is not insured by a health insurance company that has a contract with the chosen health service provider. It is also allowed not to accept the patient into care if it would result in the exceeding of the provider's tolerable workload or if it is not possible due to operational reasons, insufficient capacity or technical and material equipment of the medical facility. Tolerable workload is deemed to be exceeded when the acceptance of the new patient would lower the quality and safety of health services provided to the already admitted patients [Section 48(1) of the Act on Health Services].

The problem of rationing in a crisis might have been solved by the quoted provision if there was no Section 48(3) of the Act on Health Services, according to which health service providers are allowed neither to refuse the admission to care nor to terminate care, among other circumstances, if the patient needs urgent care or if there is a crisis situation. Moreover, providers of acute inpatient care must take into their care a patient from the emergency medical service (from an ambulance) if the life of the patient is in direct danger (Section 6(2) of Act No. 374/2011 Coll., on Emergency Medical Service). These rules mean that the provider is effectively obliged to provide urgent care whenever it is needed, despite the exceptions.

5. On what legal basis is it possible to apply the allocation criteria in practice?

Allocation decision-making needs to be performed in the framework of the provision of health services on the appropriate professional level (see below). The law does not provide any more detailed rules; there is no explicit legal basis for the application of any particular crisis allocation criteria. This fact represented perhaps the most important threat to legal certainty during the pandemic.

6. What level of legal certainty do the health professionals and the health care providers have when applying the allocation criteria?

Access to health services comes under the scope of constitutional rights, especially the right to the protection of health under Article 31 of the Charter of Fundamental Rights and Freedoms. Therefore, it needs sufficient legal grounds. The problem is that Czech law simply does not provide any legal grounds for allocation criteria

[155] Section 48(1) of Act No. 372/2011 Coll., on Health Services.

other than those previously mentioned general principles. Unfortunately, a relevant change in legislation is not realistic in foreseeable future. The problem could alternatively be solved if the case law adopted a new rule (perhaps a new legal defence), but at the moment, health professionals and providers cannot rely on it as it would mean betting their future on a mere hope.

7. What are the civil and criminal liability implications of allocation of scarce health care resources? Have there already been any related legal suits and/or criminal proceedings?

As of yet, there have been no known litigations or criminal proceedings related to health care rationing during the Covid-19 pandemic.

In general, if the outcome of the allegedly wrong prioritisation decision would consist in personal injury, the patient could have claims for compensation of both tangible and intangible harm.[156] Among the latter, the most important would be the claim for compensation for loss of faculty. The default amount of compensation for the complete impairment in all areas of life (such as in a persistent vegetative state) is 400 times the average monthly wage in a calendar year preceding the year when the health condition of the injured person was stabilised enough to assess the impairment.[157] For a health condition stabilised in 2023, this compensation exceeds 16 million CZK (approximately 670,000 EUR). If the harm is less significant, the compensation is proportionally lowered.

Another claim for compensation of intangible harm relates to pain and suffering. It is based on a table which ascribes a certain number of points to each casuistically defined injury. The value of one point equals to one per cent of the average monthly wage in the country in a year preceding the year when the pain was suffered. For harms occurring in 2023, this value is approximately 403 CZK, which means that e.g. pain associated with a foreign body in the oesophagus (retrieved endoscopically) is compensated by the amount of 12,000 CZK (approx. 503 EUR), a femoral head fracture by more than 60,000 CZK (approx. 2,500 EUR) and a skull fracture by more than 240,000 CZK (approx. 10,000 EUR). As is apparent, compensation for pain mostly covers traumatic injuries, and it is an issue of an ongoing professional debate whether the need for medical interventions might be analogously compensated (e.g. whether artificial ventilation that was a necessary part of a medical procedure required by a wrongfully occasioned injury can be compensated similarly the above-mentioned foreign body in the oesophagus).

---

156 Cf. Petr Šustek, 'Current Debates on Medical Liability in the Czech Republic' (2019) 23 *Journal de Droit de la Santé et de l'Assurance Maladie* 63–66.

157 According to the non-binding, but generally used *Methodology for compensating intangible harm to health (pain and loss of faculty pursuant to Section 2958 of the Civil Code).*

For the cases when the patient dies, the Civil Code contains two provisions on compensation of secondary damage. Under Section 2959 of the Civil Code, the spouse, parent, child or other person close to the primary victim shall be compensated if the primary victim was killed or suffered particularly serious bodily harm. Secondary victims that do not belong to the said group can sue under Section 2971, but only if their claim is justified by special circumstances under which the tortfeasor caused harm by an unlawful act. These special circumstances include breaching an important legal duty due to gross negligence or causing harm intentionally out of a desire to destroy, hurt or for other especially reprehensible motives. According to case law,[158] the default amount of compensation for the closest secondary victims is 20 times the average monthly wage in the country in the year preceding the death of the primary victim. For a death occurring in 2023, this slightly exceeds 800,000 CZK (approx. 33,500 EUR).

Both individual health professionals and institutional health service providers can also face criminal liability, including for offences against life and health (Section 140 and following of Act No. 40/2009 Coll., the Criminal Code), including homicide or grievous bodily harm caused by negligence. Legal entities can be held criminally liable if, among other conditions, the crime was committed by their employee while performing work tasks. The legal person may exculpate itself if it can prove that it used all efforts that can be justly required to avert the offence (Section 8 of Act No. 418/2011 Coll., on Criminal Liability of Legal Persons). One of the ways a legal entity can prove that is to show that it had issued and applied relevant internal documents. That is one of the reasons why internal hospital documents were so crucially important in the practice of crisis rationing during the pandemic (see above).

B. Case studies

Case 1

As a result of a rapid worsening of the epidemiological situation, the material and personal capacities have been drastically overloaded in all the hospitals in the country. Within just a few minutes, ambulances transport ten patients to one particular hospital's emergency unit. The patients all need admission to the hospital, preferably to the intensive care unit (ICU). However, only two beds are available there. Other hospitals are overwhelmed too, so it is not possible to transport patients to any of them. All of the ten newly coming patients suffer from COVID-19; they have breathing difficulties, fast-rising fever, and decreasing oxygen saturation. Nevertheless, they differ in age, comorbidities, clinical fragility, and other factors.

[158] Cf. judgment of the Supreme Court of the Czech Republic of 19 September 2018, file no. 25 Cdo 894/2018.

Theoretically, the eight patients who cannot be admitted to beds can be placed in improvised settings in the hospital corridors, laying on gurneys or mattresses on the floor. Nevertheless, it will be impossible to provide them with the care they need.

Evaluation of the case

- What criteria can be used to choose the patients who will be admitted to the beds (i.e. what are the possible allocation criteria)?
  Only medical criteria are allowed, meaning that they must be directly connected to the patients' state of health and prognosis. In other words, the decision can only be based on considerations regarding the seriousness and urgency of the patients' condition and other aspects influencing the medical indication of the intervention. Nevertheless, it is important to note that physicians should also make sure that intensive care is not "futile" or inappropriate, i.e. that it still brings more benefits than harm to the patient. Providers are not obliged to provide care that is burdensome for the patients and has very little (or no) realistic chance to help them.
  This problem was already addressed in 2010 by the *Recommendation of the Board of Directors of the Czech Medical Chamber (ČLK) No. 1/2010 on the Procedure for Deciding to Change Intensive Care to Palliative Care in Patients in the Terminal Stage Who Are Unable to Express their Will.* In this document, the medical association (whose members are all the physicians practicing in the country) explicitly states that treatment that cannot stop the progression of the disease, restore the patient's health, or avert their death is not indicated and as such should not be initiated, and if it already was started, it can be terminated. In 2020, Czech Society for Palliative Medicine published the *Opinion on the Provision of Life-Sustaining Treatment to Minor Patients*, which also stressed the need to refrain from prolongation of unnecessary suffering at the end of life.[159]
- What legal consequences can this decision have for the health professionals and the hospital? How strong is their legal certainty that there will be no adverse legal consequences if they follow the above-mentioned criteria?
  The allocation decision can have serious legal ramifications. If the rejection of a patient leads to death or serious bodily injury, the health service provider might be sued by the patient or secondary victims (mainly close relatives). Both the involved health professionals and the provider could also be held criminally liable (see above).
- What legal defences could the health professionals and the hospital use against a civil lawsuit and/or criminal prosecution for the allocation decision?
  The options of legal defence are rather limited, or, to be more precise, quite uncertain. In a situation of crisis rationing the legal defence consisting in the state

[159] Cf. Helena Krejčíková and Jan Hřídel, 'Stanovisko k poskytování život udržující léčby dětským pacientům [Opinion on the Provision of Life-Sustaining Treatment to Minor Patients]' (2020) 1 *Paliativní medicína* 26–30.

of necessity comes most readily to mind. However, in both the civil[160] and criminal[161] law it can only be applied if the danger could not have been prevented otherwise and, at the same time, if the acting person does not cause a harm which is evidently equally serious or even more serious than the averted imminent harm. From legal perspective, each human life has equal value.[162] To let a patient die so that another patient can survive would mean that the caused harm was equally serious as the averted harm, so it would not fulfil the conditions under which the state of necessity can be applied.

There is an older case law according to which in extreme situations, the defence of state of necessity can be used if one life was sacrificed to save more people. It stems from an extraordinarily horrifying case where a father forced his children to kill their grandmother (his mother-in-law) under a threat that he would otherwise murder them all.[163] The same principle could also be applied, for example, if a crew refuses to let a person embark an overcrowded lifeboat because it would sink under the weight of too many passengers.[164]

An argument might arise that withdrawing life-sustaining care from one patient may in the end save more patients who will have access to the freed scarce resources. However, these additional patients will, as a rule, access the freed resource one after another, not simultaneously, and we do not know how long each of them will use it. The state of necessity is always assessed on the basis of the individual situation in the given moment. Therefore, we need to balance the harm against the imminent benefit, not against hypothetical further benefits in the future. In most cases, the imminent benefit will consist in helping one other patient, not more of them (for example, a ventilator or an ECMO machine will be provided to another patient). In situations like that, one life would be exchanged for another life, which is not permissible under Czech law.[165]

The situation might apparently be solved with a suitable legislative change. That is, however, very unlikely to happen in the near future. In times of a crisis, emotions and stakes are too high, and when the acute crisis ends, the demand for opening such a controversial topic vanishes.

160 Section 2906 of Act No. 89/2012 Coll., the Civil Code.

161 Section 28(2) of Act No. 40/2009 Coll., the Criminal Code.

162 Cf. Petr Šustek, Tomáš Holčapek, Martin Šolc, 'Příloha 1: Právní rozbor situace nedostatku vzácných zdrojů v systému zdravotní péče [Appendix 1: Legal Analysis of a Situation of a Lack of Scarce Resources in the Health System]' (2020) 5 *Anesteziologie a intenzivní medicína* 254.

163 Cf. judgment of the Supreme Court of the Slovak Socialist Republic of 11 December 1980, file no. 3 To 72/80 (R 20/1982 tr.), or Vladimír Pelc, *Krajní nouze v trestním právu [State of Necessity in Criminal Law]* (Leges 2021) 266–269.

164 Cf. Pavel Šámal, 'Commentary to Section § 28' in Pavel Šámal et al., *Trestní zákoník I. Obecná část (§ 1–139) [The Criminal Code I. General Part (Sections 1–139]* (2nd edn, C. H. Beck 2012) 394.

165 Cf. Petr Šustek, Tomáš Holčapek, Martin Šolc, 'Příloha 1: Právní rozbor situace nedostatku vzácných zdrojů v systému zdravotní péče [Appendix 1: Legal Analysis of a Situation of a Lack of Scarce Resources in the Health System]' (2020) 5 *Anesteziologie a intenzivní medicína* 254, Vladimír Pelc, Krajní nouze v trestním právu *[State of Necessity in Criminal Law]* (Leges 2021) 102.

Alternatively, the case law could establish new rules to justify looser prioritisation criteria. For example, it could somehow find a way to apply the state of necessity after all. However, for the reasons we have already explained, this is rather unlikely to happen. The courts could also introduce a new legal defence which has not yet been used in Czech law. If this was to happen, the most likely candidate would be the so-called conflict of duties, which is also suggested as a solution by some Czech authors.[166] While this concept is known especially in German law, legal defences in Czech law are not listed exhaustively, so nothing in principle prevents the case law from adopting it. However, as of today, health professionals and hospitals cannot rely on it — there is no legal certainty that the courts would be willing to use the conflict of duties as a legal defence. Perhaps more importantly, even if they did, it is not clear whether the conflict of duties really addresses the basic question of to whom the care should be provided. It is necessary to justify the individual prioritisation decisions, not the (rather obvious) fact that not everybody can be provided with every potential manner of health care. It seems that the concept of conflict of duties is not very useful in this context since it can only work when accompanied with another legal defence justifying the particular prioritisation decision.

Additional questions

- Would it be legally permissible to lower the standard of care provided to all patients in order to provide at least basic decent care to the newly admitted patients who are placed in the hospital corridors? To what extent?

  It is without doubt that the standard of care can be lowered in a particular case if it is absolutely necessary. The standard of appropriate professional level of care is defined in the Act on Health Services.[167] It consists of three cumulative criteria. First, health services must be provided according to the rules of science and acknowledged medical procedures. Second, the individuality of the patient must be respected. Third, particular conditions and objective possibilities must be taken into account. If it becomes objectively impossible to provide care on the until-now required level of quality, the legal duty is not breached. After all, one of the most fundamental legal maxims states that nobody is obliged to do the impossible.[168]

  During a critical shortage of scarce resources, the standard of care cannot always be the same. A practical example is when health professionals who are

[166] Cf. Tomáš Doležal, 'Konflikt povinností jako okolnost vylučující protiprávnost – východisko pro úvahy o možné prioritizaci pacientů v případě nedostatku zdrojů [Conflict of Duties as a Legal Defence — A Starting Point for Consideration of Possible Patient Prioritisation in the Event of the Lack of Resources]' (*Zdravotnické právo a bioetika,* 2 November 2020) <https://zdravotnickepravo.info/konflikt-povinnosti-jako-okolnost-vylucujici-protipravnost-vychodisko-pro-uvahy-o-mozne-prioritizaci-pacientu-v-pripade-nedostatku-zdroju/> accessed 29 June 2023.

[167] Section 4(5) of Act No. 372/2011 Coll., on Health Services.

[168] Cf. Petr Šustek, Tomáš Holčapek, Martin Šolc, 'Příloha 1: Právní rozbor situace nedostatku vzácných zdrojů v systému zdravotní péče [Appendix 1: Legal Analysis of a Situation of a Lack of Scarce Resources in the Health System]' (2020) 5 *Anesteziologie a intenzivní medicína* 254.

not specialised in intensive care work in Covid-19 intensive care units, or when doctors from completely different branches of medicine work at improvised Covid-19 normal wards. Nevertheless, we have already established above that providers cannot refuse to admit to care a patient who needs urgent care or if there is a crisis situation [Section 48(3) of Act on Health Services]. Therefore, the hospital must provide the best care possible to each patient in urgent need in a given situation. In the worst-case scenario, patients may be cared for in hospital corridors, being provided with a sheet and basic available medication — but they should not be rejected altogether.

Case 2

Two patients in an ICU are suffering from COVID-19. After admission to the hospital, they were provided with the high-flow nasal oxygen therapy (HFNO). During one night, the condition of both patients starts to worsen rapidly. At dawn, it is clear that neither of them will survive without artificial ventilation. However, there is just one ventilator available.

Evaluation of the case

- What criteria can be used to choose which of the two patients will be provided with artificial ventilation and which one will be left without it, possibly to die?
  In principle, the answer does not differ from the first case study discussed above. The only permissible criteria are medical ones, i.e. the gravity and urgency of the patients' state of health and the question of whether artificial ventilation has a realistic chance of saving their life and thus providing them with real benefit rather than prolonging their suffering at the end of life.[169]
- What legal consequences can this decision have for the health professionals and the hospital? How strong is their legal certainty that there will be no adverse legal consequences if they follow the above-mentioned criteria?
  The legal consequences do not differ from the general explanation provided above. Both the health service provider (hospital) and the health professional who made the allocation decision might, at the worst case, face criminal prosecution for negligent homicide (or negligent grievous bodily harm etc.). Furthermore, the surviving patient, or the persons close to the deceased patient, might sue the provider for compensation in civil litigation. Legal certainty is relatively high as long as the prioritisation decision can be fully justified by medical criteria as discussed above; otherwise, it becomes very low.
- What legal defences could the health professionals and the hospital use against a civil lawsuit and/or criminal prosecution for the allocation decision?

[169] See the above-presented *Recommendation of the Board of Directors of the Czech Medical Chamber (ČLK) No. 1/2010 on the Procedure for Deciding to Change Intensive Care to Palliative Care in Patients in the Terminal Stage Who Are Unable to Express their Will.*

In this answer, we refer to the general discussion of legal defences above. State of necessity would not apply since one life would be exchanged for another. The courts might theoretically apply a new legal defence not yet used in Czech law, but this option seems to be rather unlikely, and nobody can safely rely on it.

- If the allocation criteria specified in your answer to the first question to this case consisted of the patients' clinical features (such as their age, clinical fragility etc.), please identify what criteria could be used for the allocation decision if all the relevant clinical features of both patients were practically the same?

If more patients come with comparably urgent need for care, the *first come, first served* rule should apply.[170] Some authors believe there should be a sort of lottery as a pure mechanism of chance.[171] However, lottery involves a direct choice made by the health services provider in organising it but there are no legal grounds for it. Furthermore, a lottery might be impractical to carry out in real-life conditions. Last but not least, a drawing of lots would be difficult to explain to patients and their loved ones and convince them of its fairness.

Case 3

There is a single extracorporeal membrane oxygenation (ECMO) device in the hospital. It is currently being used for an 84-year-old patient suffering from COVID-19, with diabetes as an underlying disease, clinical frailty score (CFS) 6–7 (moderate to severe frailty). It is possible that the patient will survive and will be discharged from the hospital if the ECMO treatment is continued. However, a younger COVID-19 patient is admitted to the hospital. This new patient is 51 years old, otherwise healthy, but her health condition has been rapidly deteriorating. Soon she will most likely need the ECMO to survive.

Evaluation of the case

- Can it be legally permissible for the hospital staff to discontinue the ECMO treatment of the older patient and provide palliative care to her in order to save

[170] Cf. Renata Černá Pařízková, Petr Šustek, Lukáš Prudil, Jolana Kopsa Těšinová, Martin Šolc, Karel Cvachovec, Ondřej Dostál, Tomáš Holčapek, Marek Vácha, Pavel Ševčík, Vladimír Černý, 'Stanovisko výboru ČSARIM 13/2020: Rozhodování u pacientů v intenzivní péči v situaci nedostatku vzácných zdrojů [Statement of the Committee of the Czech Society for Anaesthesiology, Resuscitation and Intensive Medicine no. 13/2020: Decision-Making Regarding Patients In Intensive Care in a Situation of a Lack of Scarce Resources]' (2020) 5 *Anesteziologie a intenzivní medicína* 250, 251, Petr Šustek, Tomáš Holčapek, Martin Šolc, 'Příloha 1: Právní rozbor situace nedostatku vzácných zdrojů v systému zdravotní péče [Appendix 1: Legal Analysis of a Situation of a Lack of Scarce Resources in the Health System]' (2020) 5 *Anesteziologie a intenzivní medicína* 252, 253.

[171] Cf. David Černý, Adam Doležal, Tomáš Doležal, 'Etická a právní východiska pro tvorbu doporučení k rozhodování o alokaci vzácných zdrojů při poskytování zdravotních služeb v rámci pandemie COVID-19 [Ethical and Legal Framework for the Creation of Guidelines for the Decisions Regarding Scarce Resources Allocation in the Provision of Health Services in the COVID-19 Pandemic]' 12 (2nd edn, Kabinet zdravotnického práva a bioetiky Ústavu státu a práva AV ČR, October 2020) 9 <https://zdravotnickepravo.info/wp-content/uploads/2020/10/Eticka-a-pravni-vychodiska-pro-tvorbu-doporuceni-v-ramci-COVID-19_podzim-2020.pdf> accessed 29 June 2023.

the younger and healthier patient's life? Please keep in mind that the older patient could survive if the treatment continued, but her chances may be lower than those of the younger patient.

We need to stress that it is not allowed to terminate intensive care on the basis of comparing one patient with other patients. The patient must not be taken from intensive care when she is benefitting from it simply because there are other patients who have better chances of survival. Otherwise, both the hospital and the doctor would be acting illegally and might be sued or even face criminal prosecution.

Additional question

– Suppose that there are two different scenarios: a) the older patient was admitted to the hospital and provided with the ECMO treatment, and only later, after several days, the younger patient was admitted, and b) the younger patient was admitted before the older patient, however, the older patient required ECMO treatment soon after admission while the younger patient's health condition deteriorated only after a longer time when the ECMO was already occupied (i.e. at the time when the younger patient was admitted to the hospital, she did not yet need it). Would there be any difference in the allocation decision making between these two scenarios?

  In these scenarios, the same principles still apply: the treatment is provided to a patient to whom it is indicated, and it cannot be withdrawn merely for the sake of another patient. Therefore, in the first scenario, the ECMO treatment for the older patient should only be terminated if it becomes too burdensome for her with no realistic corresponding benefit. In the second scenario, both patients are admitted to the hospital, the older patient is provided with ECMO when it is indicated, and the younger patient would need to wait for the ECMO machine until the moment when it no longer provides the older patient with more benefit than harm (i.e. when it is no longer medically indicated).

List of abbreviations

Framework

David Černý, Adam Doležal, Tomáš Doležal, 'Etická a právní východiska pro tvorbu doporučení k rozhodování o alokaci vzácných zdrojů při poskytování zdravotních služeb v rámci pandemie COVID-19 [Ethical and Legal Framework for the Creation of Guidelines for the Decisions Regarding Scarce Resources Allocation in the Provision of Health Services in the COVID-19 Pandemic]' (2nd edn, Kabinet zdravotnického práva a bioetiky Ústavu státu a práva AV ČR, October 2020) <https://zdravotnickepravo.info/wp-content/uploads/2020/10/Eticka-a-pravni-vychodiska-pro-tvorbu-doporuceni-v-ramci-COVID-19_podzim-2020.pdf> accessed 29 June 2023

Statement

Renata Černá Pařízková, Petr Šustek, Lukáš Prudil, Jolana Kopsa Těšinová, Martin Šolc, Karel Cvachovec, Ondřej Dostál, Tomáš Holčapek, Marek Vácha, Pavel Ševčík,

Vladimír Černý, 'Stanovisko výboru ČSARIM 13/2020: Rozhodování u pacientů v intenzivní péči v situaci nedostatku vzácných zdrojů [Statement of the Committee of the Czech Society for Anaesthesiology, Resuscitation and Intensive Medicine no. 13/2020: Decision-Making Regarding Patients In Intensive Care in a Situation of a Lack of Scarce Resources]' (2020) 5 *Anesteziologie a intenzivní medicína* 249–251

Bibliography

• Legislation

Act No. 40/2009 Coll., the Criminal Code, as amended

Act No. 372/2011 Coll., on Health Services and the Conditions of their Provision, as amended

Act No. 374/2011 Coll., on Emergency Medical Service, as amended

Act No. 418/2011 Coll., on Criminal Liability of Legal Persons, as amended

Act No. 89/2012 Coll., the Civil Code, as amended

Charter of Fundamental Rights and Freedoms

• Case law

Judgment of Supreme Court of the Slovak Socialist Republic of 11 December 1980, file no. 3 To 72/80 (R 20/1982 tr.)

Judgment of the Supreme Court of the Czech Republic of 19 September 2018, file no. 25 Cdo 894/2018

• Books

Vladimír Pelc, *Krajní nouze v trestním právu [State of Necessity in Criminal Law]* (Leges 2021)

Pavel Šámal et al., *Trestní zákoník I. Obecná část (§ 1–139) [Criminal Code I. General Part (Sections 1–139)]* (2nd edn, C. H. Beck 2012)

Petr Šustek, Tomáš Holčapek et al., *Zdravotnické právo [Health Law]* (Wolters Kluwer 2016)

• Articles

Renata Černá Pařízková, Petr Šustek, Lukáš Prudil, Jolana Kopsa Těšinová, Martin Šolc, Karel Cvachovec, Ondřej Dostál, Tomáš Holčapek, Marek Vácha, Pavel Ševčík, Vladimír Černý, 'Stanovisko výboru ČSARIM 13/2020: Rozhodování u pacientů v intenzivní péči v situaci nedostatku vzácných zdrojů [Statement of the Committee of the Czech Society for Anaesthesiology, Resuscitation and Intensive Medicine no. 13/2020: Decision-Making Regarding Patients In Intensive Care in a Situation of a Lack of Scarce Resources]' (2020) 5 *Anesteziologie a intenzivní medicína* 249–251

Tomáš Doležal, 'Konflikt povinností jako okolnost vylučující protiprávnost – východisko pro úvahy o možné prioritizaci pacientů v případě nedostatku zdrojů [Conflict of Duties as a Legal Defence — A Starting Point for Consideration of Possible Patient Prioritisation in the Event of the Lack of Resources]' (*Zdravotnické právo a bioetika,* 2 November 2020) <https://zdravotnickepravo.info/konflikt-povinnosti-jako-okolnost-vylucujici-protipravnost-vychodisko-pro-uvahy-o-mozne-prioritizaci-pacientu-v-pripade-nedostatku-zdroju/> accessed 29 June 2023.

Helena Krejčíková and Jan Hřídel, 'Stanovisko k poskytování život udržující léčby dětským pacientům [Opinion on the Provision of Life-Sustaining Treatment to Minor Patients]' (2020) 1 *Paliativní medicína* 26–30

Kenneth Rockwood and Olga Theou, 'Using the Clinical Frailty Scale in Allocating Scarce Health Care Resources' (2020) 3 *Canadian Geriatrics Journal* 254–259 doi: https://doi.org/10.5770/cgj.23.463

Martin Šolc, 'The Pandemic and the Law: Challenges of Covid-19 to the Ethical and Legal Paradigm of Health Care' in Pavel Šturma (ed), *Czech Yearbook of Public & Private International Law. Česká ročenka mezinárodního práva veřejného a soukromého. Vol. 12* (Česká společnost pro mezinárodní právo 2021) 371–380

Petr Šustek, 'Current Debates on Medical Liability in the Czech Republic' (2019) 23 *Journal de Droit de la Santé et de l'Assurance Maladie* 63–71

Petr Šustek, 'Czech Expert Statements on Patient Prioritisation in the Covid-19 Pandemic in International Comparison' in Pavel Šturma (ed), *Czech Yearbook of Public & Private International Law. Česká ročenka mezinárodního práva veřejného a soukromého. Vol. 12* (Česká společnost pro mezinárodní právo 2021) 345–359

Petr Šustek, Tomáš Holčapek, Martin Šolc, 'Příloha 1: Právní rozbor situace nedostatku vzácných zdrojů v systému zdravotní péče [Appendix 1: Legal Analysis of a Situation of a Lack of Scarce Resources in the Health System]' (2020) 5 *Anesteziologie a intenzivní medicína* 252–255

• Other secondary sources

David Černý, Adam Doležal, Tomáš Doležal, 'Etická a právní východiska pro tvorbu doporučení k rozhodování o alokaci vzácných zdrojů při poskytování zdravotních služeb v rámci pandemie COVID-19 [Ethical and Legal Framework for the Creation of Guidelines for the Decisions Regarding Scarce Resources Allocation in the Provision of Health Services in the COVID-19 Pandemic]' (2nd edn, Kabinet zdravotnického práva a bioetiky Ústavu státu a práva AV ČR, October 2020) <https://zdravotnickepravo.info/wp-content/uploads/2020/10/Eticka-a-pravni-vychodiska-pro-tvorbu-doporuceni-v-ramci-COVID-19_podzim-2020.pdf> accessed 29 June 2023

Dalibor Glück, 'A year into Covid-19 pandemic, Czech 'success story' becomes cautionary tale' (*Radio Prague International,* 3 January 2021) <https://english.radio.cz/a-year-covid-19-pandemic-czech-success-story-becomes-cautionary-tale-8710743> accessed 29 June 2023

Methodology on Compensation of Non-proprietary Personal Injury (Pain and Loss of Amenity in accordance with Section 2958 of the Civil Code)

Recommendation of the Board of Directors of the Czech Medical Chamber (ČLK) No. 1/2010 on the Procedure for Deciding to Change Intensive Care to Palliative Care in Patients in the Terminal Stage Who Are Unable to Express their Will

FRANCE

Maxime Lassalle[172]
University of Burgundy

Introduction

The mere existence of triage practices during the pandemic is contested in France. However, public data has been consolidated in parliamentary reports. They concluded that senior patients — especially those above 75 — were excluded from the hospitals during the pandemic.[173] In other words, French health care professionals had to allocate scarce resources. This has caught attention from the media, raising ethics questions mainly on the utilitarian approach.[174] Despite the discussions in the public media, this question was barely addressed by legal scholarship.[175]

A. Questionnaire

1. What are the criteria for the allocation of scarce health care resources in your country?

Specific criteria have been used to address the issue of the allocation of scarce health care resources during the pandemic and were based on previous health care policies and practices:[176] collegiality, respect of the patient's will, non-discrimination, pa-

---

172 Associate Professor at the University of Burgundy (maxime.lassalle@u-bourgogne.fr).

173 Catherine Deroche, Bernard Jomier and Sylvie Vermeillet, 'Santé publique : pour un nouveau départ – Leçons de l'épidémie de covid-19; Rapport n° 199 (2020-2021) fait au nom de la CE Évaluation des politiques publiques face aux pandémies, déposé le 8 décembre 2020' (*Sénat*, 8 December 2020) <www.senat.fr/notice-rapport/2020/r20-199-2-notice.html>; Julien Borowczyk and Eric Ciotti, 'Rapport d'information par la mission d'information relative à l'impact, la gestion et les conséquences dans toutes ses dimensions de l'épidémie de Coronavirus-Covid 19, n°1399' 156-163 (*Assemblée nationale*, 2 December 2020) <www2.assemblee-nationale.fr/static/15/pdf/rapport/i3633.pdf>.

174 ibid.

175 Jean Marie Crouzatier, 'Le Triage Des Malades de La Covid-19 et l'éthique Médicale' Revue de la recherche juridique. Droit prospectif 564; Jonas Knetsch and Maxime Lassalle, 'La Responsabilité Des Professionnels de Santé Face Au Tri Des Patients : Dilemme Éthique Ou Question Juridique ?' (2022) 6 Recueil Dalloz 286.

176 The concept of triage existed before: Alain Puidupin et al, 'Triage et Régulation Des Afflux' in *Agressions collectives par armes de guerre : Conduites à tenir pour les professionnels de santé*

tient's prior condition, current clinical severity, comfort, guarantee that everybody has access to health care and medical support.[177] One of these criteria, namely, the patient's previous condition, is itself distinguished in subcriteria: fragility, age ("to be taken particularly into account for covid's patient"),[178] comorbidities, neurocognitive stage, and global evolution of the patient's health situation. Age is therefore not the only criteria, but it is considered.

These criteria are used in particular regarding access to intensive care units, when it is necessary to prioritize specific patients over others. Such prioritization is the last resort measure, but is not ruled out as a matter of principle. On top of the aforementioned criteria, such a measure of allocation should be used only if transfers of patients to other hospitals are not possible and if alternative measures are not available either. In those circumstances, it is for instance possible to replace a patient already using the resources available (i. e. oxygen) with another patient with higher chances of survival. Such a measure "requires respecting the temporality of decision-making processes and the possible introduction of palliative care as well as support for families."[179] The least we can say is that this criterion is not very clear. The absence of specific rules that could be applied even in cases of emergency concerning the prioritization of particular patients over others was criticized by some practitioners in the context of the pandemic.[180]

2. What values are the allocation criteria based on?

Although the principle is equality, the necessity to apply specific criteria to face allocation of scarce resources in exceptional circumstances, such as in the case of a pandemic led to accept the principle of prioritization. Such prioritization is however based on specific values. These values are not exhaustively listed in an official text or document. Different kinds of document were published in the context of the pandemic[181] namely equity, autonomy, dignity, solidarity, and non-maleficence.[182] Transparency in the decision-making process is also a significant value. Distributive

(Ministère des Solidarités et de la Santé 2018).

177 Agence Régionale de Santé Ile de France, 'Recommandations régionales Covid 19 – Décision d'admission des patients en unités de réanimation et unités de soins critiques' (19 March 2020) <www.iledefrance.ars.sante.fr/system/files/2020-03/010_ARSIdF-CRAPS_2020-03-19_Doctrine_Criteres-admission_Soins-Critiques.pdf>

178 ibid 3.

179 ibid.

180 Pierre Biclet, 'Covid-19, Comment Gérer Un Autre Titanic?' [2020] Médecin et droit 74; see also Robin Cremer and Pascale Valette, 'Peut-on Parler de Tri Des Malades et Avec Qui ?' [2021] Ethique et santé 18.

181 See bellow para. 30.

182 Comité consultatif national d'éthique, 'Contribution du comité consultatif national d'éthique : Enjeux éthiques face à une pandémie' (13 March 2020) <www.ccne-ethique.fr/sites/default/files/2021-07/R%C3%A9ponse%20CCNE%20-%20Covid-19%20%20Def.pdf>.

justice is explicitly mentioned but must be considered in exceptional circumstances only.[183] It is understood in this context as follows:

"preserving scarce resources (such as intensive care beds) for the benefit of the greatest number and to take care of patients with or without COVID-19 for whom admission to critical care would be beneficial, to avoid deaths, lack of space."[184]

3. In what type(s) of document(s) are the allocation criteria set? Is it in binding or non-binding guidelines, in the law, or in another type of document?

No specific law has been adopted to deal with civil, administrative, or criminal liability risks. However, several non-binding guidelines have been published to address the specificities of the pandemic. One can distinguish three different types of documents. The first category of publication comes from learned societies such as the ethics council. They based their guidelines on the values that should be respected to execute allocation measures.[185] The second category of publication comes from the medical professions itself, which issued guidelines meant to help the members of those professions in practice.[186] The third category of publication comes from

183 Mission nationale Coordination Opérationnelle Risque Epidémique et Biologique (COREB), groupe « Ethique réanimation COVID19 », Société de réanimation et de Langue Française (SRLF), Société Française de Gériatrie et de Gérontologie (SFGG), Société Française d'Anesthésie et de Réanimation (SFAR), Société Française de Pathologie Infectieuse et de Langue Française (SPILF), la Société Française d'Accompagnement et de soins Palliatifs (SFAP), 'Recommandation professionnelle multi-disciplinaire (RPMO) – Aspects éthiques et stratégiques de l'accès aux soins de réanimation et autres soins critiques (SC) en contexte de pandémie Covid-19' (24 March 2020) <www.coreb.infectiologie.com/UserFiles/File/procedures/rpmo-ethique-rea-covid-19-vf-24-corr26-mar20-2.pdf>.

184 ibid 7.

185 Comité consultatif national d'éthique, 'Contribution du comité consultatif ntional d'éthique : Enjeux éthiques face à une pandémie' (13 March 2020) <www.ccne-ethique.fr/sites/default/files/2021-07/R%C3%A9ponse%20CCNE%20-%20Covid-19%20%20Def.pdf>; Comité consultatif national d'éthique, 'Enjeux éthiques de la prise en charge et de l'accès aux soins pour tous en situation de forte tension liée à l'épidémie de Covid-19' (16 Novembre 2020) <www.ccne-ethique.fr/sites/default/files/2021-07/ccne_-_saisine_triage.pdf>.

186 Mission nationale Coordination Opérationnelle Risque Epidémique et Biologique (COREB), groupe « Ethique réanimation COVID19 », Société de réanimation et de Langue Française (SRLF), Société Française de Gériatrie et de Gérontologie (SFGG), Société Française d'Anesthésie et de Réanimation (SFAR), Société Française de Pathologie Infectieuse et de Langue Française (SPILF), la Société Française d'Accompagnement et de soins Palliatifs (SFAP), 'Recommandation professionnelle multi-disciplinaire (RPMO) – Aspects éthiques et stratégiques de l'accès aux soins de réanimation et autres soins critiques (SC) en contexte de pandémie Covid-19' (24 March 2020) <www.coreb.infectiologie.com/UserFiles/File/procedures/rpmo-ethique-rea-covid-19-vf-24-corr26-mar20-2.pdf>; Comité éthique de la société française d'anesthésie et de réanimation, 'À propos des décisions médicales d'admission des patients en unité de soins critiques en contexte pandémique : quelques repères éthiques' (26 Mars 2020) <https://sfar.org/comite-ethique-a-propos-des-decisions-medicales-dadmission-des-patients-en-unite-de-soins-critiques-en-context-pandemique-quelques-reperes-ethiques/>

public administrations in charge of health issues. They released guidelines that were meant to guide practitioners in the possible event that medical professionals should make allocation decisions.[187]

The coordination of these three categories of texts has not been addressed by the legal framework so far.

4. Are providers of health care obliged by the law to provide (urgent) care to all patients? If the answer is yes, are there any legally recognized exceptions from this duty?

Access to health care is a right for everybody in French law. In particular, paragraph 11 of the Preamble to the 1946 Constitution, states that the Nation "shall guarantee to all, notably to children, mothers and elderly workers, protection of their health". However, this right is limited in practice to using "available means".[188] The meaning of this phrase is however very unclear.[189] For instance, instead of a reference to the material and financial means, it could be a mere reference to technological possibilities. Furthermore, everybody has the right to dignity at the end of her life, and "health care professionals use all the means at their disposal to ensure that this right is respected".

In any event, medical professionals are only obliged to provide urgent health care.[190] Even in that case, the obligation to provide medical care can be limited to the mere maintenance and continuity of a patient's care, since this obligation applies "whatever the circumstances"[191]. Therefore, scarcity of medical resources could be a basis for allocation of scarce resources in case of an emergency as long as minimum care is provided to everybody.[192]

187 Agence Régionale de Santé Ile de France, 'Recommandations régionales Covid 19 – Décision d'admission des patients en unités de réanimation et unités de soins critiques' (19 March 2020) <www.iledefrance.ars.sante.fr/system/files/2020-03/010_ARSIdF-CRAPS_2020-03-19_Doctrine_Criteres-admission_Soins-Critiques.pdf>

188 Art. L1110-1 Public health code.

189 Jean-Marie Pontier, 'Crise Sanitaire et Droit à La Santé' [2021] Revue de droit sanitaire et social 661.

190 Art. R4127-9 Public health code. Art. R4127-47 § 2 Public health code: "Apart from emergency cases, or if he fails in his duty of humanity, (…) a doctor has the right to refuse treatment for professional or personal reasons."

191 Art. R4127-47 § 1 Public health code: "Whatever the circumstances, continuity of patient care must be ensured".

192 In a public hospital, refusal to provide for health care is not an option, some health care have to be provided, see Xavier Bioy, Anne Laude and Didier Tabuteau, *Droit de La Santé* (4th edn, PUF 2020) 388.

5. On what legal basis is it possible to apply the allocation criteria in practice?

Since no legal reform occurred during the pandemic, an existing legal basis had to be used. The applicable legal basis was the law meant to deal with therapeutic obstinacy, namely the so-called "Leonetti" and "Claeys-Leonetti" Acts.[193] According to these Acts, the provision of health care should not be implemented or pursued if it leads to unreasonable obstinacy.[194] This legal basis allows the possibility of letting somebody die provided that some conditions are respected. In particular, such a procedure can be used only where health care appears unuseful, disproportionate, or would only artificially lengthen somebody's life. It is based on a collegial decision.

Even though experts favor this legal basis,[195] one could say that it was not meant to deal with the specific situation created by the Covid-19. In a pandemic, triage measures are different from therapeutic obstinacy. Medical professionals have to choose between people who could live provided that they received appropriate health care. If some of them needed more health care, the outcome would not be to "artificially lengthen" their lives.

One could argue that health care could not be helpful or proportionate in case of a pandemic, but it would imply comparing the respective values of at least two patients' lives. This would not imply taking into account the fact that treatments appear to be excessive regardless of financial resources, as is the case with medical obstinacy. Yet comparing two patient's lives was not the situation the so-called "Leonetti" and "Claeys-Leonetti" Acts were meant to address. For this reason, one could say that there is a contradiction between the application of this law and the principles of equality[196] and non-discrimination, which are also provided by the law.[197]

---

[193] Law « Leonetti » n° 2005-370, 22 April 2005 relative aux droits des malades et à la fin de vie; Law « Claeys-Leonetti » n° 2016-87, 2 February 2016, créant de nouveaux droits en faveur des malades et des personnes en fin de vie.

[194] Art. L1110-5-1 Public health code.

[195] See Cécile Manaouil, 'Réflexions Sur Le Tri Des Patients En Période de Crise Sanitaire' (*Dalloz Actualité*, 30 April 2020) <www.dalloz-actualite.fr/dossier/reflexions-sur-tri-des-patients-en-periode-de-crise-sanitaire>.

[196] Art. L1110-5 Public health code. See Diane Roman, '« Ils Ne Mouraient Pas Tous, Mais Tous Étaient Frappés » Le Coronavirus, Révélateur Des Ambigüités de l'appréhension Juridique de La Vulnérabilité' [2020] Revue des droits fondamentaux.
However the Council of state ruled out a claim requested the administration to establish a clear legal framework to guarantee an equal access to health care (Council of State, 15 April 2020, n°439910), see Crouzatier (n 4).

[197] Art. L1110-3 Public health code; Art. 225-1 Criminal code.

6. What level of legal certainty do the health professionals and the health care providers have when applying the allocation criteria?

Legal certainty is minimal since no law was adopted to deal explicitly with this situation.[198]

The highest administrative court in France (*Conseil d'Etat*) refused to compel the government to act and provide a clear legal framework.[199] It was seized by civil society organizations based on the high likelihood that allocation criteria would have to be used and would put practitioners at risk, for instance, of criminal or disciplinary proceedings. The civil society organizations based their claim on the principle that such important decisions should be addressed by an act of parliament and could not be left to soft law such as learned societies' guidelines. The decision of the *Conseil d'Etat* took place relatively early during the pandemic and was based on the absence of evidence that triage was already taking place.[200] One could say that triage measures did not happen in France as early as April 2020. However, it did happen later, and the legal framework was not adapted at that point.

7. What are the civil and criminal liability implications of allocation of scarce health care resources? Have there already been any related legal suits and/or criminal proceedings?

There are no known cases of legal suits related to the pandemic.[201] However, one could consider that actions taken by doctors or hospitals could be followed by legal consequences regarding their administrative or criminal liability and disciplinary proceedings.

The liability of health care providers is fault-based, whatever the context in which health care is provided.[202] There is no case law regarding the application of medical liability in exceptional circumstances and especially during a pandemic, however, the most important case at the basis of the modern approach to medical

198 Other reforms were implemented in order to deal with the provision of medical products and drugs and vaccination by doctors (Art. L3131-20 Public health code) but also to deal with the decisions made by public authorities; see Arnaud Lami, 'Covid-19, et Si on Parlait de La Responsabilité Des Professionnels de Santé ?' [2020] Jounal du droit administratif <www.journal-du-droit-administratif.fr/?p=3313>.

199 Council of State, 15 April 2020, n°439910.

200 For a sharp criticism of this decision, especially as it implicitly aknowledges that the guidelines established by learned societies were clear enough, see Xavier Bioy, 'Le Droit d'accès Aux Soins Dans Un Contexte Pandémique' [2020] AJDA 1487.

201 There are in comparison numerous procedures regarding the criminal liability of ministers for their inaction in the face of the pandemic. See Maxime Lassalle, 'La Responsabilité Pénale Ministérielle Face à Une Crise Mal Anticipée' [2020] Droit pénal 16.

202 Art. L1142-1 Public health code

liability referred to extraordinary circumstances as an exception to the duties a doctor had towards its patients.[203]

Current medical law is based on this approach but is also more detailed. There are currently two kinds of medical faults that can give ground to claims for compensation. The first one is the lack of organization of an administration. There are examples of cases where the administration was liable for insufficient organization regarding specific medical care.[204] There are, however, still uncertainties regarding the applicability of this ground for liability to the lack of organization of hospitals in the face of a global pandemic.[205] Therefore, one could wonder whether the lack of beds in intensive care units be considered a fault during a pandemic.[206]

The other kind of fault that can trigger a health professional liability is an illicit act, or an act contrary to the applicable regulation.[207] In this regard, replacing a patient with another might be considered an illicit act insofar as it contradicts the equal right to receive health care. Therefore, the question is that of the value of the criteria regarding allocation of scarce health care resources that have been established during the pandemic. Can applying the guidelines or other soft law instruments released during the pandemic be considered a fault? Can the inapplication of these guidelines be considered as a fault? In its decision regarding the absence of a legal framework regarding triage, the Council of State highlighted the importance of compliance with professional guidelines by hospitals and doctors, which seems to highlight the value of these guidelines.[208] However, the legal situation is quite ambiguous and the conciliation of the traditional principles established by the law with these guidelines and other soft law instruments should be addressed by the courts.

As far as criminal liability is concerned, one could say that triage measures could be excused based on two grounds for exemption: (1) the general excuse of necessity or (2) the specific excuse based on the so-called "Leonetti" and "Claeys-Leonetti" Acts.

Art. 122-7 of the Criminal code is the legal basis for the excuse of necessity (1). It states that "The person who, faced with a current or imminent danger which threatens himself, others or property, performs an act necessary for the protection of the person

[203] Cass. Civ, 20 May 1936, *Mercier*.

[204] See, for instance, on the lack of coordination between two hospitals: Council of State, 4° et 5°, 25 juillet 2007, n° 274682, Centre hospitalier général d'Avignon.

[205] On the uncertainties of this claims, see Thierry Dal Farra, 'La Responsabilité de l'Etat et de Ses Représentants Dans La Gestion de l'épidémie de Covid-19' [2020] AJDA 1463. It is however a kind of liability that could be developped in the future, see Hafida Belrhali, 'La Responsabilité Administrative de Demain' [2021] AJDA 1250.

[206] The main element here will be that of compliance with regulatory requirements. See, for a recent example not related to the pandemic: Cass, Civ 1., 28 February 2024, n° 22-23888.

[207] Bioy, Laude and Tabuteau (n 20) 435.

[208] This decision can be criticized for this reason: it is based on the absence of evidence of any triage and yet highlights the existence of guidelines that could guide health care professionnals. It gives an importance, which might be too high, to sources outside the standard legal framework (Bioy (n 28).

or the property, is not criminally liable unless there is a disproportion between the means employed and the seriousness of the threat." Case law is quite limited regarding the interpretation of this excuse but is very demanding.[209] For instance, in a case where a doctor on duty refused to go to the sick child's domicile because he had to visit urgently another patient, the Court of Cassation sustained a court of appeal's decision that condemned the doctor for failing to help a person in danger.[210]

As already mentioned, the so-called "Leonetti" and "Claeys-Leonetti" Acts provide for an exception (2) to the principle that medical professionals cannot stop providing health care. Therefore, it is a specific excuse for medical professionals who let somebody die. The Court of Cassation ruled that even though the specific rules regarding the decision-making process (collegiality, information of the family...) are not entirely respected, the fact that medical professionals let somebody die within the framework of this act excludes the intention to harm the patient and therefore the application of criminal law.[211]

B. Case studies

Case 1

As a result of a rapid worsening of the epidemiological situation, the material, and personal capacities have been drastically overloaded in all the hospitals in the country. Ambulances transport ten patients to one particular hospital's emergency unit within just a few minutes. The patients all need admission to the hospital, preferably to the intensive care unit (ICU). However, only two beds are available there. Other hospitals are overwhelmed too, so it is not possible to transport patients to any of them. All of the ten newly coming patients suffer from COVID-19; they have breathing difficulties, fast-rising fever, and decreasing oxygen saturation. Nevertheless, they differ in age, comorbidities, clinical fragility, and other factors.

Theoretically, the eight patients who cannot be admitted to beds can be placed in improvised settings in the hospital corridors, laying on gurneys or mattresses on the floor. Nevertheless, it will be impossible to provide them with the care they need.

Evaluation of the case

- What criteria can be used to choose the patients who will be admitted to the beds (i.e. what are the possible allocation criteria)?

  The applicable criteria regarding the decision about who will be admitted to the beds are the following: respect of the patient's will, non-discrimination, patient's previous condition, and current clinical severity, comfort, guarantee

---

209 Patrick Mistretta, *Droit Pénal Médical* (Cujas 2013) 89.

210 Cass. Crim., 4 February 1998, n° 96-81.425.

211 Cass. Crim., 5 March 2019, n°18-80.712. In this case it would not be considered as an excuse, the mental element of the criminal offence would simply not exist.

that everybody has access to health care, and medical support.[212] One of these criteria, namely, the patient's previous condition, is sub-distinguished in subcriteria: fragility, age ("to be taken particularly into account for covid's patient"), comorbidities, neurocognitive stage, and global evolution of the patient's health situation. Therefore, age is not the only criteria, but it counts as one of them. In this case, the patients will all be distinguished based on their comorbidities and clinical fragility, and their age will be taken into consideration to determine who will be admitted to beds. In theory, the other patients should be admitted to the hospital to ensure continuity of medical care. In practice, they could probably not be admitted at all, especially those who are above 75.[213]

- What legal consequences can this decision have for the health professionals and the hospital? How strong is their legal certainty that there will be no adverse legal consequences if they follow the above-mentioned criteria?
  This decision might have consequences regarding the hospital's and doctors' medical liability and their criminal liability. In its decision regarding the absence of a legal framework regarding triage, the Council of State highlighted the importance of compliance with professional guidelines by hospitals and doctors, which seems to highlight the value of these guidelines.[214] However, the nature of the allocation criteria is still unsettled since they do not have an explicit legal basis. Consequently, there is no legal certainty that there will be no adverse legal consequence.
- What legal defenses could the health professionals and the hospital use against a civil lawsuit and/or criminal prosecution for the allocation decision?
  In French law, two grounds for medical liability have to be distinguished. First, the lack of organization of an administration. There are uncertainties regarding the applicability of this ground for liability to the lack of organization of hospitals in the face of a global pandemic since, in such an exceptional situation, the lack of beds could hardly be considered a fault as long as the hospital is in compliance with existing regulatory requirements.[215]

---

212 Agence Régionale de Santé Ile de France, 'Recommandations régionales Covid 19 – Décision d'admission des patients en unités de réanimation ou de soins critiques dans un contexte d'épidémie de Covid-19' (19 March 2020) <www.iledefrance.ars.sante.fr/system/files/2020-03/010_ARSIdF-CRAPS_2020-03-19_Doctrine_Criteres-admission_Soins-Critiques.pdf>.

213 Catherine Deroche, Bernard Jomier and Sylvie Vermeillet, 'Santé publique : pour un nouveau départ – Leçons de l'épidémie de covid-19; Rapport n° 199 (2020-2021) fait au nom de la CE Évaluation des politiques publiques face aux pandémies, déposé le 8 décembre 2020' (*Sénat*, 8 December 2020) <www.senat.fr/notice-rapport/2020/r20-199-2-notice.html>; Julien Borowczyk, Eric Ciotti, 'Rapport d'information par la mission d'information relative à l'impact, la gestion et les conséquences dans toutes ses dimensions de l'épidémie de Coronavirus-Covid 19, n°1399' (*Assemblée nationale*, 2 December 2020) 156–163 <www2.assemblee-nationale.fr/static/15/pdf/rapport/i3633.pdf>.

214 This decision can be criticized for this reason: It is based on the absence of evidence of any triage and yet highlights the existence of guidelines that could guide potential health care professionnals. It gives an importance, which might be too high, to sources outside the standard legal framework (Bioy (n 28).

215 On the uncertainties of this claim, see Dal Farra (n 33). It is however a kind of liability that could be developped in the future, see Belrhali (n 33).

Second, the individual liability of the health professional. The liability of health care providers is fault-based, whatever the context in which health care was provided.[216] There is no case law regarding the application of medical liability in exceptional circumstances, especially during a pandemic. The most important case at the basis of the modern approach to medical liability referred to extraordinary circumstances as an exception to the duties a doctor had towards her patients and it is quite likely that a pandemic matches the definition of exceptional circumstances.[217] However, the existing legal framework regarding medical liability, which was modified in 2002, does not refer to exceptional circumstances. Furthermore, this legal framework was reformed again as a reaction to the pandemic, but exemptions from liability were created only to deal with the provision of medical products and drugs and vaccination by doctors.[218] It has not been extended to triage measures. In this context, the action to replace a patient with another might be considered an illicit act insofar as it contradicts the equal right to receive health care. However, in its decision regarding the absence of a legal framework regarding triage, the council of state highlighted the importance of compliance with professional guidelines by hospitals and doctors, which seems to highlight the value of these guidelines.[219] Compliance with this guidelines could therefore be used to deny the existence of a fault.

As far as criminal law is concerned, triage measures could be excused on two grounds: the general excuse of necessity and the so-called "Leonetti" and "Claeys-Leonetti" Acts. Case law is quite demanding regarding the interpretation of the excuse of necessity,[220] much less so when applying the so-called "Leonetti" and "Claeys-Leonetti" Acts.[221] One could, however, wonder whether this law could apply for somebody whose life would not have been "artificially lengthened" and had a chance to survive with the appropriate medical resources.

Additional questions

- Would it be legally permissible to lower the standard of care provided to all patients to provide at least basic decent care to the newly admitted patients who are placed in the hospital corridors? To what extent?

  The legal obligation to provide health care is limited to "available means" but, as already mentioned, the interpretation of this phrase is quite unclear. Moreover, medical professionals have to ensure "continuity of patient care"[222] whatever

[216] Art. L1142-1 Public health code.

[217] Cass. Civ, 20 May 1936, *Mercier*.

[218] Art. L3131-20 Public health code. See Lami (n 26).

[219] This decision can be criticized for this reason: It is based on the absence of evidence of any triage and yet highlight the existent of guidelines that could guide potential health care professionnals. It gives an importance, which might be too high, to sources outside the standard legal framework (Bioy (n 28)).

[220] Cass. Crim., 4 February 1998, n° 96-81.425.

[221] Cass. Crim., 5 March 2019, n°18-80.712. In this case it would not be considered as an excuse, the mental element of the criminal offence would simply not exist.

[222] Art. R4127-47 Public health code.

the circumstance. If there is no clear basis for choosing between two alternatives — high standards whatever the cicumstance, or lower standards in exceptional circumstances — the latter option would probably be the one that would be retained to ensure a continuity of health care for everybody.

Case 2

Two patients in an ICU are suffering from COVID-19. After admission to the hospital, they were provided with the high-flow nasal oxygen therapy (HFNO). During one night, the condition of both patients starts to worsen rapidly. At dawn, it is clear that neither of them will survive without artificial ventilation. However, there is just one ventilator available.

Evaluation of the case

- What criteria can be used to choose which of the two patients will be provided with artificial ventilation and which one will be left without it, possibly to die?
  Prioritization of specific patients over others should, of course, be the last resort measure but it is not ruled out as a matter of principle in this kind of situation. The criteria regarding this kind of allocation measure are very fuzzy. Such a measure should be used only if the transfer of the patient is not a possibility and if alternative measures are not available either. In those circumstances, the aforementioned soft law instruments would allow to replace a patient already using the resources available (e.g. oxygen) with another one with higher chances of survival. This is, however, conditioned.
  There is no real distinction based on the nature of the health care provided regarding the applicable criteria for allocation of scarce resources. The decision about who will get the artificial ventilation is therefore based on the same criteria as the ones which were applied to decide on who would access the hospital in case 1: respect of the patient's will, non-discrimination, patient's previous condition, and current clinical severity, comfort, guarantee that everybody has access to health care and medical support.[223] One of these criteria, namely, the patient's previous condition, is further distinguished in subcriteria: fragility, age ("to be taken particularly into account for covid's patient"[224]), comorbidities, neurocognitive stage, and global evolution of the patient's health situation. As already explained, age is not the only criteria, but it counts as one of them.
  One regional agency in charge of public health disclosed a document stating, on top of these general criteria, that this specific kind of allocation of ressources "requires respecting the temporality of decision-making processes and the

223 Agence Régionale de Santé Ile de France, 'Recommandations régionales Covid 19 – Décision d'admission des patients en unités de réanimation ou de soins critiques dans un contexte d'épidémie de Covid-19' (19 March 2020) <www.iledefrance.ars.sante.fr/system/files/2020-03/010_ARSIdF-CRAPS_2020-03-19_Doctrine_Criteres-admission_Soins-Critiques.pdf>

224 ibid 3.

possible introduction of palliative care as well as support for families."[225] This is obviously not sufficiently precise to evaluate case number 2 but shows that this specific situation was at least considered.

- What legal consequences can this decision have for the health professionals and the hospital? How strong is their legal certainty that there will be no adverse legal consequences if they follow the above-mentioned criteria?
  The principles that have been set out in case 1 also apply here.
- What legal defences could the health professionals and the hospital use against a civil lawsuit and/or criminal prosecution for the allocation decision?
  The principles that have been set out in case 1 also apply here.

Additional question

- If the allocation criteria specified in your answer to the first question to this case consisted of the patients' clinical features (such as their age, clinical fragility, etc.), please identify what criteria could be used for the allocation decision if all the relevant clinical features of both patients were practically the same?
  Even though it might be challenging to check if it was respected in practice, the only element that has been clarified is that there is no social scoring.[226] The alleged usefulness of a person in society is not taken into consideration. Similarly, the choice not to get vaccinated was not taken into account either.

Case 3

There is a single extracorporeal membrane oxygenation (ECMO) device in the hospital. It is currently being used for an 84-year-old patient suffering from COVID-19, with diabetes as an underlying disease, clinical frailty score (CFS) 6-7 (moderate to severe frailty). It is possible that the patient will survive and will be discharged from the hospital if the ECMO treatment is continued. However, a younger COVID-19 patient is admitted to the hospital. This new patient is 51 years old, otherwise healthy, but her health condition has been rapidly deteriorating. Soon she will most likely need ECMO to survive.

225 Agence Régionale de Santé Ile de France, 'Recommandations régionales Covid 19 – Décision d'admission des patients en unités de réanimation et unités de soins critiques' (19 March 2020) <www.iledefrance.ars.sante.fr/system/files/2020-03/010_ARSIdF-CRAPS_2020-03-19_Doctrine_Criteres-admission_Soins-Critiques.pdf>.

226 Mission nationale Coordination Opérationnelle Risque Epidémique et Biologique (COREB), groupe « Ethique réanimation COVID19 », Société de réanimation et de Langue Française (SRLF), Société Française de Gériatrie et de Gérontologie (SFGG), Société Française d'Anesthésie et de Réanimation (SFAR), Société Française de Pathologie Infectieuse et de Langue Française (SPILF), la Société Française d'Accompagnement et de soins Palliatifs (SFAP), 'Recommandation professionnelle multi-disciplinaire (RPMO) – Aspects éthiques et stratégiques de l'accès aux soins de réanimation et autres soins critiques (SC) en contexte de pandémie Covid-19' (24 March 2020) <www.coreb.infectiologie.com/UserFiles/File/procedures/rpmo-ethique-rea-covid-19-vf-24-corr26-mar20-2.pdf>.

Evaluation of the case

- Can it be legally permissible for the hospital staff to discontinue the ECMO treatment of the older patient and provide palliative care to her in order to save the younger and healthier patient's life? Please keep in mind that the older patient could survive if the treatment continued, but her chances may be lower than those of the younger patient.
  It is probably this situation that is primarily concerned by the application of the aforementioned "Leonetti" and "Claeys-Leonetti" Acts.[227] As already explained, some professionals believe that this is the relevant legal basis. They imply that it could be legal to withdraw treatment from someone and give it to someone else.
- If the answer to the first question is positive, what specific criteria can be used in clinical decision-making regarding replacing one patient with another with respect to a particular treatment unavailable for all?
  The principles that have been set out in case 1 and 2 also apply here.
  The above-mentioned approach is based on the same general criteria applicable to the allocation of scarce health care resources: collegiality, respect of the patient's will, non-discrimination, patient's previous condition and current clinical severity, comfort, and guarantee that everybody has access to health care and medical support.[228] One of these criteria, namely, the patient's previous condition, is further distinguished in subcriteria: fragility, age ("to be taken particularly into account for covid's patient"), comorbidities, neurocognitive stage, and global evolution of the patient's health situation. There are no further specific criteria.
- What legal consequences can this decision have for the health professionals and the hospital? How strong is their legal certainty that there will be no adverse legal consequences if they follow the above-mentioned criteria?
  The principles that have been set out in case 1 also apply here.
- What legal defences could the health professionals and the hospital use against a civil lawsuit and/or criminal prosecution for the allocation decision?
  The principles that have been set out in case 1 also apply here.

Additional question

- Suppose there are two different scenarios: a) the older patient was admitted to the hospital and provided with the ECMO treatment, and only later, after several days, the younger patient was admitted, and b) the younger patient was admitted before, the older patient, however, the older patient required ECMO treatment soon after admission while the younger patient's health condition deteriorated only after a longer time when the ECMO was already occupied (i. e. at the time when the younger patient was admitted to the hospital, she did not yet need it). Would there be any difference in the allocation decision making between these two scenarios?
  The criteria that have been proposed do not address such a specific situation.

---

227 See above § 32.

228 ibid.

Bibliography

• Legislation

Criminal code (*Code pénal*); cited as: Criminal code

Law « Leonetti » n° 2005-370, 22 April 2005 relative aux droits des malades et à la fin de vie

Law « Claeys-Leonetti » n° 2016-87, 2 February 2016, créant de nouveaux droits en faveur des malades et des personnes en fin de vie

Public health code (*Code de la santé publique*); cited as: Public health code

• Case law

Council of State

Council of State, 15 April 2020, n° 439910

Council of State, 4° et 5°, 25 juillet 2007, n° 274682, Centre hospitalier général d'Avignon

Court of cassation

Criminal chamber, 4 February 1998, n° 96-81.425

Criminal chamber, 5 March 2019, n° 18-80.712

Civil chamber, 20 May 1936, *Mercier*

Civil chamber (1), 28 February 2024, n° 22-23888

• Books

Bioy X, Laude A and Tabuteau D, *Droit de La Santé* (4th edn, PUF 2020)

Mistretta P, *Droit Pénal Médical* (Cujas 2013)

• Articles

Belrhali H, 'La Responsabilité Administrative de Demain' [2021] AJDA 1250

Biclet P, 'Covid-19, Comment Gérer Un Autre Titanic?' [2020] Médecin et droit 74

Bioy X, 'Le Droit d'accès Aux Soins Dans Un Contexte Pandémique' [2020] AJDA 1487

Cremer R and Valette P, 'Peut-on Parler de Tri Des Malades et Avec Qui ?' [2021] Ethique et santé 18

Crouzatier JM, 'Le Triage Des Malades de La Covid-19 et l'éthique Médicale' Revue de la recherche juridique' Droit prospectif 564

Dal Farra T, 'La Responsabilité de l'Etat et de Ses Représentants Dans La Gestion de l'épidémie de Covid-19' [2020] AJDA 1463

Knetsch J and Lassalle M, 'La Responsabilité Des Professionnels de Santé Face Au Tri Des Patients : Dilemme Éthique Ou Question Juridique ?' (2022) 6 Recueil Dalloz 286

Lami A, 'Covid-19, et Si on Parlait de La Responsabilité Des Professionnels de Santé ?' [2020] Jounal du droit administratif <www.journal-du-droit-administratif.fr/?p=3313>

Lassalle M, 'La Responsabilité Pénale Ministérielle Face à Une Crise Mal Anticipée' [2020] Droit pénal 16

Lefève C, 'La Pandémie, Révélateur de l'extension Du Domaine Du Tri' in Céline Worms, Jean-Christophe Mino and Martin Dumont (eds), Le soin en première ligne (PUF 2021)

Manaouil C, 'Réflexions Sur Le Tri Des Patients En Période de Crise Sanitaire' (*Dalloz Actualité*, 30 April 2020) <www.dalloz-actualite.fr/dossier/reflexions-sur-tri-des-patients-en-periode-de-crise-sanitaire>

Pontier J-M, 'Crise Sanitaire et Droit à La Santé' [2021] Revue de droit sanitaire et social 661

Puidupin A et al, 'Triage et Régulation Des Afflux' in *Agressions collectives par armes de guerre : Conduites à tenir pour les professionnels de santé* (Ministère des Solidarités et de la Santé 2018)

Roman D, '« Ils Ne Mouraient Pas Tous, Mais Tous Étaient Frappés » Le Coronavirus, Révélateur Des Ambigüités de l'appréhension Juridique de La Vulnérabilité' [2020] Revue des droits fondamentaux

• Other secondary sources

Official reports

Borowczyk J and Ciotti E, 'Rapport d'information par la mission d'information relative à l'impact, la gestion et les conséquences dans toutes ses dimensions de l'épidémie de Coronavirus-Covid 19, n°1399' (*Assemblée nationale*, 2 December 2020) <www2.assemblee-nationale.fr/static/15/pdf/rapport/i3633.pdf>

Deroche C, Jomier B and Vermeillet S, 'Santé publique : pour un nouveau départ – Leçons de l'épidémie de covid-19, Rapport n° 199 (2020-2021) fait au nom de la CE Évaluation des politiques publiques face aux pandémies, déposé le 8 décembre 2020' (*Sénat*, 8 December 2020) <www.senat.fr/notice-rapport/2020/r20-199-2-notice.html>

Guidelines and recommendations

Agence Régionale de Santé Ile de France, 'Recommandations régionales Covid 19 – Décision d'admission des patients en unités de réanimation ou de soins critiques dans un contexte d'épidémie de Covid-19' (19 March 2020) <www.iledefrance.ars.sante.fr/system/files/2020-03/010_ARSIdF-CRAPS_2020-03-19_Doctrine_Criteres-admission_Soins-Critiques.pdf>

Comité consultatif national d'éthique, 'Contribution du comité consultatif national d'éthique : Enjeux éthiques face à une pandémie' (13 March 2020) <www.ccne-ethique.fr/sites/default/files/2021-07/R%C3%A9ponse%20CCNE%20-%20Covid-19%20%20Def.pdf>

Comité consultatif national d'éthique, 'Enjeux éthiques de la prise en charge et de l'accès aux soins pour tous en situation de forte tension liée à l'épidémie de Covid-19' (16 November 2020) <www.ccne-ethique.fr/sites/default/files/2021-07/ccne_-_saisine_triage.pdf>

Comité éthique de la société française d'anesthésie et de réanimation, 'À propos des décisions médicales d'admission des patients en unité de soins critiques en contexte pandémique : quelques repères éthiques' (26 March 2020) <https://sfar.org/comite-ethique-a-propos-des-decisions-medicales-dadmission-des-patients-en-unite-de-soins-critiques-en-context-pandemique-quelques-reperes-ethiques/>

Haut Conseil de la Santé Publique, 'Avis relatif à la prise en charge des cas confirmés d'infection au virus SARS-CoV21' (5 March 2020)

Haut Conseil de la Santé Publique, 'Avis relatif à la prévention et à la prise en charge des patients à risque de formes graves de COVID-19 ainsi qu'à la priorisation des tests diagnostiques' (31 March 2020)

Mission nationale Coordination Opérationnelle Risque Epidémique et Biologique (COREB), groupe « Ethique réanimation COVID19 », Société de réanimation et de Langue Française (SRLF), Société Française de Gériatrie et de Gérontologie (SFGG), Société Française d'Anesthésie et de Réanimation (SFAR), Société Française de Pathologie Infectieuse et de Langue Française (SPILF), la Société Française d'Accompagnement et de soins Palliatifs (SFAP), 'Recommandation professionnelle multi-disciplinaire (RPMO) – Aspects éthiques et stratégiques de l'accès aux soins de réanimation et autres soins critiques (SC) en contexte de pandémie Covid-19' (24 March 2020) <www.coreb.infectiologie.com/UserFiles/File/procedures/rpmo-ethique-rea-covid-19-vf-24-corr26-mar20-2.pdf>

ITALY

Roberto Pucella and Massimo Foglia
University of Bergamo

A. Questionnaire

1. What are the criteria for the allocation of scarce health care resources in your country?

It has been estimated that in the most critical period between the 5th and the 25th of March 2020 in the provinces of Bergamo-Lodi-Brescia-Cremona (the so-called red zone) for every single bed in intensive care, there were almost 10 patients queuing up for it. The terrible emergency triggered by the Covid-19 brings us up against such a shortage, and the dramatic problem of how best to manage health resources to ensure the right to health referred to in the Italian Constitution.

With regard to the possibility to establish criteria that should guide healthcare professionals in this "tragic choice"[229], the Statute n. 833 of 1978, founding the Italian National Health Service,[230] establishes that *"The National Health Service encompasses all the functions, facilities, services and activities directed at the promotion, maintenance and recovery of physical and mental health of the entire population,* ***regardless of social or individual conditions, and in a way which ensures the equality of the citizens.*** *"*[231]

So, together with the constitutional principles, the law prescribes that care must be ensured according to universalistic and egalitarian criterion.

---

[229] On this issue see Guido Calabresi, *Tragic Choices* (W. W. Norton & Company 1978).

[230] For an outline of the Italian Health Care System, see Alessandro Pietro Scarso and Massimo Foglia, '*Medical Liability in Italy*' in Bernhard A Koch (ed), *Medical Liability in Europe. A Comparison of Selected Jurisdictions* (De Gruyter 2011) 329ff.

[231] For a broader analysis of the issue, see Roberto Pucella, 'Scelte tragiche e dilemmi giuridici a tempi della pandemia' 2020 (3) Nuova giur. civ. comm., Special Issue 24; Giulio Ponzanelli, 'I danni subiti da CoViD-19 tra regole di responsabilità civile e piani no fault' ivi 137; Claudio Scognamiglio, 'La pandemia CoViD-19, i danni alla salute ed i limiti della responsabilità civile' 140; Carlo Casonato, 'Health At The Time Of Covid-19: Tyrannical, Denied, Unequal Health' (2020) 3 BioLaw Journal 315; Marcello Maggiolo, 'Coronavirus and Medical Liability' in E Hondius, M Santos Silva, A Nicolussi, P Salvador Coderch, C Wendehorst and F Zoll (eds), *Coronavirus and the Law in Europe* (Intersentia 2021); Guido Smorto, '*The Right to Health and Resource Allocation. Who Gets What and Why in the COVID-19 Pandemic*' (2020) 20 *Global Jurist* 59 <https://doi.org/10.1515/gj-2020-0040>.

In March 2020, the Italian Society of Anesthesia, Analgesia, Resuscitation and Intensive Therapy (SIAARTI) issued the document entitled "clinical ethics recommendations for the allocation of intensive care treatments, in exceptional, resource-limited circumstances."[232] *The document establishes guidelines on the access to the intensive care units in situations of scarce resources, as happened due to Covid-19 pandemic. The core principle is not new: the basic rule "first come, first served"* is replaced by the "clinical suitability" criterion, according to which the patient more likely to have more benefits from the treatment must be cured.

This is the same principle that is applied in *triage* practices, where the severity of the reported disease justifies the priority in healthcare delivery.

In a situation where the scarcity of resources not only affects the priority but also the possibility to cure someone, the criterion in the allocation of the scarce resource is identified by the SIAARTI in the chances of survival, depending on the age of the person and the presence of previous pathologies (or, in other words, comorbidities).

On the other hand, the Italian National Bioethical Committee evaluates the «clinical criterion» to be the most appropriate reference point for the allocation of the same resources: any other selection criterion, such as for example age, sex, condition and social role, ethnicity, disability and so on, is deemed ethically unacceptable by the Committee.[233]

Now, it goes without saying that: first, those "guidelines" are not mandatory (as they are not laid down by the lawmaker nor administrative bodies); second, they cannot — as a general rule — prevent any physician or medical institutions from civil or criminal liability.[234]

2. What values are the allocation criteria based on?

The SIAARTI guidelines appears to adopt a utilitarian approach, which typically favours the healthy and young. While this logic may appear to be agreeable to a certain extent, it should be emphasized, however, that it is precisely the elderly — who tend to be excluded from medical care in a context of insufficient resources — who have contributed most to the creation of the health care system that now places them at a disadvantage in the framework of the distribution of social burdens and benefits; a different criterion instead — that inspires the document of the Italian National

232 See *Italian Society of Anesthesia, Analgesia, Resuscitation and Intensive Therapy* (SIAARTI), 'Clinical ethics recommendations for the allocation of intensive care treatments, in exceptional, resource-limited circumstances' (*SIIARTI*, 16 March 2020).

233 See Italian National Bioethical Committee, 'Covid 19: Clinical Decision-Making In Conditions Of Resource Shortage And The "Pandemic Emergency Triage" Criterion' (*Italian Committee for Bioethics*, 8 April 2020) <https://bioetica.governo.it/en/opinions/opinions-responses/covid-19-clinical-decision-making-in-conditions-of-resource-shortage-and-the-pandemic-emergency-triage-criterion/>.

234 For detailed information, see R Pucella 28ff.

Bioethical Committee — admits that the scarce resource was assigned to the most serious patient or the one who first entered the waiting list, thereby offering the greatest guarantee of safeguarding, according to justice, people's dignity.

This is the "clinical" criterion, which identifies the current urgency and necessity as the only criterion that must govern the physician's conduct in treating the patient in need of care; any other canon of selection, such as age, sex, social status and role, ethnicity, disability and so on must be considered, according to the Italian National Bioethical Committee, ethically unacceptable.

It should be noted that, even irrespective of the pandemic, in Italy the criterion of "first come, first served" is out of date whenever the circumstances of the case require it: the criterion (so-called triage) operating in Italy assigns a priority of care regardless of the time of the patients acceptance into the healthcare facility, expressed with colors that represent urgency in healthcare provision. This is an utilitarian approach inasmuch as it assigns the priority of care to the one who (receiving it immediately) is more likely to overcome the pathological condition.

The difference from the Covid infection is that in the triage system all the patients, even with different timing, will receive the needed treatment, meanwhile the Covid experience has shown that the lack of timely treatment to some patients has, unfortunately, resulted in death.

The most striking aspect is the idea that a fundamental right such as health can be sacrificed, despite the fact that the guidelines make it clear that this represents the *extrema ratio* and that, in any case, the physician's professional autonomy always allows him or her to consider each individual case in its precise specificity, without being bound by rigidly prefixed parameters.

However it is necessary to ask whether it is really a "sacrifice". Sacrificing health is an active conduct, implying a voluntary act or a decision; but if in a healthcare facility for every ICU bed there are 10 applicants and the bed can be assigned to only one of those ten, can we really say that the health of the other nine has been sacrificed?

The real issue then is not that of "sacrifice", but that of the inevitability of the situation and the impossibility of resolving it any other way.

3. In what type(s) of document(s) are the allocation criteria set? Is it in binding or non-binding guidelines, in the law, or in another type of document?

As mentioned in question 1, the State has not published legally binding allocation criteria in respect of the COVID-19 pandemic. The SIAARTI guidelines represent the most important document because they adopt the criterion that poses the greatest complexity from an ethical and moral point of view; the document of the Italian National Bioethics Committee, on the other hand, applies the traditional criterion according to which whoever needs a medical treatment at a given moment must be treated without further evaluation. Both these "guidelines" are not mandatory (as they are not laid down by the lawmaker nor administrative bodies); second, they cannot — as a general rule — prevent any physician or medical institutions from civil or criminal liability.[235]

4. Are providers of health care obliged by the law to provide (urgent) care to all patients? If the answer is yes, are there any legally recognised exceptions from this duty?

There is no doubt that health care providers must ensure the necessary care for each patient. There are several principles that regulate this: the most important is expressed in Article 32 of the Italian Constitution, which protects health as a fundamental right of the individual and interest of the community.

But then the protection of the patient is ensured at the level of the contractual relationship, that is the contract of hospitalization, which binds the patient to the public or private health care facility that treats him or her.

The patient is, therefore, entitled to receive treatment appropriate to their condition and needs. The most problematic aspect concerns the hypothesis in which the health service cannot be assured (or cannot be fully assured) for reasons that are not attributable to the health care staff member or the healthcare facility; here the problem is to understand whether the combination of circumstances that has put health care systems in every part of the world under stress constitutes a circumstance marked by unpredictability and in the face of which it was not possible to take countermeasures such as to avoid the very serious complex of harmful consequences that world experience has delivered to us.

The prevailing opinion is that the disruptive force of the Covid-19 pandemic, together with the lack — for a long time — of an adequate medical response, constitutes that condition of impossibility of performance which, under art. 1218 ICC (or by reason of the state of necessity, as others have held), makes the physician's failure to perform, nor his or her conduct criminally punishable.

This conclusion could be reached even though some scholars argued that a pandemic was not a totally unforeseeable event; and it is noted that every patient could be cured, perhaps by being admitted to another healthcare facility (even in a foreign country) where the one of first admission is congested.

Obviously, a different situation is the one that may concern cases of non-compliance of medical provision: think of the hypothesis of non-Covid patients admitted to the same hospital environments where Covid patients were; or the case of doctors who, having tested positive for the virus, or having come into contact with positive family members, nevertheless went to the workplace; or the case of failure to adequately sterilize environments; in these cases, liability is justified by applying the ordinary criterion of fault.

---

235 For detailed information, see R Pucella 28ff.

In conclusion: the "tragic choices" that Italian doctors have been forced to make are not "exceptions" to the duty to treat patients.

The "exception", in fact, presupposes a faculty of choice between conduct — that which is due — and its deviance (that which was held); in the case at hand, however, the doctors were precluded from this possibility of choice and the only possibility granted to them was to choose how to "measure out" the scarce resource made available to them.

Here a principle highlighted by the Italian Constitutional Court intervenes: *"[...] it is not, as a rule, the lawmaker that can directly and specifically establish what therapeutic practices are permitted, with what limits and under what conditions. Since the practice of medical art is based on scientific and experimental acquisitions, which are constantly evolving, the basic rule in this matter and constituted by the autonomy and responsibility of the physician who, always with the consent of the patient, makes professional choices based on the state of knowledge available."*

It seems, therefore, clear that the criteria by which to allocate the very scarce intensive care resources in a time of medical emergency can only be established at the medical-scientific level, while respecting constitutional principles in all cases.

5. On what legal basis is it possible to apply the allocation criteria in practice?

As mentioned in the previous answer, there is no "legal basis" for the application of allocation criteria, because they are not subject to legislative norms. Instead, they are placed to the physician's autonomy and responsibility and to ethical and deontological criteria, such as the already cited "recommendations", which do not have an actual legal basis.

6. What level of legal certainty do the health professionals and the health care providers have when applying the allocation criteria?

The position of the physician is not qualified by the respect of the allocation criteria, because the already cited documents (SIAARTI and the Italian National Bioethical Committee recommendations) are not guidelines. These latter can define the doctor's conduct as diligent, in the sense that the doctor who respects them correctly performs his duty of care. The allocation criteria of scarce resources, instead, do not define the quality of the physician performance, from the technical-executive point of view, but express the compliance of his conduct with ethical criteria.

According to the overriding approach, the abidance by the recommendations do not release the physician from liability, but the general principle concerning contractual obligations (art. 1218 ICC) according to which the debtor (in this case the physician) does not bear the negative consequences of their conduct when the improper performance was due to an impossibility of performance resulting from a cause not attributable to the physician themself.

Moreover, it is a common opinion that, faced with the shortage of medical aids (ventilators, beds in ICU, etc.) or the lack of health personnel able to cope with the exceptional need for health care in the difficult months of 2020 and 2021, the physician's fault cannot be proposed.

A different issue on which conclusions appear less certain is that concerning the possible organizational negligence of public and private health structures.

7. What are the civil and criminal liability implications of allocation of scarce health care resources? Have there already been any related legal suits and/or criminal proceedings?

The patient (or his relatives if he has died) who has suffered damage for not having received timely treatment has three means of protection: civil liability, criminal liability and liability deriving from codes of ethics and guidelines.

In Italian court cases criminal liability is invoked with less frequency for several reasons: usually the injured party is more interested in receiving compensation for the damage suffered than to see the physician sentenced to a penalty. The actual reason why in the Italian system criminal liability is less applied is that the liability assessment is based on a stricter causal criterion, the one of "beyond any reasonable doubt". This explains why in Italy the vast majority of criminal proceedings against physicians end with filing or absolution; not to mention that criminal proceedings last longer than civil trials, that are already very long.

The civil trial, instead, is based on a looser causal criterion, the one of "more probable than not"; in addition to this, in Italy the liquidation criteria of the damage to health and moral suffering (also of relatives) are very advantageous compared to other European countries and encourage the injured party to start a court proceeding. Moreover, until 2017, the civil action for damages was convenient also in terms of the burden of proof on the plaintiff, who had only to prove the damage suffered and not the fault of the physician, both with regard to the health care facility and to the individual health care professional; in many cases the causal link was (and still is) ascertained through jurisprudential presumptions (for example, if the health condition of the patient has worsened after therapy, this suggests that the doctor was wrong). Both the physician and the health care facility's liability had contractual nature; the law n. 24 of 2017 made the burden of proof of the physician's liability harder, because the rules of non-contractual liability are now applied, which prescribe to give concrete proof of the fault and the causal link. It is still too early to understand if this change — aimed at avoiding compensatory over-exposure phenomena of individual physicians, with all that follows (defensive medicine, insurance overexposure, instrumentalization of informed consent, etc.) — will have achieved its result.

As for the responsibility deriving from codes of ethics, it can be ascertained independently by the Medical Association, possibly also on the recommendation of the injured patient; the procedure, of internal nature, can end with a punitive measure (censorship, recall, suspension from salary for a certain period of time); however, it does not have a significant deflating force and is most regarded when the physician's conduct is reprehensible (for neglect, carelessness, inattention) than harmful.

Covid-19's impressive effect on the life and health of people is certainly a greedy opportunity in terms of professional liability, so much so that in April 2020, the National Forensic Council invited the Bar Associations to monitor the "unworthy behavior" of certain lawyers, who were willing to encourage judicial actions against doctors who, at the same time and with dedication, saved the lives of thousands of people.

The law no 76/2021, entered into force on the 1st of June 2021, has introduced the so called "Criminal shield" for physicians and health professionals, during the Covid emergency (Art. 3–3bis); the rule states that during the state of epidemiological emergency, the facts referred to in Articles 589 and 590 of the IPC (manslaughter and negligent personal injury) are punishable only in cases of gross negligence if consumed in the exercise of a health profession and caused by an emergency situation. The norm specifies that the gross negligence must be assessed taking into account the limited scientific knowledge, the shortage of the human and material resources actually available in relation to the number of cases to be treated, and the lesser degree of experience and technical knowledge possessed by the non-specialist personnel employed to cope with the emergency.

This rule, specifically adopted to solve the serious liability problems resulting from the Covid-19 epidemic, is in addition to the general provision in the new art. 590 sexies of the IPC, according to which the criminal liability of the physician is excluded when the damage has been caused by inexperience, but the recommendations provided for by the Guidelines or, in the absence of these, by good clinical practice provisions were abided.

However, this provision has not prevented the initiation of legal proceedings aimed at ascertaining the medical liability for the death or the severity of the injuries suffered by patients suffering from Covid.

In relation to this, it must be considered that the most widely used procedural tool was the so called Preventive Technical Assessment, a technical consultancy entrusted by the judge before judgment and aimed at ascertaining whether there were shortcomings from a technical-executive point of view.

Moreover, those court proceedings were mainly aimed at ascertaining not the liability of the individual health worker, but the lack of management and organization of the health care facility and in general of the entire "Health System".

This is the reason why, up to now, these attempts have been rejected by the judges who have observed that the "system" gaps is something unrelated to what can be ascertained with a technical consultancy.

The Court of Rome is currently considering a case brought by about 200 families, mostly from Lombardy, aimed at establishing the inadequacy of the Italian health policy in dealing with the Covid emergency.

B. Case studies

Case 1

As a result of a rapid worsening of the epidemiological situation, the material and personal capacities have been drastically overloaded in all the hospitals in the country. Within just a few minutes, ambulances transport ten patients to one particular hospital's emergency unit. The patients all need admission to the hospital, preferably to the intensive care unit (ICU). However, only two beds are available there. Other hospitals are overwhelmed too, so it is not possible to transport patients to any of them. All of the ten newly coming patients suffer from COVID-19; they have breathing difficulties, fast-rising fever, and decreasing oxygen saturation. Nevertheless, they differ in age, comorbidities, clinical fragility, and other factors.

Theoretically, the eight patients who cannot be admitted to beds can be placed in improvised settings in the hospital corridors, laying on gurneys or mattresses on the floor. Nevertheless, it will be impossible to provide them with the care they need.

Evaluation of the case

- What criteria can be used to choose the patients who will be admitted to the beds (i.e. what are the possible allocation criteria)?
  As mentioned above, the applicable criteria seem to be two: the "utilitarian" criterion, according to which the treatment must be assured to those patients that seem to guarantee the most favourable outcome (because younger or without comorbidity); and the "clinical" criterion, according to which the treatment must be assured to those who, at that moment, need it most (the older person, who could bear less than others the delay in the treatment).
  It could be more sensitive the case where the patients were not all admitted at the same time; here the utilitarian criterion (and this is an example taken from the SIAARTI Recommendations) could induce not to occupy one of the vacant places, even if there were patients needing it, when it is reasonable to assume that a person with a better outcome of healing will soon be admitted.
  We do not know that this last criterion has ever found real application.
- What legal consequences can this decision have for the health professionals and the hospital? How strong is their legal certainty that there will be no adverse legal consequences if they follow the above-mentioned criteria?
  Unfortunately the choice to allocate a scarce resource does not ensure release from liability of the physician or of the health care facility, because the unfortunate event (death, injury) always urges the search for a guilty party, both from the criminal and the civil point of view, and not because there are no suitable

rules to protect medical operators from liability, as it will be said in subsequent answers. This is the reason why criminal trials take place, even if from statistics emerges that only a small percentage of them lead to a conviction.
In Covid cases, an additional issue is the organizational liability, which mostly involves the health care facilities, but fosters the idea that also the physician did not what was necessary to save the patient.

– What legal defences could the health professionals and the hospital use against a civil lawsuit and/or criminal prosecution for the allocation decision?

Art. 5 of the law no 24/2017 on medical liability provides for "good clinical practices and guidelines" and establishes that: *"The healthcare workers, in the execution of health services [...], must abide by the guidelines issued by private and public bodies as well as by the scientific societies [...]. In the absence of the above recommendations, the healthcare workers must adhere to good clinical care practices."*

Now, should the SIAARTI recommendations be equated to the guidelines laid down in Art. 5 of the Statute above mentioned, on one hand the health professionals' criminal liability should be excluded and, on the other, the civil consequences should be determined in relation to their abidance to these guidelines.

However, in our opinion, the two sets of rules cannot be placed on the same level because they have a different ratio and functions: law no 24/2017 guidelines define the adequacy of a possible and due performance, meanwhile the SIAARTI recommendations concern the decision imposed by the scarcity of resources, where the performance of the healthcare professional becomes impossible because he or she cannot deliver the service to all those who need it.

Therefore, negligence is not the adequate standard to evaluate the healthcare professionals conduct and guidelines are not the right instrument to justify sacrifices of the right to health.

Some scholars have suggested the application of art. 2236 ICC according to which whenever the performance to be carried out involves "the solution of technical problems of special difficulty", the debtor is not liable for damages, except in cases of intent or gross negligence; or art. 2045 ICC on the state of necessity. However, in our view, also these qualifications are not completely satisfactory, because the performance of the healthcare professional is not just limited but rather impossible.

Others have claimed that, rather than the healthcare professionals, the healthcare facilities should be liable for negligence, identifying the misconducts in management deficiencies, such as the insufficient sanitization of hospital environments, inappropriate isolation protocols or ineffectiveness of treatments. However, the burden of proof will be extremely hard to satisfy in the event of a lawsuit.

Think about the single patient trying to prove that he or she was infected during the hospitalization; or for the non-Covid patient to prove that the cancellation of their scheduled surgery for the benefit of patients in life-threatening conditions, was determined by a negligent misconduct. Nor claims for the ineffectiveness of treatments appear to be actionable because the virus is almost totally unknown (at least it was at that time), therefore it was inevitable that off-label treatments would have been delivered.

Hence, it is to our belief that the most appropriate interpretation seems to be the impossibility of performance for a cause not imputable to the debtor, according to art. 1218 ICC.

In relation to healthcare facilities, the liability could be almost objective (so in terms of strict liability), when the lack of resources could have been foreseeable and therefore avoidable. In any case, it will be difficult to charge healthcare facilities with an order to compensate damages, because even though at the beginning of this year the gravity of the situation was clear, it would still have been impossible for them to properly prepare to fight it.

The impossibility of performance due to the scarcity of resources obliged healthcare professionals to take non-avoidable tragic choices. Of course: the recommendations mentioned previously cannot create priorities among rights that cannot be reduced (such as the right to health); they rather define guidelines to help healthcare professionals in taking such choices, identifying those who can have access to the treatments and those who cannot.

Additional questions

- Would it be legally permissible to lower the standard of care provided to all patients in order to provide at least basic decent care to the newly admitted patients who are placed in the hospital corridors? To what extent?

  Assuming that a better rationalization of a scarce resource (for example a drug) can allow to treat, albeit with less effectiveness, more patients in need simultaneously, it would seem possible.

  But this solution can only apply if it does not end up harming the collective health. However, it would have been very hardly applicable to the damages caused by this pandemic that did not allow "mild" treatments or reduced therapies, but needed specific aids (respirators, oxygen masks, helmets, antivirals) that could not be "rationed".

Case 2

Two patients in an ICU are suffering from COVID-19. After admission to the hospital, they were provided with the high-flow nasal oxygen therapy (HFNO). During one night, the condition of both patients starts to worsen rapidly. At dawn, it is clear that neither of them will survive without artificial ventilation. However, there is just one ventilator available.

Evaluation of the case

- What criteria can be used to choose which of the two patients will be provided with artificial ventilation and which one will be left without it, possibly to die?

The same considerations that have already been expressed apply here: in the face of the impossibility of allowing both patients to fight for survival, physicians will have to choose to whom to offer the scarce resource; on equal terms the "utilitarian" one would be the most considered criterion; the resource will be assigned to the one of the two that will present better prospects of survival.

- What legal consequences can this decision have for the health professionals and the hospital? How strong is their legal certainty that there will be no adverse legal consequences if they follow the above-mentioned criteria?
  See above the previous answer.
- What legal defences could the health professionals and the hospital use against a civil lawsuit and/or criminal prosecution for the allocation decision?
  See above the previous answer.
- If the allocation criteria specified in your answer to the first question to this case consisted of the patients' clinical features (such as their age, clinical fragility, etc.), please identify what criteria could be used for the allocation decision if all the relevant clinical features of both patients were practically the same?
  Physicians cannot "draw straws" to decide who, between the two patients that are in the same condition (age, severity, comorbidity), must prevail (and having the possibility of healing). In this case, physicians should identify a prevalence criterion anyway that suggests that one of the two has better chances to succeed; nothing excludes that other factors, quite secondary, but ethically, morally or socially significant, can have a role in this difficult choice (for example, the scarce resource could be given to the mother of a small child rather than the childless one; or to the doctor who became ill in an attempt to save many lives rather than the "anonymous" person; or, and unfortunately, to the famous person or with an important social role rather than the unemployed or the homeless).

Case 3

There is a single extracorporeal membrane oxygenation (ECMO) device in the hospital. It is currently being used for an 84-year-old patient suffering from COVID-19, with diabetes as an underlying disease, clinical frailty score (CFS) 6–7 (moderate to severe frailty). It is possible that the patient will survive and will be discharged from the hospital if the ECMO treatment is continued. However, a younger COVID-19 patient is admitted to the hospital. This new patient is 51 years old, otherwise healthy, but her health condition has been rapidly deteriorating. Soon she will most likely need ECMO to survive.

<u>Evaluation of the case</u>

- Can it be legally permissible for the hospital staff to discontinue the ECMO treatment of the older patient and provide palliative care to her in order to save the younger and healthier patient's life? Please keep in mind that the older patient could survive if the treatment continued, but her chances may be lower than those of the younger patient.

In Italy it is not allowed to interrupt a life-saving treatment; much debate has arosed in relation to cases in which this happened at the direct request of the interested party, based on specific reasons that the legal system deems necessary. Therefore, in Italy it would not be allowed to stop the life-saving treatment to assign it to another individual; it would be regarded as crime of murder: a different case is when the treatment can be suspended without jeopardizing the life or physical integrity of the person who is deprived of it (such as the respirator that is removed to the patient now in recovery and no longer in need of it).

Additional question

- Suppose there are two different scenarios: a) the older patient was admitted to the hospital and provided with the ECMO treatment, and only later, after several days, the younger patient was admitted, and b) the younger patient was admitted before the older patient, however, the older patient required ECMO treatment soon after admission while the younger patient's health condition deteriorated only after a longer time when the ECMO was already occupied (i. e. at the time when the younger patient was admitted to the hospital, she did not yet need it). Would there be any difference in the allocation decision making between these two scenarios?

  The crucial issue does not concern the difference in time of hospitalization, but the fact that interrupting a life-saving treatment, whatever the reason for which it is done, causes the death of the patient which is not allowed by the Italian law. Those who are assisted by a life support cannot be deprived of it, except at their request and under certain conditions required by the law; this is in order to avoid not only the murder of patients on the basis of uncontrollable medical or bioethical reasons, but also euthanasia practices, which are not allowed in Italy. In conclusion, the patient assisted by a life-saving mechanism cannot be deprived of it, except on the assumption that he no longer needs it.

The list of abbreviations

ICU	Intensive Care Unit
SIAARTI	Italian Society of Anesthesia, Analgesia, Resuscitation and Intensive Therapy

Bibliography

• Legislation

Civil Code (*Codice civile*), Gazzetta Ufficiale n. 79 del 4. 4. 1942; cited as: ICC

Constitution of the Italian Republic (*Costituzione Della Repubblica Italiana*), Gazzetta Ufficiale n. 298 del 27. 12. 1947; cited as: Italian Constitution

Law no 833/1978, Establishment of the Italian National Health Service (*Legge 23 dicembre 1978, n. 833, Istituzione del servizio sanitario nazionale*), Gazzetta Ufficiale n. 360 del 28. 12. 1978

Law no 24/2017, Provisions on the safety of care and the assisted person, as well as on the professional responsibility of health professions (*Legge 8 marzo 2017, n. 24, Disposizioni in materia di sicurezza delle cure e della persona assistita, nonché in materia di responsabilità professionale degli esercenti le professioni sanitarie*), Gazzetta Ufficiale n. 63 del 17. 3. 2017; cited as: law no 24/2017

Law no 76/2021, Urgent measures for the containment of the COVID-19 epidemic, in the field of anti-SARS-CoV-2 vaccinations, justice and public competitions (*Legge 28 maggio 2021, n. 76, Recante misure urgenti per il contenimento dell'epidemia da COVID-19, in materia di vaccinazioni anti SARS-CoV-2, di giustizia e di concorsi pubblici*), Gazzetta Ufficiale n. 128 del 31. 5. 2021; cited as: law no 76/2021

Penal Code (*Codice penale*), Gazzetta Ufficiale n. 251 del 26. 10. 1930; cited as: IPC

• Case law

Trib. Rovigo, ord. 1° marzo 2021

Trib. Torino, ord. 6 maggio 2021

Trib. Foggia, decr. 4 ottobre 2021

Trib. Foggia, ord. 21 dicembre 2021

Trib. Cuneo, ord. 18 gennaio 2022

Trib. Bologna, ord. 26 aprile 2022

• Books

Calabresi G, *Tragic Choices* (W. W. Norton & Company 1978)

Maggiolo M, 'Coronavirus and Medical Liability' in E Hondius, M Santos Silva, A Nicolussi, P Salvador Coderch, C Wendehorst and F Zoll (eds), *Coronavirus and the Law in Europe* (Intersentia 2021)

Scarso A P, Foglia M, 'Medical Liability in Italy' in B A Koch (ed), *Medical Liability in Europe. A Comparison of Selected Jurisdictions* (De Gruyter 2011)

• Articles

Casonato C, 'Health At The Time Of Covid-19: Tyrannical, Denied, Unequal Health' (2020) 3 BioLaw Journal 315

Ponzanelli G, 'I danni subiti da CoViD-19 tra regole di responsabilità civile e piani no fault' 2020 (3) Nuova giur. civ. comm., Special Issue 137

Pucella R, 'Scelte tragiche e dilemmi giuridici a tempi della pandemia' 2020 (3) Nuova giur. civ. comm. 24

Scognamiglio C, 'La pandemia CoViD-19, i danni alla salute ed i limiti della responsabilità civile' (2020) 3 Nuova giur. civ. comm., Special Issue 140

Smorto G, 'The Right to Health and Resource Allocation. Who Gets What and Why in the COVID-19 Pandemic' (2020) 20 Global Jurist 59 <https://doi.org/10.1515/gj-2020-0040>

• Other secondary sources

Italian National Bioethical Committee, 'Covid 19: Clinical Decision-Making In Conditions Of Resource Shortage And The "Pandemic Emergency Triage" Criterion' (*Italian Committee for Bioethics*, 8 April 2020) <https://bioetica.governo.it/en/opinions/opinions-responses/covid-19-clinical-decision-making-in-conditions-of-resource-shortage-and-the-pandemic-emergency-triage-criterion/>

Italian Society of Anesthesia, Analgesia, Resuscitation and Intensive Therapy (SIAARTI), 'Clinical ethics recommendations for the allocation of intensive care treatments, in exceptional, resource-limited circumstances' (*SIAARTI*, 16 March 2020)

PORTUGAL

Carla Barbosa[236]
University of Coimbra

Introduction

Portugal, in the context of the pandemic resulting from the emergence and spread of the SARS-CoV-2 virus, went from a relatively quiet situation — in the spring of 2020 — to the real chaos — in the winter of 2020–21.

When the first European cases arose, we were under the belief that Portugal, located at the southwesternmost point in Europe and bordering only with Spain, stood at an advantageous point when compared with other European countries. Its remaining territory was of no concern as it bordered the Atlantic Ocean. It is perhaps for this very reason that the first infected individuals appeared later than in many other European countries like Italy, Spain, France, etc. As the numbers of infected people increased and frightening news arrived from Italy, with regard to Europe, civil society in Portugal immediately reacted by demanding its governmental and health leaderships to take immediate action. Perhaps for this reason — namely strong pressure from civil society — Portugal adopted protective measures early when compared with the rest of European countries. Many of the measures were implemented before there was news of deaths by Covid 19 in Portugal and when the number of known infected people was still quite low. We knew that we could not escape this pandemic, so the objective was to expand the number of infected people in time so that we could avoid very high peaks that would lead to the rupturing of our health system, as happened, for example, in Italy and Spain.

Thus, the first wave of the pandemic did not pose any major problems regarding the scarce resources available in the health sector — this despite the fact that the Portuguese Government, on that date, acquired several medical supplies such as personal protective equipment and ventilators to face an eventual scarcity that would arise.

In Portugal, in the first wave of the pandemic, the health system was not really *put to the test*, nor did it suffer from pressure situations as in other European countries.

---

[236] Researcher at the Biomedical Law Center of the Faculty of Law of the University of Coimbra — cbarbosa@fd.uc.pt.
Special thanks to Nadav Hillebrand for the English revision.

The public health policies adopted reduced the transmission chains with epidemic control in the first wave. At the same time, the decision to suspend or decrease the programmed activity, focusing on the response to the epidemic, helped in the health care response.

We thus witnessed, in this first phase, a decrease in the access of non-Covid patients,[237] but also the number of patients with Covid-19 was below expectations, which allowed an adequate response.

Meanwhile, the summer and early autumn months passed, with a collective demobilization on the part of society and a slowing down of government measures, which led to the fact that, despite there having been a decrease in cases, these never dropped in sufficient numbers, during the summer period.

In November, Portugal went through a second wave, harder than the first, felt in the spring. New levels of numbers of daily infections and deaths were reached. However, although here we have already felt our National Health Service accusing the pressure of a number of high cases daily, there was an answer that does not, yet, jeopardize health resources.

The real health crisis in Portugal arose in December 2020, with a sharp increase in January/February 2021. On January 15 we became the country with the highest number of daily infections per million inhabitants and the country with the second largest number deaths, also per million inhabitants.

And it was at this moment, that society, health establishments, health professionals were confronted with the scarcity of resources in health and with the need to make options that compel us to mobilize and analyze ethical-legal principles.

A. Questionnaire

1. Health resource allocation criteria

Questions: What were the criteria for the allocation of scarce health resources in your country and in what type of document were they set?; What values are the allocation criteria based on?; In what type(s) of document(s) are the allocation criteria set? Is it in binding or non-binding guidelines, in the law, or in another type of document?

In Portugal there is a mixed health system, with different payment models, that is, a model based on the National Health Service (Serviço Nacional de Saúde — SNS) financed through the State budget; a model based on social insurance financed by professionally-funded health funds; a model based on individually-funded voluntary insurance and a model based on direct payments.[238]

[237] In May 2020, there was an indication that 1.4 million consultations would have been missed and 51,000 surgeries would have been postponed.

[238] About the Portuguese health system please see Jorge Simões and António Correia de Campos, *O Percurso da Saúde: Portugal na Europa* (Almedina 2011).

The health system includes public, private and social providers. The SNS is particularly relevant because it is universal in nature. As such, improving the efficiency and effectiveness of the SNS has underpinned a wide range of measures and reforms that have been implemented in recent years.

After 33 years, the SNS has become a collective asset of Portuguese society, contributing to the improvement of health indicators (reducing child mortality, increasing life expectancy, etc.) and placing Portugal in the first positions of the international ranking in terms of the quality of care provided in our country. Especially since the end of the 90s, the reform process has contributed to achieving these goals through technological advances, the strengthening of primary health care and the introduction of integrated continuous care. However, in a context of crisis, critical areas and priorities remain to be addressed: a) geographic and social inequalities in access to health care; b) co-presence, alongside the SNS, of other public and private care subsystems that can accentuate health inequalities; c) scarce mechanisms for citizen participation.

The SNS, financed through taxes, provides universal coverage and a wide range of benefits. Costs are shared, with non-reimbursed expenses generally higher than the European average, although more than half the population is exempt.

However, resources continue to be scarce and inadequate to the needs of the population, demanding on part of the population, in addition to tax charges, a strong share in health expenses.

This scarcity was accentuated by the pandemic. Portugal does not normally have legislation that provides for the criteria for allocating resources in the event of a shortage of resources.

For several years now (almost a decade) the Portuguese Observatory of Health Systems (OPSS) refers the existence of "multiple indications of implicit rationing" (not providing adequate care without this being the result of explicit guidance by the National Health Service, resulting from ongoing budgetary restraint).[239]

"The scarcity of resources that characterizes health systems requires that priority decisions be made that translate into choices between alternative programs/ services and/or between patients or groups of patients. In the absence of a price mechanism, the establishment of priorities enshrines a way of allocating scarce resources in the health care market, translated into rationing. Traditionally, in public health systems, resource allocation decisions have been made at a discretionary level, especially by doctors. However, the growing limitation of resources, coupled with an increase in patient expectations, calls for more explicit forms of rationing that are socially legitimized. Internationally, the development of explicit prioritization processes has proven to be difficult and controversial."[240]

[239] 2012 Spring Report of the Portuguese Observatory on Health Systems: Observatório português dos sistemas de Saúde, 'Relatório de primavera 2012' (*OPSS*) <http://opssaude.pt/relatorios/relatorio-de-primavera-2012/>

[240] Micaela Moreira Pinho, 'Racionamento dos cuidados de saúde: problemática inerente' (2008) 3 Cadernos de Saúde Pública 690–695.

In the context of the pandemic, the Government decided, however, to issue Guidelines, through the Ministry of Health, to suspend scheduled and non-priority activity. The last of these diplomas, Order No. 574-A/2021, determines that hospital establishments of the National Health Service (SNS) pass their Contingency Plans to the maximum level and suspend the programmed non-urgent assistance activity that can revert in reinforcing care for critically ill patients.

Justifying this measure with the emergence and spread of the SARS-CoV-2 virus in Portugal, which determined the need to ensure the prevention, containment, mitigation and treatment of COVID-19, through the adoption of a set of exceptional and temporary measures response to the pandemic. In January 2021, the date of publication of the referred diploma, Portugal recorded a notification rate accumulated to 14 days above 900 cases per 100,000 inhabitants and an average number of secondary cases resulting from an infected case, measured as a function of time, R (t), above 1.

These factors put the health system, and in particular the National Health Service (SNS), under high pressure, especially in hospitalization (hospitalization in infirmary and hospitalization in intensive care, both with occupancy rates, in January, which were situated between 85% and 96%). In January/February 2021, the highest number of COVID-19 hospitalizations in SNS institutions was reached, since the beginning of the pandemic.

Considering the epidemiological situation, the occupation of infirmary and intensive care beds and the need to guarantee a response to a demand that it was expected to increase, and with the aim of ensuring the mobilization of all qualified health professionals to a response aligned with the demand for care observed was then published guidelines for resource allocation.

According to these guidelines, hospital establishments of the National Health Service (SNS) should ensure the promptness of the response to COVID-19 and the best possible balance of the various care responses, especially at the level of Intensive Care. To implement this prioritization, health establishments: *"a) passed their Contingency Plans to the maximum level and proceeded to their review and expansion, in order to maximize the response of the hospital capacity to the local, regional and national epidemiological situation, in articulation with the National Response Monitoring Committee in Medicine Intensive Care (CARNMI) and the respective Regional Health Administrations; b) suspended the programmed non-urgent care activity that can revert to reinforcing care for critically ill patients, provided that such suspension, due to its nature or clinical priority, does not imply risk of life for users, severe limitation of its prognosis and or limitation access to periodic or surveillance treatments, namely in the context of monitoring pregnancy, exacerbation of chronic or other diseases; c) proceeded with the deferral of scheduled surgical activity of normal priority; d) promoted the allocation of human resources for Intensive Care Medicine, in order to maximize the response capacity in this area, in accordance with the suspension and deferral of care activity carried out, following a proposal by CARNMI and always in conjunction with the clinical management of each unity."*

Considering the foregoing in terms of resource allocation, the Portuguese Government has given total priority to combating the pandemic, relegating to the background all other pathologies that need hospital monitoring. This fact has resulted in a high increase in mortality in Portugal due to other pathologies than those resulting from infection by the SARS-CoV-2 virus. In the balance made by the National Statistics Institute, between March 2 and December 27 (2020) 99,356 deaths were recorded in Portugal, which represents an additional 12,852 when compared to the average of the last five years. Of these, only 52 % — that is 6,677 — died from covid-19.

It is obvious that the monitoring of the remaining pathologies did not cease to exist. The Portuguese Ministry of Health even had to clarify that the dispatch sent to hospitals does not order urgent or very priority surgery to be suspended and does not apply to hospitals such as the Portuguese Institute of Oncology (IPO) (exclusively dedicated to the treatment of cancer patients). The Ministry of Health (MS) ensures that *"the deferral of surgical activity will always be made through clinical evaluation and ensuring that the user's prognosis is not limited"*. It also notes that the priority oncological surgery must take place within 45 days after the surgical indication, noting that the order is valid until January 31. According to the Health Ministry, *"the Order does not apply to hospitals such as IPOs, which, according to the network, are available to receive patients who require priority surgery during the period of application of the order"*. However, resources are not elastic and the real scarcity, in Portugal, in January/ February 2021, was felt mainly in the level of human resources. The institutions have tried to increase the hospitalization capacity, but this "increase in beds" was not accompanied by an increase in the hiring of health professionals since there was also no availability of these *in the market*.

Regarding the allocation of resources, we cannot fail to mention here, given its importance the CNEDM58 guidance[241] of the Portuguese Medical Association, which makes ethical considerations and recommendations related to the situations caused by the pandemic.

This guidance, despite having been enacted in April 2020, was only made public in October of that same year (since in April the situation improved and the question of scarcity of resources was never raised). In the aforementioned guideline, the Portuguese Medical Association refers that in the face of a scenario of insufficient resources for all those who need it, it may be necessary to follow the principles to be applied in "catastrophe medicine" scenarios. And, considering this fact, the National Council of Medical Ethics and Deontology of the Portuguese Medical Association prepared the document with some ethical guidelines. After listing several

241 O Conselho Nacional de Ética e Deontologia Médicas da Ordem dos Médicos, 'CNEDM58. Considerações E Recomendações Éticas Relacionadas Com As Situações Provocadas Pela Pandemia Covid-19' (*Ordem dos Médicos*) <https://ordemdosmedicos.pt/wp-content/uploads/2020/11/Parecer-CNEDM58vf-páginas-1-4.pdf>.

principles to be respected by doctors, the opinion states that in case of scarcity in access to resources, especially in intensive care, the options to be made should be guided by criteria of proportionality and distributive justice.

The criteria apply to all patients who require intensive care, not only to patients infected with the new coronavirus. The Opinion states that the following cannot be priority criteria: the order of arrival of the application for admission or arrival at the hospital emergency services.

A case by case assessment will have to be carried out. Which means that, although many of the patients are elderly, this fact, in itself, can never be used as a criterion. The presence of co-morbidities and the functional status of multiple organs must be carefully assessed, along with age. In addition, patients where the benefit is minimal and unlikely due to advanced or terminal illness should not, as in non-emergency situations, undergo intensive therapy. All decisions to limit access must be duly substantiated and result from a consensus of the health team. This decision must be communicated (to himself — whenever possible — and to family members) and recorded in the process.

2. Resource allocation and universal care obligation

Questions: Are providers of health care obliged to provide (urgent) care to all patients? Are there any legally recognised exceptions from this duty?

Considering the above, namely the guidelines of the Ministry of Health and the Portuguese Medical Association, we verify that care should be provided to all urgent patients (*Covid and non Covid*). However, in reality, such care may not be adequate and sufficient because it depends on existing resources.

There will be some urgent cases that will therefore not have the necessary follow-up. Therefore, it is almost possible to state that only emerging cases will-expectedly, have immediate and adequate monitoring (and this if given there are resources that can be allocated).

In Report No. 5/2020 — OAC, of October 2020,[242] therefore, even before the serious third wave, the Court of Auditors (Tribunal de Contas) warns that one of the biggest current challenges of the National Health Service (SNS) is to balance the response to a second phase of higher incidence of the Covid-19 pandemic with guaranteed assistance to non-Covid patients without the sharp increase in waiting times.

This report, carried out between March and July 2020, on the management of the pandemic by the Ministry of Health, highlights, among other aspects, the need for recognition in the SNS of the best administrative practices for the reorganization of services, as well as the review and adjustment of contingency plans.

242 José António Carpinteiro and Pedro Fonseca, 'COVID-19 – Impacto na atividade e no acesso ao SNS – Relatório No. 5/2020 – OAC 2.ª Secção' (*Tribunal de Contas*, October 2020) <www.tcontas.pt/pt-pt/ProdutosTC/Relatorios/relatorios-oac/Documents/2020/relatorio-oac-2020-05.pdf>

"It is at stake the need to know and evaluate the 'trade-off' of the allocation of resources to the treatment of patients with COVID-19, in view of the needs for diagnosis and treatment of other diseases, even if not urgent (recovery of the programmed activity)."[243] *The Court considers that the recovery of the activity not performed will have to occur in a context of additional care in clinical practice, with the risk that the installed capacity in the SNS will not be sufficient to cope with this increase in demand without the sharp increase in waiting times.*

The activity of the SNS providers in the months from March to May 2020 was thus lower than that registered in the same period of 2019, with emphasis on the reduction in the scheduled surgical activity (–58%, 93,300 surgeries), in the activity of hospital emergency services (–44%, 683,389 visits) and the first outpatient medical consultations (–40%, 364,535 consultations). New user registrations for outpatient hospital visits (referenced by primary health care) and for surgery have been markedly reduced. Until May 2020, only 67% of the requests for consultation were made and 42% of the registrations for surgery occurred in the same period of 2019.

The average waiting times for users on the list also worsened between December 31, 2019 and May 31, 2020: i) in external consultations, from 100 to 171 days, with about 69% of those registered on 31/05/2020 to wait beyond the Maximum Guaranteed Response Times (TMRG); ii) in those enrolled for surgery, from 106 to 147 days, with about 43% of those enrolled on 31/05/2020 exceeding the TMRG. The surgeries performed in May 2020 also registered some deterioration in compliance with the TMRG, although it remained relatively close to the values recorded in previous years.

In the most urgent surgeries (priorities 3 and 4, oncological and non-oncological disease), compliance with the TMRGs improved (in the first half of 2020), due to the focus of activity on these patients, compared to the least urgent.

We witnessed two types of scarcity: human resources and equipment with a special focus on the first resources, humans. Entities, such as the Portuguese Medical Association, and the Portuguese Nurses Association have even advised doctors and nurses to ask for "excuse for civil liability" to express disagreement with the lack of conditions for the provision of health care. In fact, these entities have warned that the increase in the number of patients hospitalized with covid-19 was being done "at the expense of beds for 'non-covid' patients and without an adequate increase in the number of doctors, nurses and other health professionals, putting at risk all the patients".

3. Legal foundations for resource allocation in health

Questions: On what legal basis is it possible to apply the allocation criteria in practice? For example, can the health professionals and the providers of health care successfully claim that they acted in the state of necessity?

[243] ibid.

The Constitution of the Portuguese Republic protects the right to health as a fundamental right, within the scope of economic, social and cultural rights (article 64).

According to our fundamental law, everyone has the right to health protection and the duty to defend and promote it (1). The right to health protection is achieved through the creation of a universal, general and free national health service (the National Health Service — Serviço Nacional de Saúde), through the creation of economic, social and cultural conditions that guarantee the protection of children, youth and elderly, for the systematic improvement of living and working conditions, as well as the promotion of physical and sporting, school and popular culture and also for the development of health education for the people (2). In order to ensure the right to health protection, the State is primarily responsible for: a) guaranteeing access for all citizens, regardless of their economic condition, to the care of preventive, curative and rehabilitation medicine; b) guarantee rational and efficient medical and hospital coverage throughout the country; c) orient its action towards the socialization of medicine and the medical-medicine sectors; d) discipline and control the business and private forms of medicine, articulating them with the national health service; e) discipline and control the production, marketing and use of chemical, biological and pharmaceutical products and other means of treatment and diagnosis (3).

The protection of health is therefore protected as a fundamental right of the people and a duty of the State. It is a right that has two aspects: *"one, of a negative nature, which consists of the right to require the State (or third parties) to refrain from any act that harms health; another, of a positive nature, which means the right to state measures and benefits aimed at disease prevention and treatment"*.[244] However, the question is to know how far this State's duty goes since health needs are practically infinite, but the resources available are not, and health, despite being a fundamental and especially important good, is not the only good that a society has to maintain. Considering this fact, and taking into account that there are several health needs of the population, the difficulty is how resources should be allocated, since, as we mentioned, we are facing finite resources, and to that extent an absolute scarcity.

Our Constitution determines this access to the national health service in a universal, general and free way, which justifies the mobilization of the principle of equality. This means that all Portuguese citizens must be included in this access, without distinction. Under the legislation of the Rights and Duties of Users (of Users of Health Services), users of health services are entitled to receive, promptly or within a period of time considered clinically acceptable, depending on the case, the health care they need. Users are also entitled to the provision of the most appropriate and technically correct health care (Article 4).

But, given the scarcity of resources, is this possible?

[244] José Joaquim Gomes Canotilho and Vital Moreira, *Constituição da República Portuguesa – Anotada – Volume I* (4th edn, Coimbra Editora 2007) 825.

In reality, the answer will have to be negative. Considering, in particular, Order No. 574-A/2021, which determines that hospital establishments of the National Health Service (SNS) pass their Contingency Plans to the maximum level and suspend the programmed non-urgent assistance activity that can be used to reinforce care for critical patients, we have effective parameters for allocating resources: human and equipment.

For example, in the case of cancer patients, the General Directorate of Health through Standard 009/2020, of 2 April 2020, established, in view of the scarcity of resources, priorities in performing surgeries.[245]

Thus, it will be these documents already mentioned — Order No. 574-A/2021 and Standard 009/2020, of April 2, 2020 — that will serve as a legal basis for the allocation of resources.

The problem will arise when, reaching a point, that obeying all these legally established criteria (through hard law and soft law instruments) health professionals are faced with situations in which even in emergency or urgent situations it is no longer possible to meet all the demand. At that moment, there will no longer be any legal support, within the scope of these decrees just mentioned, in which health professionals can sustain their decisions, having, however, to continue taking them. This is where we ask: how to justify the performance of health professionals? Ethically, the performance of these professionals can be supported by the aforementioned opinion issued by the Portuguese Medical Association. But what about the legal point of view?

The Portuguese Medical Association and the Portuguese Nurses Association advise their professionals to issue declarations of non-responsibility and forward them for filing with the respective Associations and also to report situations of anomalous service operation with the intention that the responsibility of these professionals can

245 According to Ordinance 153/2017 and considering the date of the surgical indication as the date of the multidisciplinary decision that it is essential, the following prioritization methodology is proposed: 1. Deferred Urgency (72 hours counted from the surgical indication): the Clinical criteria without recommended organizational modeling. 2. Very Priority (15 consecutive days counted from the surgical indication): a) Epithelial malignant neoplasms of the upper aerodigestive system, in which the surgery to be performed is predictably curative (excluding surgical intervention for diagnosis); b) Malignant neoplasms whose surgery to be performed is part of a multimodal therapeutic plan in which the surgery is expected to be of curative intention (excluding surgical intervention for diagnosis or staging); c) Malignant germ cell neoplasms in which the surgery is expected to be of curative intent (excluding surgical intervention for diagnosis or staging); d) Non-haematological neoplasms with aggressive biological behavior and for which a multidisciplinary group consultation considers that the surgery to be performed is predictably curative (excluding surgical intervention for diagnosis). e) Hematological neoplasms. 3. Priority (45 consecutive days counting from the surgical indication): a) Malignant neoplasms of the lung for curative therapy of primary neoplasms; b) Malignant epithelial neoplasms of the esophagus for curative treatment of primary neoplasms; c) Epithelial malignant neoplasms of the stomach for curative therapy of primary neoplasms; d) Malignant neoplasms of the exocrine pancreas for curative therapy of primary neoplasms; e) CNS malignant neoplasms. 4. Normal (60 consecutive days counted from the surgical indication): a) Remaining neoplasms, whose surgical plan foresees intervention of curative intention.

be somehow exempted. However, the legal value of these statements is practically nil. The question that may be asked is whether it will be possible to use a more generic instrument, such as the right of necessity, that would remove any punishment, from the criminal and civil point of view, of these professionals?

The state of necessity is a cause of exclusion of illegality from a conduct that sacrifices the goods or interests of a third party in order to avoid a current danger of injury to the goods or interests of the author or third parties that are objectively superior to the sacrificed goods or interests.

The figure of the state of necessity, which presupposes a conflict between holders of legal assets and interests, which are, as a rule, lawful, which is resolved with the prevalence of one of them by means of a weighting judgment, covers a civil and a criminal dimension, being regulated in article 339 of the Civil Code (CC) and in article 34 of the Penal Code (CP).

In the civil plan, according to Menezes Cordeiro, the state of need is *"the situation in which a person is constrained to destroy or damage someone else's object, in order to remove the danger of manifestly superior damage, either to the agent or to a third party".*[246] However, as Rodrigues Nunes points out, this notion must be complemented since *"of the letter of the Law seems to result that the agent will only act in a state of necessity and his conduct will only be justified when he destroys or damages (but no longer when he uses) 'things' (that is, only when he sacrifices legal assets of a patrimonial nature, but no longer when sacrificing legal personality assets) and provided that the damage to be avoided is clearly greater than the damage caused."*[247]

Therefore, considering these requirements it seems to us that it is not possible to mobilize the right of necessity in the civil plan. Not only are we not dealing with heritage assets, but there is a situation of preserving the life or health of two people, with scarce resources, the rights at stake will be of equal value. Therefore, there is no restriction on a right to preserve another manifestly superior one.

However, notwithstanding, we will not be able to mobilize this figure as we will see, nor will it be possible to civilly condemn health professionals.

At the criminal level, the state of necessity can be presented as an exclusion clause for illegality, but also as an exclusion clause for guilt.

The right of necessity, as a cause of justification and exclusion clause of illegality, is provided for in Article 34 of the Penal Code (CP), in the following terms: *"It is not unlawful for a fact practiced as an adequate means to remove a current danger that threatens the agent's or third party's legally protected interests, when the following requirements are met: a) the danger situation has not been voluntarily created by the agent, unless to protect the interests of third parties; b) there is*

246 António Menezes Cordeiro, *Tratado de Direito Civil Português, I, Parte Geral, Tomo IV* (Almedina 2019) 439.

247 Duarte Alberto Rodrigues Nunes, 'O estado de necessidade em Direito civil' (*Julgar online*, March 2017).

a significant superiority of the interest to be safeguarded in relation to the sacrificed interest; c) it is reasonable to impose on the victim the sacrifice of his interest in consideration of the nature or the value of the threatened interest."

It is necessary, in Criminal Law, to distinguish the state of justifying need (objective), from the state of excusing need (subjective) provided for in article 35 of the CP, which refers to us in its paragraph 1, who acts without fault whoever practices an illegal act appropriate to remove a current danger, which is not otherwise removable, that threatens the life, physical integrity, honor or freedom of the agent or third party, when it is not reasonable to demand, under the circumstances of the case, different behavior.

However, whether one speaks of the state of excusing or justifying need, it does not seem possible to mobilize it. In the state of justifying need, the requirement for the defense of a substantially superior legal asset fails us, while the apologetic attentive to the content of this justification cause, it seems to us that it is remote since there is no practice, by any health professional, of an act that aims to ward off current danger.

The foregoing considerations seem to lead us to an understanding that in the present case it is not possible to rule out any possible liability based on the use of the figure of the right to necessity, but is it possible to find other solutions in the law?

In truth, it does not seem to us that these health professionals can be held responsible, individually, for the options taken in view of the scarce resources in accordance with the existing legal regime in Portugal, as we will see below.

It should also be noted that the state of necessity should also be considered in constitutional terms when linked to a social or emergency disorder. The state of emergency is a state of exception to the current constitutional regime, namely as regards the protection of fundamental rights that can only be declared, in all or in part of the national territory, in situations of effective or imminent aggression by foreign forces, serious threat or disturbance of the democratic constitutional order or public calamity. It allows suspending the exercise of certain fundamental rights, giving public authorities the power to take the necessary measures to restore constitutional normality.

It is incumbent upon the President of the Republic to declare a state of emergency, after hearing the Government and obtained the authorization from the Assembly of the Republic. The state of emergency usually refers to a localized situation (such as an epidemic), so it can only lead to the suspension of rights, freedoms and guarantees with concrete relevance to that situation (in the case of an epidemic, the right to freedom, for example).

However, the enactment of a state of emergency in no case may affect the rights to life, personal integrity, personal identity, civil capacity and citizenship, non-retroactivity of criminal law, guarantees of defense of defendants and freedom of conscience and religion.

4. Possible civil and criminal liability of professionals and entities in times of resource scarcity and resource allocation

Questions: What level of legal certainty do the health professionals and the providers of health care have when applying the allocation criteria? What are the civil and criminal liability implications of allocation?

4.1. The right to health protection and the distribution of resources

What is certain is that health professionals, in abstract terms, have no guarantee of their non-responsibility. In fact, for this reason they tried to make use of the aforementioned declarations of non-liability. In Portugal, contrary to what happened in other countries, no legislation has been published that would exempt health professionals from liability in situations of scarcity of resources.

Article 64 of the Constitution of the Portuguese Republic enshrines the right to health protection and the duty to defend and promote it and stipulates how that right should be realized. Such an important mission was delivered by the constituent legislator to the National Health Service ("SNS"). The SNS has a matrix with a universal and general character, which means that anyone should be able to access the health services provided by them, and that these services must incorporate the majority of the existing health services necessary for the protection of the health of users and beneficiaries of the SNS. However, the tendency of free services provided by the SNS is, however, limited by the economic and social conditions of the citizens.

Considering this fact and, in spite of the existence of a public and private system of assistance care in Portugal, in the scope of health, it is in terms of the allocation of resources, within the scope of public health institutions, that we will refer and address the question of the health professionals liability and the responsibility of public health establishments, that is, ultimately the responsibility of the State itself.

4.2. Civil liability

"Medical activity in public health establishments (...) is part of an institutional framework of a public nature: it constitutes the exercise of a public function, develops under the aegis of public law rules (...)."[248] To that extent, this relationship between public hospitals (article 1, paragraph 1), doctors (article 1, paragraph 4) and patients has its own regime known as the State's Non-Contractual Liability Regime (hereinafter Regime) that is provided for in Law No. 67/2007, of 31 December. This Regime determines, through paragraph 1 of article 1, that the regulation in question

[248] Diogo Freitas do Amaral, 'Natureza da Responsabilidade Civil por Actos Médicos praticados em Estabelecimentos públicos de saúde' in José de Oliveira Ascensão et al, *Direito da Saúde e Bioética* (Lex 1991) 129.

applies to damages resulting from the exercise of the various functions of the State. This Regime applies *"to actions and omissions adopted in the exercise of public authority prerogatives or regulated by provisions or principles of administrative law"* (article 1, paragraph 2).

Within the scope of this responsibility *"it is not a question of any personal action or omission by its author, who coincidentally also holds a State body or other legal person, its employee or agent, or even its worker, but a fact included in the performance of the function and, therefore, a fact that not only legally configures the performance of an individual, but also — simultaneously, by law — the performance of the Public Administration itself in pursuit of a given public interest."*[249]

The Portuguese system of civil liability continues to maintain the paradigm based on the primacy of responsibility based on the fault of the agent, for which *"there is a civil liability of the Administration and, as such, a duty to indemnify, when five assumptions are verified, expressly or implicitly resulting of Articles 7, I, 8, I and II, of Law 67/2007: the voluntary fact, the illegality, the fault, the damage and the causal link."*[250]

Article 8 of Law No. 67/2007 establishes that the holders of bodies, employees and agents are responsible for damages resulting from unlawful actions or omissions, committed by them with intent or with diligence and zeal manifestly inferior to those to which were obliged. It follows from this normative provision that we will have joint liability (from the agent and the institution) in those situations in which we are faced with acts committed with intent or serious guilt. The regime of Law no. 67/2007, of 31 December, for what it is important to appreciate here, can be summarized in the following terms: for the damages caused by slight negligence practiced by the holders of the organs, the agents and other public legal persons in the exercise of their functions and because of that exercise, the State or other public legal persons respond, directly and exclusively, to the victim; for the damages caused by acts practiced by those same entities (holders of administrative bodies or agents) under the same conditions (in the exercise of their functions and because of them), but committed with intent or gross negligence, the State or other public legal persons and the agents respond jointly to the injured party.[251]

The judgment of guilt presupposes, moreover, the existence of a standard behavior to be observed in certain circumstances against which the conduct of the agent will be assessed. Only in case of non-conformity between that behavior that the agent could and should have had and what he/she actually did, may there be a possible censorship. In the situations analyzed, of possible scarcity of resources, there is,

---

249 Raquel Carvalho, 'N.º 1 Artigo 7.º – Responsabilidade exclusiva do Estado e demais pessoas coletivas de direito público' *in Comentário ao Regime da Responsabilidade Civil Extracontratual do Estado e demais Entidades Públicas* (Universidade Católica Editora, 2013) 175.

250 Marcelo Rebelo de Sousa and André Salgado de Matos, *Direito Administrativo Geral – Tomo III. Responsabilidade Civil Administrativa* (1st edn, Dom Quixote 2008) 19.

251 In these cases, the State may have a right of return on the agent who acted with intent or gross negligence.

abstractly, no repair that can be undermined by the conduct of health professionals who act according to the normal standards of diligence and care. Because of this, the doctor whose clinical procedure is in accordance with the technical/scientific standard of the performance required of the average professional, does not violate any objective duty of care, in the circumstances of the specific case.

The civil liability institute is thus based on the concept of fault, which remains the backbone of the civil liability system, expressly stipulating the law that there is only an obligation to indemnify regardless of fault in the cases specified in the law. We cannot, however, fail to place here a possible liability for service failure. This is a liability based on Article 7 (2) of the Regime. Article 7, paragraphs 3 and 4, of the aforementioned Law no. 67/2007 enshrines a regime of liability of the Administration for *abnormal operation of the service*, which has an innovative scope.

"From the reading of the content of this precept, it immediately and unequivocally results in the conclusion that there is a liability which, being guided by a depersonalization of illegality and guilt, is direct, exclusive and has an objective character." In reality, *"the administrative organization designed to satisfy the general interest of the community fell short of what would reasonably be expected and due, given the circumstances surrounding the illegality perpetrated and the median result models, regardless of the agent's actual fault (...)." "The occurrence of damages reveals, under any circumstances, an abnormal functioning of the service, either because the injury results from failures attributable to the service globally considered, or because it was one of its employees or agents that incurred the violation of technical rules or a duty general care, although it was not possible to identify the person responsible."*[252]

In the words of Mário Aroso de Almeida,[253] with the introduction of the *service's abnormal functioning* institute, *"it is ensured that the Administration is not only responsible for damages resulting from specific illicit and culpable conduct of determined agents, but, in general, for damages resulting from its functioning that injured person has no obligation to endure, because they would not be caused by a service that works normally, that is, according to average result standards."*

In other words, *"the fault of the service must be assessed in the abstract, given the standard of average behavior that would be required in the circumstances of the case. This analysis of circumstances is formatted for situations in which the damage is attributed to financial constraints or scarcity of other material and human resources that are not attributable to the service."*[254]

252 Ana Pereira Sousa, 'A culpa do serviço no exercício da função administrativa' (2012) 1 *Boletim da Ordem dos Advogados* 335 <https://portal.oa.pt/upl/%7B54c06115-8834-4732-80bd-d5741c-bae04d%7D.pdf>.

253 Mário Aroso de Almeida in Rui Medeiros (eds), *Comentário ao Regime da Responsabilidade Civil Extracontratual do Estado e demais Entidades Públicas*(Universidade Católica Editora 2013) 219–223.

254 Tiago Viana Barra, 'A responsabilidade civil administrativa do estado' (2011) 1 Boletim da Ordem dos Advogados 111 <www.oa.pt/upl/%7B915b1a77-e7cb-48fa-9b7c-3399815c19dd%7D.pdf>.

So, *"in the area of liability for the abnormal functioning of the service, there is a presumption of illegality against public entities and in exclusive terms, this does not mean that the consideration of guilt should always be irrelevant. If there is intent or serious fault of the holder of the organ, official or agent, he/she is jointly and severally liable with the State and public entities should proceed with the right of recourse in order not to burden the taxpayer."*[255]

Aroso de Almeida tells us that two types of situations are at issue here: the *collective* fault and the *anonymous* fault. *"Collective guilt would cover cases in which the damage cannot be directly attributed to the concrete behavior of an employee, but results from a global action that involves a dispersed liability for different sectors of the public administration."* In turn, *"anonymous fault would include situations in which the damage is attributable to the action of a specific employee, but it is not possible to ascertain the personal authorship of the injurious fact"*.[256] The *"anonymous foul exists in situations where the injury cannot fail to determine the identity of that agent and, therefore, ascertain the personal authorship of the injurious fact"*.[257] In this case, *"the production of the damages shows the existence of an* ***abnormal functioning of the service****, insofar as it can be said that if the service, through that indeterminate agent, had worked as it should, the damages would not have occurred".*

"It is above all in the domain of omissions of conduct that tend to occur situations of abnormal functioning of the service, since it is primarily in this domain that the most difficult to establish the connection between the damage and the concrete conduct of an agent that can be individualized." "As is clear from paragraph 4 [of this art. 7], the lack of service must be assessed in the abstract, taking into account average income standards that would be required to be observed in the circumstances of the specific case." (...) It seems, therefore, to understand that there will be no liability when the damages can be attributed to a scarcity of human, material or financial resources — but this (...) only insofar as the service has the minimum resources that it is reasonable to demand for (the resources that in a normal situation would be adequate to avoid the damage produced)."[258]

"Of course, in order to have Aquilian liability, in addition to illegality and guilt, there must be a (appropriate) causal link between fact and harm. If we work with a notion of omission of prospective surveillance and renew the omission in vigilando, the burden of proving the impossibility will rest with the public entity (removing guilt) and this impossibility is largely due to an irresistible external event (removing causality) — cf. paragraph 3 of article 10 of the Regime, by reference to paragraph 1 of article 493 of the Civil Code. But even if these arguments do not succeed, you

---

255 ibid.

256 Carlos Alberto Cadilha, *Regime da Responsabilidade Civil Extracontratual do Estado e demais entidades públicas – Anotado* (1st edn, Coimbra Editora 2008) 132.

257 Mário Aroso de Almeida in Rui Medeiros (eds), *Comentário ao Regime da Responsabilidade Civil Extracontratual do Estado e demais Entidades Públicas* (Universidade Católica Editora 2013) 219–223.

258 ibid.

can, in subsidiary support, claim that the damage (hospitalization; lasting physical failure; death) most likely would have always occurred, by checking for causes other than COVID infection19 and/or by behavior of the patient. injured, thus removing or reducing the liability."[259]

If a possible civil liability is complex, criminal does not lag behind in terms of complexity of analysis.

4.3. Criminal liability

Life is the first of the fundamental rights to be protected under the Constitution of the Portuguese Republic.[260] *"The right to life is closely linked to other rights (and principles) such as the dignity of the human person (...), personality development (...) physical and psychological integrity (...) and equality (...). Equality, in this context, means the equal constitutional dignity of all life."*[261]

The high demand for health resources in view of the scarce existing supply, namely with regard to human resources, may lead to legal assets such as life and physical integrity not being adequately protected. Better, do not have the accompaniment that you would have in a normal situation in which we were not facing the practice of catastrophe medicine. This fact implies not only profound ethical constraints for doctors who are placed in a position to choose who to treat when, in reality, they have promised to keep absolute respect for Human Life from the beginning, even under threat[262] (…) but also eventual legal issues.

From a criminal point of view and starting from a simplistic analysis, we wonder if these professionals will not commit a crime of homicide, a crime of offense to physical integrity or even a crime of failure to help. We understand that it is not. As the health professional is placed in a situation of scarcity of resources (whether they are human resources or equipment) and there is not enough response to the demand, these professionals will have nothing left but to choose ... They are faced with a conflict of duties: the duty to try to save citizen A and the duty to try to save citizen B. There are no means to be able to save both.

This fact will lead us to affirm that there is no unlawful fact. It is not unlawful for those who, in the event of a conflict in the fulfillment of legal duties or legitimate orders from the authority, satisfy a duty or order of equal or greater value than the duty or order they sacrifice (Article 36 of the Penal Code — CP). Article 36 of the CP acts as a cause of justification that is assessed as to illegality.

This conflict brings a conceptual difficulty that needs to be clarified. In situations where a health professional is faced with a shortage of resources, we are facing

---

259 Carla Amado Gomes, 'Responsabilidade civil extracontratual do Estado e(m) estado de emergência: Dez breves notas' (2020) 7 ePública – Revista Eletrónica de Direito Público 170.

260 Through the provisions of article 24 of the Constitution of the Portuguese Republic.

261 José Joaquim Gomes Canotilho and Vital Moreira, *Constituição da República Portuguesa Anotada – Volume I* (4th edn, Coimbra Editora 2007) 448.

262 Hippocratic Oath.

a conflict of interest or a state of need? Conceição Ferreira da Cunha tells us that *"we are facing problems that fall under the concept of 'conflict of duties, in a broad sense', when it comes to a third party in a position (and with a legal duty) to decide; and when faced with situations of need (states of need), when it comes to acting in an attempt to survive"*. The Author even gives us the example of conflict of duties, stating that this "conflict of duty in the strict sense" may occur *"when, for example, the doctor, being in front of two seriously ill patients, can only treat one of them"*.[263]

The essential difference will be that for the state of necessity, justification could only work whenever there was a preservation of a legal asset of a significantly higher value, whereas, in the conflict of interests, provided for in paragraph 1 of article 36 of the Penal Code, the values just need to be equal. As mentioned above, all "lives" have an equal dignity, so we could never operate the state of need here since, in our example, patient A's life is not superior to patient B's and vice versa.

Jorge de Figueiredo Dias tells us that *"as in the right of necessity (...) also in the conflict of duties, the result of weighting (equality of duties, superiority or inferiority of the duty fulfilled) must not result simply from the hierarchy of legal assets colliding, but the global and concrete weighing of conflicting interests"*.[264]

This will lead to the fact that the practiced fact cannot be considered illegal because the health professional just does not fulfill the duty of trying to save A because he is trying to save B.

As for access to ventilators, that is, since health professionals are faced with a situation in which there are more patients in need of ventilation than available machines, we should mobilize here what was written by Conceição Ferreira da Cunha who states that when *"such conflict arises, there will be no doubt about the priority of the patient who has chances of survival, as well as it seems reasonable that the duty to save those who have better chances of survival should be imposed as a priority (compared to those who have a reduced or doubtful possibility of being saved)"*. The Author defends that it will not be necessary to "strictly and strictly respect the order of priority of admission to the hospital" and that the criterion presented (que patient who have better chances of survival) will always be preferable to the criterion "first come, first served" or the rule of the draw "practiced in North American institutions."[265]

However, if there are several lives or physical integrity of several people at risk, with an equal dignity of all human lives and a duty to safeguard the lives and health of these people, we may be facing not only a conflict of duties — one doctor for two sick; a machine for two patients — but also a situation of necessity that underlies this conflict of duties, as stated by Maria da Conceição Cunha Rodrigues.

263 Maria da Conceição Ferreira da Cunha, *Vida contra vida – conflitos existenciais e limites do direito penal* (Coimbra Editora 2009) 28ff.

264 Jorge de Figueiredo Dias, *Direito penal – Parte Geral – Tomo I – Questões fundamentais, a doutrina geral do crime* (Coimbra Editora 2004) 438.

265 Maria da Conceição Ferreira da Cunha, *Vida contra vida – conflitos existenciais e limites do direito penal* (Coimbra Editora 2009) 262ff.

The Author states that such situations may *"arise independently of the conflict of duties, or may, in other cases,"* collide *"to some extent with the conflict of duties (more precisely, with the rules for their resolution), (...)"*. In fact, the duties of saving, which are imposed on the decision-making agent, exist exactly for the protection of people in need, with certain rules regarding the prevalence of some duties in relation to others and, in extreme cases, the complete imponderability of the duties in conflict, granting freedom of choice to the decision-making agent"[266].

In conclusion, criminal law cannot require the doctor to do the impossible. The general principle *impossibilium nulla est obligatio* (or *ultra posse nemo tenetur*) — no duty in the event of real impossibility — also applies in medical and criminal law. If a patient needing ventilation cannot be treated due to the lack of a (free) ventilation place and due to the lack of an effective transfer option, there is no criminal liability. The (very few) resources that are still available and the decision to allocate have to be made (therefore *ex ante*). For factual reasons, the doctor cannot fulfill all (equivalent) duties to act. In the doctrine of criminal law, there is talk of a so-called "conflict of duties": the doctor treats as many patients as the available resources, so he is not accused of illegality for not treating all patients — because his is not possible for him.

B. Case studies

Case 1

As a result of a rapid worsening of the epidemiological situation, the material and personal capacities have been drastically overloaded in all the hospitals in the country. Within just a few minutes, ambulances transport ten patients to one particular hospital's emergency unit. The patients all need admission to the hospital, preferably to the intensive care unit (ICU). However, only two beds are available there. Other hospitals are overwhelmed too, so it is not possible to transport patients to any of them. All of the ten newly coming patients suffer from COVID-19; they have breathing difficulties, fast-rising fever, and decreasing oxygen saturation. Nevertheless, they differ in age, comorbidities, clinical fragility, and other factors.

Theoretically, the eight patients who cannot be admitted to beds can be placed in improvised settings in the hospital corridors, laying on gurneys or mattresses on the floor. Nevertheless, it will be impossible to provide them with the care they need.

<u>Evaluation of the case</u>

- What criteria can be used to choose the patients who will be admitted to the beds (i.e. what are the possible allocation criteria)?
  According to CNEDM58 — ethical considerations and recommendations related to situations caused by the covid pandemic19 of the Portuguese Medical

266 ibid 293ff.

Association, in situations of extreme uncontrolled progression of the pandemic, a limitation of existing resources is possible, namely assisted ventilation, and it is necessary to establish screening of patients who will have access to these resources. In this situation, doctors need to make the difficult decision to condition this access, maximizing its benefits. This decision should take into account clinical and risk assessment criteria including those of intensive care medicine, as well as the greater probability of treatment effectiveness and expected survival (age, co-morbidities, etc.), with proportionality and distributive justice.
In these cases, the defined protocol follows the deontological rules of medicine and meets ethical principles with which the vast majority of the population agrees: the most urgent cases are treated first and, for the same level of urgency, a precedence criterion is applied.

- What legal consequences can this decision have for the health professionals and the hospital? How strong is their legal certainty that there will be no adverse legal consequences if they follow the above-mentioned criteria?
  As we mentioned in chapter 5, there is no guarantee for health professionals that they are not sued for the options taken. In fact, Portugal has not adopted legal mechanisms to exclude liability. However, the general legal mechanisms existing in the Portuguese legal system allow us to conclude that it will be very difficult to hold a professional (who acts according to the appropriate scientific technical standards) or hospital establishments in the face of a situation of scarcity.
- What legal defences could the health professionals and the hospital use against a civil lawsuit and/or criminal prosecution for the allocation decision?
  In the case of health professionals and health establishments in relation to civil liability, the requirements set out in the Portuguese legal system are not met. In particular, we cannot claim that there is any unlawful fact or fault of the agent here. Specifically, regarding the establishments, the eventual liability is also ruled out (a possible "faut du service") because these hospital units had the appropriate means to respond to a normal situation. The abnormal character that leads to an excess of demand and removes the possible liability (for further development see subchapter B, of Chapter 5).
  As for criminal liability, this will be removed because we are witnessing a conflict of duties. This fact will lead us to affirm that there is no unlawful fact. It is not unlawful for those who, in the event of a conflict in the fulfillment of legal duties or legitimate orders from the authority, satisfy a duty or order of equal or greater value than the duty or order they sacrifice (Article 36 of the Penal Code — CP) (for further developments see subchapter C, of Chapter 5).

<u>Additional questions</u>

- Would it be legally permissible to lower the standard of care provided to all patients in order to provide at least basic decent care to the newly admitted patients who are placed in the hospital corridors? To what extent?

According to CNEDM58 (ethical considerations and recommendations related to the situations caused by the covid pandemic19 of the Portuguese Medical Association) assistance care must be framed in the fundamental principle of human dignity and in the principle / condition of vulnerability imposed by the difficult balance between the individual good and the common good that this situation imposes on us. The ethical principles that should guide ethical and deontological action in this pandemic include: beneficence and non-maleficence, which include the duty to take good care of and to manage adequate resources (and available in emergency), justice as equity, proportionality, responsibility, truth, transparency and consistency. In addition, it is recommended that prudence, common sense, dialogue, collaboration and solidarity should also always be present in the decision-making process.

Case 2

Two patients in an ICU are suffering from COVID-19. After admission to the hospital, they were provided with the high-flow nasal oxygen therapy (NFNO). During one night, the condition of both patients starts to worsen rapidly. At dawn, it is clear that neither of them will survive without artificial ventilation. However, there is just one ventilator available.

Evaluation of the case

- What criteria can be used to choose which of the two patients will be provided with artificial ventilation and which one will be left without it, possibly to die?
  According to CNEDM58 (ethical considerations and recommendations related to the situations caused by the covid-19 pandemic of the Portuguese Medical Association) in the extreme situations of uncontrolled progression of the pandemic, in which there is a limitation of existing resources, namely assisted ventilation, and in which it is necessary to screening of patients who will have access to these resources, doctors need to condition this access, maximizing its benefits. This decision should take into account clinical and risk assessment criteria including those of intensive care medicine, as well as the greater probability of treatment effectiveness and expected survival (age, co-morbidities, etc.), with proportionality and distributive justice.
- What legal consequences can this decision have for the health professionals and the hospital? How strong is their legal certainty that there will be no adverse legal consequences if they follow the above-mentioned criteria?
  The answer will be the same as in question 2 of the previous case.
- What legal defences could the health professionals and the hospital use against a civil lawsuit and/or criminal prosecution for the allocation decision?
  The answer will be the same as in question 3 of the previous case.

Additional question

- If the allocation criteria specified in your answer to the first question to this case consisted of the patients' clinical features (such as their age, clinical fragility,

etc.), please identify what criteria could be used for the allocation decision if all the relevant clinical features of both patients were practically the same?
It is clear that the triage criteria — the order of arrival of the application for admission or arrival at hospital emergency services — cannot be priority criteria. The support of any means of extracorporeal oxygenation (ECMO), should be reserved for strictly selected cases and with a reasonable expectation of relatively rapid abandonment; or that the limitation or suspension of controlled or assisted ventilation, or endo-tracheal extubation or of the non-invasive route, does not in itself constitute an indication to suspend the remaining treatment.

Case 3

There is a single extracorporeal membrane oxygenation (ECMO) device in the hospital. It is currently being used for an 84-year-old patient suffering from COVID-19, with diabetes as an underlying disease, clinical frailty score (CFS) 6–7 (moderate to severe frailty). It is possible that the patient will survive and will be discharged from the hospital if the ECMO treatment is continued. However, a younger COVID-19 patient is admitted to the hospital. This new patient is 51 years old, otherwise healthy, but her health condition has been rapidly deteriorating. Soon she will most likely need ECMO to survive.

Evaluation of the case

- Can it be legally permissible for the hospital staff to discontinue the ECMO treatment of the older patient and provide palliative care to her in order to save the younger and healthier patient's life? Please keep in mind that the older patient could survive if the treatment continued, but her chances may be lower than those of the younger patient.
  In the case of decisions to suspend curative attitudes, the doctor cannot abandon any patient who needs their care and must always ensure adequate monitoring.
  Disconnecting an ECMO treatment implies a very well thought out decision in a multidisciplinary team where the action is guided by the clinical situation, the prognosis, the ethical principles and the respect for the patient's dignity.
  In the case presented, there are no clinical criteria that could lead to the discontinuation of ECMO treatment for a patient, so that discontinuation cannot exist.
- If the answer to the first question is positive, what specific criteria can be used in clinical decision-making regarding replacing one patient with another with respect to a particular treatment unavailable for all?
  The answer was negative.
- What legal consequences can this decision have for the health professionals and the hospital? How strong is their legal certainty that there will be no adverse legal consequences if they follow the above-mentioned criteria?
  Impaired by the negative answer.
- What legal defences could the health professionals and the hospital use against a civil lawsuit and/or criminal prosecution for the allocation decision?

A possible liability could be questioned as to the patient who comes in second and ECMO treatment will not be available. Therefore, the weighting of any liability will have the same answer as in question 3 of case 1.

Additional question

- Suppose there are two different scenarios: a) the older patient was admitted to the hospital and provided with the ECMO treatment, and only later, after several days, the younger patient was admitted, and b) the younger patient was admitted before the older patient, however, the older patient required ECMO treatment soon after admission while the younger patient's health condition deteriorated only after a longer time when the ECMO was already occupied (i. e. at the time when the younger patient was admitted to the hospital, she did not yet need it). Would there be any difference in the allocation decision making between these two scenarios?
  No.

Conclusion

The pandemic brought developed countries to a reality unfortunately experienced, in their daily lives, in the so-called underdeveloped countries: the scarcity of resources. Considering the evolution of medicine, it would not be imaginable to think of European countries, or of the USA faced with a lack of means to assist its citizens. But, this is what happened. Portugal lived this reality. The scarcity of these human and technical resources poses several difficulties, be they of management or ethical-legal. However, it is necessary to take options. It is, above all, necessary to help those who are in the front line "of the battle" — the health professionals — to practice this catastrophe medicine. We must assist them by providing instruments that clearly offer the guidelines that guide their performance when faced with greater demand considering the available resources.

In Portugal, the existing legal regime, in an abstract analysis, does not allow civil liability for either individual professionals or the institutions themselves. Also, from the criminal point of view, this liability of professionals is removed.

The removal of individual responsibility is achieved through general mechanisms provided by law without the need to mobilize any specific legal device (which, in the Portuguese case, does not even exist). Humanely, thankfully it is. In this difficult period when the health professional has to make decisions that, most likely, will torment them throughout their lives, it would be unacceptable that they could still be confronted with any legal liability (civil or criminal).

Bibliography

• Legislation

Constitution of the Portuguese Republic (*Constituição da República Portuguesa*), 25 April 1976; cited as: Constitution of the Portuguese Republic

Ordinance 153/2017 of May 4 (*Portaria n.º 153/2017 de 4 de maio*); cited as: Ordinance 153/2017

• Books

Aroso De Almeida M, in Rui Medeiros (eds), *Comentário ao Regime da Responsabilidade Civil Extracontratual do Estado e demais Entidades Públicas* (Universidade Católica Editora 2013)

Cadilha C A, *Regime da Responsabilidade Civil da Responsabilidade Civil Extracontratual do Estado e demais entidades públicas – Anotado* (1st edn, Coimbra Editora 2008)

Carvalho R, 'N.º 1 Artigo 7.º – Responsabilidade exclusiva do Estado e demais pessoas coletivas de direito público' in *Comentário ao Regime da Responsabilidade Civil Extracontratual do Estado e demais Entidades Públicas* (Universidade Católica Editora 2013)

Gomes Canotilho J J and Moreira V, *Constituição da República Portuguesa – Anotada – Volume I* (4th edn, Coimbra Editora 2007)

Ferreira da Cunha M da C, *Vida contra vida – conflitos existenciais e limites do direito penal* (Coimbra Editora 2009)

Figueiredo Dias J de, *Direito penal – Parte Geral – Tomo I – Questões fundamentais, a doutrina geral do crime* (Coimbra Editora 2004)

Freitas do Amaral D, 'Natureza da Responsabilidade Civil por Actos Médicos praticados em Estabelecimentos públicos de saúde' in José de Oliveira Ascensão et al, *Direito da Saúde e Bioética* (Lex 1991)

Menezes Cordeiro A, *Tratado de Direito Civil Português, I, Parte Geral, Tomo IV* (Almedina 2019)

Simões J and Correia de Campo A, *O Percurso da Saúde: Portugal na Europa* (Almedina 2011)

Sousa M R de and Matos A S de, *Direito Administrativo Geral – Tomo III. Responsabilidade Civil Administrativa* (1st edn, Dom Quixote 2008)

• Articles

Amado Gomes C, 'Responsabilidade civil extracontratual do Estado e(m) estado de emergência: Dez breves notas' (2020) 7 ePública – Revista Eletrónica de Direito Público 170

Barra T V, A responsabilidade civil administrativa do estado (2011) 1 Boletim da Ordem dos Advogados 111 <www.oa.pt/upl/%7B915b1a77-e7cb-48fa-9b7c-3399815c19dd%7D.pdf>

Pinho M M, 'Racionamento dos cuidados de saúde: problemática inerente' (2008) 3 Cadernos de Saúde Pública 690

Sousa A P, 'A culpa do serviço no exercício da função administrativa' (2012) 1 Boletim da Ordem dos Advogados 335 <https://portal.oa.pt/upl/%7B54c06115-8834-4732-80bd-d5741cbae04d%7D.pdf>

• Other secondary sources

Carpinteiro J A and Fonseca P, 'COVID-19 – Impacto na atividade e no acesso ao SNS – Relatório No. 5/2020 – OAC 2.ª Secção' (*Tribunal de Contas*, October 2020) <www.tcontas.pt/pt-pt/ProdutosTC/Relatorios/relatorios-oac/Documents/2020/relatorio-oac-2020-05.pdf>

Nunes D A R, 'O estado de necessidade em Direito civil' (*Julgar online*, March 2017) <http://julgar.pt/o-estado-de-necessidade-em-direito-civil/>

O Conselho Nacional de Ética e Deontologia Médicas da Ordem dos Médicos, 'CNEDM58. Considerações E Recomendações Éticas Relacionadas Com As Situações Provocadas Pela Pandemia Covid-19' (*Ordem dos Médicos*) <https://ordemdosmedicos.pt/wp-content/uploads/2020/11/Parecer-CNEDM58vf-páginas-1-4.pdf>

Observatório português dos sistemas de Saúde, 'Relatório de primavera 2012' (*OPSS*) <http://opssaude.pt/relatorios/relatorio-de-primavera-2012/>

SERBIA

Marija Karanikić Mirić
University of Belgrade

A. Questionnaire

1. What are the criteria for the allocation of scarce health care resources in your country?

The COVID-19 pandemic has provoked unparalleled changes in demand and uncertainties in production and distribution of medical resources used to treat COVID-19 itself and related conditions. The imbalance between supply and demand for healthcare resources in hospital settings (such as qualified medical workers, specialised medical equipment and medicines under shortage) is rapidly growing in many countries across the world. This raises some essentially normative questions: How should medical institutions and healthcare professionals distribute healthcare resources in short supply among their patients? How can insufficient medical resources be allocated fairly during the COVID-19 pandemic? Who should be given precedence when there is not enough medical resources for everyone in need? Is it possible to have allocation or prioritisation criteria that are both fair and efficient?

Medical institutions and healthcare professionals deal with these hard yet necessary choices on daily basis. In Serbia, they make these difficult decisions not only under psychological stress and time pressure, but also under a great deal of legal uncertainty. The existing medical protocols seem to have been written under the premise of sufficiency, meaning that they solely define the conditions under which one qualifies for certain type of medical service or medicine. As a rule, they do not address the situation where medical professional needs to decide who, among the persons in need, should receive the treatment, and who must remain deprived.

Healthcare in Serbia is delivered by means of a universal health care system. The system is managed by the National Health Insurance Fund, which covers all citizens and permanent residents. The percentage of funds spent on healthcare is at the level of European Union (EU) countries, but in absolute terms, it is many times lower. Private health expenditure in Serbia is also significant. The number of physicians is lower than the EU average, but the difference is not pronounced. When comparing the numbers of other medical personnel, however, the difference is larger, which indicates that the quality of hospital care is much lower than in developed countries.

When it comes to number of hospital beds, Serbia scores very well, which means that physical capacities exist, but data for 2014 indicates that they are less exploited than in most EU countries. Only 68% of these resources were utilized at that time. When comparing medical technology, Serbia lags behind most of the EU countries. Life expectancy in Serbia is as much as 5.5 years shorter than in the EU. The legislative reforms have mandated, and are yet to implement, a basic level of health services for all people, but at varying levels of co-payment. Services not covered may be supplemented by private insurance. The medical staff report that current concerns in the field of healthcare are poor funding for primary care and inadequate equipment and supplies, insufficient salaries, and substandard continuing medical education. The emphasis is still on curative instead on preventive care.[267]

There are different procedures and protocols for classic triage situations in disaster medicine, for when there is a large number of injured persons that need to be screened, and when the priority of patients' treatments needs to be determined — usually by the severity of their condition or likelihood of recovery with and without treatment. However, there are yet no official guidelines for rationing decisions in situation where the spread of COVID-19 has created shortages of medical supplies for both COVID and non-COVID patients. The impending scarcity of medical resources is not only the issue of a relatively large influx of COVID-19 patients requiring intensive care and ventilation, but also the issue of obstructed access to ordinary medical care, since it is becoming more and more difficult to timely receive regular health services.

Rationing decisions are somewhat intrinsic for medical profession. There was an old case in former Yugoslavia of a local village doctor who did not allow the woman in labour to be transported by ambulance to the town hospital 30 km away.[268] The courts held the doctor's decision was prudent and well-balanced. The doctor was in charge of the population of thousands of potential patients, and had one medically equipped vehicle. To make such decision, several criteria had to be taken into account (the medical condition of the woman, the expected development of that condition, the regular needs of the village area for their sole ambulance, etc.).

There are no specific formal criteria for allocation of scarce medical resources during the COVID-19 pandemic in Serbia. No comprehensive official instructions for such decision-making has been introduced, and only a few rationing principles are scattered across the protocols. This does not mean that the prioritisation decisions are not being made, but rather that it is hard to extract the principles or the criteria which are being observed or used in the process. In addition, we still do not have any court decisions or decisions of professional bodies applying general standards of medical profession to the specific COVID-19 situations of scarcity. So,

[267] The whole paragraph according to: Lara Lebedinski, 'How effective is healthcare in Serbia?' (*Monitoring social situation in Serbia – MONS*, 26 January 2018), http://mons.rs/how-effective-is-healthcare-in-serbia accessed 22 May 2021.

[268] Mirko Gjurašin, 'Autorizovano izlaganje' [2002] Godišnjak tribina Pravnog fakulteta u Zagrebu i Kluba pravnika grada Zagreba (Pravni fakultet u Zagrebu 2002) 71.

one can only speculate about the manner in which general standards of professional conduct would be utilised in this particular context.

The existence of a clear protocol for ethically and morally delicate situations of allocation of deficient medical resources would be of immense assistance to health professionals. It would make it easier for them to make critical decisions under time pressure and in stressful situations. Also, it would help the professionals to deal with loss and sense of personal liability for an unwanted outcome; and it would definitely give them opportunity to defend themselves from legal liability. Obviously, it would be much easier to make decisions under legal certainty, where health professionals would know that, in general, they may not be held legally liable, as long as they are conscientiously following the official protocols and settled standards of medical profession.

Medical professionals are bound by the *Code of Medical Ethics of the Medical Chamber of Serbia* (CME in further text).[269] CME prescribes the principle of diligence (conscientiousness) and the principle of equality. In addition, it sets out the duty of medical professionals to act rationally and cost-effectively.

Under the principle of diligence, contained in Article 4 of CME, the duty of a medical doctor is to perform his professional activity conscientiously, in line with the standards of medical profession and with the necessary care, in accordance with the principles of medical ethics and the principles of humanity. The doctor should always keep in mind the absolute obligation to protect human life and health, respecting the basic principle of medical ethics 'first, do not harm (*primum, non nocere*)'.

In addition, under the principle of equality (Article 5 of CME) a medical doctor is obliged to provide medical assistance to everyone equally, regardless of their age, gender, race, nationality, religion, social status, education, social origin, political or other beliefs, property status, language, culture, type of illness, mental or physical disability, or other personal trait, respecting the human rights and dignity of every human being.

According to Article 9 of CME, a medical doctor is obliged to participate in the organization and provision of medical assistance in case of emergency, including epidemics, mass accidents, natural and other disasters. And, when making a professional decision, medical doctor should behave rationally and cost-effectively, in order to achieve the best results in relation to the available financial resources (Article 15 of CME).

Furthermore, every doctor is obliged to always and everywhere provide emergency medical assistance to a person who is in imminent danger to life and health, within the limits of his abilities and knowledge, and regardless of whether he is on duty or not and whether he is explicitly asked for help or not. If a patient or an injured person needs medical assistance that the doctor is not able to provide, he is obliged to take appropriate measures to assure that the patient gets adequate medical assistance (Article 8 of CME).

---

[269] Kodeks medicinske etike Lekarske komore Srbije, *Službeni glasnik RS*, 104/2016.

The protocols of Serbian Association of Anaesthesiologists and Intensivists include *Diagram of initial care for the COVID-19 patients with respiratory failure and their admission to the intensive care unit* (DIC in further text).[270] The prescribed triage procedure states that patients with very reduced functional reserve, disseminated malignancy, extreme life ages combined with severe clinical picture, severe neurological disorders, or in coma, in which no recovery is expected despite the applied mechanical ventilation, can be referred to supportive therapy and care, instead of being admitted to the intensive care unit (ICU). In other words, the prescribed triage on admission to the ICU allows for prioritizing the patients based on their age, comorbidities and clinical frailty, in conjunction with their prognosis. On admission to the ICU, it is permissible to maximize benefits by shifting resources to the patients with better prognosis.

However, there is no permission for the healthcare workers to remove patients from ICU beds and ventilators (without their consent) to give the resources to other patients who have a better chance of surviving for longer. This practice would be unlawful and discriminatory, may qualify as infliction of bodily harm and lead to both criminal and civil liability. The patient would need to give consent for such removal, or it would have to be the case of ventilation not being clinically indicated any more. Should the postponement of imminent death only cause inhumane prolongation of suffering for a dying patient, Article 67 of CME stipulates that the medical doctor may effectively reduce treatment to mitigation of the patient's suffering, but only if the patient has ability to reason, and if he willingly and freely refuses further treatment.

The spread of COVID-19 has left Serbia with so many patients requiring medical treatment, and some of them in need of intensive care and ventilation, that the capacity of hospitals, and especially the intensive care units, was not sufficient at one point. The non-COVID patients were facing premature releases from the medical facilities, their stay at hospitals was being shortened, and the COVID patients were being released at the earliest possibility.[271] The triage among the COVID patients was necessary at that time. The criteria included: severity of acute respiratory distress, concomitant diseases that may worsen the patient's prognosis, patient's general condition and prognosis.

270 COVID-19 Preporuke, www.uais.rs/covid-19-preporuke-2 accessed 22. May 2021; Dijagram inicijalnog zbrinjavanja bolesnika s respiratornom insuficijencijom, www.uais.rs/wp-content/uploads/2020/03/9.COVID-19.Dijagram_inicijalnog_zbrinjavanja_bolesnika.pdf accessed 22. May 2021.

271 For instance, on 18 April 2020 a protocol has been changed (and such changes are regular as means od adapting to changes in epidemiological situation): a patient being treated for COVID-19 at a hospital, or in a temporary facility for the accommodation and treatment of patients with COVID-19 infection, will be discharged after the first control test (PCR swab finding) shows a negative result and if the patient is in a good general condition. The patient will be obliged to continue compulsory home isolation for a further period of 14 days. The second control test (PCR swab finding) will be taken after the expiration of the mandatory home isolation, *i.e.*, after the expiration of 14 days from the day of discharge by the competent health centre.

In addition, Article 5 of CME clearly states what *may not* be taken into account: age, gender, race, nationality, religion, marital status, social status, education, social origin, political or other beliefs, property status, language, culture, mental or physical disability, etc. For instance, the age of a patient may not be the sole criterion for triage, but may be taken into account for the purposes of assessing the patient's general condition and prognosis.

During the most severe outbreak of the epidemic, the health authorities were trying to expand capacities (by setting up improvised medical facilities and building new provisional hospitals), and also to make optimum use of the capacity available, for example by assigning certain medical institutions under the COVID regime, coordinating intensive care beds and switching patients. At that time, the lowering of the standard of health care provided to all patients was necessary, in order to provide at least decent basic care to all admitted patients, as there have been reports of people literally placed in the hospital corridors.

For instance, the *Protocol of securing airway in patients with COVID-19* (enacted by Serbian Association of Anaesthesiologists and Intensivists) explicitly allows for the number of team members to depend on the number of cases in the hospital. Due to the high risk of intubation procedure, two anaesthesiologist and one anaesthetist should be present as an already trained team. However, in case of mass influx of patients, the most experienced anaesthesiologist may be accompanied with only one team member.[272]

To give another example of settling for the possibility of substandard medical care so as to achieve maximum utility across the population: On 24 March 2020, the Government allowed that, during the state of emergency, the medical devices that are not manufactured in accordance with the prescribed standards may be procured for the purposes of the effective control of the epidemic and for the treatment of the patients with COVID-19. The criterions were lowered when the resources were insufficient: the devices that had not been tested to the standards that normally apply became acceptable, so as to provide at least some medical care to the maximum number of people.[273]

Allocation decisions put huge psychological burden on medical professionals. This burden could be alleviated by having clear protocols and guidelines on the criteria by which these decisions should be made. Until now, Serbian Resuscitation Council has adopted *Ethical principles and recommendations for prehospital emergency care during the COVID-19 pandemic in the Republic of Serbia[274] (SRCEP in further text). This document provides for collegial support, so that no one has to make these delicate decisions alone.*

[272] Obezbeđivanje disajnog puta kod pacijenata s COVID-19, www.uais.rs/wp-content/uploads/2020/03/2. COVID-19_Preporuke_za_intubaciju_SIAARTI_adaptacija.ver_.1.4.-1.pdf accessed 22 May 2021.

[273] Uredba o posebnim tehničkim zahtevima, standardima i primeni medicinskih sredstava za vreme vanrednog stanja nastalog usled bolesti COVID-19 izazvane virusom SARS-CoV-2, *Službeni glasnik RS* 41/2020.

[274] Etička načela i preporuke za prehospitalno urgentno zbrinjavanje tokom pandemije COVID-19 u Republici Srbiji, https://www.serrc.rs/text.php?opcijaA=txt&strana=115 accessed 22 May 2021.

SRCEP orders that every decision related to stopping or not starting resuscitation must be a team decision, with mandatory presence of the leader of the team, and maintains that in ethical terms there is no difference between 'not initiating resuscitation' (e.g. intubation) and 'stopping resuscitation' (*e.g.* extubation). SRCEP also states that all patients should receive standard medical care for as long as the circumstances allow.

However, in specific situations where the resuscitation teams face a lack of resources due to the increased number of COVID-19 sufferers, the priorities need to be re-considered in relation to the expected outcome and the required resources for both COVID and non-COVID patients. SRCEP concludes that ethical decisions in such situations are difficult and complex. The principle of 'first-come, first-served' remains fair in these cases. Furthermore, Charlson Comorbidity Index[275] may be of an informative nature. The medical records of individual cases must be properly kept, and all clinical decisions must be documented, preferably in a separate registry, in order to ensure transparency at all times.

SRCEP further prescribes that the medical professionals who have participated in making difficult ethical decisions should undergo appropriate debriefing and prolonged psychological support. The medical professionals who are unwilling or unable to accept this kind of ethical framework should be redirected to the areas of non-clinical support.

2. What values are the allocation criteria based on?

In normal circumstances, immediate treatment is given to those who are critically-ill, and others are delayed. Among those that are delayed, seriously-ill are given precedence over the slightly-ill patients, and the ones with no chance of survival receive palliative care only. In situations involving a large number of injured or infected people and limited medical resources, epidemiologists act in a way that the largest number of people survive. They try to ensure that incidence of illness and death within the population is the lowest possible. However, it is hard for medical professionals dealing with singular patients to take this general population oriented approach, as it may mean denying the treatment to an individual at their care.

Since the rationing system is non-explicit, and there are no written guidelines on giving priority to one patient over another when resources are limited, one may be tempted to look at the teaching materials and check the instructions given to future medical professionals. Medical students at the University of Belgrade are taught that consequentialism is acceptable under scarcity. It is permissible to weigh the prognosis of a patient against other patients' prognosis to make a prioritisation decision.

---

275 This is a specific method of categorizing comorbidities of patients, which can be used to measure the comorbidity of individual episodes of hospital care.

If there is only one dialysis device, the university textbook asserts that precedence should be given to a 25-year-old waiting for transplantation over a 75-year-old with a number of concomitant diseases and a bad prognosis. And, if two patients are the same (of the same age, same comorbidities and same prognosis), which is very rare, several different material principles of justice may come into play. However, the textbook does not provide a formula or a guideline, but leaves it to each medical professional to personally weigh in on all aspects of an individual case, in order to make the least unjust rationing decision.[276]

So, medical students at the University of Belgrade learn that rationing decisions may be based on the ideas of consequentialism. Some of the special medical protocols discreetly hold the consequentialist approach as well. For instance, SRCEP adopts the consequentialist approach when it comes to rationing decisions, and promotes the aggregate well-being or welfare (maximum utility across the population) as a desired outcome.

The provisions of SRCEP stipulate that general ethical principles do not change in COVID-19 pandemic. The 'best interest' of the patient must always come first. According to the principles of fairness and equality, every patient has the right to equal medical treatment. Although the ethical considerations include achieving the best results and overall balance in terms of minimizing harm to the patient, it is equally important for the society as a whole to allocate available resources. In certain situations, this may mean 'the best medical care for the maximum number of people' (the notion of distributive justice). In a state of emergency, ethical decisions require specific approach due to the existing imbalance between the need for and the supply of healthcare resources. Under these circumstances, healthcare professionals should have relevant decisions about patient interventions at their disposal. The provisions of SRCEP affirm that most often such decisions will be based on some contextual (additional) parameters, such as safety, availability and resource needs, as well as the expected outcome for each patient individually.

3. In what type(s) of document(s) are the allocation criteria set? Is it in binding or non-binding guidelines, in the law, or in another type of document?

The law is silent on the issue of rationing principles in healthcare: there are no outright legal instructions for prioritization decisions in hospital setting in Serbia. By failing to set formal criteria for allocation of scarce medical resources, the legislator leaves this matter to the associations of healthcare professionals and medical and scientific institutions. Therefore, some rationing principles are dispersed across the codes of medical ethics, medical protocols and other documents of this kind. However, even the codes and protocols do not set explicit criteria for rationing decisions.

276 Karel Turza, *Medicina i društvo: Uvod u medicinsku etiku* (Libri Medicorum 2015), 56, 66, 88.

The occasional allocation principles may only be deduced from some documents adopted by the associations of medical professionals.

For instance, the Medical Chamber of Serbia adopted CME in 2016, in which it affirms the principles of diligence and equality, but also states that medical doctor should behave rationally and cost-effectively, in order to achieve the best results in relation to the available financial resources.

Furthermore, DIC (recently approved by the Serbian Association of Anaesthesiologists and Intensivists) allows for prioritizing the patients based on their age, comorbidities and clinical frailty, in conjunction with their prognosis.

In addition, SRCEP (introduced by the Serbian Resuscitation Council) tries to reconcile the imperative to minimize harm to an individual patient, with the need to allocate available resources in a rational manner. This document affirms that sometimes resources must be apportioned in a way that brings *"the best medical care for the maximum number of people"*.

The codes and protocols bring some legal certainty to healthcare professionals, as they can be taken into account in any proceedings in which it is necessary to determine whether the healthcare professional has acted in accordance with the standards of medical profession and with due professional diligence.

4. Are providers of health care obliged by the law to provide (urgent) care to all patients? If the answer is yes, are there any legally recognised exceptions from this duty?

According to the Health Protection Act (HPA in further text)[277] the public interest in healthcare in Serbia includes: prevention, suppression and elimination of epidemics of infectious diseases; emergency medical care to persons of unknown residence and other persons who otherwise do not hold the right to emergency medical treatment; prevention and elimination of the health consequences of crisis and emergency situations. These activities are fully funded from the budget of the Republic of Serbia. HPA assures the right to healthcare to each citizen, and also to foreign citizens and stateless persons who are permanently or temporarily residing in Serbia. These individuals also have a duty to protect and improve their own health, the health of others and the living and working conditions of everyone. A person passing through the territory of Serbia also has the right to emergency medical care.[278]

The healthcare institutions are obliged by law to provide emergency medical care to everyone, and to organize and implement measures in case of crisis and emergency situations. Private practices are also obliged to provide emergency medical care, and to participate, at the invitation of the competent state authority, in

277 Zakon o zdravstvenoj zaštiti, *Službeni glasnik RS*, 25/2019, Article 17.

278 HPA, Article 3.

prevention and suppression of infectious diseases, and in protection and rescue of the population in case of crisis and emergency situations.[279]

Under the Health Insurance Act (HIA in further text),[280] the patients treated for infectious diseases are covered by health insurance, even if they do not normally qualify for the status of an insured person. In addition, HPA provides that for the foreigners suffering from infectious diseases, which require a person to be placed under medical supervision in accordance with the regulations governing the protection of the population against infectious diseases, health care costs will be reimbursed from the budget of the Republic of Serbia.[281]

HPA prescribes a duty of a healthcare professional to render healthcare services in keeping with professional standards, guidelines of good practice, medical protocols and codes of professional ethics. Moreover, healthcare professionals assume professional, ethical, criminal, civil and disciplinary liability for their work, in line with the law.[282]

HPA also prescribes that healthcare professionals may exercise conscientious objection: they may refuse to provide healthcare services which are contrary to their conscience, beliefs, or international rules of medical ethics. However, healthcare professionals can not refuse to provide *emergency* medical care by reason of their conscientious objection.[283]

In addition to everything said, every medical doctor is obliged under CME to always and everywhere provide emergency medical assistance to a person who is in an imminent danger to life and health, within the limits of his abilities and knowledge, and regardless of whether he is on duty or not, and whether he is explicitly asked for help or not. If a patient or injured person needs medical assistance that a doctor is not able to provide, the doctor is obliged to take appropriate measures to assure that the patient gets adequate health care (Article 8 CME). Furthermore, medical doctor is obliged to participate in the organization and provision of medical assistance in cases of emergency, including epidemics, mass accidents, natural and other disasters (Article 9 CME).

5. On what legal basis is it possible to apply the allocation criteria in practice?

As said before, healthcare professionals are legally bound to render healthcare services in line with the professional standards, guidelines of good practice, medical protocols and codes of professional ethics, and they bear professional, ethical, criminal, civil and disciplinary liability for their work.[284]

---

279 HPA, Article 62 para. 1(1, 2 and 9) and Article 42 para. 1(1 and 2).
280 Zakon o zdravstvenom osiguranju, *Službeni glasnik RS*, 25/2019, Article 16, para. 1(5).
281 HPA, Article 239 para. 1(4).
282 HPA Article 155.
283 HPA Article 156.
284 HPA Article 155.

The decisions of medical professionals, their acts and omissions, are evaluated against the standard of a hypothetical reasonable and very diligent expert of pertinent specialization. Ordinary negligence in a professional context is always measured against the higher (objective) standard of appropriate conduct. In civil proceedings, the rebuttable statutory presumption of fault applies,[285] and in order to refute this presumption, a medical professional would have to prove that he acted in accordance with the standard of reasonable and very careful expert of relevant specialization.

Medical professionals are expected to abide by the standards of medical profession. In the context of allocation of scarce healthcare resources, their legal position would be much better, if there were explicit official protocols or guidelines for rationing decisions. Unfortunately, there are no such protocols. The court may appoint a medical expert after the fact, with the request to clarify the standards of professional behaviour under the circumstances of the case.

Medical doctors may use specialized standards of medical profession, such as admission protocols and triage procedures, to prioritize among the patients on admission. In such cases, medical professionals could try to protect themselves from legal liability by proving that they have abided by professional standards, and that a hypothetical reasonable and exceptionally diligent health expert of relevant specialization would decide or do the same under the circumstances. In the absence of more specific guidelines and protocols for the situations of insufficiency of resources, health professionals have to resort to the general standards of medical profession.

6. What level of legal certainty do the health professionals and the health care providers have when applying the allocation criteria?

The existence of a clear protocol for ethically and morally delicate situations would be of immense assistance to health professionals. It would make it easier for them to make critical decisions under time pressure and in stressful situations. Also, it would help the professionals deal with loss and sense of personal liability for an unwanted outcome. It would be much easier to make rationing decisions knowing that medical workers may not be held legally liable as long as they are diligently following the official protocols and settled standards of medical profession. However, the allocation criteria are not explicitly codified in Serbia. If there are any rationing principles, they are fragmentary and scattered across the protocols. The reader is never certain if she is deducing the rationing criteria from the protocols, or reading the criteria into these documents.

[285] Zakon o obligacionim odnosima (Law of Obligations – *LO*), *Službeni list SFRJ*, br. 29/78, 39/85, 45/89, 57/89, *Službeni list SRJ*, 31/93, *Službeni list SCG*, 1/2003, *Službeni glasnik RS*, 18/2020, Article 154, para. 1.

In addition, the mere adherence to guidelines and protocols, where there are any, strongly supports that the health professional did not act negligently, but it does not exclude every possibility of his fault. In other words, a medical doctor may be liable for negligence, even if his behaviour was not in violation of any professional guidelines or protocols. And also, there are yet no court decisions or decisions of professional bodies applying general standards of medical profession to the specific COVID-19 situations of scarcity. So, it is fair to conclude that medical professionals make rationing decisions under a high level of legal uncertainty.

7. What are the civil and criminal liability implications of allocation of scarce health care resources? Have there already been any related legal suits and/or criminal proceedings?

As stated before, HPA imposes a duty to medical workers to provide healthcare services in line with professional standards, guidelines of good practice, medical protocols and codes of professional ethics. HPA also specifies that medical workers assume professional, ethical, criminal, civil and disciplinary liability for their work, in line with the law. However, neither civil nor criminal proceedings have been initiated so far against any medical professional or healthcare institution in connection with the rationing decisions in hospital setting during the COVID-19 pandemic. There have only been several criminal proceedings against patients for non-compliance with the health regulations during the epidemic (violation of home isolation).[286]

a) Disciplinary liability of medical professionals.

Under Article 185 of HPA, a medical professional may temporarily lose their professional licence in disciplinary proceedings before the corresponding professional chamber, for committing a professional error and thus causing harm to a patient or worsening the condition of the patient's health. HPA defines professional error as negligent performance of health services, which results in injury, impairment, deterioration of health or loss of a body part of the patient. The notion of professional error includes the instances of non-compliance with the established standards of medical profession. A professional error may be made by omission. Medical professional may also temporarily lose the professional licence for being convicted to imprisonment of six month or longer for an intentional criminal offence, or for being convicted to imprisonment for a criminal offence against human health (either intentional or negligent).

---

[286] Presuda Višeg suda u Užicu, Kz 139/2020, 4 November 2020; Presuda Vrhovnog kasacionog suda, Kzz 1516/2020, 20 January 2021. See: Krivični zakonik (Criminal Code, CC in further text), *Službeni glasnik RS*, 85/2005, 88/2005, 107/2005, 72/2009, 111/2009, 121/2012, 104/2013, 108/2014, 94/2016, 35/2019, Article 248.

b) Criminal liability of medical professionals.

A medical doctor or other medical worker may be criminally liable for negligent provision of medical care, if he uses obviously inadequate means and devices, or obviously inadequate method of treatment, or fails to observe appropriate standards of hygiene, or acts obviously unconscientiously, and thereby causes deterioration of a person's health. The punishment shall be imprisonment of three months to three years. If the same offence is committed out of criminal negligence, the prescribed punishment is either a fine (a monetary penalty) or imprisonment of up to one year.[287]

A medical doctor may also be criminally liable for failure to provide medical assistance, if he refuses, contrary to his duty, to provide medical assistance to a person that is in need of such assistance and in immediate danger of death, serious bodily injury or serious impairment of health. The punishment shall be either a fine or imprisonment of up to two years. If the offence resulted in serious bodily injury or serious impairment of health, the prescribed punishment is imprisonment of six months to five years, and if the consequence was death, the penalty shall be imprisonment of one to eight years.[288]

The unlawfulness of human actions may be excluded by necessity in Serbian criminal law. CC prescribes that an act will not constitute criminal offence, if it was committed in necessity, because the condition of unlawfulness will not have been met. And, the necessity exists where the act is committed for the purpose of the committer averting from his good, or from the good of another person, a concurrent unprovoked danger which could not be otherwise repelled, provided that, in so doing, the harm done is not greater than the harm that was avoided. Furthermore, a committer who caused the danger himself, but out of negligence, or who exceeded the limitations of necessity, may have their penalty mitigated. Where a committer exceeded the limitations of necessity under particularly mitigating circumstances, punishment may be remitted. Finally, necessity does not exist where the committer had a duty to expose himself to the danger which threatened.[289]

Furthermore, the patient's consent may not exclude the liability of a medical doctor for negligent provision of medical assistance. Also, a medical doctor cannot avoid the duty to provide medical assistance by invoking the risk of infection, that is to say, the possibility to be infected himself in the course of providing medical assistance to the patient.[290]

When it comes to rationing decisions in hospital settings, the scholars of criminal law estimate that, among the available criminal offences, it would be the easiest to establish liability for the negligent provision of medical assistance (Article 251

[287] CC, Article 251; Zoran Stojanović, *Komentar Krivičnog zakonika* (Službeni glasnik 2016), 772–778; Ljubiša Lazarević, *Komentar Krivičnog zakonika Republike Srbije* (Savremena administracija 2006), 661–665.

[288] CC, Article 253; Z. Stojanović (2016), 778–780; Lj. Lazarević (2006), 667–670.

[289] CC, Article 20.

[290] Lj. Lazarević (2006), 665, 668.

CC).[291] The conditions for such liability include a manifest negligence of the physician or other medical professional, demonstrated in their gross disregard for the accepted medical standards in the provision of emergency and intensive medical care, which has caused deterioration of the patient's health. Here, even the slightest shortening of life is sufficient to ascertain causation and liability for death as a consequence.[292]

Medical doctor has a legal duty to provide emergency medical assistance to a person who is in an imminent danger to life or health, *i.e.*, a duty to act in a certain manner, and in line with the applicable standards, in order to prevent damaging effects to human life and bodily integrity. And where there is more then one person in danger and not enough resources to provide everyone with the much needed assistance, a doctor may find herself in a morally challenging situation of being forced to make a choice. So, at least in theory, the question may arise of possible criminal liability for a rationing decision that deviates from the established generally binding criteria. And, exactly for this type of situations, some legal systems have developed the institute of the so-called collision of duties, which may constitute either an independent cause for exclusion of unlawfulness, or a type of necessity. The collision of duties directed towards the goods or legally protected interests of equal values is a much needed separate defence to a criminal charge in the legal systems in which necessity may be invoked only if one of the endangered goods or interests is more significant or valuable than another. There are no rules on collision of duties in Serbian legislation, and the courts may only consider applying the rules on necessity in these situations. However, the rules on necessity in Serbian law allow for the exclusion of unlawfulness in cases where the threatened goods are of equal values (for instance, two human lives).[293]

Under Serbian statutory provisions on necessity, the court should not only compare abstract values of the endangered goods (*e.g.* human life is always more valuable than bodily integrity or property interest), but also the impending harms. The harm that was eventually inflicted must not be greater than the harm that was effectively avoided. And, for comparison of the potential harms, some additional criteria may be taken into account, such as the gravity of danger the goods are exposed to, the severity of medical condition of each patient, their age, prognosis and concomitant diseases, etc. *Vuković* convincingly stresses out that it is not that two (or more) lives are in collision; it is that two (or more) lives are in danger, and the danger may be scored or graded.[294] It would be nearly impossible to show that one life should

291 Responsibility for murder is less likely, although the doctor is regularly aware that giving priority to another patient, or removing the patient from the treatment, may lead to his death. The criminal offense of negligent provision of medical care has both intentional and negligent form. However, it is undisputed in Serbian legal doctrine that the intentional form includes only indirect intent (*dolus eventualis*), and not direct intent (*dolus directus*). Everything according to: Igor Vuković, 'Kolizija dužnosti kao osnov opravdanja u okolnostima pandemije' [2020], 2 Crimen 132, 133.

292 I. Vuković (2020), 133.

293 The whole paragraph is based on: I. Vuković (2020), 133–134.

294 According to: I. Vuković (2020), 135–136.

have been given preference over another and that some other person (and not the alleged victim) should have been deprived of the treatment instead; in other words, that the treatment should have been provided to the alleged victim to the detriment of another patient. Nonetheless, Vuković insists that this is not the issue of comparing two lives, but the issue of comparing the two perils.

To sum up, the conditions of criminal liability for making a necessary rationing decision in the situation of scarcity caused by pandemic would include manifest negligence on the part of a physician or other medical worker, demonstrated in gross disregard for the established standards of medical profession, which resulted in deterioration of the patient's health. The medical worker could try to invoke necessity as a defence, by showing that the allocation decision was made with a view of averting a concurrent unprovoked danger from one patient, which could not be otherwise repelled and that, in doing so, the harm done to another patient was not greater than the harm which threatened the patient who received the treatment. And, according to the country's leading criminal law scholars, when deciding on the existence of necessity, it is legitimate not only to compare the abstract values of the endangered goods, but also to compare the gravity of approaching harms.

In the absence of statutory norms and court practice, prominent legal scholars in Serbia have not closed off the possibility of removing one patient from the ICU bed and ventilator in order to provide these resources to another patient who has a better chance of surviving for longer. *Vuković* points out that the rules of medical profession require constant review of the health condition of the patients connected to ventilators. And if the rules on necessity apply in these cases, at least according to Serbian criminal law, not only the value of the endangered goods must be compared, but also the gravity of the dangers, as well as the impending harms. This means that some additional relevant criteria need to be taken into account, such as the chance of improving health of a patient by keeping him on the ventilator, the duration of his treatment in relation to how many other people could be saved over the same period of time, the probability of survival, etc.[295]

Finally, and as said before, medical doctors may use standards of their profession, such as admission protocols and triage procedures, to relieve themselves from legal liability by proving that they have abided by the well-settled standards of medical profession. If a medical doctor adheres to the given standard of medical profession, it is less likely that his conduct would be assessed as negligent by the court, as there is no breach of duty for which he would be held accountable.[296] But, the allocation criteria are not explicitly codified in Serbia. If there are any rationing principles, they are fragmentary and scattered across the medical guidelines and

295 I. Vuković (2020), 142.

296 Medical error implies disregard for either the generally accepted medical standard, if any, or the general standard of care, which the court may establish under the circumstances by appointing a medical expert. Igor Vuković, 'Pojam lekarske greške i krivična odgovornost' [2013], 10 Pravni život 639, 641. See also: Marija Karanikić Mirić, 'Krivica kao osnov deliktne odgovornosti lekara u građanskom pravu' [2013], 10 Pravni život, 623.

protocols. And in any case, the physician's adherence to the settled standards of medical profession indicates that there was no negligence on his side, but criminal proceedings against him are still possible.

For instance, the Supreme Court of Cassation held that a medical doctor may be criminally liable for negligent provision of medical care, even if his actions were not in violation of the relevant national guide of good clinical practice. The existing national guides of good clinical practice are relevant only in the context of moral obligation of medical doctors to apply all available knowledge and achievements of modern medicine in the process of diagnosis and treatment. The prosecution does not have to prove that a medical doctor has acted contrary to the applicable national clinical guidelines in order to prove that his actions were negligent.[297]

c) Civil liability of medical professionals.

Actions for damages against medical professionals in Serbia are consistently brought in tort. It is considered that in the state-owned medical institutions patients do not enter into a contract either with the institution, or with the health care professional who treats them, and they are commonly covered by the mandatory health insurance. A patient may, at least in theory, bring an action for breach of contract against a private institution. However, there are no such cases as yet: when it comes to medical malpractice, the patients routinely bring claims in tort against both the private and the state health institutions.[298]

The healthcare professionals as employees are reasonably protected from direct tort liability to the patients and their relatives, and from the recourse claims of medical institutions as employers. This protection comes from the general statutory rules on employer's vicarious liability:[299]

The direct claim in tort against medical doctors or nurses requires a proof of their intent. The existence of tortious intent must be proven by the plaintiff, *i.e.*, the patient. Furthermore, the employer's recourse claim necessitates a proof of either intent or gross (professional) negligence of the medical professional as a tortfeasor. The existence of the qualified fault of the health professional (his gross negligence or intent) must be proven by his employer (the medical institution) in the recourse proceedings.

So, it is very hard to establish direct tortious liability of the medical professional who has acted in the course of his employment: a medical doctor or nurse shall be directly liable for damage caused during the course of their employment only if there was the highest degree of fault on their side, which the injured party must prove. In such cases, the employer and his employee shall be jointly and severally liable towards the victim; none of them can use the liability of another as a defence against the injured party.

---

297 Presuda Vrhovnog kasacionog suda, Kz 1129/2014, 19 November 2014.

298 Everything according to: M. Karanikić Mirić (2013), 623; Marija Karanikić Mirić, *Serbia* in (Britt Weyts, IEL Tort Law, Kluwer Law International 2019).

299 LO, Articles 170 and 171.

The conditions of vicarious liability of the healthcare institution for damage caused by their employees (the medical staff) are, first of all, moral and/or material damage suffered by the patient; secondly, the causal link between the action (including omissions) of the employee and the damage incurred by the patient; and finally, the medical worker needs to be at fault. There is a rebuttable statutory presumption of the employee's ordinary (professional) negligence. And, which is important, the presumed degree of the medical professional's fault is sufficient for establishing vicarious liability of the healthcare institution as his employer. It is difficult to prove causation in the cases of medical malpractice before Serbian courts. The courts heavily rely on medical expert witnesses in these matters.

The objective standard of legitimate social expectations to act as a reasonable and diligent person is elevated in professional setups. If damage is caused by a medical professional in the course of, or in connection to providing medical care or assistance to a patient, the medical professional is considered to be at fault if, under the given circumstances, he has failed to act as a hypothetical reasonable and very careful professional of corresponding specialization.[300] The statutory presumption of ordinary professional negligence applies. However, and as said before, the rebuttably presumed degree of fault of a medical professional is not sufficient for establishing his direct liability to the patient. The injured party must prove tortious intent of the medical professional, before the court may ascertain his liability.

If the health professional suffers from certain individual shortcomings, weaknesses or lack of knowledge, which prevents him from reaching the heightened professional standard of reasonableness and care, this may not excuse him from liability. And, if the health professional has possession of some additional special skills, knowledge or insight, which renders him even more capable and knowledgeable than normally requested, the measure of what is legitimately expected from him further elevates, and he shall be obliged to employ all of his extra capacities for the benefit of his patient.

The health institution may relieve itself from vicarious liability by proving that there was no fault on the side of its employee. The institution may not be excused from liability by proving lack of its own fault, for example, by proving that it has diligently chosen, supervised and instructed its employee. The way in which the health institution itself behaved bears no relevance.

The patients and their relatives may have their separate claims for compensation against the healthcare institutions and professionals. In case of death of a person, the court may award equitable compensation for psychological pain to the members of the deceased's immediate family: his spouse or cohabitant; parents; children; and also to brothers and sisters who have lived with the deceased in a shared household. And, in case of particularly serious disability of a person, the court may award

300 In detail: Miodrag V. Orlić, 'Evolucija shvatanja o krivici (u srpskom pravu) sa osvrtom na pojam profesionalne krivice' [2010] in Mirko Vasiljević (ed.) Private Law Reform in South East Europe: Liber Amicorum Christa Jessel-Holst 263.

equitable compensation for psychological pain to his spouse or cohabitant, parents and children.[301] In addition, in case of loss of support, the court shall award indemnity in the form of annuities to a person who was supported, or entitled to demand support from the deceased. When deciding on the amount of the annuities, the court shall take all circumstances of the case into account, but in any case, the awarded sum cannot exceed the amount the injured party would have been receiving from the deceased, had he not died.[302]

Under the stated conditions, one may assume that medical professionals, along with healthcare institutions as their employers, could be held liable for moral and material damage caused by their decisions on allocation of scarce medical resources during pandemic, provided that a hypothetical reasonable and very diligent expert of corresponding medical specialization would have made a different rationing decision under the same circumstances. And, if the medical professional was conscientiously following the official protocols and settled standards of medical profession, it will be less likely that his conduct (the allocation decision he made in scarcity) would be assessed as negligent by the court.

The courts have generally rejected the idea of strict liability of medical doctors and other health professionals for medical malpractice.[303] Health professional *liability insurance* is available in Serbia, but it is not mandatory.

In addition to everything, there are special rules of Serbian tort law on liability in emergency cases, *i.e.*, special liability in tort for omitting to render help to a person whose life or bodily integrity is in obvious peril, if the help needed could be rendered without danger to self *or others*. The rules apply both to medical professionals and non-professionals, with the difference that legitimate expectations of reasonableness, diligence and self-exposure to danger are significantly higher towards the medical professionals.[304] These provisions are exceptionally rarely used in practice, if ever. It is a type of fault-based liability of a person who causes foreseeable damage, by failing to help another person whose life or bodily integrity is in an obvious danger. Liability for the failure to rescue may be established solely if the assistance could have been rendered without risk to oneself or to others. The general rebuttable statutory presumption of fault does not apply in this case.[305] The court may exonerate the tortfeasor from duty to compensate, or reduce the awarded compensation, *on the grounds of equity*.[306] This kind of tort liability is excluded per

301 LO, Article 201.

302 LO, Article 194.

303 Some authors advocate strict liability for damages caused to the medical research participants and to the blood donors. For example: Jakov Radišić, *Medicinsko pravo* (Nomos 2004), 170.

304 LO, Article 182. Marija Karanikić Mirić, 'Građanskopravna odgovornost zbog uskraćivanja pomoći' in Đorđe Ignjatović (ed.), *Kaznena reakcija u Srbiji* (III deo, Pravni fakultet Univerziteta u Beogradu 2013), 187.

305 Đorđe Nikolić, 'Odgovornost zbog uskraćivanja neophodne pomoći' [1992] 9–10 Pravni život, 1337, 1343.

306 Vladan Stanković, 'Član 182. Odgovornost zbog uskraćivanja neophodne pomoći' in Slobodan Perović and Dragoljub Stojanović (eds.), Komentar Zakona o obligacionim odnosima (Pravni

definition, if rendering assistance to one person would mean putting another person in peril. However, and at least in theory, since these provisions are virtually never actually used, it should be considerably easier for the non-professionals to exonerate themselves from this type of tort liability, then for the professionals (*e.g.* medical doctors and nurses, policemen, firefighters). In any case, this institute has received much more attention in legal theory then in the practice of the courts in Serbia.

Furthermore, one should examine the relevance of impossibility of performance. It is important to reiterate here that actions for damages against medical professionals in Serbia are consistently brought in tort. There is a clear and important distinction in Serbian law between tortious liability (liability in delict, extra-contractual liability) and liability for violation or failure of a pre-existing duty to the other party to the obligation. The latter kind of liability is usually called contractual liability, though the infringed pre-existent duty in question does not have to be a contractual duty. Parties to the obligation must exercise due care in performing their commitments to one another.[307] In general, they have to observe the standard of a hypothetical diligent person, businessperson or professional, depending on the context. However, this principle may only be invoked if the parties are already mutually legally bound.

Insofar as tortious liability is concerned, it is considered that there are no pre-existing obligations between the parties, and the obligation (to compensate for the damage) arises from the very fact that damage to one was caused by the conduct of another. The codified principle of *neminem laedere*[308] applies as a general standard of behaviour that runs to all others, irrespective of any prior legally recognized mutual relationship.

As many other European legal systems, Serbian law accepts the principle 'impossibilium nulla obligatio est', meaning that there is no obligation to perform the impossible. If objective impossibility of performance is initial, the obligation may not even arise, and if impossibility subsequently occurs, the obligation will cease to exist. Therefore, the obligation terminates *ipso lege*, if its performance becomes objectively impossible due to the circumstances for which the debtor is not liable.[309]

In the context of liability in tort, there is no obligation among the parties prior to the occurrence of damage, so impossibility as a defence would not be appropriate to these situations. Also, in a hypothetical setting where a physician must allocate a scarce resource (*e.g.* a ventilator) to one of the two of his patients in need, the physician cannot reasonably point out against any of the two patients that it was impossible to provide them with assistance. It was 'only' impossible to provide

fakultet u Kragujevcu 1980); Đorđe Nikolić, 'Član 182. Odgovornost zbog uskraćivanja neophodne pomoći' in Slobodan Perović (ed.), Komentar Zakona o obligacionim odnosima (Savremena administracija 1995), 422–433; Stojan Cigoj, 'Član 182. Odgovornost zbog uskraćivanja neophodne pomoći' in Borislav T. Blagojević and Vrleta Krulj (eds.), Komentar Zakona o obligacionim odnosima (Savremena administracija 1983), 682–683.

307 LO, Article 18.

308 LO, Article 16.

309 LO, Article 354, para. 1.

assistance to both of them at the same time, so the physician would have to justify the allocation decision he had made.

Finally, where damage is caused in the state of necessity, the injured party (*i.e.*, a third person who was injured in the event of averting the approaching damage) is entitled to seek compensation from the person who is at fault for the state of necessity, that is, from the one who has wrongfully created the danger.[310] These are the situations where one person (the 'rescuer') has taken measures to protect himself or others from an imminent danger, that is, from the impending harm to property, life, body, health, etc. In the course of this action, the rescuer has sustained damage, or has caused damage to another. The rescuer may be excused from liability, under the conditions that (1) the impending harm could not have been avoided in other way than by the harmful conduct in question, and that (2) the damage he has caused is still smaller or less significant than the damage which was averted. In other words, a tortfeasor shall be excused from liability if he proves that he has caused damage in a state of emergency, with a view of escaping an imminent danger of an even more serious and significant impending damage to self or others. Moreover, liability shall lie with the person who has created the hazard, or the risk of damage, that is, with the one who is at fault for the state of necessity. This person shall be liable for damages originating from the attempts to overcome the state of necessity, and suffered by the rescuer, or by the persons in need of rescue. In the context of the COVID-19 epidemic and the liability for damage caused by making an allocation decision under the conditions of scarcity, there is no person that could be held liable for the epidemic, but one could at least contemplate about the existence of a person liable for the exact case of scarcity.

B. Case studies

Case 1

As a result of a rapid worsening of the epidemiological situation, the material and personal capacities have been drastically overloaded in all the hospitals in the country. Within just a few minutes, ambulances transport ten patients to one particular hospital's emergency unit. The patients all need admission to the hospital, preferably to the intensive care unit (ICU). However, only two beds are available there. Other hospitals are overwhelmed too, so it is not possible to transport patients to any of them. All of the ten newly coming patients suffer from COVID-19; they have breathing difficulties, fast-rising fever, and decreasing oxygen saturation. Nevertheless, they differ in age, comorbidities, clinical fragility, and other factors.

Theoretically, the eight patients who cannot be admitted to beds can be placed in improvised settings in the hospital corridors, laying on gurneys or mattresses on the floor. Nevertheless, it will be impossible to provide them with the care they need.

---

310 LO, Article 161, para. 2.

Evaluation of the case

- What criteria can be used to choose the patients who will be admitted to the beds (*i.e.*, what are the possible allocation criteria)?
  The prescribed triage on admission to the ICU, as per DIC, allows for prioritizing the patients based on their age, comorbidities and clinical frailty, in conjunction with their prognosis. On admission to the ICU, it is permissible to maximize benefits by shifting resources to patients with better prognosis. The patients with very reduced functional reserve, disseminated malignancy, extreme life ages combined with severe clinical picture, severe neurological disorders, or in coma, in which no recovery is expected despite the applied mechanical ventilation, can be referred to supportive therapy and care, instead of being admitted to the ICU.
- What legal consequences can this decision have for the health professionals and the hospital? How strong is their legal certainty that there will be no adverse legal consequences if they follow the above-mentioned criteria?
  It is hard to say, given that the allocation criteria are not explicitly codified in Serbia. If there are any rationing principles, they are fragmented and dispersed across the medical guidelines and protocols. When a health professional follows the given standards of his profession, it is less likely that his conduct would be assessed as negligent by the court. However, it is not positive that he will avoid liability simply by proving that he has followed some professional guidelines and protocols. In other words, the adherence to guidelines and protocols, where there are any, strongly supports the claim that there was no negligence on the health professional's side, but it does not exclude every possibility that he has acted in a negligent manner under the existing circumstances.
- What legal defences could the health professionals and the hospital use against a civil lawsuit and/or criminal prosecution for the allocation decision?
  In civil proceedings, the health professionals and the hospital could claim that a hypothetical reasonable and very diligent expert of corresponding medical specialization would have made the same rationing decision under the existing circumstances, or they could try to prove that the impending harm could not have been avoided in other way than by the damaging conduct and that the damage caused by the health professional is still smaller or less significant than the damage which was averted. In criminal proceedings, the health professional could try to prove that he acted out of necessity.

Additional questions

- Would it be legally permissible to lower the standard of care provided to all patients in order to provide at least basic decent care to the newly admitted patients who are placed in the hospital corridors? To what extent?
  During the most severe outbreak of the epidemic, the lowering of the standard of healthcare provided to all patients was necessary in order to provide at least basic care to all admitted patients. Actually, there have been some reports of people literally placed in the hospital corridors. Therefore, in the course of the epidemic,

certain protocols were relaxed in terms of lowering the standard of care, in order to provide medical assistance to as many people as possible. For instance, the *Protocol of securing airway in patients with COVID-19* explicitly states that in case of mass influx of patients, the most experienced anaesthesiologist may be accompanied with only one team member, instead of two. Similarly, at some point it was permitted to import medical devices which had not been tested to the standards that normally apply. In any case, the content of reasonable expectations depends on the circumstances. It seems that it would be permissible in a hospital setting to lower the standard of care provided to all the patients, as long as it could be said that a hypothetical reasonable and very diligent professional of the relevant specialization would act the same under the same circumstances. Of course, the extent of such relaxation of standards is not prescribed. One may only turn to general principles and assume that lowering of the standard of care would not be permitted when it starts to threaten the life of the admitted patients.

Case 2

Two patients in an ICU are suffering from COVID-19. After admission to the hospital, they were provided with the high-flow nasal oxygen therapy (HFNO). During one night, the condition of both patients starts to worsen rapidly. At dawn, it is clear that neither of them will survive without artificial ventilation. However, there is just one ventilator available.

Evaluation of the case

- What criteria can be used to choose which of the two patients will be provided with artificial ventilation and which one will be left without it, possibly to die?
  On admission to the ICU, it is permissible to maximize benefits by shifting resources to patients with better prognosis. The prescribed triage *on admission* to the ICU allows for prioritizing the patients based on their age, comorbidities and clinical frailty, in conjunction with their prognosis (DIC). It appears that the same criteria could be used in the described hypothetical situation.
- What legal consequences can this decision have for the health professionals and the hospital? How strong is their legal certainty that there will be no adverse legal consequences if they follow the above-mentioned criteria?
  As said before, when a health professional follows the given standards of his profession, it is less likely that his conduct would be assessed as negligent by the court. However, it is not assured that he will avoid liability simply by proving that he has followed medical guidelines and protocols.
- What legal defences could the health professionals and the hospital use against a civil lawsuit and/or criminal prosecution for the allocation decision?
  In civil proceedings, the health professionals and the hospital could claim that a hypothetical reasonable and very diligent expert of corresponding medical specialization would have made the same rationing decision under the existing circumstances, or they could try to prove that the impending harm could not have

been avoided in other way than by the damaging conduct and that the damage caused by the health professional is still smaller or less significant than the damage which was averted. In criminal proceedings, the health professional could try to prove that he acted out of necessity.

Additional question

- If the allocation criteria specified in your answer to the first question to this case consisted of the patients' clinical features (such as their age, clinical fragility, etc.), please identify what criteria could be used for the allocation decision if all the relevant clinical features of both patients were practically the same?
  This is extremely hard to say. The 'first-come, first-served' principle seems unsuitable for the described factual setting, and there are no explicit guidelines for the situation where all the relevant clinical features of both patients are virtually the same. The university textbook on medical ethics, used at the most prominent faculty of medicine in the country, maintains that if two patients are the same (of the same age, same comorbidities and same prognosis), which is very rare, then several different material principles of justice may come into play. However, the textbook does not offer a formula or a guideline for this situation, but explicitly leaves it to the medical professional alone, to personally weigh in on all aspects of the individual case, in order to make the least unjust allocation decision.

Case 3

There is a single extracorporeal membrane oxygenation (ECMO) device in the hospital. It is currently being used for an 84-year-old patient suffering from COVID-19, with diabetes as an underlying disease, clinical frailty score (CFS) 6–7 (moderate to severe frailty). It is possible that the patient will survive and will be discharged from the hospital if the ECMO treatment is continued. However, a younger COVID-19 patient is admitted to the hospital. This new patient is 51 years old, otherwise healthy, but her health condition has been rapidly deteriorating. Soon she will most likely need ECMO to survive.

Evaluation of the case

- Can it be legally permissible for the hospital staff to discontinue the ECMO treatment of the older patient and provide palliative care to her in order to save the younger and healthier patient's life? Please keep in mind that the older patient could survive if the treatment continued, but her chances may be lower than those of the younger patient.
  The triage procedure prescribed by DIC affirms that on the admission to the ICU the patients with very reduced functional reserve, disseminated malignancy, extreme life ages combined with severe clinical picture, severe neurological disorders, or in coma, in which no recovery is expected despite the applied mechanical ventilation, can be referred to supportive therapy and care, instead of being admitted to the ICU. It seems that the same criteria would apply in the described

hypothetical situation, and that it would not be permissible to discontinue the ECMO treatment of the older patient in order to try to save the younger and healthier patient's life, as long as the older patient could survive if the treatment continued. It appears that there is no permission for the healthcare workers to remove patients from the ongoing treatment in order to provide the treatment to other patients who have a better chance of surviving for longer. This practice would be unlawful and discriminatory, may qualify as infliction of bodily harm and lead to both criminal and civil liability. Even when the postponement of imminent death only causes inhumane prolongation of suffering for a dying patient, Article 67 of CME stipulates that the medical doctor may effectively reduce treatment to mitigation of the patient's suffering, *only if* the patient has ability to reason, and if he willingly and freely refuses further treatment. However, in the absence of statutory norms and court practice, some prominent legal scholars remain open for the possibility of removing one patient from the treatment in order to provide the treatment to another patient who has a better chance of surviving for longer. *Vuković* points out that the standards of medical profession require constant review of the health condition of the patients connected to ventilators. And if the rules on necessity apply in these cases, at least according to Serbian criminal law, *Vuković* asserts that not only the value of the endangered goods must be compared, but also the gravity of the dangers and the impending harms. This means that additional criteria need to be taken into account, such as the chance of improving health of a patient by keeping him on the ventilator, the duration of his treatment in relation to how many other people could be saved over the same period of time, the probability of survival, etc.

- If the answer to the first question is positive, what specific criteria can be used in clinical decision-making regarding replacing one patient with another with respect to a particular treatment unavailable for all?

  There are no written protocols for this situation. *Vuković* asserts that specific criteria for this type of situations should include: the chance of improving health of a patient by keeping him on the ventilator, the duration of his treatment in relation to how many other people could be saved over the same period of time, the probability of survival, etc.
- What legal consequences can this decision have for the health professionals and the hospital? How strong is their legal certainty that there will be no adverse legal consequences if they follow the above-mentioned criteria?

  The health professionals and the hospital would expose themselves to an elevated risk of liability for the consequences of the decision to discontinue the ECMO treatment of the older patient who could survive if the treatment continued, even if it was for the purposes of trying to save the younger and healthier patient. The level of their legal certainty in prioritizing like this would be exceptionally low.
- What legal defences could the health professionals and the hospital use against a civil lawsuit and/or criminal prosecution for the allocation decision?

  It seems that it would be very hard to escape liability in this situation.

Additional question

- Suppose there are two different scenarios: a) the older patient was admitted to the hospital and provided with the ECMO treatment, and only later, after several days, the younger patient was admitted, and b) the younger patient was admitted before the older patient, however, the older patient required ECMO treatment soon after admission while the younger patient's health condition deteriorated only after a longer time when the ECMO was already occupied (*i.e.*, at the time when the younger patient was admitted to the hospital, she did not yet need it). Would there be any difference in the allocation decision-making between these two scenarios?

  It appears that there would be no difference in the allocation decision-making between the two scenarios.

The list of abbreviations

CC	Criminal Code
CFS	Clinical frailty score
CME	Code of Medical Ethics of the Medical Chamber of Serbia
COVID-19	Coronavirus disease of 2019
DIC	Diagram of initial care for the COVID-19 patients with respiratory failure and their admission to the intensive care unit
ECMO	Extracorporeal membrane oxygenation
EU	European Union
HFNO	High-flow nasal oxygen therapy
HIA	Health Insurance Act
HPA	Health Protection Act
ICU	Intensive care unit
LO	Law of Obligations
SRCEP	Ethical principles and recommendations for prehospital emergency care during the COVID-19 pandemic in the Republic of Serbia

Bibliography

• Legislation

COVID-19 Preporuke, www.uais.rs/covid-19-preporuke-2 accessed 22. May 2021.

Dijagram inicijalnog zbrinjavanja bolesnika s respiratornom insuficijencijom (*Diagram of initial care for the COVID-19 patients with respiratory failure and their admission to the intensive care unit*), www.uais.rs/wp-content/uploads/2020/03/9.COVID-19.Dijagram_inicijalnog_zbrinjavanja_bolesnika.pdf accessed 22. May 2021.

Etička načela i preporuke za prehospitalno urgentno zbrinjavanje tokom pandemije COVID-19 u Republici Srbiji (*Ethical principles and recommendations for prehospital*

emergency care during the COVID-19 pandemic in the Republic of Serbia), https://www.serrc.rs/text.php?opcijaA=txt&strana=115 accessed 22 May 2021.
Kodeks medicinske etike Lekarske komore Srbije (*Code of Medical Ethics of the Medical Chamber of Serbia*), *Službeni glasnik RS*, 104/2016.
Krivični zakonik (*Criminal Code*), *Službeni glasnik RS*, 85/2005, 88/2005, 107/2005, 72/2009, 111/2009, 121/2012, 104/2013, 108/2014, 94/2016, 35/2019.
Obezbeđivanje disajnog puta kod pacijenata s COVID-19 (*Protocol of securing airway in patients with COVID-19*), Serbian Association of Anaesthesiologists and Intensivists, www.uais.rs/wp-content/uploads/2020/03/2.COVID-19_Preporuke_za_intubaciju_SIAARTI_adaptacija.ver_.1.4.-1.pdf accessed 22 May 2021.
Uredba o posebnim tehničkim zahtevima, standardima i primeni medicinskih sredstava za vreme vanrednog stanja nastalog usled bolesti COVID-19 izazvane virusom SARS-CoV-2, *Službeni glasnik RS* 41/2020.
Zakon o obligacionim odnosima (*Law of Obligations*), *Službeni list SFRJ*, br. 29/78, 39/85, 45/89, 57/89, *Službeni list SRJ*, 31/93, *Službeni list SCG*, 1/2003, *Službeni glasnik RS*, 18/2020.
Zakon o zdravstvenoj zaštiti (*Health Protection Act*), *Službeni glasnik RS*, 25/2019.
Zakon o zdravstvenom osiguranju (*Health Insurance Act*), *Službeni glasnik RS*, 25/2019.

• Case law

Presuda Višeg suda u Užicu, Kz 139/2020, 4 November 2020
Presuda Vrhovnog kasacionog suda, Kz 1129/2014, 19 November 2014
Presuda Vrhovnog kasacionog suda, Kzz 1516/2020, 20 January 2021

• Books

Lazarević L, *Komentar Krivičnog zakonika Republike Srbije* (Savremena administracija 2006).
Karanikić Mirić M, *Serbia* in (Britt Weyts, IEL Tort Law, Kluwer Law International 2019).
Radišić J, *Medicinsko pravo* (Nomos 2004).
Stojanović Z, *Komentar Krivičnog zakonika* (Službeni glasnik 2016).
Turza K, *Medicina i društvo: Uvod u medicinsku etiku* (Libri Medicorum 2015).

• Articles

Cigoj S, 'Član 182. Odgovornost zbog uskraćivanja neophodne pomoći' [1983] Borislav T. Blagojević and Vrleta Krulj (eds.), Komentar Zakona o obligacionim odnosima 681.
Gjurašin M, 'Autorizovano izlaganje' [2002] Jakša Barbić (ed.), Godišnjak tribina Pravnog fakulteta u Zagrebu i Kluba pravnika grada Zagreba.
Karanikić Mirić M, 'Građanskopravna odgovornost zbog uskraćivanja pomoći' [2013] Đorđe Ignjatović (ed.), Kaznena reakcija u Srbiji III deo 187.
Karanikić Mirić M, 'Krivica kao osnov deliktne odgovornosti lekara u građanskom pravu' [2013] 10 Pravni život, 623.
Nikolić D, 'Član 182. Odgovornost zbog uskraćivanja neophodne pomoći' [1995] Slobodan Perović (ed.), Komentar Zakona o obligacionim odnosima 421.

Nikolić D, 'Odgovornost zbog uskraćivanja neophodne pomoći' [1992] 9–10 Pravni život, 1337.

Orlić M V, 'Evolucija shvatanja o krivici (u srpskom pravu) sa osvrtom na pojam profesionalne krivice' [2010] Mirko Vasiljević (ed.) Private Law Reform in South East Europe: Liber Amicorum Christa Jessel-Holst 263.

Stanković V, 'Član 182. Odgovornost zbog uskraćivanja neophodne pomoći' [1980] Slobodan Perović and Dragoljub Stojanović (eds.), Komentar Zakona o obligacionim odnosima 540.

Vuković I, ' Kolizija dužnosti kao osnov opravdanja u okolnostima pandemije' [2020], 2 Crimen 132.

Vuković I, ' Pojam lekarske greške i krivična odgovornost' [2013], 10 Pravni život 639.

- **Other secondary sources**

Lebedinski L, 'How effective is healthcare in Serbia?' (*Monitoring social situation in Serbia – MONS*, 26 January 2018), http://mons.rs/how-effective-is-healthcare-in-serbia accessed 22 May 2021.

SOUTH AFRICA

Bernard Wessels
Stellenbosch University

A. Questionnaire

1. What are the criteria for the allocation of scarce health care resources in your country?

The State has not yet provided health care practitioners with legally binding criteria for the allocation of scarce health care resources during the COVID-19 pandemic. In the absence of such national legally-binding criteria, it would appear that most health care practitioners make use of the criteria developed by the Critical Care Society of Southern Africa (CCSSA), (the CCSSA Guidelines),[311] which will be briefly summarised below.[312]

The first point to make regarding resource allocation is that the CCSSA Guidelines envisage each hospital to set up a triage team, who is supposed to be responsible for implementing the guidelines.[313] Where resources allow it, this team should consist of an acute care physician triage officer, an acute care nuse and an administrator.[314]

Secondly, it should be noted that the CCSSA Guidelines are to be applied to all critically ill patients who meet the 'usual indications for ICU beds',[315] and not merely to COVID 19-patients. This means that, when presented with any patient who arrives at hospital and who appears to be in need of critical care, the first health care responders must initially stabilise the patient in question.[316] Along with stabi-

---

311 Critical Care Society of Southern Africa (CCSSA), 'Allocation of Scarce Critical Care Resources During the COVID-19 Public Health Emergency in South Africa' (2 April 2020) <https://criticalcare.org.za/wp-content/uploads/2020/06/V3-2020-May-05-Allocation-of-Scarce-Critical-Care-Resources-During-the-COVID-19-Public-Health-Emergency-in-South-Africa-FINAL-.pdf> accessed 8 June 2020.

312 Although these guidelines appear to be adopted generally in South Africa, they have also been criticised. A full evaluation of such criticism falls outside the scope of this contribution, but see generally Jerome Amir Singh and Keymanthri Moodley, 'Critical care triaging in the shadow of COVID-19: Ethics consideration' (2020) 110 SAMJ 355, 356–357.

313 CCSSA (n 1) 3.

314 CCSSA (n 1) 3.

315 CCSSA (n 1) 4.

316 CCSSA (n 1) 4.

lisation, temporary ventilatory support may also be offered.[317] Once this has been done, the triage team must be called in and tasked to assess the patient for critical resource allocation.[318]

Insofar as resource allocation by the triage team is concerned, the first step requires the team to determine whether a patient requires care in the Intensive Care Unit (ICU).[319] ICU treatment will generally be required where the patient is regarded as critically ill and in need of ventilatory support, or if they require other organ support that can only be found in the ICU.[320] Patients who do not fall within this category, will continuously be monitored outside the ICU and may be reconsidered for ICU treatment at a later stage.[321]

Hereafter, it must be determined whether a patient consents to ICU treatment.[322] Where a critically ill patient does indeed consent, the triage team will be called upon to make an assessment 'of the likelihood of care in the ICU being beneficial.'[323] In this regard, the CCSSA Guidelines state that '[p]atients will not be considered for admission to critical care beds where further therapy is deemed to be futile.'[324] Futility, in turn, is not necessarily related to the degree or pattern of acute organ dysfunction, but takes into account the long-term outcome of treatment.[325] Some examples of futility include brain death, chronic, terminal and irreversible illness as well as irreversible, severe brain damage.[326]

Assuming that none of these futility factors are present in a particular situation and that the patient is likely to benefit from ICU treatment, then the next step for the triage team is to award the patient a score using the so-called Clinical Frailty Scale (CFS).[327] The general idea seems to be that patients with a CFS score of 6 or more

317 CCSSA (n 1) 4.
318 CCSSA (n 1) 4.
319 CCSSA (n 1) 5.
320 CCSSA (n 1) 5.
321 CCSSA (n 1) 5.
322 CCSSA (n 1) 5.
323 CCSSA (n 1) 5.
324 CCSSA (n 1) 5.
325 CCSSA (n 1) 5.
326 CCSSA (n 1) 5.
327 In the South African context, BM Morrow, 'Critical care triage during the COVID-19 pandemic in South Africa: A constitutional imperative!' (2020) 110 SMJ 1176, 1177–1178 writes as follows about frailty and the CFS: *"Frailty is defined as a multidimensional syndrome characterised by a decline in physiological and cognitive reserve, which increases susceptibility to adverse events and poor outcome. There is currently no gold standard for diagnosing frailty. Although the term 'frailty' is most commonly associated with age, this syndrome has also been described in younger cohorts of patients admitted to ICUs. Increased frailty markers have been shown to be highly predictive of poor ICU outcome, including longer duration of ICU and hospital stay, increased post-discharge disability, and increased short- and longer-term mortality. [...] The CFS is a well-established, robust and valid judgement-based assessment tool, frequently used in the ICU, based on information provided by the patient, family or medical records. We acknowledge that the CFS has not been locally validated and that the graphics used in the tool might be negatively slanted against the elderly. We therefore recommend that the CFS should be formally adapted and validated for use in the SA context, with*

will 'be offered a management plan excluding ICU',[328] while patients with a CFS score of below 6 'are prioritized further'.[329] This means that only the patients in this last-mentioned category are really taken into consideration when it comes to the allocation of scarce resources. To decide whether a patient in this category should receive such resources, they must undergo further assessment to determine their 'priority scoring for ICU access.'[330]

It is at this stage that the triage team will use the so-called Sequential Organ Failure Assessment (SOFA) to rate a patient. Using the SOFA, the patient is given a score between 1 and 4 to determine the likelihood of surviving until hospital discharge.[331] In addition, a patient is also allocated a score between 1 and 4 to determine the likelihood of achieving longer-term survival based on the presence or absence of comorbid conditions that may influence survival.[332] Some of the comorbidities listed in the CCSSA Guidelines include Alzheimer's disease, cancer, renal disease and chronic lung disease.[333]

These scores are then added together to produce the patient's total priority scoring for ICU treatment, which may range from 1 to 8.[334] A lower score (between 1 and 3) indicates a higher likelihood of benefiting from critical care, and patients within this category therefore receive priority treatment.[335] An intermediate score (4–5) means that a patient will receive critical care resources if there are available resources after all the patients in the priority group (1–3) have been allocated critical care resources. Finally, a score between 6–8 means that a patient will only receive critical care resources if all other patients in the preceding groups have received resources.

Importantly, if there are so-called 'ties' between patients within the same priority groups, the CCSSA Guidelines determine that the following factors must be considered. First, attention must be given to life-cycle considerations and priority should generally be given to younger patients. This is based on the notion that younger patients have 'had less opportunity to live through life's stages.'[336] A second factor to be considered is whether the patient in question 'perform tasks that are vital to the public health response — specifically those whose work supports the provision of acute care to others.'[337] A person in this category is likely to receive 'heightened priority.'[338]

---

appropriate public stakeholder input, to become more socially and culturally acceptable." See also the CCSSA (n 1) 5, where it is stated that the CFS is not applicable in patients with stable long-term disabilities (for example, cerebral palsy), learning disabilities or autism.

328 CCSSA (n 1) 5.

329 CCSSA (n 1) 5.

330 Singh and Moodley (n 2) 356.

331 CCSSA (n 1) 5.

332 CCSSA (n 1) 5.

333 CCSSA (n 1) 7.

334 CCSSA (n 1) 7.

335 CCSSA (n 1) 7–8.

336 CCSSA (n 1) 8.

337 CCSSA (n 1) 8.

338 CCSSA (n 1) 8.

Finally, the CCSSA Guidelines indicate that, where a patient was triaged with the effect that he or she will not receive scarce healthcare resources, it must be kept in mind that they should still be awarded medical care. Such care may include intensive symptom management and psychosocial support.[339] Also, they should be continuously reassessed to evaluate whether changes in resource availability or the patient's clinical status would warrant provision of critical care services.

In conclusion, it is worth emphasising that a clear set of criteria for resource allocation is of critical importance during any healthcare crisis, including the Covid-19 pandemic. While the CCSSA Guideliness afford practical guidance, it would be preferable if such criteria could be included in a national prioritsation plan authored by the State (Department of Health), which would provide certainty to health care practitioners.

2. What values are the allocation criteria based on?

The CCSSA Guidelines appears to adopt a utilitarian approach, which typically favours the healthy and young.[340] This central idea seems to be to save as many lives as possible and improve patients' years of post-treatment life.[341] Some ethicists have pointed out that the values that underpin the allocation of scarce resources during the COVID-19 pandemic differ from the normal context in the following way: instead of focusing on the individual and concentrating solely on that person's likelihood of benefiting from treatment (like practitioners would in normal circumstance), the focus has now shifted to the well-being of the broader community, 'with most disaster triage guidelines using utilitarian principles aiming to provide the greatest benefit for the greatest number of people.'[342]

The issues surrounding the values upon which the CCSSA Guidelines have been based are very complex and cannot be discussed in detail within this questionnaire. At this stage, it may be mentioned that such a debate would involve evaluating the role of patient autonomy, the conflict between non-maleficence (avoiding harm) and beneficence (doing good), the apparent tension between values such as justice/fairness and efficiency, while topics such as public safety, public interest, transparency, and trust must also be considered.

339 CCSSA (n 1) 8.

340 Singh and Moodley (n 2) 355. See also CCSSA (n 1) 4.

341 Singh and Moodley (n 2) 355. See also Keymanthri Moodley et al, 'What could "fair allocation" during the Covid-19 crisis possibly mean in Sub-Saharan South Africa?' (2020) 50 Hastings Center Report 33, 33–35.

342 Morrow (n 17) 1177.

3. In what type(s) of document(s) are the allocation criteria set? Is it in binding or non-binding guidelines, in the law, or in another type of document?

As mentioned in question 1, the State (Department of Health) has not published legally binding allocation criteria in respect of the COVID-19 pandemic. However, the CCSSA Guidelines, discussed in question 1, appear to be generally followed in practice.

4. Are providers of health care obliged by the law to provide (urgent) care to all patients? If the answer is yes, are there any legally recognised exceptions from this duty?

The legal basis upon which health care is provided in South Africa and limitation of the state's duty to provide access to the constitutional right to health care:
Firstly, it is important to distinguish between the bases upon which health care providers in the public and private health care sectors are obliged to provide medical care to their patients. Arguably, the legal basis for providing medical care in the private health care sector is the contract that is concluded between the patient and the private health care provider. However, in the case of the public health care sector, the legal basis for providing health care may be found in sections 27(1)(a) and (2) of the Constitution, which read as follows: 'Everyone has the right to have access to health care services, including reproductive health care. […] The state must take reasonable legislative and other measures, within its available resources, to achieve the progressive realisation of each of these rights.'[343]

At this stage, it is important to note that South African constitutional law distinguishes between positive and negative constitutional duties.[344] Put simply, this means that, regarding positive duties, the State must 'respect, protect, promote and fulfil the rights in the Bill of Rights.'[345] On the other hand, insofar as negative duties are concerned, the State must not interfere with the constitutional rights of people, including the rights entrenched in section 27(1). Where there is a breach of the

343 The right to access to health care, as set out in section 27 of the Constitution, is one of the human rights identified in chapter of the Constitution, i.e. the Bill of Rights. All of the rights in the Bill of Rights are justiciable. The inclusion of socio-economic rights (like the right to access to health care) as justiciable rights in the Constitution socio-economic rights are regarded as crucial to facilitating the fundamental transformation of South African society. For an examination of the implications of the transformative nature of the South African Constitution for the adjudication of socio-economic rights, see generally S Liebenberg, *Socio-Economic Rights: Adjudication under a transformative Constitution* (Juta 2010).

344 Ignatius Michael Rautenbach and Roxan Venter, *Rautenbach-Malherbe Constitutional Law* (7th ed, LexisNexis 2018) 437–438.

345 Section 7(2) of the Constitution.

negative duty, ie where the State interferes with the right to access to health care,[346] it is not the end of the matter, and the State will be provided with an opportunity to justify such an infringement. This may be done through section 36(1) of the Constitution, which stipulates that the rights in the Bill of Rights 'may be limited only in terms of law of general application to the extent that the limitation is reasonable and justifiable in an open and democratic society based on human dignity, equality and freedom, taking into account all relevant factors,' which includes the nature of the right, the importance of the purpose of the limitation, the nature and extent of the limitation, the relation between the limitation and its purpose and less restrictive means to achieve the purpose.

However, the State's constitutional duty to provide access to health care services under section 27(2) of the Constitution is regarded as a positive constitutional duty.[347] Furthermore, as the language in section 27(2) reflects, the State has a qualified positive duty to give effect to the right to access to health care services.[348] Indeed, it refers to 'reasonable legislative [...] measures', 'available resources' and 'progressive realisation'. Rautenbach explains how these terms have been given content to by the courts in the following way.[349] First, 'reasonable legislative and other measures' are understood as imposing a duty on the State to establish coherent programmes which '(a) are capable of facilitating the realisation of the rights, (b) allocate responsibilities and tasks to the different spheres of government, (c) ensure that appropriate resources are available; (d) are implemented in a reasonable way; and (e) provide for those whose needs are most urgent.'[350] Secondly, when it is said that the State must ensure the '[p]rogressive realisation of the right' in question, it means 'that it is recognised that the rights cannot be realised immediately, but that the State is required to move as expeditiously and effectively as possible towards the goal.'[351] Of course, it means that, where the State has failed to take steps to realise the right in question, then the courts will 'require it to take such steps.'[352] It seems clear that, where no provisions have been made for 'those most desperately in need,'[353] the State's inaction will be regarded as unreasonable. Thirdly, the reference to '[w]ithin available resources' further limits the

346 An example of where this may happen is 'where the state closes a clinic already providing basic health care to people in a district, making it more difficult or impossible for them to access health care'— see Pierre De Vos & Warren Freedman (eds), *South African Constitutional Law in Context* (2nd ed, OUP 2020) para 17.7.3.

347 Rautenbach and Venter (n 34) 437–438.

348 See generally Liebenberg (n 33) 82; De Vos and Freedman (n 36) para 17.7.3.

349 See Rautenbach and Venter (n 34) 438. See also De Vos and Freedman (n 36) para 17.7.3; *Soobramoney v Minister of Health* 1998 (1) SA 765 (CC); *Government of the Republic of South Africa v Grootboom* 2001 (1) SA 46 (CC); *Khosa v Minister of Social Development; Mahlaule v Minister of Social Development* 2004 (6) SA 505 (CC); *Mazibuko v City of Johannesburg* 2010 (4) SA 1 (CC).

350 Rautenbach and Venter (n 34) 438; *Mazibuko v City of Johannesburg* 2010 (4) SA 1 (CC). See also Liebenberg (n 33) 132–227.

351 Rautenbach and Venter (n 34) 438.

352 Rautenbach and Venter (n 34) 438.

353 Rautenbach and Venter (n 34) 438.

State's positive duty to further the relevant right. Importantly, particularly in the context of the Covid-19 pandemic, this means that 'the rate at which the goal is achieved and the reasonableness of the measures employed, are governed by the availability of resources.'[354] In other words, when resources are limited, the courts will expect rationing and prioritisation as inevitable measures.[355] Notwitshtanding, the rationing decisions, prioritisation and allocation criteria are indeed subject to judicial control and oversight.[356]

All of this seems to mean that the positive duty on the State to provide access to health care has been qualified and, ultimately, where someone alleges that the State has failed to comply with its positive duty under section 27(2) of the Constitution, a different model of review will be adopted than what is the case where a negative constitutional duty has been infringed. Ultimately, the approach that is adopted to determine whether an infringement of the positive duty in section 27(2) can be justified, is the so-called reasonableness review.[357] In this regard, as Liebenberg notes:

"[T]he central question that the Court asks is whether the means chosen are reasonably capable of facilitating the realisation of the socio-economic rights in question. The Court's approach is designed to allow government a margin of discretion relating to the specific policy choices adopted to give effect to socio-economic rights."[358]

In this regard, she refers to the seminal judgment in *Government of the Republic of South Africa v Grootboom*, where it was stated as follows:[359]

"A court considering reasonableness will not enquire whether other more desirable or favourable measures could have been adopted, or whether public money could have been better spent. The question would be whether the measures that have been adopted are reasonable. It is necessary to recognise that a wide range of possible measures could be adopted by the state to meet its obligations. Many of these would meet the requirement of reasonableness. Once it is shown that the measures do so, this requirement is met."

If we apply all of this to the COVID-19 context, it may be said that, where a public health care facility (eg a State hospital) allegedly breaches its constitutional duty to provide access to health care, it seems that the crucial question will be whether the State (in this instance the State hospital in question) conducted itself reasonably in the circumstances. Moreover, the highest court in the country, the Constitutional Court, has indicated that a significant measure of deference must be given to the medical authorities in devising and applying the criteria for the allocation of scarce health care resources.[360] Also, the consensus view appears to be that courts 'will be

354 Rautenbach and Venter (n 34) 438.
355 Rautenbach and Venter (n 34) 438.
356 Rautenbach and Venter (n 34) 438.
357 See De Vos and Freedman para (n 36) 17.7.3.1.1; Rautenbach and Venter (n 34) 443–445.
358 Liebenberg (n 33) 151.
359 2001 (1) SA 46 para 41.
360 See *Soobramoney v Minister of Health* 1998 (1) SA 765 (CC); *Government of the Republic of South Africa v Grootboom* 2001 (1) SA 46 (CC); Liebenberg (n 33) 34–76.

slow to interfere with rational decisions taken in good faith by the political organs and medical authorities whose responsibility it is to deal with such matters.'[361]

The constitutional right to emergency medical treatment and its potential limitation: Insofar as emergency or urgent medical treatment is concerned, it is important to emphasise that section 27(3) of the Constitution imposes a duty, which is framed in negative terms, on health care providers, which dictates that they may not refuse emergency medical treatment.[362] It is not a positive duty that compels them to provide emergency medical treatment. Furthermore, unlike sections 27(1) and (2), it would appear that section 27(3) applies not only to the State (ie the provision of health care services in the public health care sector), but also to private natural and juristic persons (ie the provision of health care services in the private health care sector).[363] In the leading judgment on section 27(3), the Constitutional Court dismissed the 'argument that s 27(3) should be construed [...] so as to encompass a right to life-saving treatment at State expense where a patient is unable to afford private treatment.'[364] Also, and important in the Covid 19-context, the Constitutional Court has suggested that the right to emergency medical treatment is restricted to currently available emergency medical facilities.[365] So, there would be no infringement of the right if there simply are no emergency medical facilities or scarce resources available. In short, the Constitutional Court has confirmed that there is a duty on health care providers to provide emergency medical treatment, but it also indicated that limited available resources would constitute a valid and justifiable basis for limiting access to, or refusing, emergency medical treatment for patients.

5. On what legal basis is it possible to apply the allocation criteria in practice?

Insofar as the COVID-19 pandemic is concerned, there is no legally binding document that sets out allocation criteria for scarce health care resources during the pandemic. As explained in questions 1 and 3, the CCSSA Guidelines, which is implemented by public and private health care facilities in South Africa, provides non-binding recommendations. An analysis of the case law surrounding section 27 of the Constitution (see also question 4 above), however, would seem to suggest that

[361] *Soobramoney v Minister of Health* 1998 (1) SA 765 (CC) para 29; Liebenberg (n 33) 137.

[362] Section 27(3) of the Constitution states as follows: 'No one may be refused emergency medical treatment.'

[363] See P Carstens and D Pearmain, *Foundational Principles of South African Medical Law* (LexisNexis 2007) 221–226.

[364] Liebenberg (n 33) 135.

[365] Liebenberg (n 33) 136. See also *Soobramoney v Minister of Health* 1998 (1) SA 765 (CC) para 19: 'What the section requires is that remedial treatment that is necessary and available be given immediately to avert that harm.'

the particular section affords a legal basis to allocate certain scarce resources to certain individuals and to deny them to others — as long as the decision to do so was reasonable in the circumstances.[366]

6. What level of legal certainty do the health professionals and the health care providers have when applying the allocation criteria?

While it may be said that most health care practitioners appear to be aware of the fact that the CCSSA Guidelines exist, the guidelines are not legally binding and provide room for discretion regarding their application. Although the guidelines aim to provide a firm, objective basis for rationing, there will always be scope for human discretion and judgment to be exercised, which brings with it a level of uncertainty.

7. What are the civil and criminal liability implications of allocation of scarce health care resources? Have there already been any related legal suits and/or criminal proceedings?

Firstly, there has not yet been civil or criminal legal proceedings instituted against a health care practitioner or facility arising from the allocation of scarce health care resources. However, there has been widespread fraud and corruption related to the procurement of PPE equipment and other goods used in the fight against COVID 19-pandemic.[367]

Insofar as the criminal and civil liability implications of allocation of scarce health care resources are concerned, the normal legal rules would apply.[368] It is perhaps easiest to illustrate the working of these rules, if attention is given to the facts of scenario number 1 of the questionnaire. Suppose that one of the patients who was not offered a bed, dies and suppose further that (a) the health practitioner who made the decision is criminally pursued for culpable homicide by the State and (b) the health practitioner and the hospital is sued in civil law (the law of delict) by the

366 See also, for example, *Soobramoney v Minister of Health* 1998 (1) SA 765 (CC); *Government of the Republic of South Africa v Grootboom* 2001 (1) SA 46 (CC).

367 See, for example: 'In South Africa, covid-19 has exposed greed and spurred long-needed action against corruption' (*Transparency International*, 4 September 2020) <www.transparency.org/en/blog/in-south-africa-covid-19-has-exposed-greed-and-spurred-long-needed-action-against-corruption#> accessed 14 June 2021.

368 With regard to criminal liability, see generally Jonathan M Burchell, *Principles of Criminal Law* (5th ed, JUTA 2016); Gerhard Kemp (ed), *Criminal Law in South Africa* (3rd ed, OUP 2018). Regarding delictual (civil) liability, see Max Loubser and Rob Midgley (eds), *The Law Law of Delict in South Africa* (3rd ed, OUP 2017); Johann Neethling and J Potgieter, *Law of Delict* (8th ed, LexisNexis 2020).

dependents of the deceased for the harm (loss of support and maintenance) that they suffer arising from the person's death.

Essentially, insofar as criminal liability is concerned, the State will be tasked to prove, beyond reasonable doubt, that the requirements for the particular crime (culpable homicide) was indeed proven. This means proving the basic elements of criminal liability, namely conduct, accountability, causation, wrongfulness and fault (more specifically: negligence). If the State is indeed successful, the practitioner in question will be sentenced appropriately. Insofar as civil (delictual/tortious) liability is concerned, the dependants may institute a civil/delictual claim against the hospital and/or health practitioner in question. In doing so, the plaintiff will be required to prove the five elements for civil/delictual liability on a balance of probabilities: harm, conduct, causation, wrongfulness and fault (in this case: negligence). The claim may be instituted directly against the hospital itself, or the plaintiff may seek to hold the hospital vicariously liable for the delict committed by its employee (the healthcare practitioner) during the course and scope of his employment.

Although much more may be said about the application of each of the requirements for criminal and civil (delictual) liability, it may be worthwhile to make the following brief observations about fault, which must be proven regardless of whether one deals with criminal or civil proceedings, and because it will arguably present a significant hurdle facing litigants and a central issue in determining civil and criminal liability.

In South African law, fault can manifest in one of two ways: intention or negligence.[369] In the type of scenario mentioned here, South African law would hold that the hospital or health practitioner did not act intentionally.[370] The crucial question would therefore be (both in the context of civil and criminal law): did the doctor or the hospital in question act negligently by allocating certain resources to certain patients? In this regard, it is important to understand that the law treats professional people differently insofar as the test for negligence is concerned.[371] Ordinarily, when assessing negligence, the central question is whether or not the defendant's conduct matches the standard of conduct that may be expected from a reasonable person within the particular circumstances under consideration.[372] However, when professionals are sued, and negligence falls to be determined, the question is whether the defendant's conduct matches the standard of conduct that could be expected from a reasonable professional person within the specific circumstances.[373] In other

369 This is true of criminal and delictual (civil) liability — see generally Burchell (n 58); Loubser and Midgley (n 58) 137–176.

370 Here it must be noted that, for purposes of criminal and delictual (civil) liability, intention consists of (a) the direction of will and (b) consciousness of wrongfulness. It may be said that the health practitioner in question lacked both components.

371 Loubser and Midgley (n 58) 325–327; *Van Wyk v Lewis* 1924 AD 438; *Mouton v Die Mynwerkersunie 1977 (1) SA 119 (A).*

372 See, for example, *Sea Harvest Corporation (Pty) Ltd v Duncan Dock Cold Storage (Pty) Ltd* 2000 (1) SA 827 (SCA); Loubser and Midgley (n 58) 154–155.

373 Loubser and Midgley (n 58) 325–327; *Van Wyk v Lewis*; *Mouton v Die Mynwerkersunie.*

words, the standard of conduct against which the defendant's conduct is measured is adjusted so as to take into account the level of skill and knowledge of the professional involved. Therefore, where the defendant is a health practitioner, the question is not whether he or she conducted herself in line with the standard of conduct that may be expected from the reasonable person, but rather whether he or she behaved like the reasonable health practitioner would have within the specific circumstances. Furthermore, particular attention is given to the branch of the profession in which the health practitioner operates. For example, if the health practioner is a heart surgeon, the question that falls to be determined is whether the defendant behaved like the reasonable heart surgeon would have conducted him- or herself in the circumstances.

It bears further emphasis that negligence is a fact-based enquiry and much will depend on the evidence that is advanced by the parties in court. Indeed, the particular circumstances of each case will be of extreme importance. The fact that health care practitioners are operating within the context of a worldwide pandemic, which places significant strains and substantial stumbling-blocks in front of practitioners and health care facilities will be of much relevance. Also, adherence to applicable standard guidelines or criteria by the defendant will be of much consequence.[374] Therefore, if the practitioner in question applied the criteria set out in the CCSSA Guidelines, it would go a long way in proving that the doctor or hospital acted reasonably within the particular circumstances, although by itself it will not be entirely conclusive. In short, these guidelines are seen as the reasonable standard practice within the critical care community, and adherence to such standard practice would imply reasonable behaviour. Where a court (faced with deciding criminal or civil liability) decides that the hospital or practitioner in question behaved reasonably, there will be no civil or criminal liability.

B. Case studies

Case 1

As a result of a rapid worsening of the epidemiological situation, the material and personal capacities have been drastically overloaded in all the hospitals in the country. Within just a few minutes, ambulances transport ten patients to one particular hospital's emergency unit. The patients all need admission to the hospital, preferably to the intensive care unit (ICU). However, only two beds are available there. Other hospitals are overwhelmed too, so it is not possible to transport patients to any of them. All of the ten newly coming patients suffer from COVID-19; they have breathing difficulties, fast-rising fever, and decreasing oxygen saturation. Nevertheless, they differ in age, comorbidities, clinical fragility, and other factors.

374 Loubser and Midgley (n 58) 167.

Theoretically, the eight patients who cannot be admitted to beds can be placed in improvised settings in the hospital corridors, laying on gurneys or mattresses on the floor. Nevertheless, it will be impossible to provide them with the care they need.

Evaluation of the case

- What criteria can be used to choose the patients who will be admitted to the beds (i.e. what are the possible allocation criteria)?
  The allocation criteria set out in the CCSSA Guidelines (see the response to question 1 above).
- What legal consequences can this decision have for the health professionals and the hospital? How strong is their legal certainty that there will be no adverse legal consequences if they follow the above-mentioned criteria?
  Given the overall lack of resources available as a result of the COVID-19 pandemic, and assuming that the hospital and/or health care practitioner in question applied the CCSSA Guidelines within what appears to be an emergency situation, one may conclude that there is a very strong possibility that courts will regard the conduct in question as reasonable. Put differently, if the hospital and/or doctor in question behaves reasonably — eg by applying the criteria in the CCSSA Guidelines — their behaviour will not be regarded as negligent.[375] And without negligence (fault), liability (in civil and criminal law) cannot follow.
- What legal defences could the health professionals and the hospital use against a civil lawsuit and/or criminal prosecution for the allocation decision?
  Apart from defending themselves by arguing that they behaved reasonably and therefore lacked fault, the health professionals and/or hospital are likely to raise the defence of necessity, which will be aimed at negating the requirement for wrongfulness (both in civil and criminal law). More specifically, necessity is a defence that can be raised to justify the infringement of the legally recognised interest of an innocent person.[376] To be successful in this regard, the defendant practitioner or hospital would have the onus to prove that the state of necessity existed or that it was imminent; that the legally recognised right or interest of the defendant or another person was actually endangered; and that the defendant's conduct (ie infringing on the rights of an innocent person) was necessary and reasonable within the particular circumstances.[377] Arguably, these requirements have been met in the factual scenario, and therefore the hospital/practitioner's decision that the eight patients cannot be admitted to beds (and other scarce resources), and the concomitant infringement upon their right to their bodily integrity, life and dignity, may be justified in this instance. A South African court is therefore likely to find that there is no wrongfulness in the particular scenario. Also, and particularly insofar as civil law (law of delict) is concerned, because the defence of necessity is aimed at negating the element of wrongful-

375 See also the answer to question 7 above.

376 See Loubser and Midgley (n 58) 213–217; Neethling and Potgieter (n 58) 112–123.

377 Loubser and Midgley (n 58) 213–217; Neethling and Potgieter (n 58) 119–120.

ness, the court will also be entitled to take into account legal and public policy considerations and constitutional rights and norms to assess whether liability must indeed be imposed on the defendant practitioner or hospital.[378] A very important policy consideration in this regard will be the fact that, within the state of emergency brought about by the COVID-19 pandemic, there is a clear lack of scarce medical resources.

Additional questions

- Would it be legally permissible to lower the standard of care provided to all patients in order to provide at least basic decent care to the newly admitted patients who are placed in the hospital corridors? To what extent?
  As Neethling and Potgieter states, 'the state of necessity gives [the defendant] the power to act in a way which, in the absence of necessity, would have infringed [the plaintiff's] right and would have been wrongful.'[379] This means that the defence of necessity effectively provides the practitioner/hospital with the right to infringe upon the rights of all patients within the hospital (ie providing them with a different or lowered standard of care), and simultaneously restricts those patients' respective rights to their bodily integrity, health, etc in order to provide basic decent care to the newly admitted patients who are placed in the hospital corridors. Because necessity is raised where the rights of innocent persons are infringed upon, the law requires a certain degree of proportionality.[380] What this means is that, generally, 'the interest sacrificed must not be more valuable than the interest protected.'[381] Of course, it is not possible to lay down strict rules for proportionality, and much will depend upon the circumstances of the case.[382] In this particular example, it would appear as though there is proportionality between the interests infringed upon (the rights relating to life, health and bodily integrity of the patients in the hospital) and the rights that are sought to be protected (the rights relating to life, health and bodily integrity of the patients who are admitted and placed in the hospital corridor.) It should be noted, however, that the courts would not sanction gross improportionality or the unreasonable infringement of harm to patients who have been taken up earlier in the hospital.

Case 2

Two patients in an ICU are suffering from COVID-19. After admission to the hospital, they were provided with the high-flow nasal oxygen therapy (HFNO). During one night, the condition of both patients starts to worsen rapidly. At dawn, it is clear

378 See Wessels, 'Wrongfulness in pure economic loss cases: the "traditional approach" and the "new approach"' (2020) 83 THRHR 151–170; Wessels, 'Establishing legal certainty in novel pure economic loss cases' (2020) 83 THRHR 318–342.

379 Neethling and Potgieter (n 58) 117.

380 See Loubser and Midgley (n 58) 216–217; Neethling and Potgieter (n 58) 120–121.

381 Neethling and Potgieter (n 58) 120.

382 Neethling and Potgieter (n 58) 120–121.

that neither of them will survive without artificial ventilation. However, there is just one ventilator available.

Evaluation of the case

- What criteria can be used to choose which of the two patients will be provided with artificial ventilation and which one will be left without it, possibly to die?
  The allocation criteria set out in the CCSSA Guidelines (see the response to question 1 above). The CCSSA Guidelines also cater for situations where there are so-called 'ties', ie where, as in the scenario presented here, there are two patients who apparently fall within the same priority groups. As indicated in the response to question 1 above, in such instance, the CCSSA Guidelines determine that the following factors must be considered. First, attention must be given to life-cycle considerations and priority should generally be given to younger patients. This is based on the notion that younger patients have 'had less opportunity to live through life's stages.'[383] A second factor to be considered is whether the patient in question 'perform tasks that are vital to the public health response — specifically those whose work supports the provision of acute care to others'.[384] A person in this category is likely to receive 'heightened priority'.[385]
- What legal consequences can this decision have for the health professionals and the hospital? How strong is their legal certainty that there will be no adverse legal consequences if they follow the above-mentioned criteria?
  The principles that have been briefly set out in case 1 also apply here.
- What legal defences could the health professionals and the hospital use against a civil lawsuit and/or criminal prosecution for the allocation decision?
  The principles that have been briefly set out in case 1 also apply here.

Additional question

- If the allocation criteria specified in your answer to the first question to this case consisted of the patients' clinical features (such as their age, clinical fragility, etc.), please identify what criteria could be used for the allocation decision if all the relevant clinical features of both patients were practically the same?
  Presumably, if all clinical features are practically the same, regard will be had to whether one of the patients are involved in the public health care response to COVID-19 pandemic.[386] Such a person is likely to receive 'heightened priority'.[387]

Case 3

There is a single extracorporeal membrane oxygenation (ECMO) device in the hospital. It is currently being used for an 84-year-old patient suffering from COVID-19,

383 CCSSA (n 1) 8.
384 CCSSA (n 1) 8.
385 CCSSA (n 1) 8.
386 CCSSA (n 1) 8.
387 CCSSA (n 1) 8.

with diabetes as an underlying disease, clinical frailty score (CFS) 6–7 (moderate to severe frailty). It is possible that the patient will survive and will be discharged from the hospital if the ECMO treatment is continued. However, a younger COVID-19 patient is admitted to the hospital. This new patient is 51 years old, otherwise healthy, but her health condition has been rapidly deteriorating. Soon she will most likely need ECMO to survive.

Evaluation of the case

- Can it be legally permissible for the hospital staff to discontinue the ECMO treatment of the older patient and provide palliative care to her in order to save the younger and healthier patient's life? Please keep in mind that the older patient could survive if the treatment continued, but her chances may be lower than those of the younger patient.

  Based on the fact that one of the underlying values of the allocation criteria set out in the CCSSA Guidelines appear to be that priority should generally be given to younger patients,[388] it is conceivable that preference may be given to the younger patient in this particular scenario. Following these guidelines may be regarded as reasonable conduct, which means that there may possibly be no criminal or civil implications.
- If the answer to the first question is positive, what specific criteria can be used in clinical decision-making regarding replacing one patient with another with respect to a particular treatment unavailable for all?

  Generally, the allocation criteria set out in the CCSSA Guidelines (see the response to question 1 above) will also apply here. As indicated earlier, it is at this stage that the triage team will use the so-called Sequential Organ Failure Assessment (SOFA) to rate a patient. Using the SOFA, each patient is given a score between 1 and 4 to determine the likelihood of surviving until hospital discharge.[389] In addition, a patient is also allocated a score between 1 and 4 to determine the likelihood of achieving longer-term survival based on the presence or absence of comorbid conditions that may influence survival.[390] These scores are then added together to produce the patient's total priority scoring for ICU treatment, which may range from 1 to 8.[391] A lower score (between 1 and 3) indicates a higher likelihood of benefiting from critical care, and patients within this category therefore receive priority treatment.[392] An intermediate score (4–5) means that a patient will receive critical care resources if there are available resources after all the patients in the priority group (1–3) have been allocated critical care resources. Finally, a score between 6–8 means that a patient will only receive critical care resources if all other patients in the preceding groups have received resources.

388 CCSSA (n 1) 8.
389 CCSSA (n 1) 5.
390 CCSSA (n 1) 5.
391 CCSSA (n 1) 7.
392 CCSSA (n 1) 7–8.

- What legal consequences can this decision have for the health professionals and the hospital? How strong is their legal certainty that there will be no adverse legal consequences if they follow the above-mentioned criteria?
  The principles that have been briefly set out in case 1 also apply here.
- What legal defences could the health professionals and the hospital use against a civil lawsuit and/or criminal prosecution for the allocation decision?
  The principles that have been briefly set out in case 1 also apply here.

Additional question

- Suppose there are two different scenarios: a) the older patient was admitted to the hospital and provided with the ECMO treatment, and only later, after several days, the younger patient was admitted, and b) the younger patient was admitted before the older patient, however, the older patient required ECMO treatment soon after admission while the younger patient's health condition deteriorated only after a longer time when the ECMO was already occupied (i. e. at the time when the younger patient was admitted to the hospital, she did not yet need it). Would there be any difference in the allocation decision making between these two scenarios?
  Unfortunately, this question requires technical insight and medical expertise into ECMO, which I do not have. I would prefer therefore not to venture a guess and have decided not to answer this question.

The list of abbreviations

CCSSA	Critical Care Society of Southern Africa
COVID	Coronavirus Disease
CFS	Critical Frailty Scale
ICU	Intensive Care Unit
SOFA	Sequential Organ Failure Assessment
PPE	Personal Protective Equipment

Bibliography

• Legislation

The Constitution of the Republic of South Africa Act 108 of 1996; cited as: the Constitution

• Case law

Government of the Republic of South Africa v Grootboom 2001 (1) SA 46 (CC)

Khosa v Minister of Social Development; Mahlaule v Minister of Social Development 2004 (6) SA 505 (CC)

Mazibuko v City of Johannesburg 2010 (4) SA 1 (CC)
Mouton v Die Mynwerkersunie 1977 (1) SA 119 (A)
Sea Harvest Corporation (Pty) Ltd v Duncan Dock Cold Storage (Pty) Ltd 2000 (1) SA 827 (SCA)
Soobramoney v Minister of Health 1998 (1) SA 765 (CC)
Van Wyk v Lewis 1924 AD 438

• Books

Burchell JM, *Principles of Criminal Law* (5th ed, JUTA 2016)
Carstens P and D Pearmain, *Foundational Principles of South African Medical Law* (LexisNexis 2007)
De Vos P and W Freedman (eds), *South African Constitutional Law in Context* (2nd ed, OUP 2020)
Kemp G (ed), *Criminal Law in South Africa* (3rd ed, OUP 2018)
Liebenberg S, *Socio-Economic Rights: Adjudication under a transformative Constitution* (JUTA 2010)
Loubser M & R Midgley (eds), *The Law Law of Delict in South Africa* (3rd ed, OUP 2017)
Neethling J & J Potgieter, *Law of Delict* (8th ed, LexisNexis 2020)
Rautenbach IM & R Venter, *Rautenbach-Malherbe Constitutional Law* (7th ed, LexisNexis 2018)

• Articles

—— 'In South Africa, covid-19 has exposed greed and spurred long-needed action against corruption' (*Transparency International*, 4 September 2020) <www.transparency.org/en/blog/in-south-africa-covid-19-has-exposed-greed-and-spurred-long-needed-action-against-corruption#> accessed 14 June 2021
Moodley K et al, 'What could "fair allocation" during the Covid-19 crisis possibly mean in Sub-Saharan South Africa?' (2020) 50 Hastings Center Report 33
Morrow BM, 'Critical care triage during the COVID-19 pandemic in South Africa: A constitutional imperative!' (2020) 110 SAMJ 1177
Singh JA & K Moodley, 'Critical care triaging in the shadow of COVID-19: Ethics consideration' (2020) 110 SAMJ 355
Wessels, 'Wrongfulness in pure economic loss cases: the "traditional approach" and the "new approach"' (2020) 83 THRHR 151
Wessels, 'Establishing legal certainty in novel pure economic loss cases' (2020) 83 THRHR 318

• Other secondary sources

Critical Care Society of Southern Africa (CCSSA), 'Allocation of Scarce Critical Care Resources During the COVID-19 Public Health Emergency in South Africa' (2 April 2020) <https://criticalcare.org.za/wp-content/uploads/2020/06/V3-2020-May-05-Allocation-of-Scarce-Critical-Care-Resources-During-the-COVID-19-Public-Health-Emergency-in-South-Africa-FINAL-.pdf> accessed 8 June 2020

SPAIN

Albert Ruda
University of Girona

Introduction

This paper examines the way in which Spain addressed the scarcity of health care resources during the Covid-19 outbreak. First, it provides an overview of the legal framework, including the Constitutional and statutory provisions (Section II). Then, the specific regulatory framework which was passed to cope with the pandemic is summarized (Section III). After that, the issue of the allocation of scarce resources is discussed (Section IV). The paper ends with some conclusions (Section V).

The purpose of the paper is to show that Spanish law was largely unprepared to cope with the pandemic in general and triage in particular. The Spanish legislature embarked on a frantic enterprise to issue extremely detailed legislation on a plethora of aspects, however clear criteria upon which triage could be done remained absent. A state of alarm was declared on two occasions and the general population was subjected to draconian restrictions for months. However, it must be questioned whether all this disregarded that there were already other regulatory mechanisms to deal with the crisis. Moreover, eventually the state of alarm turned to have infringed the Constitution. As regards the particular issue of scarce resource allocation, Spanish law seems to have also been rather ill equipped. An important discussion on the matter took place, due to the lack of clear-cut guidelines; this happened at a time when vulnerable persons were subjected to a harsh treatment — if not left to their fates — which is hardly compatible with their fundamental rights. Worse than that, it may be wondered whether Spain has learnt any lessons from the havoc caused by both the pandemic as such and the blatant inability of its public authorities. The paper discusses whether, should another pandemic take place, Spain would be better equipped to deal with it.

A. Statutory framework

From a constitutional perspective, the normative scaffolding with which Spanish law faced the pandemic was rather meagre. The Spanish Constitution (*Constitución*

Española, CE), from 1978,[393] does not mention epidemics or pandemics. There is a section on individuals' rights, some of which are considered to be fundamental and thus enjoying a higher degree of protection. This includes the possibility to file an appeal (*recurso de amparo*) before the Constitutional Court (*Tribunal Constitucional*, TC) in case of violation thereof (Art. 53 CE).

Whereas the right to an equal treatment (Art. 14 CE) is a fundamental right (Art. 53.2 CE), the right to health (Art. 43) is not.[394] Art. 50, which refers to the care of the elderly people, is also protected in a less intense manner than fundamental rights. This is also the case of consumers' rights (Art. 51.1), which includes consumers' right to health. Human dignity is enshrined in a specific provision (Art. 10 CE) as the 'basis of the political order and social peace'. However, it is also left out of the Chapter on fundamental rights (Arts. 14 to 30).

One may wonder whether triage of patients as a result of resources scarcity may be in contradiction with the principle of equality. This principle does not actually prevent every difference in treatment. Differences may occur, but they should be based upon objective and reasonable grounds. Artificial and unjustified differences are therefore prohibited by the Spanish Constitution. The equality principle is also established in ordinary legislation, in particular in the General Act on Health Care 1986,[395] according to which the access to health care services should occur in conditions of effective equality (Art. 3.2). Age can be a differentiating factor upon which differences may be made; nevertheless, such factor is subject to the strictest scrutiny (Decision of the Constitutional Court [*Sentencia del Tribunal Constitutional*, STC] 63/2011, of 16 May).[396] The Spanish Constitutional Court has stated that the prohibition of discrimination upon age should not prevent one from taking other personal circumstances into account (STC 69/1991, of 8 April).[397]

As regards the right to health (Art. 43 CE), it may be striking that it is not a fundamental right. In fact, it is not even a true right, since it is recognized within the Chapter on the 'governing principles of social and economic policy' (Title I, Chapter III, CE). Therefore, such a 'right' does not have an objective content which the individual could rely upon as the basis of a claim before the Constitutional Court. Principles like this one are merely meant to guide the general policy of the State. The right to health may be developed by way of ordinary statutes (instead of "organic"[398] ones) and a preferen-

393 An official translation into English can be found under Boletín Oficial del Estado, "The Spanish Constitution", Madrid: BOE, without date, <https://www.boe.es/legislacion/documentos/ConstitucionINGLES.pdf>.

394 This is a response to Question no. 4 of the Questionnaire.

395 Act (Ley) 14/1986, of 25 April, Ley 14/1986, de 25 de abril, *General de Sanidad* (Official Gazette [*Boletín Oficial del Estado,* BOE] no. 102, 29.4.1986).

396 The decision (in Spanish) can be found under <https://hj.tribunalconstitucional.es/es/Resolucion/Show/6845>.

397 <https://vlex.es/vid/1-14-15356743>.

398 In this context, organic means that the act at skate requires an absolute majority at the lower Chamber of the Spanish Parliament to be passed, instead of the regular simple majority (pursuant to Art. 81.2 CE).

tial and speedy procedure to protect it before the courts is lacking. The appeal before the Constitutional Court (*amparo*) is also unavailable as a result of such categorization. In spite of all this, one should not consider that the right to health does not exist at all under Spanish law. Indeed, such a right should prevent, for instance, private organizations from establishing prioritization criteria in the case of scarce resources.[399]

Moreover, public authorities have a duty to protect it (Art. 43.2 CE). That right is construed as an 'active principle' which is the basis for other rights (life, personal integrity, privacy, etc.). Besides that, one should bear in mind that in Spain a there is universal health system. Therefore, scarce resource allocation is not exceptional but actually the rule.[400] Spanish courts are well aware that resources are not unlimited. As a result, there may be waiting lists for certain surgery operations.

As pointed out above, Spain has a general statutory framework concerning health protection. The most important statute to this regard is the Public Health Act from 2011.[401] It provides that every person has a right to equal treatment (Art. 6.1). In accordance to that, there is a ban on discrimination because of birth, racial or ethnic origin, sex, religion, convictions or opinions, age, disability, sexual identity or orientation, illness, 'or any other personal or social condition or circumstance'.

The Act provides on an explicit basis that illness as such cannot be the ground for a different treatment (Art. 6.3). Such differences can only be based on (i) the treatment as such, (ii) objective limitations to personal freedom derived from the treatment (e.g. no physical activities…), or (iii) public health. Therefore, the Public Health Act does not fully exclude the possibility of triage among patients but merely prohibits that triage occurs on the basis of certain specific factors. Age as such is not mentioned but it is excluded as a relevant factor on an implicit basis.

B. The state of alarm

The possibility that public authorities declare a state of alarm is provided for in the Spanish Constitution (Art. 116). Pursuant to the same, the legislature will provide for the statutory regime on the state of alarm. The latter must be decreed by the Spanish Government. Therefore, if one takes into account that the territorial structure of the Spanish state is akin to a federal state, the previous means that the regional authorities (Autonomous Communities [*Comunidades Autónomas,* CCAA]) lack such a power. Moreover, the duration of the state of alarm must be maximum 15 days; the extension of such a period requires approval by the lower Parliamentary Chamber (Congress of Deputies [*Congreso de los Diputados*]). The state of the

399 See Federico De Montalvo Jääskeläinen and Vicente Bellver Capella, "La Bioética en los tiempos del coronavirus: una reflexión acerca de algunos dilemas éticos-legales de la pandemia a partir del Informe del Comité de Bioética de España", in Elena Atienza Macías and Juan Francisco Rodríguez Ayuso (eds.), *Las respuestas del Derecho a las crisis de salud pública* (Dykinson 2020) 243, 255.

400 See Montalvo and Bellver, *op. cit.*, 246.

401 Act 33/2011, of 4 October, *General de Salud Pública* (BOE no. 240, 5.10.2011).

alarm may have the territorial scope which may be determined by the Government. Therefore, the latter may decree that there is a state of alarm in, let's say, the region of Madrid, but not in Andalusia. The effects of the declaration of a state of alarm themselves are not laid down by the Constitution.[402]

The statutory development of the state of alarm is provided by an Act from 1981, namely, the Act on the states of alarm, exception and siege.[403] The state of alarm declaration must be based on 'extraordinary circumstances which make maintaining of normality by ordinary means of the authorities in charge impossible' (Art. 1.1). An example of such situation is a health crisis such as an epidemic (Art. 4.b). The measures adopted in the framework of such declaration should be those indispensable and proportionate to the circumstances (Art. 1.2). Interestingly, victims of damage caused as a result of acts and provisions adopted during such a state may claim compensation according to the laws (Art. 3.2).[404]

Before the pandemic, there was very little experience with regard to the functioning of states of alarm. In fact, there was just one precedent, consisting in a general strike by air controllers in 2010. In that occasion, the Spanish Government ordered the military to take control of the situation to put an end to the ensuing chaos; air controllers were actually taken out of their homes to the airport at gunpoint. However, this was an issue of public order, not a health issue. It has been suggested that the constitutional State was in a state of shock, as a result of the lack of preparation to cope with the pandemic.[405]

The first state of alarm due to the Covid-19 outbreak was decreed in March 2020 by way of a Royal Decree,[406] this is, a regulation issued by the Spanish Government.[407] The initial duration provided for such a state was three months (14.3.2020-21.6.2020). Measures adopted included (inter alia): a) the limitation of the freedom of movement; b) in person activities were suspended (except for essential ones); c) the reinforcement of health measures (Art. 12); d) the Spanish Government retained the control of health provision services to ensure the best distribution of personal and technical means, and e) it was established that vulnerable persons should be taken into account. In addition

402 On exceptional states under Spanish law generally see the classical work by Pedro Cruz Villalón, *Estados excepcionales y suspensión de garantías*, (Tecnos 1984).

403 Organic Act (*Ley Orgánica,* LO) 4/1981, of 1 June, de los estados de alarma, excepción y sitio (BOE no. 134, 5.6.1981).

404 See Albert Ruda, "Tort Law and the Coronavirus: Liability for Harm Caused by the COVID-19 Outbreak", in Ewoud Hondius, Marta Santos Silva, Andrea Nicolussi, Pablo Salvador Coderch, Christiane Wendehorst and Fryderik Zoll (eds.), *Coronavirus and the Law in Europe* (Intersentia Online 2021) <https://www.intersentiaonline.com/permalink/4987572baac823522e7a3b5ecffd952b>.

405 See Enrique Arnaldo Alcubilla, "España: tres meses y una semana bajo el estado de alarma", in Enrique Arnaldo Alcubilla and Raúl Canosa Usera (eds.), *El Derecho Constitucional ante el Covid-19. Las diferentes respuestas en el ámbito comparado* (Wolters Kluwer 2020) 271, 276.

406 Royal Decree (*Real Decreto,* RD) 463/2020, of 14 March, *por el que se declara el estado de alarma para la gestión de la situación de crisis sanitaria ocasionada por el COVID-19* (BOE no. 67, 14.3.2020).

407 On such a declaration see Albert Ruda, "Spain", in Ernst Karner and Barbara C. Steininger (eds.), *European Tort Law 2020* (Springer, 2021) 612, with further references.

to that, Spanish Ministries were appointed as authorities in charge to issue any orders, decisions, provisions or instructions necessary to guarantee the provision of all services to protect persons, goods and places (Art. 4.3 I). Again, such acts, provisions and measures should pay attention to vulnerable persons (Art. 4.3. II). That state of alarm was extended in time several times and eventually lasted six months.

After a summer break, in which the general situation seemed to improve, a second state of alarm was decreed in October 2020.[408] That state of alarm was also extended.[409] Instead of several short extensions, the Spanish Government opted for a longer extension, of six months. That the Spanish Constitution provides — as mentioned above — that the state of alarm should be decreed for 15 days maximum (Art. 116.2 CE) did not apparently constitute an obstacle. The Spanish legal scholarship has often criticized the poor technique and blatant disregard of the most elementary principles of public law by the avalanche of regulations issued by the Spanish Government during the pandemic. Thousands of pages in the Official Gazette have been filled with provisions, the usefulness of which is questionable.[410] Legal certainty has been sacrificed on the altar of public health protection.[411] Since the coalition Government had a rather weak position in the Parliament, one may assume that it intended to provide an image of strength by decreeing very harsh measures. Government representatives even boasted that the Spanish lockdown was the strictest in the world. What they forgot is that they were not merely restricting constitutionally protected freedoms, but even suppressing them completely without an adequate legal backup and even a factual need for it. This is the reason why the decrees of state of alarm were challenged before the Spanish Constitutional Court and eventually declared unconstitutional.[412]

C. Allocation of scarce resources

1. The battle of the reports

The issue of the allocation of scarce resources during the pandemic has resulted in what could be described as 'The battle of the reports'.[413] This was so because there

[408] RD 926/2020, of 25 October, *por el que se declara el estado de alarma para contener la propagación de infecciones causadas por el SARS-CoV-2* (BOE no. 282, 25.10.2020).

[409] RD 956/2020, of 3 November, *por el que se prorroga el estado de alarma declarado por el Real Decreto 926/2020, de 25 de octubre, por el que se declara el estado de alarma para contener la propagación de infecciones causadas por el SARS-CoV-2* (BOE no. 291, 4.11.2020).

[410] See for instance the criticism by Fernando Savater, "Editorial. Plagas", (2020) 271 Claves de Razón Práctica 7.

[411] Instead of many see Joan Manuel Trayter Jiménez, "Derecho administrativo sancionador, estado de alarma y COVID-19", in David Blanquer (ed.), *COVID-19 y Derecho público* (Tirant 2020) 243, 241, 256, 262.

[412] On such a declaration and its effects see Albert Ruda, "Spain", in Ernst Karner and Barbara C. Steininger (eds.), *European Tort Law 2021* (Springer 2022) .

[413] This is a response to Question no. 1 of the Questionnaire.

were no general guidelines from the Spanish Government and Spanish bibliography on the issue was actually very meagre.[414] Therefore, a plethora of organizations started issuing their own recommendations and protocols, including: a) the Spanish Society of Geriatrics and Gerontology; b) the Bioethics Working Group within the Spanish Society of Internal and Critical Medicine and Coronary Units; c) the Health Ministry; d) the Spanish Society of Bioethics and Medical Ethics; e) the Spanish Bioethics Committee; f) the Health Care Ethics Committee (CEA, by its initials in Spanish) at the Clinic Hospital in Barcelona; g) the Observatory of Bioethics and Law at the University of Barcelona, and h) the Central Commission of Deontology of the Medical Organization.

From a legal scholarly perspective, there has been hardly any discussion about triage. This is obviously a moral or philosophical issue, on which legal criteria may be adopted. According to one scholarly opinion, the law cannot solve all moral dilemmas which the fight against a pandemic may pose; however, it is added, the law may lay down some of the 'variables in the equation', by establishing which factors are legally relevant as regards prioritization of access to a scarce resource in the pandemic context.[415] This standpoint assumes that there can be prioritization and that it is legally possible to define some parameters according to which that could be carried out. However, it has also been suggested that it is not possible to provide a clear-cut solution to all those dilemmas, since one cannot give a value to human life, because of the legal protection of human dignity.[416] The reports mentioned above address such a difficult issue in different ways.[417]

a) The Spanish Society of Geriatrics and Gerontology (SEGG) issued a document called "General recommendations related to difficult ethical decisions and the adequacy of the health care provision intensity / admission to the ICUs in exceptional crisis situations". This was the result of the consensus of 24 different organizations.[418] The document at stake contains many recommendations which refer to different aspects of health care provision in the pandemic. According to the same, one should prioritize maximization of: (i) survival at discharge from hospital; (ii) number of life years saved, and (iii) the chances of living at each of life stages. However, age as such should not be the only element to be considered in the assignation strategies.[419] Triage

414 For an overview see O. Rubio et al, "Recomendaciones éticas para la toma de decisiones difíciles en las unidades de cuidados intensivos ante la situación excepcional de crisis por la pandemia por COVID-19: revisión rápida y consenso de expertos" (2020) 44 *Medicina Intensiva* 439 <https://www.ncbi.nlm.nih.gov/pmc/articles/PMC7158790/>.

415 See César Cierco Seira, "Derecho de la salud pública y COVID-19", in David Blanquer (ed.), *COVID-19 y Derecho público* (Tirant 2020) 25, 52.

416 Again, see Cierco Seira, *op. cit.*, 53 and Montalvo and Bellver, *op. cit.*, 251.

417 This is a response to Question no. 2 of the Questionnaire.

418 See Sociedad Española de Geriatría y Gerontología (SEGG), "Recomendaciones generales relacionadas con las decisiones éticas difíciles y la adecuación de la intensidad asistencial / ingreso en las unidades de cuidados intensivos en situaciones excepcionales de crisis" (2020) <https://www.segg.es/media/descargas/CONSENSO-RECOMENDACIONES-UCI-COVID-19.pdf>.

419 This is a response to the Additional Question of the Questionnaire.

should be based on distributive justice, to which a specific section of the document is devoted. The SEGG refers to the principle of cost / opportunity, meaning that one should avoid allocating resources on a 'first come, first served' basis. However, from a critical perspective, this seems to imply that medical professionals should wait just in case another patient appears which requires the scarce resource more than the one who arrived earlier. This may amount to a deprivation of medical attention to the one who arrived first. Apart from that, the SEGG's document concludes that maximization of the benefit to the common good (*maximizar el beneficio del bien común*) should guide the criteria applied to Intensive Care Units (ICU) allocation. That entails saving the biggest number of socially valuable lives. If conflict between Covid-19/non-Covid-19 patients arises, it is the one who would benefit most from treatment who should be treated.

SEGG's criteria were the object of fierce criticism, to the point where the SEGG's president issued a statement. According to the same, no vulnerable elderly person had been denied high level hospital care as a result of the SEGG's guidelines.[420]

b) The Spanish Society of Internal and Critical Medicine and Coronary Units (*Sociedad Española de Medicina Intensiva, Crítica y Unidades Coronarias,* SEMICYUC) issued a series of Ethical Recommendations regarding ICUs.[421] Such society considers that an exceptional situation where there is an imbalance between clinical needs and effective resources availability is a catastrophe where decisions should be adopted on the basis of distributive justice (*justicia distributiva*) and an "adequate assignation" of health care resources.[422] According to the same, patients with cognition impairments (dementia or other degenerative illnesses) are not subsidiary of invasive mechanical ventilation (Recommendation no. 4). In case of elderly people, one should take the possibility of survival free from disability into account (before survival alone) (Recommendation no. 17). This is consistent with the idea that one should maximize the number of people saved as well as survival without a disability and the number of life years saved.[423] However, the same Recommendations establish as a prioritization criterion the "number of years adjusted to quality" *(años de vida ajustados a la calidad)* or QALY (Quality-adjusted life years). They conclude that one should take "the social value of the ill person into account".

These set of recommendations has been criticized because they aim at saving the highest number of socially valuable persons. The mere idea of having to establish who is socially valuable should be rejected. It is argued that such a criterion may

420 See Dependencia.info, "SEGG: 'No se ha negado la atención hospitalaria de alto nivel a ningún anciano vulnerable'", 8 June 2020 <https://dependencia.info/noticia/3620/salud/segg:-no-se-ha-negado-la-atencion-hospitalaria-de-alto-nivel-a-ningun-anciano-vulnerable.html>.

421 See Grupo de Trabajo de Bioética de la SEMICYUC, "Recomendaciones éticas para la toma de decisiones en la situación excepcional de crisis por pandemia Covid-19 en las unidades de cuidados intensivos", 2020, <https://semicyuc.org/wp-content/uploads/2020/03/%C3%89tica_SEMICYUC-COVID-19.pdf>. The elaboration process of this document is explained by Rubio *et al., op. cit.,* 441 ff.

422 See SEMICYUC, *op. cit.,* 3.

423 See Rubio *et al., op. cit.,* 443.

provide unacceptable cover to prioritizing those in power.[424] Moreover, those recommendations are deemed to follow a utilitarian perspective, which the critics say that is hard to reconcile with the Spanish Constitution and bioethics principles.[425]

In particular, it is deplorable that SEMICYUC's recommendations may lead to people with disabilities being relegated due to the mere fact that they are depending on another person.[426] This may be a violation of the New York Convention on the Rights of Persons with Disabilities (CRPD), of which Spain is a party.[427] The recommendations at stake would leave in a worse condition those who, after hypothetically receiving medical treatment, would stay in a permanent vegetative state. This is contrary to human dignity (enshrined in Art. 10 CE). To this regard, the Spanish Committee of Representatives of Persons with Disabilities (CERMI, by its initials in Spanish)[428] issued a document[429] in which they rejected discrimination against persons with disabilities. According to the same, one should never deny access to intensive medicine to such persons, since they have a right to be provided health care in ICUs whenever their illness so requires. Where disability is not clinically relevant, it should not actually play a role with regard to health care provision, CERMI concluded. CERMI requested from the Spanish Ombudsman (*Defensor del Pueblo*) that scientific recommendations such as the aforementioned are rejected as a valid basis for any clinical decisions. The Spanish Ombudsman replied that such recommendations lack any official character and are blatantly contrary to the Spanish legal system.[430]

c) The Spanish Health Ministry issued a Report on the ethical aspects of the Covid-19 pandemic.[431] According to it, the measures adopted should be based on the principles of equity, non-discrimination, solidarity, justice, proportionality and

[424] See Iñigo De Miguel Beriain, "Triaje en tiempos de pandemia: un análisis a partir de las limitaciones del marco jurídico español", in Elena Atienza Macías / Juan Francisco Rodríguez Ayuso (eds.), *Las respuestas del Derecho a las crisis de salud pública* (Dykinson 2020), 229, 230.

[425] See Montalvo and Bellver, *op. cit.*, p. 246 and 249.

[426] Again, see De Miguel, *op. cit.*, 231.

[427] Ratification Instrument (*Instrumento de Ratificación*) of 23 November 2007, *de la Convención sobre los derechos de las personas con discapacidad, hecho en Nueva York el 13 de diciembre de 2006* (BOE no. 96, 21.4.2008).

[428] See Comité Español de Representantes de Personas con Discapacidad (CERMI), <https://www.cermi.es/>.

[429] CERMI, "Argumentario de urgencia para las organizaciones del movimiento CERMI sobre atención sanitaria adecuada sin discriminaciones por razón de discapacidad en la crisis de la pandemia del coronavirus", April 2020, <https://www.cermi.es/es/actualidad/novedades/argumentario-de-urgencia-para-las-organizaciones-del-movimiento-cermi-sobre>.

[430] See CERMI, "El Defensor del Pueblo dice que 'no es aceptable' que sociedades científicas recomienden el sacrificio de personas con discapacidad por falta de medios", 27 March 2020, <https://www.cermi.es/es/actualidad/noticias/el-defensor-del-pueblo-dice-que-no-es-aceptable-que-sociedades-cient%C3%ADficas>.

[431] Ministerio de Sanidad, "Informe del Ministerio de Sanidad sobrelos aspectos éticos ensituaciones de pandemia: ElSARS-CoV-2", 2 April 2020, <https://www.sanidad.gob.es/profesionales/saludPublica/ccayes/alertasActual/nCov/documentos/AspectosEticos_en_situaciones_de_pandemia.pdf>.

transparency, inter alia. Scarce resources allocation should be based on objective, generalizable, transparent, public and consensus criteria (in addition to the individual circumstances of each patient). The general criteria laid down by the Ministry are: 1) non-discrimination on the basis of criteria other than the objective chances of survival, based on evidence; 2) the principle of maximum benefit re the recovery of human lives; 3) the seriousness of the patient's condition (ICUs); 4) the objective chances of saving the patient with regard to her previous health state, and 5) that triage on the basis of age is 'absolutely' forbidden.[432]

d) The Spanish Society of Bioethics and Medical Ethics (*Asociación Española de Bioética y Ética Médica,* AEBI),[433] a private organization, issued a document titled "Bioethical Considerations regarding Covid-19"[434] in March 22, 2020. According to the same, prioritization should be based on: (i) the seriousness of the patient's condition, prognosis and evolution; (ii) Every patient should be assessed on the basis of what is more adequate for the same (disability is rejected as a criterion); and (iii) age should not be used as the sole or even the main criterion.

e) The Spanish Bioethics Committee, an official commission with an independent nature,[435] issued its own report in March 25, 2020.[436] According to it, several criteria used by the recommendations aforementioned are deemed inadmissible. Utilitarianism is rejected.[437] The report considers that one cannot discuss what makes a person socially valuable or not. The Committee is in favor of what is called a 'mixed model'. This takes into consideration social utility, equity, and protection against vulnerability, in addition to the individual circumstances. However, age as such cannot be a criterion to deny treatment. Doctors should assess every patient. The only exception of positive discrimination allowed should be children (the principle of the so-called 'superior interest of the minor' is referred to).[438] Age can be used as a prioritization criterion, but not to decide who gets medical treatment. Disability as such is also not allowed as a criterion, otherwise this would be in contradiction with the New York Convention, mentioned above.[439]

---

432 This is also the point of view held by Carlos María Romeo Casabona and Asier Urruela Mora, "La gestión de soportes vitales escasos en contextos de pandemia. Reflexiones acerca de la aplicación de triajes en el marco del COVID-19" (2020) 50 Revista de Bioética y Derecho 99 <https%3A%2F%2Fscielo.isciii.es%2Fpdf%2Fbioetica%2Fn50%2F1886-5887-bioetica-50-00099.pdf>„ 109, who were, by the way, the two main drafters of the Spanish Health Ministry report.

433 <http://aebioetica.org>.

434 AEBI, "Consideraciones bioéticas ante el Covid-19 de AEBI", 22 March 2020, <https://www.cibir.es/files/biblioteca/COVID-19-aebi.pdf>

435 See its website under <http://www.comitedebioetica.es>.

436 Comité de Bioética de España (CBE), "Informe del Comité de Bioética de España sobre los aspectos bioéticos de la priorización de recursos sanitarios en el contexto de la crisis del coronavirus", Madrid: CBE, 2020 <http://assets.comitedebioetica.es/files/documentacion/Informe%20CBE-%20Priorizacion%20de%20recursos%20sanitarios-coronavirus%20CBE.pdf>.

437 See also Montalvo and Bellver, *op. cit.,* 246 (both authors are members of the Committee, and Montalvo is actually its president).

438 See also Montalvo and Bellver, *op. cit.,* 262 and Romeo andUrruela, *op. cit.,* 106.

439 Also see Montalvo and Bellver, *op. cit.,* 262.

f) The Health Care Ethics Committee (CEA, by its initials in Catalan) at the Clinic Hospital in Barcelona also published a "Document on the adequacy of vital support treatment during the period of the SARS-CoV-2 pandemic", also in March 2020.[440] The document starts from the basis that in an emergency situation it is more pressing to prioritize access to beds in ICUs for those patients who may derive a larger benefit, so health care professionals face ethical dilemmas without any absolute rules solving the latter. Therefore, decisions should not be adopted on the basis of who is it possible to cure from a utilitarian perspective, but who will be in the best situation to overcome the illness.[441] The CEA is in favor of assessing the life expectancy of each individual patient as well as the benefit expected, in particular with regard to the expected quality of life. Therefore, the CEA does not intend to prioritize saving as many lives as possible but it introduces a quality of life criterion. In order to decide whether a patient may enter an ICU, a global assessment of the whole patient is required (recommendation no. 1). This should include the assessment of the patient's functional and cognitive situation as well as their previous comorbidity. Withdrawal of assigned resources is provided for according to the patient's clinical evolution (recommendation no. 4), but no mention is made to resources' scarcity. CEA is also in favor of decisions adoption by an ad hoc committee.[442]

g) The Observatory of Bioethics and Law (*Observatorio de Bioética y Derecho,* OBD) at the University of Barcelona issued a set of recommendations in March 2020.[443] The document aims at providing guidance to professionals in the area of health care to patients in a critical condition. The OBD assumes that under such circumstances the individual rights of patients may have to endure a restriction. Therefore, in an emergency setting, *"professionals must prioritize their duty to the community over the duty of respect for the individual"*. However, this "change from patient-centered care to population-focused care" should be in line with some previous, general and transparent guidelines.[444] Triage should take place only after all intra- and extra-hospital resources have been exhausted.[445] Prioritization should be established in advance and no patient should be ever abandoned.[446] As to the guidelines, the OBD recommends an early proactive assessment of patients who may be

---

440 Comitè d'Ètica Assistencial – Hospital Universitari Clínic Barcelona, "Document sobre adequació del tractament de suport vital en el període de pandèmia SARS-CoV-2", Barcelona: Hospital Clínic, 2020 <https://www.uch.cat/documents/hclinic-cea-uci-covid-19-v.1-20-03-20.pdf>.

441 CEA, *op. cit.,* 1.

442 CEA, *op. cit.,* 2; similarly, Romeo andUrruela, *op. cit.,* 105.

443 Observatorio de Bioética y Derecho de la Universidad de Barcelona, "Recomendaciones para la toma de decisiones éticas sobre el acceso de pacientes a unidades de cuidados especiales en situaciones de pandemia. Documento de consenso del OBD", Barcelona: Universitat de Barcelona, 2020 <http://www.bioeticayderecho.ub.edu/sites/default/files/documents/doc_recom-decisiones-pandemia.pdf>.

444 OBD, *op. cit.,* 32.

445 OBD, *op. cit.,* 33.

446 OBD, *op. cit.,* 36 (recommendation no. 3)

potential candidates for ICU admission; an evaluation of the patient's comorbidity; prioritization according to specific criteria and a decision in advance as to when a treatment which has already been initiated may be changed to a lower-level treatment; limitation of life support treatment will be assessed in patients who are developing unfavorably; decisions ideally to be taken by a triage committee; dynamical reassessment of the guidelines; end of life care to be ensured to all patients, as well as emotional support measures for personnel involved in decision-making.[447] In addition to this guidelines, OBD states that decisions not to allow admission to a ICU should be assessed dynamically *"in order to adapt the exceptional criteria to the current situation"*.[448]

h) The Central Commission of Deontology of the Medical Organization *(Comisión Central de Deontología de la Organización Médica)*[449] *issued a Report with regard to the prioritization of decisions on the ill people in a critical condition in a health catastrophe.*[450] *According to the same, establishing priorities is not only necessary but unavoidable when resources become scarce. In such a setting, the use of resources should be guided by an idea of solidarity among regions. Therefore, in a country of Spain where there may be important differences between one region and another, it is important that triage does not take place if there still remain resources available at a different place in the country.*[451] *Moreover, establishing life expectancies in the short term is acceptable in order to avoid "therapeutic obstinacy"; however, in the mid-term, using criteria such as the chronological one (i.e. the age) is a "very risky decision which should be taken in an exceptional manner only"*. To this regard, the Report states that one should take into consideration *"the usual valuation instruments but never the own clinical impression only"*. Therefore, each decision should be taken as regards an individual patient only, it is concluded.[452] They also emphasize that any criteria used should be transparent but it should be the public authorities which should disseminate information instead of scientific committees, to avoid unnecessary social unrest or alarm.[453]

From a general perspective, one may wonder what the value of such protocols and recommendations actually is.[454] They are nothing more than mere recommendations, therefore lacking in binding force. Scientific societies can provide technical opinions but cannot adopt political or legal decisions. Prioritization protocols can

---

447 OBD, *op. cit.*, 36–37.

448 OBD, *op. cit.*, 37.

449 <https://www.cgcom.es>.

450 Organización Médica Colegial de España (OMC), "Informe en relación a la priorización de las decisiones sobre los enfermos en estado crítico en una catástrofe sanitaria", 23 March 2020, <https://www.cgcom.es/media/2819/download>.

451 Also see Romeo and Urruela, *op. cit.*, 102–103. Nevertheless, it may be submitted that in a situation like the Covid-19 pandemic where the health system collapsed as a whole the idea that one may transfer patients from a region to another may be just an illusion.

452 OMC, *op. cit.*, 5.

453 OMC, *op. cit.*, 5.

454 This is a response to Question no. 3 of the Questionnaire.

only be passed by the Ministry of Health, pursuant to Royal Decree Act 6/2020, on certain urgent measures in the economic sphere and to protect public health (Art. 4).[455] The latter norm amended an Organic Act from 1986 on special public health measures.[456] According to the amended provision (new Art. 4),

When a medicine, a health product or any product necessary for the protection of health is affected by exceptional supply difficulties and to guarantee its best distribution, the State Health Administration may temporarily:

a) Establish centralized supply by the Administration.
b) Condition its prescription to the identification of risk groups, performance of analytical and diagnostic tests, completion of protocols, sending information to the health authority on the course of treatment or other similar particularities.

It may be suggested that this provision provides a statutory basis for the application of triage protocols.[457] However, the lack of clear guidance by the public authorities paved the way for the flourishing of a number of protocols from several private organizations, as shown above. Apart from the Health Ministry, only the Spanish Bioethics Committee had an official nature.[458] The result of such a diversity of instruments is uncertainty as to how to operate in practice.[459] On the one hand, having a previously drafted set of guidelines may help health care professionals in that at least they are assisted to some extent to face moral and ethical dilemmas.[460] From this perspective, such kind of protocols and recommendations may be useful in reducing collateral damage such as stress on the side of health care staff.[461] Moreover, recommendations and protocols may be informative as regards the public, so everyone may know well in advance what can be expected in an emergency situation. Protocols may be of limited help when situations evolve and change. Therefore, recommendations should be open and professionals should seek the backup from ethical committees or, probably even better, *ad hoc* committees, as far as possible.[462]

On the other hand, some of the criteria used by some protocols are hard to reconcile with existing legislation, as has already been pointed out in part. Generally speaking, in a pandemic one may use the following criteria: a) saving the highest number of lives possible; b) saving the highest number of life years possible; c) maximizing the life years taking the quality of life into account. However, only

455 Royal Decree-Act (*Real Decreto-ley*, RDL) 6/2020, of 10 March, *por el que se adoptan determinadas medidas urgentes en el ámbito económico y para la protección de la salud pública* (BOE no. 62, 11.3.2020).

456 LO 3/1986, of 14 April, *de Medidas Especiales en Materia de Salud Pública* (BOE no. 102, 29.4.1986).

457 This is a response to Question no. 5 of the Questionnaire.

458 To be more precise, it is the only commission with a legal authorization to issue bioethical reports; see Montalvo and Bellver, *op. cit.*, 246.

459 This is a response to Question no. 6 of the Questionnaire.

460 Similarly, see OBD, *op. cit.*, 33.

461 See Rubio *et al.*, *op. cit.*, 444; similarly, Romeo and Urruela, *op. cit.*, 103.

462 See De Miguel, *op. cit.*, 233–234. Also, in favor of decisions' adoption by a triage committee, OBD, *op. cit.*, 36 (recommendation no. 5) and Romeo and Urruela, *op. cit.*, 105.

the first of the three is in conformity with the fundamental rights and the values enshrined in the modern Constitutions.[463]

In general, scarce resources should only be used by those for whom such resources may be of use. If an illness may be treated without having to use a given resource, the latter should be kept for those patients who really need it. Similarly, with the case of futile treatments, which happen when the resource is used although the patient has no real chances to survive.[464] For instance, the SEGG recommendations, referred to above, state that futile treatments should be avoided.[465] There is no reason to maintain a treatment which has become futile. Obviously, what may be futile can only be decided in the light of the individual circumstances of the case and it may be extremely difficult to define; if directives could be issued regarding what is going to be deemed futile, they should be made public. Transparency is essential to this regard.[466]

It may also be kept in mind that some patients may have rejected life support in advance; on a general basis, access to a resource should be provided to those patients who accept it.[467] The patient's autonomy is protected by the law.[468] What should not be accepted is that a resource is reserved in advance and kept aside on a precautionary basis so a patient in need will be deprived of the same merely because that very resource may become necessary at a later stage for another patient.[469] That could amount to a violation of the equality of treatment principle. Therefore, all patients with the same needs should be treated equally. To that end, one should assess each patient on an individual basis. In Spanish literature, some scholars endorse the use of a clinical assessment instrument called SOFA (Sequential Organ Failure Assessment). The latter provides a model according to which each patient may be given a score upon which access to an ICU may be provided or not. Such a scoring system may be followed but not in an automatic manner; one should always keep the whole circumstances of the individual patient in mind.[470] However, it may be taken into consideration that SOFA is not advised to be used in isolation to exclude a patient from receiving interventions, and therefore will not assist in the triage process which typically took place during the pandemic.[471] At any rate, those

[463] See De Miguel, *op. cit.,* 230.

[464] See De Miguel, *op. cit.,* 234.

[465] SEGG, *op. cit.,* 2.

[466] Similarly see Romeo and Urruela, *op. cit.,* 104, according to whom transparency prevents that some patients are preferred or treated better than others. Also see Marta Consuegra Fernández and María Casado, "El triaje de los pacientes de COVID-19" (2020) *527 Investigación y Ciencia 56.*

[467] See Romeo and Urruela, *op. cit.,* 105.

[468] In particular see Act 41/2002, of 14 November, *básica reguladora de la autonomía del paciente y de derechos y obligaciones en materia de información y documentación clínica* (BOE no. 274, 15.11.2002).

[469] Again, see De Miguel, *op. cit.,* 234, with further references.

[470] See Romeo and Urruela, *op. cit.,* 110.

[471] See TRACIE — Healhcare Emergency Preparedness Information Gateway, "SOFA Score: What it is and How to Use it in Triage", December 2020, <https://files.asprtracie.hhs.gov/documents/aspr-tracie-sofa-score-fact-sheet.pdf>.

patients who do not make it to an ICU should also not be abandoned but provided medical attention or palliative care.[472]

Nevertheless, there may be two qualifications to the equal treatment principle. One has already been mentioned and is the case of health care professionals. The rationale behind this is that this is the best way to protect the health of all, as suggested by the Spanish Bioethics Committee.[473] Such perspective is based on the assumption that some people have an instrumental value or a multiplier effect, in the sense that they are more valuable not intrinsically but because of they carry out activities which are essential for society. The Committee admits that there may be other professionals who also assume risks in the framework of the pandemic.[474] However, it is argued that health care professionals stand out among all of them since they actually risk their lives to save others. This may be true in some circumstances; however, in the case of the Covid-19 it was soon evident that professionals who got infected took some time to get back to work, and some could not even do it. Thus, the idea that one should save them to preserve the others may be based on a wrong assumption.[475]

Moreover, it may be submitted that the Spanish Bioethics Committee, which threw utilitarianism as a guiding principle through the window, is letting utilitarian considerations in through the door, inasmuch as the medical profession and other professions in the health care sector are deemed more important than others. As a result of this utilitarian valuation, the life of a doctor becomes more worth keeping than, for instance, the one of a member of the military or a firefighter, although the latter may put their lives at risk not only in a pandemic, but on a permanent basis. Those in favor of giving priority to health care professionals have no other option than giving the same to these other categories of professionals as well.[476] Nevertheless, it may be submitted that we are entering a very muddy arena this way. Which professions are more risky or worthy than others may be the object of controversy; many professionals may suggest they are the real heroes. Even within health care professionals, one could say that a pediatrician may be more worth saving than a general doctor due to the superior interest of the child.

The second qualification to the equality principle is the case of minors. Again, the Spanish Bioethics Committee holds that children should have a preference access to medical treatment, on the basis of the 'superior interest of the child' (pursuant to the Organic Act on the legal protection of minors[477] and international law). According

472 Again, see Romeo and Urruela, *op. cit.*, 110; similarly, Consuegra and Casado, *op. cit.*, 56.

473 Also see De Miguel, *op. cit.*, 237.

474 In a similar vein, Montalvo and Bellver, *op. cit.*, 263, suggest that it is important that the morale of such professionals is kept high and to that end one should assure them that in case needed they will receive all the attention and care.

475 Similarly, Romeo and Urruela, *op. cit.*, 107.

476 As happens with De Miguel, *op. cit.*, 238 or Romeo and Urruela, *op. cit.*, 108.

477 LO 1/1996, of 15 January, *de Protección Jurídica del Menor, de modificación parcial del Código Civil y de la Ley de Enjuiciamiento Civil* (BOE no. 15, 17.1.1996).

to that Act, *"In the event that all the competing legitimate interests cannot be respected, the best interest of the minor must prevail over any other legitimate interest that may occur"* (Art. 2.4 II LO 1/1996). This being said, fortunately the Covid-19 pandemic did not have a relevant impact on the children population so triage was not necessary among children.[478]

In any case, it is not the task of scientific committees and the like to establish prioritization criteria. They may contribute to scientific discussion but the legal protection of the right to health should not be left in the hands of private associations.[479] Moreover, these protocols usually fail to solve the case where two patients have exactly the same clinical features and resources are scarce.[480]

2. Chaos in practice

The Spanish Government was clearly unprepared to deal with the pandemic crisis. The public administrations did not have enough means to tackle the same. Obviously, the probability of a pandemic was not unknown, certainly not to public authorities. Pandemic have existed for centuries and there were still fresh examples from recent times.[481] However, the fact is that public hospitals lacked a sufficient number of ventilators for the number of patients, not to talk about protective devices and equipment for the medical personnel. The lack of political leadership resulted in a tension between the central government and some of the regions. In particular, conflicts arose in Madrid and Catalonia. Leaving aside the latter — since the tensions were partly attributable to preexisting political issues in the context of the pro-independence movement — the situation was particularly serious in Madrid.

The Health Ministry of Madrid regional Government issued an internal protocol in March 23, 2020.[482] Similar protocols were adopted in other regions such as Catalonia.[483] The Madrid protocol included the recommendation that elderly people (i.e., those 80 years old or older) in a seriously fragile state or with a serious or moderate dementia should not be sent to hospitals but kept at their homes. Such criterion may

478 See Romeo and Urruela, *op. cit.,* 105.

479 See Montalvo and Bellver, *op. cit.,* 255.

480 This is a response to Case no. 2 of the Questionnaire.

481 For a general overview, see Sonia De Miguel Fernández and Juan Carlos Ruiz de la Roja, *Coronavirus. Prevención, pandemia y contención* (Catarata 2020) 11 ff.

482 This was revealed by a press article by Elena G. Sevillano, "Madrid elaboró un protocolo para no derivar al hospital a pacientes domiciliarios", *El País* 10 June 2020 <https://elpais.com/sociedad/2020-06-09/madrid-elaboro-un-protocolo-para-no-derivar-al-hospital-a-pacientes-domiciliarios.html>.

483 See P. Gabilondo *et al.,* "De Canarias a Castilla y León, autonomías que limitaron la hospitalización de ancianos", *El Confidencial,* 21 June 2020 <https://www.elconfidencial.com/espana/2020-06-21/canarias-castilla-leon-autonomias-ingreso-vital-hospital-ancianos_2647963/>; Ignasi Jorro, "Médicos y expertos exigen a Torra parar el triaje y pedir auxilio al Gobierno", *El confidencial,* 2 April 2020, <https://cronicaglobal.elespanol.com/vida/ancianos-mayores-coronavirus-cataluna_334590_102.html>.

have been based on the assumption that the elderly may be infected at hospitals and therefore it was safer to keep them where they were — or simply that they were of less social value. The protocol also relied upon criteria which were not of medical but merely bureaucratic or administrative ones, such as whether the patient had a private insurance policy or the degree to which they were dependent on another person. These are purely arbitrary and discriminatory criteria.[484] The protocol was amended at a later stage[485] but still some cases (terminal patients) were kept at their homes or in nurseries in cases where going to hospital was not recommended. The Madrid protocol is a disgraceful case of discrimination on the basis of age. According to the Spanish Bioethics Committee, the age criterion should only be relied upon in order to prioritize, but not to deny or limit health care provision and access to certain measures of life support.[486] Similarly, it has been suggested that "chronological age" as such cannot be used as a criterion to exclude patients from ICUs or more generally to adopt health care decisions.[487] There seems to be a consensus that one should take "biological age" into account, where other variables like the degree of fragility of the patient is considered, instead.[488] Moreover, the protocol may have been resulted in the death of many elderly people for want of an adequate medical attention at hospital. This is a serious failure by public authorities. Even in a state of emergency the State has a duty to protect human rights.[489]

It is open to question whether such conduct on the side of the public authorities may give rise to any liabilities at all from a legal perspective. The Public Prosecutor rejected to file criminal charges against the regional authorities of Madrid. From a tort law perspective, medical liability is based on fault as a rule (Art. 1902 ff of the Civil Code, [*Código Civil,* CC]). However, Spanish legislation also provides that public administrations are liable on a strict basis, irrespective of fault. This being so, the fact is that case law always analyzes public authorities' liability from a fault perspective. The previous is important in a country like Spain, where most hospitals are public. It has been suggested that modern hospitals were, paradoxically, badly

---

484 See Milagros Pérez Oliva, "La peor medicina de catástrofe" (2002) El País <https://elpais.com/opinion/2020-06-14/la-peor-medicina-de-catastrofe.html>.

485 See Público, "La Comunidad de Madrid también dio orden de no derivar a hospitales a pacientes domiciliarios", 10 June 2020 <https://www.publico.es/politica/comunidad-madrid-dio-orden-no-derivar-hospitales-pacientes-domiciliarios.html>.

486 See also De Miguel, *op. cit.,* 231 and Romeo and Urruela, *op. cit.,* 108.

487 See Clara Bonanada *et al.*, "Coronavirus: la emergencia geriátrica de 2020. Documento conjunto de la Sección de Cardiología Geriátrica de la Sociedad Española de Cardiología y la Sociedad Española de Geriatría y Gerontología" (2020) 73 Revista Española de Cardiología 569 <https://www.revespcardiol.org/es-coronavirus-emergencia-geriatrica-2020-documento-articulo-S030089322030172X>.

488 See Rubio *et al., op. cit.,* 443.

489 As emphasized by Carlos Ayala Corao, "Algunos efectos de las restricciones adoptadas por el Covid-19 para el Estado de Derecho, la democracia y los derechos humanos con especial énfasis en las Américas", in Enrique Arnaldo Alcubilla and Raúl Canosa Usera (eds.), *El Derecho Constitucional ante el Covid-19. Las diferentes respuestas en el ámbito comparado* (Wolters Kluwer 2020) 51, 70.

prepared to cope with the pandemic patients. Whereas old hospitals are said to have large rooms where several patients may stay, more modern ones follow an 'attention quality' and 'one chamber per patient' approach, which implies that there is a lower availability of ventilators and oxygen inlet devices.[490] At any rate, there is no liability for force majeure (Art. 1105 CC). Nevertheless, public authorities may be held liable for damage caused by their actions or omissions in the face of force majeure; therefore, if they fail to act or their measures cause damage to third persons, they may have to compensate for the same.[491]

Failure to treat a patient medically can also amount to a crime (Art. 196 of the Spanish Criminal Code [*Código Penal*, CP]).[492] State of necessity is available as a defence,[493] as would probably happen in a case where there was a need to spare the resource for a later patient, but not as a ground for ex-post triage (which could amount to a homicide).[494] According to criminal legal scholarship, a patient must be provided with the resources available, so denying a resource for a hypothetical later use could amount to a crime of deprivation of medical assistance (Art. 196 CP) as mentioned before. Once a resource is assigned to one patient, it cannot be withdrawn from the same. However, this may be inconvenient where it is realized that the initial assignation was suboptimal. A correction at a later stage, by way of resource reassignation, is incompatible with Spanish criminal law, although from a theoretical perspective is what one should do in order to save as many lives as possible.[495] As it seems, such reassignation happened in practice and was actually one of the issues which caused more uproar in the public opinion against medical staff during the pandemic.[496] Moreover, if reassignation is excluded, a physician may take more time to assign a given resource, in anticipation for any other potential patients which may require the same in the future. This may result in people dying because of not having been provided the resource at stake when they needed it.

To date, it is not entirely clear whether Spanish public administrations will be held liable for damage related to the pandemic.[497] Of course, one should bear in

[490] See José Antonio Suñé Cano, "Directrices de la Organización Mundial de la Salud ante retos de l asistencia sanitaria hospitalaria derivados de la pandemia de Covid-19", in Gabriela Cobo del Rosal and Jesús María Navalpotro (eds.), *Derechos fundamentales en estado de alarma: una aproximación multidisciplinar* (Dykinson 2020)105, 117.

[491] For further detail see Ruda, "Tort Law and the Coronavirus", *op cit.*

[492] LO 10/1995, of 23 November, *del Código Penal* (BOE no. 281, 24.11.1995). This is a response to Question no. 7 of the Questionnaire.

[493] This is a response to Case no. 1 of the Questionnaire.

[494] This is a response to Case no. 3 of the Questionnaire. See Montalvo and Bellver, *op. cit.,* 254, according to whom ethical conflicts posed by *ex post* triage are even more serious than with regard to *ex ante* triage.

[495] See De Miguel, *op. cit.,* 235–236.

[496] See Diana Fresno, "Los médicos defienden su actuación frente a los triajes: 'El objetivo siempre ha sido salvar vidas'",*Voz Pópuli,* 20 June 2020 <https://www.vozpopuli.com/sanidad/medicos-niegan-criterio-atencion-coronavirus_0_1365764619.html>.

[497] On this issue, see David Blanquer Criado, "Los daños por la COVID-19 (responsabilidad patrimonial; ordenación y privación de derechos)", in David Blanquer (ed.), *COVID-19 y Derecho público*

mind that difficult decisions had to be taken under difficult circumstances.[498] However, where there was clearly a negligent conduct liability should arise.

An example that the Spanish public authorities failed to fulfil their duties is the case decided by the Decision of the Spanish Supreme Court (*Sentencia del Tribunal Supremo,* STS) of 8 October 2020 (No. 3024/2020). The claim had been filed by the State Confederation of Medical Unions (*Confederación Estatal de Sindicatos Médicos*, CESM) on the basis of the inactivity by the Spanish Health Ministry. In particular, the claimant organization claimed that the Ministry had failed to provide the means required to fight the pandemic so medical professionals were exposed to a higher risk of contagion.

Health provision professionals complain, in particular, that they were unprepared, badly equipped, and risked their lives to save others. There is a reciprocity argument here, since by assuming a higher risk they should also be preferred when medical treatment is provided and resources are scarce. To this regard, the Spanish Bioethics Committee has adopted the view that those professionals should be given priority in medical treatment, and this is also the way to better protect the population in general — as already pointed out. According to this perspective, health provision professionals are socially valuable because of the activity they carry out (not because of the persons as such). The problem with this perspective is that it may leave aside other people who were exposed to a similar risk, like other hospital staff (cleaning, concierges, etc.), as well as other professionals outside the health sector, like police and security forces. Going even further, it may be open to discussion why some categories of professionals are more valuable than others; why, for instance, a supermarket cashier is worth less than a nurse.

Conclusions

In sum, Spain was rather ill equipped to face a pandemic like the Covid-19 one as a country. From a statutory or regulatory perspective, Spanish law already had the instruments needed to cope with it. In particular, legislation on health protection provided some mechanisms which allowed public authorities to deal with the situation. However, from an economic perspective it soon became obvious that resources available were insufficient. Moreover, public authorities did not address the whole situation in a proper manner. First, a plethora of normative instruments, in particular through Royal Decree-Acts, was issued. This caused confusion and uncertainty. Second, the Spanish Government made use of a state of alarm declaration. However, eventually this turned to be a wrong decision, not only because the restrictions of rights which were decreed would have required a much more stringent normative cover (a state of emergency), but also because a state of alarm was actually not

(Tirant 2020) 399.

498 See De Miguel, *op. cit.*, 233.

necessary at all. Largely the same politicians who proved unable to navigate this crisis stay in power and no liabilities have been assumed.

As regards resources scarcity, first of all it is undeniable that public authorities had failed to prepare for the pandemic from the point of health care provision. In the case of Spain, it may be taken into consideration that the financial crisis from 2008 took a particularly high toll. However, after the crisis ended in 2014 the risk of a new pandemic coming was already known. Although public authorities have a duty to protect public health, privatization of hospitals and public cutoffs have been going on in several regions such as Madrid or Catalonia for many years now. This resulted in nothing less than chaos when the Covid-19 outbreak took place in March 2020. It is obvious that those professionals in the front line, like physicians and nurses, were exposed to an excessive risk; many paid with their lives. To make things worse, ventilators and ICUs were insufficient in the worst days of the pandemic. Medical professionals had to face such resources' shortage with no clear protocols and the first protocols issued were rather problematic.

A number of protocols which include guidance on triage and resources' rationing have indeed been issued during the pandemic. Such protocols may get outdated soon because of the evolution of the pandemic itself. Moreover, there may be contradictions and uncertainties resulting from them. There is a general tendency to allow utilitarianism perspectives into the protocols' recommendations, as in the case where some types of professionals are given preference over others. However, utilitarian points of view are largely rejected by the Spanish Bioethics Committee. According to the latter, utilitarian theories are incompatible with fundamental rights as enshrined in the Spanish Constitution.[499] This may be seen as an echo of the classic debate between Kantian deontologism and utilitarianism (or consequentialism) in its different forms.[500] Be it as it may, the parties involved in health care provision and authorities in charge of decision adoption should make clear on which criteria they decided to ration resources. Politicians who did not measure up to the job should be held accountable and victims of bad decisions should get compensation and redress. More importantly, lessons should be drawn from the whole pandemic experience so Spain and other countries are better prepared in the future. Although the situation is not the same than before the pandemic, still several issues need to be addressed, like reassignation, the use of SOFA, or what collectives should be preferred, if any, *inter alia*.

499 Also see Montalvo and Bellver, *op. cit.*, 251–252.

500 Instead of many see Tom L. Beauchamp and James F. Childress, *Principles of Biomedical Ethics* (7th edn., New York / Oxford: Oxford University Press, 2013) p. 354 ff.

The list of abbreviations

AEBI	Spanish Society of Bioethics and Medical Ethics (*Asociación Española de Bioética y Ética Médica*)
BOE	Official Gazette (*Boletín Oficial del Estado*)
CBE	Spanish Bioethics Committee (*Comité de Bioética de España*)
CC	Civil Code (*Código Civil*)
CE	Spanish Constitution
CEA	Health Care Ethics Committee
CERMI	Committee of Representatives of Persons with Disabilities
CESM	Confederation of Medical Unions (*Confederación Estatal de Sindicatos Médicos*)
CP	Criminal Code (*Código Penal*)
CRPD	Convention on the Rights of Persons with Disabilities
LO	Organic Act (*Ley Orgánica*)
QALY	Quality-adjusted life years
OBD	Observatory of Bioethics and Law (*Observatorio de Bioética y Derecho*)
OMC	Collegiate Medical Organization of Spain (*Organización Médica Colegial de España*)
RDL	Royal Decree-Act (*Real Decreto-ley*)
SEGG	Spanish Society of Geriatrics and Gerontology (*Sociedad Española de Geriatría y Gerontología*)
SEMICYUC	Spanish Society of Internal and Critical Medicine and Coronary Units (*Sociedad Española de Medicina Intensiva, Crítica y Unidades Coronarias*)
SOFA	Sequential Organ Failure Assessment
STC	Decision of the Spanish Constitutional Court (*Sentencia del Tribunal Constitutional*)
TC	Spanish Constitutional Court (Tribunal Constitucional)

Bibliography

• Legislation

Act (Ley) 14/1986, of 25 April, Ley 14/1986, de 25 de abril, *General de Sanidad* (Official Gazette [*Boletín Oficial del Estado,* BOE] no. 102, 29.4.1986)

Act (Ley) 41/2002, of 14 November, *básica reguladora de la autonomía del paciente y de derechos y obligaciones en materia de información y documentación clínica* (BOE no. 274, 15.11.2002)

Act (Ley) 33/2011, of 4 October, *General de Salud Pública* (BOE no. 240, 5.10.2011)

Organic Act (*Ley Orgánica,* LO) 4/1981, of 1 June, de los estados de alarma, excepción y sitio (BOE no. 134, 5.6.1981)

Organic Act (*Ley Orgánica,* LO) 3/1986, of 14 April, *de Medidas Especiales en Materia de Salud Pública* (BOE no. 102, 29.4.1986)

Organic Act (*Ley Orgánica,* LO) 10/1995, of 23 November, *del Código Penal* (BOE no. 281, 24.11.1995)

Organic Act (*Ley Orgánica,* LO) 1/1996, of 15 January, *de Protección Jurídica del Menor, de modificación parcial del Código Civil y de la Ley de Enjuiciamiento Civil* (BOE no. 15, 17.1.1996)

Ratification Instrument (*Instrumento de Ratificación*) of 23 November 2007, *de la Convención sobre los derechos de las personas con discapacidad, hecho en Nueva York el 13 de diciembre de 2006* (BOE no. 96, 21.4.2008)

Royal Decree-Act (*Real Decreto-ley*, RDL) 6/2020, of 10 March, *por el que se adoptan determinadas medidas urgentes en el ámbito económico y para la protección de la salud pública* (BOE no. 62, 11.3.2020)

Royal Decree (*Real Decreto,* RD) 463/2020, of 14 March, *por el que se declara el estado de alarma para la gestión de la situación de crisis sanitaria ocasionada por el COVID-19* (BOE no. 67, 14.3.2020)

Royal Decree (*Real Decreto,* RD) 926/2020, of 25 October, *por el que se declara el estado de alarma para contener la propagación de infecciones causadas por el SARS-CoV-2* (BOE no. 282, 25.10.2020)

Royal Decree (*Real Decreto,* RD) 956/2020, of 3 November, *por el que se prorroga el estado de alarma declarado por el Real Decreto 926/2020, de 25 de octubre, por el que se declara el estado de alarma para contener la propagación de infecciones causadas por el SARS-CoV-2* (BOE no. 291, 4.11.2020)

• Case law

Decision of the Constitutional Court (*Sentencia del Tribunal Constitutional*, STC) 63/2011, of 16 May

Decision of the Supreme Court (*Sentencia del Tribunal Supremo,* STS) of 8 October 2020 (No. 3024/2020).

STC 69/1991, of 8 April

• Books

Beauchamp T L and Childress J F, *Principles of Biomedical Ethics* (7th edn., New York / Oxford: Oxford University Press, 2013)

De Miguel Fernández S and Ruiz de la Roja J C, *Coronavirus. Prevención, pandemia y contención* (Madrid: Catarata 2020)

Villalón P C, *Estados excepcionales y suspensión de garantías* (Madrid: Tecnos 1984)

• Articles

Arnaldo Alcubilla E, 'España: tres meses y una semana bajo el estado de alarma', in E Arnaldo Alcubilla and R Canosa Usera (eds.), *El Derecho Constitucional ante el Covid-19. Las diferentes respuestas en el ámbito comparado* (Wolters Kluwer, 2020)

Ayala Corao C, 'Algunos efectos de las restricciones adoptadas por el Covid-19 para el Estado de Derecho, la democracia y los derechos humanos con especial énfasis en las Américas', in E Arnaldo Alcubilla and R Canosa Usera (eds.), *El Derecho Constitucional ante el Covid-19. Las diferentes respuestas en el ámbito comparado* (Wolters Kluwer 2020)

Blanquer Criado D, 'Los daños por la COVID-19 (responsabilidad patrimonial; ordenación y privación de derechos)', in D Blanquer (ed.), *COVID-19 y Derecho público* (Tirant 2020)

Bonanada C et al, 'Coronavirus: la emergencia geriátrica de 2020. Documento conjunto de la Sección de Cardiología Geriátrica de la Sociedad Española de Cardiología y la Sociedad Española de Geriatría y Gerontología' (2020) 73 Revista Española de Cardiología 7

Canosa Usera R, 'El marco internacional y supranacional de la reacción estatal europea ante la emergencia sanitaria', in E Arnaldo Alcubilla / Raúl Canosa Usera (eds.), *El Derecho Constitucional ante el Covid-19. Las diferentes respuestas en el ámbito comparado* (Wolters Kluwer 2020)

Cierco Seira C, 'Derecho de la salud pública y COVID-19', in David Blanquer (ed.), *COVID-19 y Derecho público* (Tirant 2020)

Consuegra Fernández M and Casado M, 'El triaje de los pacientes de COVID-19' (2020) 527 Investigación y Ciencia *56*

De Miguel Beriain I, 'Triaje en tiempos de pandemia: un análisis a partir de las limitaciones del marco jurídico español', in Elena Atienza Macías / Juan Francisco Rodríguez Ayuso (eds.), *Las respuestas del Derecho a las crisis de salud pública* (Dykinson 2020)

De Montalvo Jääskeläinen F and Bellver Capella V, 'La Bioética en los tiempos del coronavirus: una reflexión acerca de algunos dilemas éticos-legales de la pandemia a partir del Informe del Comité de Bioética de España', in Elena Atienza Macías / Juan Francisco Rodríguez Ayuso (eds.), *Las respuestas del Derecho a las crisis de salud pública* (Dykinson 2020)

Romeo Casabona C M and Urruela Mora A, 'La gestión de soportes vitales escasos en contextos de pandemia. Reflexiones acerca de la aplicación de triajes en el marco del COVID-19' (2020) 55 Revista de Bioética y Derecho 99

Rubio O et al, 'Recomendaciones éticas para la toma de decisiones difíciles en las unidades de cuidados intensivos ante la situación excepcional de crisis por la pandemia por COVID-19: revisión rápida y consenso de expertos' (2020) 44 Medicina Intensiva 439

Ruda A, 'Spain', in Ernst Karner / Barbara C. Steininger (eds.), *European Tort Law 2021* (Springer 2022)

Ruda A, 'Spain', in Ernst Karner / Barbara C. Steininger (eds.), *European Tort Law 2020* (Springer 2021)

Ruda A, 'Tort Law and the Coronavirus: Liability for Harm Caused by the COVID-19 Outbreak', in E Hondius, M Santos Silva, A Nicolussi, P Salvador Coderch, C Wendehorst andF Zoll (eds.), *Coronavirus and the Law in Europe* (Intersentia Online 2021)

Savater F, 'Editorial. Plagas' (2020) 271 Claves de Razón Práctica 7

Suñé Cano J A, 'Directrices de la Organización Mundial de la Salud ante retos de l asistencia sanitaria hospitalaria derivados de la pandemia de Covid-19', in G Cobo del Rosal and J M Navalpotro (eds.), *Derechos fundamentales en estado de alarma: una aproximación multidisciplinar* (Dykinson 2020)

Trayter Jiménez J M, 'Derecho administrativo sancionador, estado de alarma y COVID-19', in D Blanquer (ed.), *COVID-19 y Derecho público* (Tirant 2020)

• Other secondary sources

Pérez Oliva M, 'La peor medicina de catástrofe' (2020) *El País* <https://elpais.com/opinion/2020-06-14/la-peor-medicina-de-catastrofe.html>

SWITZERLAND[501]

Dr. Inesa Fausch
Swiss Institute of Comparative Law
University of Basel

A. Questionnaire

1. What are the criteria for the allocation of scarce health care resources in your country?

The Swiss Academy of Medical Science (SAMS[502]) Guidelines on the COVID-19 pandemic: triage for intensive-care treatment under resource scarcity (SAMS Triage Guidelines)[503] set the criteria for Intensive Care Unit (ICU) triage for the point in time at which resources become scarce and decisions must be made as to their rationing. The guidelines are applicable to all patient categories, including both COVID-19 patients and other patients in need of treatment. The SAMS Guidelines also outline the two phases where triage decisions shall be taken: (i) on admission (extent and duration of treatment, determination of pathway, e.g. ICU treatment or palliative care) and (ii) during the ICU stay (daily evaluation with regard to the continuation of treatment, limitation of treatment intensity or duration, modification of treatment goal and palliative care)[504].

The triage decisions shall be based on the principles of medical ethics such as equity (otherwise known as non-discrimination, i.e. absence of any unjustified unequal treatment on the grounds of age, sex, residence, nationality, religious affiliation, social or insurance status, or disability), preserving as many lives as possible, and protecting the health care professionals involved. The latter entails providing medical professionals with maximum protection against infection, physical and psychological stress.

---

501 "Research was conducted and its findings are limited to data available before 1. April, 2021".

502 SAMS was founded under private law in accordance with Art. 80 ff. of the Swiss Civil Code (ZGB; SR 210) of 10 December 1907 (status as of 1 January 2021) and is supported by the Confederation as a member of the Association of SAMS and a research funding institution in accordance with Art. 4 let. a and Art. 7 Para. 1 let. c of the Federal Act on the Promotion of Research and Innovation (FIFG; SR 420.1) of 14 December 2012 (status as of 1 January 2020).

503 Guidance on the application of Section 9.3 of the SAMS Guidelines «Intensive-care interventions» (2013), revised version 3.1., status as of 17 December 2020.

504 SAMS Triage Guidelines, pt II, Art. 4, para 4.1.

According to the SAMS Triage Guidelines, when a triage decision has to be made, the highest priority is to be given to patients who will benefit most from the ICU stay[505]. Upon the ICU admission, the highest priority is to be given to patients whose prognosis with regard to hospital discharge could good with intensive care, but poor otherwise, i.e. to patients who will benefit most from intensive care.[506] Thus, the short-term survival prognosis is a *decisive criterion* for the purpose of triage[507], which is to save as many lives as possible. In general, for patients in need of intensive care, a poor short-term prognosis is not be automatically inferred from age, disability or dementia alone. If a patient is to be given a lower priority with regard to intensive care, there must always be specific risk factors for increased mortality and hence a poor short-term prognosis.[508] However, age and disability require specific attention as both are often linked with a poor short-term prognosis, comorbidities or clinical frailty.

a) Patient age

Age as a criterion *per se* is regarded as controversial. Before 17th of December, 2020, when the SAMS Triage Guidelines were amended, SAMS Triage Guidelines from 20th of March, 2020 stated that *age* shall be considered as a risk factor. According to the older version of SAMS Triage Guidelines, age should be taken into account indirectly evaluating the "short-term prognosis" as older people tend to suffer from co-morbidities more frequently.[509] During the COVID-19 pandemic, age has been a risk factor for mortality and therefore has to be taken into consideration,[510] with an exception if a patient is over 85 years old. Namely, according to the SAMS Triage Guidelines from 20th of March, 2020, if there are no ICU beds available, a patient should not be admitted to the ICU if he or she meets at least one of several non-admission criteria.[511] These include, among others, an age of more than 85 years. Concomitant illness (co-morbidities) is therefore not envisaged as an additional criterion if the patient is over 85 years old. This has triggered a wave of negative reactions[512], especially considering the internal contradiction where SAMS advise that age is not to be regarded as the only factor, yet it is treat-

505 *Ibid.* Art. 1.

506 *Ibid.* Art. 3.

507 *Ibid.* Art. 3.

508 *Ibid.* Art. 3.

509 SAMS Triage Guidelines, earlier version as of 20 March 2020, pt II, art 3.

510 *Ibid.*

511 The criteria for non-admission criteria are listed in an earlier version of the SAMS Triage Guidelines dated 20 March 2020, pt II, art 4.3.

512 See for instance, Interview with Prof. Dr. Bijan Fateh-Moghadam, Professor of Fundamentals of Law and Life Sciences Law, Faculty of Law, Basel University, 'Covid-19 und Intensivmedizin: «Wir brauchen eine öffentliche Diskussion über die gerechte Verteilung von lebensrettenden Ressourcen»' <https://www.unibas.ch/de/Aktuell/News/Uni-Research/Covid-19-und-Intensivmediz-in-Wir-brauchen-eine-oeffentliche-Diskussion-ueber-die-gerechte-Verteilung-von-lebensretten-den-Ressourcen.html> accessed 2 March 2021; also Simon Hehli, 'Alle über 85-Jährigen einfach sterben lassen? Die Richtlinien für die Corona-Behandlungen lösen harsche Kritik aus' (*NZZ,* 30

ed as such if the patient's age exceeds 85 years[513]. As a consequence, the SAMS Triage Guidelines were amended. In the version of SAMS Triage Guidelines from 17th of December, 2020, an age of 85 or more is not regarded as the sole criterion for triage but is linked with a score of 6 or more on the age-related Clinical Frailty Scale[514] (CFS).[515] Thus, age-related frailty is a relevant criterion for poor short-term prognosis and is taken into consideration once the patient's frailty is assessed in accordance with the CFS.

b) Disabilities

According to the SAMS Triage Guidelines, a disability is not in itself a factor of prognostic relevance. However, persons with disabilities may have comorbidities which are associated with the disability directly (e.g. respiratory insufficiency in a person with multiple disabilities) or indirectly (e.g. cancer in a person with quadriplegia)[516]. People with disabilities dependence on assistance for daily activities is not correlated with the short-term prognosis[517]. The CFS has not been validated for the assessment of frailty in persons with disabilities[518].

In case if ICU treatment is not offered or is discontinued because of triage situation, this must be openly communicated to a patient with limited capacity or to the relatives authorised to represent them, who must be provided with the appropriate information about the decision-making process and, if possible, other options should be suggested for further discussion, possibly supplemented by, for example, hospital pastoral care or psychological support.[519]

2. What values are the allocation criteria based on?

The SAMS Triage Guidelines refer to the four widely recognised principles of medical ethics, namely, beneficence, non-maleficence, respect for autonomy and equity. The patient is given a central role as scarce resources must never be allocated for a treatment which a patient does not wish to receive. In practice, if health care

---

October 2020) <https://www.nzz.ch/schweiz/triage-richtlininen-in-den-spitaelern-loesen-harsche-kritik-aus-ld.1584225?reduced=true> accessed 2 March 2021.

513 Lic.iur. Mark-Anthony Schwestermann, 'Diskriminierende Altersgrenze für die Behandlung von COVID-19 Patienten/-innen' (*humanrights.ch,* 1 April 2020) <https://www.humanrights.ch/de/ipf/menschenrechte/alter/diskriminierung-altersgrenze-coronavirus> accessed 2 March 2021.

514 According to Church, S., Rogers, E., Rockwood, K. *et al.*, 'A scoping review of the Clinical Frailty Scale' (2020) 20, 393 *BMC Geriatr* 20, 393 <https://doi.org/10.1186/s12877-020-01801-7> accessed 11 March 2021: the Clinical Frailty Scale (CFS) is a judgement-based frailty tool that used to evaluate specific domains including comorbidity, function, and cognition to generate a frailty score ranging from 1 (very fit) to 9 (terminally ill).

515 SAMS Triage Guidelines, pt II, art 4.3.

516 *Ibid.* art 3.

517 *Ibid.* art 3.

518 *Ibid.* art 3.

519 *Ibid.* art 5.

resources become scarce and every patient cannot receive the requisite treatment, the SAMS Triage Guidelines[520] provide for prioritization on the basis of the following fundamental principles:

a) *Equity*, which means that health care resources needs to be allocated without discrimination on the grounds of age, sex, residence, nationality, religious affiliation, social or insurance status, or disability. The procedure of resource allocation needs to be fair, justified and transparent.
b) *Preserving as many lives as possible*, which means that once there is not enough place in the ICU, decisions shall be made so as to save as many lives as possible.
c) *Protecting the professionals involved*, which means that health care professionals must be protected against infection and excessive physical or psychological stress.

3. What type(s) of document(s) set the allocation criteria: binding or non-binding guidelines, laws, or other type(s) of document(s)?

Although during the first wave of the COVID-19 in Switzerland the reduction in elective procedures[521] and an increase in intensive care unit (ICU) capacity (particularly ventilator-equipped beds) along with public health (behavioural) measures[522] ordered by the federal government were sufficient to prevent health care resources from becoming scarce on a national level[523], Swiss legal acts provide for the allocation of scarce resources.

With regard to COVID-19, numerous legal acts were either implemented or issued, such as the Epidemics Act[524] or the Ordinance on the Coordinated Medical Service[525] , which formed the basis for the legal framework that could be applied in the event of a pandemic, though later Switzerland adopted COVID-19 specific legal

[520] *Ibid.* art 1.

[521] According to Art. 10a Para. 2 of the Ordinance 2 of 13 March 2020 on Measures to Combat the Coronavirus (COVID-19) (COVID-19 Ordinance 2, 818.101.27) (status as of 17 March 2020; since revoked) stated that: 'Healthcare facilities such as hospitals and clinics, medical practices and dental practices must discontinue all non-urgent medical procedures and therapies'.

[522] Hospital capacities are updated and available on the Website: until now (5 January 2021) the hospitals have not been overwhelmed beyond their capacity <https://www.covid19.admin.ch/de/hosp-capacity/icu>.

[523] Covid-19 pandemic: triage for intensive-care treatment under resource scarcity; Guidance on the application of Section 9.3 of the SAMS Guidelines «Intensive-care interventions» (2013), Revised version 3.1, 17 December 2020 <sams.ch/en/coronavirus> accessed 2 March 2021.

[524] Federal Act on the Control of Communicable Diseases in Humans (Epidemics Act, 818.101) of 28 September, 2012 (status of 25 June 2020).

[525] Ordinance on the Coordinated Medical Service (VKSD, 501.31) of 27 April, 2005 (status of 1 February 2016).

acts, including the COVID-19 Act[526], the COVID-19 Ordinance 3[527], the COVID-19 Special Situation Ordinance[528] and others. The numerous guidelines include the SAMS Triage Guidelines, the Recommendations from the Swiss Society of Emergency and Rescue Medicine on Prehospital triage and care under resource scarcity in the hospital sector (particularly in intensive care) during the COVID-19 pandemic, the Recommendations from the Swiss Society of Emergency and Rescue Medicine — Update V3 (SSERM Guidelines)[529], the Guidelines from the Federal Council Commissioner for the Coordinated Medical Service (KSD), and the Guidelines from the Office of the Coordinated Medical Service *"National coordination in the event of a massive influx of patients in intensive care units during the COVID-19 pandemic"* (Guidelines on national coordination)[530]. The aforementioned legal acts clarify the restrictions with regard to COVID-19 and provide guidelines for operation in a situation where resources are scarce. It is necessary to emphasize that the SAMS Triage Guidelines are one of the most detailed sources for health care practitioners who need to decide whether the triage situation applies. As provisions of private law, SAMS Triage Guidelines are not legally binding, but they do have a certain legal effect.[531] As there are numerous SAMS guidelines on various issues, their nature also differs. In some cases, for instance, when regulating euthanasia or reproductive medicine, legal acts must be adopted instead of the SAMS guidelines. However, if regulation is missing and/or reference is made to SAMS guidelines that regulate ethical issues to protect fundamental human rights, the SAMS guidelines shall have legal precedence.[532] Moreover, the Federal Court has long recognised the legitimacy and relevance of the SAMS guidelines[533], which may be used by the

526 Federal Act on the Statutory Principles for Federal Council Ordinances on Combating the COVID-19 Epidemic (COVID-19 Act, 818.101.24), as of 25 September 2020 (status of 19 December 2020). Art.1 of the COVID-19 Act states that this Act regulates the special powers granted to the Federal Council to combat the COVID-19 epidemic and to respond to the effects of the measures taken to combat the disease on society, on the economy and on the public sector.

527 Ordinance 3 on Measures to Combat the Coronavirus (COVID-19) (COVID-19 Ordinance 3, 818.101.24) of 19 June 2020 (status as of 8 February 2021). Art. 1 Para. 1 this Ordinance orders the measures applicable to the population, organisations and institutions to combat the coronavirus and specifies which of these measures must be taken on a canton-wide level.

528 Ordinance on Measures during the Special Situation to combat the COVID-19 Epidemic (COVID-19 Special Situation Ordinance, 818.101.26) of 19 June 2020 (status as of 8 February 2021).

529 As of 12 November, 2020, revised 3rd version, <https://www.sgnor.ch/home/covid-19/>.

530 *In German "Der Beauftragte des Bundesrates für den Koordinierten Sanitätsdienst KSD, Geschäftsstelle Koordinierter Sanitätsdienst, Nationale Koordination bei massivem Zustrom von Patienten in Intensivstationen während der COVID-19-Pandemie"*, status as of 16 June, 2020.

531 Michelle Salathé, 'Die Bedeutung der ärztlichen Unabhängigkeit in der Vollzugsmedizin', <www.samw.ch> p. 68.

532 David Rüetschi, 'Die Medizinisch-ethischen Richtlinien der SAMW aus juristischer Sicht' (2004) 85:23, Schweizerische Ärztezeitung / Bulletin des médecins suisses / Bollettino dei medici svizzeri, p. 1222–1223.

533 Please compare to BGE 98 Ia 508ff. decision from 28.06.1972; BGE 115 Ia 234ff. decision from 15.03.1989; BGE 119 Ia 460ff. decision from 22.12.1993; BGE 121 V 289ff. decision from 13.12.1995; *Supra* 32.

Federal Court as a basis for judicial decisions.[534] The guidelines are widely recognised among doctors. They therefore not only serve as a framework for decisions health care practitioners must make in delicate and complicated situations, but also contain a summary of the legal provisions applicable in law enforcement medicine.[535]

In Switzerland, different types of situations are possible where the issue of allocating scarce resources could arise, i.e. a special situation and an exceptional situation. Article 6, Paragraph 2 of the Epidemics Act states that in the event of a special situation, the necessary measures could be ordered by Federal Council after consulting the cantons[536]. In the event of an exceptional situation, the Federal Council may order the necessary measures for the entire country or for individual parts thereof without a consultation (Article 7 of the Epidemics Act). Throughout the period when the special or extraordinary situation applies[537], the issue of resource scarcity is crucial. The allocation of scarce resources is regulated by several acts.

According to Article 3 Paragraph 4 of the COVID-19 Act, in order to guarantee the hospital capacity required to treat COVID-19 cases and to implement other urgent medical tests and treatment, the cantons may be authorised (i) to prohibit or restrict non-urgent medical tests and treatment, (ii) to take further measures to guarantee the capacity required. Moreover, Article 25, Paragraph 1 of COVID-19 Ordinance 3 states that the cantons shall ensure that a sufficient capacity (in particular, beds and specialist staff) are available in the inpatient departments of hospitals and clinics for COVID-19 patients and for other urgently required medical examinations and treatment, in particular in the intensive care units and the general internal medicine departments. For this purpose, they may require hospitals and clinics: (i) to make their inpatient capacities available immediately or on demand; and (ii) to restrict or suspend non-urgent medical procedures and treatments[538]. Hospitals and clinics must ensure that supplies of medical products for COVID-19 patients and for other urgently required medical examinations and treatment are always available in their outpatient and inpatient departments.[539] Even though making sure that an adequate quantity of essential medical products and access to proper care remain accessible to the population[540] is a priority, medical resources may still become

534 *Supra* 32.

535 Michelle Salathé, Die Bedeutung der ärztlichen Unabhängigkeit in der Vollzugsmedizin, www.samw.ch, p. 68.

536 The information on measures applied by the cantons might differ and are available here: www.ch.ch https://www.bag.admin.ch/bag/de/home/krankheiten/ausbrueche-epidemien-pandemien/aktuelle-ausbrueche-epidemien/novel-cov/massnahmen-des-bundes.html#1794075501> accessed 12 February 2021.

537 During the COVID-19 pandemic, the Federal Council declared an extraordinary situation on 13 March 2020, followed by a special situation on 19 June 2020, in accordance with the Epidemics Act.

538 Covid-19 Ordinance 3 in Art. 25, para 2.

539 *Ibid.*, Art. 25, para 3.

540 Art. 1 Para. 2 of the Covid-19 Ordinances 2 and 3 respectively.

scarce. In order to ensure that the tasks pertaining to patient care can, in the event of a massive influx of patients into critical structures such as ICUs, be also carried out in the best possible way during an extraordinary or special situation, coordination at the national level is indispensable[541]. In this case, the Federal Council can order coordination at a federal level in the event of incidents that affect several cantons, the whole of Switzerland or countries close to the border (Article 1, Paragraph 3 as well as Article 9, Paragraph 3 of the VKSD). The national coordination of ICUs, which is the responsibility of the national coordination unit, is intended to ensure that an optimum balance is maintained between urgent need and the deployment and (or) use of the limited resources available. More specifically, this includes the optimum utilisation of any intensive medical treatment capacity, i.e. the respective places in intensive care units (ICUs) and the means of transport available for intensive care patients.[542]

The responsibility for the triage and admission of patients always remains *local* and lies with the respective hospital and its ICU[543]. The national coordination centre[544] of ICUs[545] shall arrange for the transfer of patients throughout Switzerland who have already undergone triage and have been admitted for intensive care to other certified or recognised ICUs with sufficient capacity as a first priority, and to treatment beds on an *ad hoc* basis as a second priority[546]. Where possible, the patients' cultural and linguistic background is also taken into consideration by arranging transfers primarily within the language regions[547]. Only when the established channels within cantons or regions can no longer allow for any further patient transfers or capacity balancing, those responsible for the ICUs turn to the national coordination unit for *supraregional or nationwide* transfers and capacity balancing[548]. This means that at first, the transfer of patients is arranged on a local scale, i. e. on a cantonal or regional level, and if this is no longer possible, on a supraregional or nationwide level. In a situation where resources are scarce, measures such as an increase in the number of ICU beds across Switzerland, ICU coordination and the suspension of elective procedures shall be applicable[549]. In addition, efforts are made to assess the availability of ICU capacity in collaboration with authorities and hospitals abroad[550].

541 Guidelines on national coordination, p. 1.

542 *Ibid.*

543 *Ibid.* p. 1–2.

544 The coordination centre acts on requests for places where intensive care can be provided or for transfer transportation. After approval by the transferring and receiving intensive care units, it organises the necessary transportation and ensures that the hospitals are informed.

545 In collaboration with various health system agents, the Coordinated Medical Services of the Swiss Armed Forces has established a system for national ICU coordination. A central coordination body is to ensure that optimum use is made of the ICU capacity available across Switzerland: <https://www.vtg.admin.ch/de/organisation/astab/san/ksd/nki.html> accessed on 12 February 2021.

546 Guidelines on national coordination, p. 2.

547 *Ibid.*, p. 5.

548 *Ibid.*, p. 2.

549 SAMS Triage Guidelines, pt II, Art. 4, para 4.2.

550 *Ibid.*

Conversely, if sufficient resources are available, Swiss ICUs should admit patients from neighbouring countries who are facing triage situations[551].

4. Are health care providers bound by law to provide (urgent) care to all patients, and, if so, are there any legally recognised exceptions from this duty?

In principle, everyone in Switzerland is obliged to provide emergency aid in the event of "immediate danger to life" (Article 128 of the Swiss Criminal Code[552]). According to Article 128 of the Swiss Criminal Code, *"any person who fails to offer aid to another whom he has injured or to another who is in immediate life-threatening danger, in circumstances where the person either could reasonably have been expected to offer aid, any person who prevents or hinders others from offering aid, is liable to a custodial sentence not exceeding three years or to a monetary penalty"*.

For practising medical professionals with a university degree, aside from Article 128 of the Swiss Criminal Code, there is a professional duty to "render assistance in urgent cases" (Article 40 let. g of the Federal Act on the University Medical Professions (MedBG)[553]). Article 40 let. g of the MedBG states that *"persons who exercise a university medical profession at their own professional responsibility provide assistance in urgent cases and participate in emergency services in accordance with cantonal regulations"*. Emergencies are therefore defined not only as life-threatening conditions, but as any illness whose treatment cannot be delayed. As a result, in such cases, a physician is under the obligation to accept the order or duty to treat, even if no specific treatment order has been issued. However, one should not make the mistake of assuming that Article 40 let. G of the MedBG extends this duty to any medically indicated treatment[554], as a health care professional may refuse to care for or treat a patient in non-emergency cases[555]. One could say that the so-called principle of "competing duty to act" is recognised as an exception from the duty to offer treatment. The supra-legal justification for the conflict of duties exists if two legal duties coincide in the same situation so that the party under the obligation cannot fulfil one of them without violating the other. In the case of two competing duties to act, whoever chooses the higher duty or one of two equivalent duties at the expense

551 *Ibid.*

552 Swiss Criminal Code (StGB, 311) of 21 December 1937 (status as of 1 July 2020).

553 Federal Act on the University Medical Professions, *in German*: Bundesgesetz über die universitären Medizinalberufe (MedBG, SR 811.11) of 23 June 2006 (status as of 1 February 2020).

554 Regina E. Aebi-Müller, 'Behandlungspflichten und Behandlungsentscheide bei Ressourcenknappheit' (2021) 1 Jusletter, para 12, p. 6; Gächter T, Rütsche B, Gesundheitsrecht, Ein Grundriss für Studium und Praxis', (4th edn, Helbing Lichtenhahn Verlag, Basel 2018), point 316; Poledna T, Berger B, Öffentliches Gesundheitsrecht, (Stämpfli, Bern 2002), point 117.

555 Poledna T, Berger B, *Öffentliches Gesundheitsrecht*, (Stämpfli, Bern 2002), point.112; compare also Büchler A, Michel M, *Medizin – Mensch – Recht, Eine Einführung in das Medizinrecht der Schweiz*, (2nd edn, Schulthess, Zürich/Basel/Genf 2020), p. 83.

of the other does not act unlawfully[556]. This means that health care practitioners who are unable to provide urgent care for every patient due to scarce resources are exempted from the liability for not doing so.

5. On what legal basis is it possible to apply the allocation criteria in practice?

To apply the allocation criteria it is necessary to know the capacity of a hospital and the utilization thereof. In Switzerland, the Coordinated Medical Service (KSD) regularly collects data on hospital capacity in 150 hospitals for acute patients. They assess the situation at a federal level and enable a regional-to-national balance of hospital capacity utilization to be maintained.[557]

Once it is obvious that there is no capacity left to provide treatment and triage decisions must be made, health care practitioners apply the SAMS Triage Guidelines accordingly.

6. What level of legal certainty do health professionals and health care providers have when applying the allocation criteria?

The health care professionals applying the allocation criteria could refer to the SAMS Triage Guidelines. However, the guidelines are not legally binding, and, moreover, there is currently no direct link between them and the Epidemics Act, the COVID-19 Act or the COVID-19 Ordinance 3. This, of course, leaves health care practitioners with a sense of insecurity, as doctors cannot rely on the SAMS Triage Guidelines alone to evade their legal obligation if there is a discrepancy between a legal principle and medical ethics under the SAMS Triage Guidelines.[558] As of today, no case law is available; therefore, it is not quite possible to assess the potential adverse legal consequences of the decisions taken by a health care practitioner on the basis of the SAMS Triage Guidelines.

Nevertheless, triage decisions demand that a health care professional be decisive. As the SAMS Triage Guidelines are the ones that provide detailed information, they are the current framework to refer if triage situation arise. According to the SAMS Triage Guidelines, the criteria of fair prioritisation and fair processes must

556 BGE 130 IV 7 decision from 28.11.2003, p. 20.

557 The data are updated on a daily basis and published on the COVID-19 website of the Federal Office of Public Health (FOPH) at 2 p.m. at the latest: <https://www.vtg.admin.ch/de/aktuell/coronavirus/spitalkapazitaeten.html>

558 According to the Statement of the Federal Council, 'Transparente und klar geregelte Verfahren bei der Verabschiedung von medizinisch-ethischen Richtlinie' (18 November 2020) <https://www.parlament.ch/de/ratsbetrieb/suche-curia-vista/geschaeft?AffairId=20204082> , accessed on 4 March 2021.

be applied at all times and in a transparent manner. Triage decisions should be made when there is sufficient information to confirm that there is indeed a situation of scarcity.[559] Individual decisions must be amenable to examination: they must be documented in writing, and must include a statement of the reasons and the name of the person responsible. Any deviation from the specified allocation criteria must be documented in a similar fashion. In addition, mechanisms should be in place for the subsequent review of conflicts.[560]

The SAMS Triage Guidelines also regulate the decision-making process. Namely, the decision must be made by experienced professionals and, if possible, within a mixed professional team that encompasses several different specializations, rather than by individuals. Ultimately, however, the responsibility is borne by the most senior ICU specialist present.[561] In the event of a discrepancy between the opinion of the referring physician and that of the responsible ICU physician as to the indication for an intensive care measure, clarification or agreement must be sought through direct communication. If this is impossible, the responsible ICU physician must act as a gatekeeper and assume the responsibility.[562]Additional criteria, such as allocation by lottery, the "first come, first served" principle, and the prioritisation of persons expected to have more quality-adjusted life years are not to be applied[563].

7. What are the implications for civil and criminal liability as far as the allocation of scarce health care resources is concerned? Have there already been any related lawsuits and/or criminal proceedings?

The SAMS Triage Guidelines, which provide the criteria for resource allocation, do not mention any potential civil or criminal liability arising to a health care professional responsible for the allocation. Switzerland lacks a clear legal basis for medical triage decisions in the event of an overloaded health care system. However, it is also quite challenging to determine whether general liability rules, whether civil or criminal, are applicable to resource allocation, considering that the health care professional is forced to act under extraordinary circumstances.

Potential triage situations place a great responsibility on health care practitioners or providers. An analysis of the Swiss Criminal Code revealed that a health

559 Ehni H-J, Wiesing U, Ranisch R, 'Saving the most lives — A comparison of European triage guidelines in the context of the COVID-19 pandemic' (2021) 35:125–134 Bioethics <https://onlinelibrary.wiley.com/doi/pdfdirect/10.1111/bioe.12836?download=true>, p. 128.

560 SAMS Triage Guidelines pt II, Art. 5.

561 *Ibid.*

562 According to SAMS Guidelines on intensive care measures, 2018 <https://www.samw.ch/dam/jcr:-48fab1c2-3a14-4bdb-b881-8e60979c1b47/richtlinien_samw_intensivmedizinische_massnahmen.pdf>, p. 38.

563 SAMS Triage Guidelines, pt II, Art. 3.

care professional may not be held criminally liable for triage decisions. First of all, criminal liability could only arise provided the conditions of Article 40 let. g of the MedGB and Article 128 of the Criminal Code are fulfilled. While Article 40 let. g of the MedBG states the professional duty to "render assistance in urgent cases", Article 128 of the Criminal Code provides that a person could be subject to a criminal penalty only in cases where he or she has failed to render such an assistance, i.e. to offer aid to another person who is in immediate life-threatening danger, in circumstances where the person could **reasonably** have been expected to offer such aid. In a triage situation, there is no "reasonable" possibility to offer aid due to the lack of resources. In such cases, the health care professionals only fulfill one of the competing duties to act.[564] In addition, an offence of omission of a required treatment is only punishable if, according to the circumstances of the offence, the same charge may be levelled against the person in question had he or she committed the offence through an active act, i.e. *"person who fails to comply with a duty to act, on the basis of the elements of the offence concerned, his conduct is, in the circumstances, as culpable as it would have been had if she or* ***he actively committed the offence****"*.[565] Thus, in a triage situation the health care practitioner cannot be accused of a criminal offence if he or she omits the treatment required. As mentioned above, under such circumstances, the treatment is not given due to the competing duties to act.[566]

As far as civil liability is concerned, a doctor who is faced with a dearth of resources and is therefore unable to complete his or her duty, does not commit a breach of contract or a breach of the duty of care,[567] even if he or she would have had to offer a certain service to a certain patient had sufficient resources been available[568].

---

564 Please compare to Regina E. Aebi-Müller, 'Behandlungspflichten und Behandlungsentscheide bei Ressourcenknappheit, in: Jusletter 1. Februar 2021, para 14, p. 7; Stefan Maeder, in: Niggli and Wiprächtiger (eds), *Basler Kommentar Strafrecht* (Part I, 4th edn, Basel 2019) Art. 128 Point 69. The supra-legal justification of the conflict of duties exists if two legal duties coincide in the same situation so that the party under the obligation is unable to fulfil one of them without violating the other. Whoever, in the case of two competing duties to act, has the higher or even only the or equivalent duty at the expense of the other, does not act unlawfully (BGE 130 IV 7 decision from 28.11.2003, p. 20).

565 Regina E. Aebi-Müller, 'Behandlungspflichten und Behandlungsentscheide bei Ressourcenknappheit' (2021) 1 Jusletter, para 14, p. 7; Art 11 para 3 StGB; Alexander Marcel, Louis Frédéric Muskens, in: Niggli and Wiprächtiger (eds), *Basler Kommentar Strafrecht* (Part I, 4th edn, Basel 2019) Art 11 Point 6.

566 Regina E. Aebi-Müller, 'Behandlungspflichten und Behandlungsentscheide bei Ressourcenknappheit' (2021) 1 Jusletter, para 14, p. 7.

567 In case of contractual relationship between the physician and the patient, the physician's liability is essentially based on Art. 97 et seq. of the Code of Obligations, 220 (Federal Act on the Amendment of the Swiss Civil Code, Part Five: The Code of Obligations as of 30 March 1911 (status as of 1 February 2021), with the provisions in Art. 41 et seq. of the Code of Obligations cumulatively applicable. In absence of contractual relationship, two types of liability are possible: liability based on the management of affairs without a mandate, as stated in Art. 419 et seq., of the Code of Obligations and liability in tort as stated in Art 41 et seq., of the Code of Obligations.

568 Regina E. Aebi-Müller, 'Behandlungspflichten und Behandlungsentscheide bei Ressourcenknappheit' (2021) 1 Jusletter, para 16, p. 8.

As medical care is determined by specific circumstances, there is no breach of the duty of care, so that the doctor, the hospital, the canton's hospitals in general or the canton itself are liable for the ensuing material or non-material damages.[569]

However, health care practitioners can be found liable or responsible for their actions, i.e. criminal and civil liability in a triage situation could still arise if these actions are unlawful. One such example would be acting in a manner defined as discriminatory under the SAMS Triage Guidelines, i.e. taking decisions based solely on the patient's age. Clearer rules of triage could enable health care practitioners to work and protect them from the serious liability risks involved once a decision is made to choose one patient among several and to treat that particular patient but not the others. It is believed that, even if far more detailed rules could certainly be provided, the current SAMS Triage Guidelines as well as the relevant provisions of criminal and civil law provisions give one a certain security standard upon which to act, i.e. enable health care practitioners to take lawful decisions on whom to treat in a situation where resources are scarce. Currently there is no case law available to evaluate this question.

B. Case studies[570]

Case 1

Due to the rapid worsening of the epidemiological situation, hospitals across the country have become drastically overloaded and their material and personal capacity has been strained. Ambulances bring as many as ten patients to the emergency unit of one particular hospital. All the patients need to be hospitalised, preferably in the intensive care unit (ICU). However, only two beds are available there. Other hospitals are overwhelmed too, so the patients cannot be transported to any of them. All of the ten newly arrived patients suffer from COVID-19; they have breathing difficulties, fast-rising fever, and decreasing oxygen saturation. Nevertheless, they differ in age, comorbidities, clinical fragility, and other factors.

Theoretically, the eight patients who cannot be admitted to beds can be placed in improvised settings in the hospital corridors, laying on gurneys or mattresses on the floor. Nevertheless, it will be impossible to provide them with the care they require.

<u>Evaluation of the case</u>

- What criteria can be used to choose the patients who will be admitted to the beds (i.e. what are the possible allocation criteria)?

569 *Ibid.*

570 The case studies are based on the current laws and guidelines (as of 5 March 2021). Please note that these are adapted as the situation changes. Each case is individual and is handled on a case-by-case basis after a careful evaluation and estimation by the responsible professionals. The solutions presented are solely the opinion of the author and are subject to change in accordance with the developing legal framework, medical practice and overall situation.

If possible, the evaluation is performed in a prehospital setting as well as upon admission to the hospital.

Prehospital environment.

It is believed that the frailty factor could already be evaluated in a pre-hospital setting. The prehospital setting often presents an opportunity to obtain the objective parameters pertaining to the frailty of a patient from patients themselves or from their relatives.[571]After admission to the hospital, this task may become more difficult due to the patient's deterioration or inability to contact the next of kin responsible.[572] Frailty-Scores are typically validated for people > 65 years and should reflect the patient's status in the period prior to the acute deterioration.[573] Despite the fact that some information on the patient could be available in a prehospital setting, it is often minimal or even contradictory. Diagnostic options are few and the patient's prehospital condition (particularly in the context of hypotension, hypothermia, intoxication, etc.) can either improve or worsen in a highly dynamic manner.[574] Therefore, serious and fair decisions can only be made at a later point in time, if at all, by obtaining additional information.[575] For these reasons, critically ill or injured patients almost always must be brought to an emergency ward even if ICU capacity is known to be lacking.[576]

Hospital setting.

There are several factors that could lead to the hospital admission. One of the decision making points regarding hospital admission (whom to admit and when) could be dynamic of respiratory deterioration (SpO2) observed in critically ill patients.[577] In justified cases, the proposed limitations can and should be waived despite a major shortage of resources in the hospital sector.[578] Secondly, the 4C Mortality Score[579] may also be applied in uncertain cases. This score, however, cannot be used in a prehospital environment, due to the unavailability of diagnostic test results such as urea or CRP.[580] Thirdly, if ICU capacity, including additional external beds, is no longer sufficient, only patients who require

[571] SSERM Guidelines, p. 4.
[572] *Ibid.*
[573] *Ibid.*
[574] *Ibid.*
[575] *Ibid.*
[576] *Ibid.*
[577] *Ibid.*, p. 5.
[578] *Ibid.*
[579] The 4C Mortality Score and 4C Deterioration models are risk stratification tools that predict in-hospital mortality or in-hospital clinical deterioration (defined as any requirement of ventilatory support or critical care, or death) for hospitalised COVID-19 patients, produced by the ISARIC4C consortium. According to ISARIC 4C Consortium <https://isaric4c.net/risk/> accessed on 5 March 2021, also

S. R. Knight, A. Ho, R. Pius, I. Buchan, G. Carson, T. Met Drake et al. 'Risk stratification of patients admitted to hospital with covid-19 using the ISARIC WHO Clinical Characterisation Protocol: development and validation of the 4C Mortality Score' (2020) 370 *BMJ* <doi:10.1136/bmj.m3339>.
[580] SSERM Guidelines, p. 5.

mechanical ventilation (or another specific intensive-care intervention, such as hemodynamic support with vasoactive agents or continuous renal replacement therapy) are to be admitted. In such situations, the utmost restraint is to be exercised in the application of cardiopulmonary resuscitation following cardiac arrest, except for situations where an excellent outcome is to be expected[581]. Last but not least, another important criterion is a short-term survival prognosis, or, in other words, the maximum benefit the patient could get from intensive care. For ICU admission, the top priority should be given to patients whose prognosis with regard to hospital discharge is poor without ICU but good otherwise; so as to enable medical professionals to save as many lives as possible.

In addition, the SAMS Triage Guidelines[582] provide detailed criteria for admission to an ICU, whose capacity may be in one of two stages, stage A or stage B[583]. In the initial stage of ICU admission the patient must fulfill any of the following criteria, namely: (i) requirement for invasive ventilatory support, (ii) requirement for hemodynamic support with vasoactive agents (e.g. noradrenalineequivalent dose >0.1 μg/kg/min) or (iii) requirement for another specific intensive-care intervention (e.g. continuous renal replacement therapy). If one of the aforementioned requirements are met, then the following criteria shall apply in connection with stage A or stage B, depending on which stage is present.

If stage A applies, the patient must meet one of the following exclusion criteria: (i) patient wishes (advance directive, etc.) against ICU treatment, (ii) age-related CFS score ≥7 and age > 65, (iii) age-related CFS score ≥6 and age > 85, (iii) unwitnessed cardiac arrest, recurrent cardiac arrest, or cardiac arrest with no return of spontaneous circulation, (iv) severe, rapidly progressive, incurable condition (e.g. neurodegenerative disease or cancer) with high short-term mortality similar to the other patient groups mentioned in Stage A or (v) chronic conditions such as: NYHA class IV heart failure which persists despite optimal treatment, COPD GOLD 4 (D) leading to more than two hospital admissions in one year, liver cirrhosis, Child-Pugh class C, Charlson comorbidity score ≥5 or (vi) severe circulatory failure, which is treatment-resistant despite the management of the acute phase, including an increased dose of vasoactive agents (hypotension and/or persistent inadequate organ perfusion). Moreover, the 4C Mortality Score may additionally be employed. A score of >15 indicates high mortality.[584]

If Switzerland is in stage B, *additional* exclusion criteria shall apply, namely, (i) age-related CFS score ≥6 and age > 65, (ii) severe trauma with high short

581 SAMS Triage Guidelines, pt II, para 4.2. as well as the recommendations of the Swiss Society of Emergency and Rescue Medicine (SSERM): Prehospital triage and care under resource scarcity in the hospital sector (particularly in intensive care) during the COVID-19 pandemic, www.sgnor.ch/home/covid-19, accessed on 12 March 2021.

582 SAMS Triage Guidelines, pt II, para 4.3.

583 Stage A means that the ICU beds are available, but capacity is limited, while stage B means that ICU beds are no longer available.

584 SAMS Triage Guidelines, pt II, para, 4.3.

term-mortality, (iii) severe burns with inhalation injury, (iv) an NIHSS score > 14 after appropriate treatment for acute stroke, (iv) chronic conditions such as NYHA class III or IV heart failure despite optimal treatment or COPD GOLD 4 (D) or COPD A–D with either FEV1 <25% or cor pulmonale, or home oxygen therapy (long-term oxygen therapy), liver cirrhosis, Child-Pugh class C with refractory ascites or encephalopathy > stage I, Charlson comorbidity score ≥4, (v) the patient's age is > 75 and meets at least one of the following criteria: liver cirrhosis, Child-Pugh class B or C *or* stage IV chronic kidney disease (KDIGO) (eGFR <30 mL/min/1.73 m2) or NYHA class >II heart failure or age-related CFS score is ≥5. Please note that according to the SAMS Triage Guidleines no cardiopulmonary resuscitation is to be performed in the ICU in stage B.
The allocation shall be made in a fair and transparent manner by applying the ethical principles outlined in the SAMS Triage Guidelines.[585]

- What legal consequences can this decision have for the health professionals and for the hospital? How strong is the legal certainty that there will be no adverse legal consequences if they follow the above-mentioned criteria?
  The guidelines are not legally binding. However, they are an accepted source of reference. It is important to perform the processes in question in a fair and transparent matter. The decisions must be made by the persons responsible and thoroughly documented, i.e. the documents must address the reasons for granting a particular patient priorirty or refusing to do so. In such cases, neither hospitals nor health care practitioners can be accused of a criminal offence in a triage situation if the required treatment is omitted. As mentioned above, under such circumstances, the requisite treatment is not provided due to competing duties to act.[586]
- What legal defences could the health professionals and the hospital use against a civil lawsuit and/or criminal prosecution for a decision related to the allocation of resources?
  The answer to the question is provided in Answer No. 7 of this Report.

<u>Additional questions</u>

- Would it be legally permissible to lower the standard of care provided to all patients in order to provide at least basic decent care to the newly admitted patients who are placed in the hospital corridors? If so, to what extent?
  There are no legal provisions regulating this issue.

Case 2

Two patients in an ICU are suffering from COVID-19. After admission to the hospital, they were provided with high-flow nasal oxygen therapy (NFNO). One night,

[585] SAMS Triage Guidelines,

[586] Regina E. Aebi-Müller, 'Behandlungspflichten und Behandlungsentscheide bei Ressourcenknappheit' (2021) 1 Jusletter, para 14, p. 7.

the condition of both patients began to deteriorate rapidly. By dawn it became clear that neither of them would survive without artificial ventilation. However, there is just one ventilator available.

Evaluation of the case

- Which criteria can be used to choose which of the two patients will be provided with artificial ventilation and which one will not, and might possibly die as a result?

  The laws as well as the guidelines do not specify any particular criteria to be used upon admission as far as specialized medical devices are concerned (in this case, artificial ventilation) in a situation where resources are scarce.

  It is presumed that one could rely on the principles outlined in the SAMS Triage Guidelines as guidance for triage during the patient's ICU stay in the aforementioned situation daily and interprofessionally. Each patient is evaluated separately and not compared with the others.

  The SAMS Triage Guidelines provide for 3 steps of evaluation[587].

  During step No. 1 the presence of a criterion for transfer from the ICU are evaluated, namely, (i) careful re-evaluation of whether the continuation of intensive-care treatment corresponds to the patient's (presumed) wishes, (ii) the patient has been extubated or exhibits spontaneous breathing after tracheotomy. In these cases, the patient is transferred from ICU as soon as possible for further treatment. *During step No. 2*, the presence of the following three criteria are evaluated depending on the condition the patient is being treated for after a period of stabilisation. Namely, (i) stabilisation or improvement of oxygenation and ventilation, (ii) stabilisation or improvement of hemodynamics, (iii) stabilisation or improvement of underlying organ dysfunction. ICU treatment is continued only if all three of the aforementioned criteria are fulfilled. *Step No. 3* is then implemented differently in stage A and stage B[588].

  In stage A, ICU treatment is discontinued if so much as one of the criteria applies, even though all the three criteria of step No. 2 are met. Namely, ICU treatment is discontinued if (i) recurrent cardiac arrest occurs during the patient's ICU stay despite initially successful resuscitation or (ii) additional significant organ failure occurs during the patient's ICU stay, leading to an even poorer short-term prognosis.

  In stage B, ICU treatment is discontinued if so much as one of the criteria applies, even though all the three criteria of step No. 2 are met. Namely, (i) no improvement in the patient's respiratory or hemodynamic status is observed (stabilisation is not sufficient) or (ii) cardiac arrest occurs during the ICU stay (thus in Stage B, cardiopulmonary resuscitation should not be attempted) or (iii) persistent or progressive failure of two other organs apart from the lungs is present.

587 SAMS Triage Guidelines, pt II, para 4.4.

588 As described above, stage A means that some ICU beds are available but the unit's capacity is limited, while stage B means that ICU beds are no longer available.

The SAMS Triage Guidelines specify that in cases where one of these criteria is present, the discontinuation of ICU treatment leads to the patient being transferred into palliative care.

- What legal consequences can this decision have for the health professionals and for the hospital? How strong is the legal certainty that there will be no adverse legal consequences if they follow the above-mentioned criteria?
  The answer to the question is provided in Answer No. 6 of this Report.
- What legal defences could the health professionals and the hospital use against a civil lawsuit and/or criminal prosecution for a decision related to the allocation of resources?
  The answer to the question is provided in Answer No. 7 of this Report.

Case 3

There is a single extracorporeal membrane oxygenation (ECMO) device in the hospital. It is currently being used for an 84-year-old patient suffering from COVID-19, with diabetes as an underlying condition and a clinical frailty score (CFS) 6–7 (moderate to severe frailty). The patient may survive and be discharged from the hospital if the ECMO treatment is continued. However, a younger COVID-19 patient is admitted to the hospital. This new patient is 51 years old, otherwise healthy, but her condition has been rapidly deteriorating. Soon she will most likely need ECMO to survive.

Evaluation of the case

- Would it be legally permissible for the hospital staff to discontinue the ECMO treatment of the older patient and provide palliative care to her in order to save the life of the younger and healthier patient? Please keep in mind that the older patient could survive if the treatment continued, but her chances may be lower than those of the younger patient.
  The situation would be solved differently at stage A and stage B. The criterion of age alone or a brief estimation of the patient's condition would not provide enough information for a decision to be made. To make the triage decision, the conditions of both patients would have to be evaluated separately, daily, and interprofessionally, according to the SAMS Triage Guidelines, by applying detailed criteria as decribed in Case No. 2, Answer to Question No. 1.
  The medical utility of intensive care is to be evaluated on the basis of the clinical course, partly in order to allow decisions to be made regarding the possible transition from curative treatment to palliative care. This applies to all (i.e. both Covid-19 and non-Covid-19) patients receiving ICU treatment when resources are exhausted.[589] The more scarce the resources become, the more stringently one has to apply the criteria listed in Case No. 2, Answer to Question No. 1.[590]

[589] SAMS Triage Guidelines, pt II, para 4.4.
[590] SAMS Triage Guidelines, pt II, para 4.4.

- If the answer to the first question is positive, which specific criteria can be used in clinical decision-making as regards replacing one patient with another when a particular treatment is unavailable for all?
  There is no criteria that could lead to the replacement of one patient with another. As mentioned above, the condition of each patient must be evaluated separately, after which one has to make a decision as to whether or not to continue the treatment.
- What legal consequences can this decision have for the health professionals and for the hospital? How strong is the legal certainty that there will be no adverse legal consequences if they follow the above-mentioned criteria?
  The answer to the question is provided in Answer No. 6 of this Report.
- What legal defences could the health professionals and the hospital use against a civil lawsuit and/or criminal prosecution for a decision related to the allocation of resources?
  The answer to the question is provided in Answer No. 7 of this Report.

The list of abbreviations

Art.	Article
BMC Geriatr	BMC Geriatrics Journal
BMJ	British Medical Association Journal
CFS	Clinical Frailty Score
COPD	Chronic Obstructive Pulmonary Disease
ECMO	Single extracorporeal membrane oxygenation
edn	Edition
ed / eds	Editor / Editors
eGFR	Estimated glomerular filtration rate
ff.	Following pages
GOLD	Chronic Obstructive Lung Disease
Ibid.	Ibidem
ICU	Intensive care unit
ISARIC	International Severe Acute Respiratory and Emerging Infection Consortium
KDIGO	Chronic kidney disease
KSD	Coordinated Medical Service
let.	Letter
MedBG	Federal Act on the University Medical Professions
NIHSS	National Institutes of Health Stroke Scale, or NIH Stroke Scale
NYHA	New York Heart Association Functional Classification
No.	Number
p.	Page
para	Paragraph
pt	Part
SAMS	Swiss Academy of Medical Science

StGB	Swiss Criminal Code
SSERM	Swiss Society of Emergency and Rescue Medicine
WHO	World Health Organisation

Bibliography

• Legislation

Federal Act on the Control of Communicable Diseases in Humans (Epidemics Act, 818.101), as of 28 September, 2012 (status of 25 June, 2020)

Federal Act on the Promotion of Research and Innovation (FIFG; SR 420.1) as of 14 December 2012 (status as of 1 January 2020)

Federal Act on the Statutory Principles for Federal Council Ordinances on Combating the COVID-19 Epidemic (COVID-19 Act, 818.101.24), as of 25 September, 2020 (status of 19 December, 2020)

Federal Act on the University Medical Professions, *in German*: Bundesgesetz über die universitären Medizinalberufe (MedBG, SR 811.11) as of 23 June 2006 (status as of 1 February 2020)

Ordinance 2 of 13 March 2020 on Measures to Combat the Coronavirus (COVID-19) (COVID-19 Ordinance 2, 818.101.27) (status as of 17 March 2020; since revoked)

Ordinance 3 on Measures to Combat the Coronavirus (COVID-19) (COVID-19 Ordinance 3, 818.101.24), as of 19 June 2020 (status as of 8 February 2021)

Ordinance on Measures during the Special Situation to combat the COVID-19 Epidemic (COVID-19 Special Situation Ordinance, 818.101.26), as of 19 June 2020 (status as of 8 February 2021)

Ordinance on the Coordinated Medical Service (VKSD, 501.31), as of 27 April, 2005 (status of 1 February, 2016)

Swiss Civil Code (ZGB; SR 210) as of 10 December 1907 (status as of 1 January 2021)

Swiss Criminal Code (StGB, 311) as of 21 December 1937 (status as of 1 July 2020)

• Case law

BGE 98 Ia 508 decision from 28.06.1972

BGE 115 Ia 234 decision from 15.03.1989

BGE 119 Ia 460 decision from 22.12.1993

BGE 121 V 289 decision from 13.12.1995

BGE 130 IV 7 decision from 28.11.2003

• Books

Büchler A and, Michel M, *Medizin – Mensch – Recht, Eine Einführung in das Medizinrecht der Schweiz*, (2nd edn, Schulthess, Zürich/Basel/Genf 2020)

Gächter T and, Rütsche B, *Gesundheitsrecht, Ein Grundriss für Studium und Praxis*', (4th edn, Helbing Lichtenhahn Verlag, Basel 2018)

Niggli and Wiprächtiger (eds), *Basler Kommentar Strafrecht,* pt I (4th edn, Basel 2019)

Poledna T and, Berger B, *Öffentliches Gesundheitsrecht*, (Stämpfli, Bern 2002)

- **Articles**

E. Aebi-Müller R E, 'Behandlungspflichten und Behandlungsentscheide bei Ressourcenknappheit' (2021) 1 Jusletter

Rüetschi D, 'Die Medizinisch-ethischen Richtlinien der SAMW aus juristischer Sicht' (2004) 85:23, Schweizerische Ärztezeitung / Bulletin des médecins suisses / Bollettino dei medici svizzeri

- **Other secondary sources**

Church S., Rogers E., Rockwood K. et al., 'A scoping review of the Clinical Frailty Scale' (2020) 20, 393 BMC Geriatr 20, 393 <https://doi.org/10.1186/s12877-020-01801-7>

Ehni H-J, Wiesing U, Ranisch R, 'Saving the most lives — A comparison of European triage guidelines in the context of the COVID-19 pandemic' (2021) 35:125–134 Bioethics <https://onlinelibrary.wiley.com/doi/pdfdirect/10.1111/bioe.12836?download=true>

Hehli S, 'Alle über 85-Jährigen einfach sterben lassen? Die Richtlinien für die Corona-Behandlungen lösen harsche Kritik aus' (*NZZ,* 30 October 2020) <https://www.nzz.ch/schweiz/triage-richtlininen-in-den-spitaelern-loesen-harsche-kritik-aus-ld.1584225?reduced=true>

Interview with Prof. Dr. Fateh-Moghadam B, 'Covid-19 und Intensivmedizin: «Wir brauchen eine öffentliche Diskussion über die gerechte Verteilung von lebensrettenden Ressourcen»' <https://www.unibas.ch/de/Aktuell/News/Uni-Research/Covid-19-und-Intensivmedizin-Wir-brauchen-eine-oeffentliche-Diskussion-ueber-die-gerechte-Verteilung-von-lebensrettenden-Ressourcen.html>

Knight S R, Ho A, Pius R, Buchan I, Carson G, T. Met Drake et al. 'Risk stratification of patients admitted to hospital with covid-19 using the ISARIC WHO Clinical Characterisation Protocol: development and validation of the 4C Mortality Score' (2020) 370 *BMJ* <doi:10.1136/bmj.m3339>

Lic.iur. Schwestermann M-A, 'Diskriminierende Altersgrenze für die Behandlung von COVID-19 Patienten/-innen' (*humanrights.ch,* 1 April 2020) <https://www.humanrights.ch/de/ipf/menschenrechte/alter/diskriminierung-altersgrenze-coronavirus>

Salathé M, 'Die Bedeutung der ärztlichen Unabhängigkeit in der Vollzugsmedizin', <www.samw.ch>

Statement of the Federal Council, 'Transparente und klar geregelte Verfahren bei der Verabschiedung von medizinisch-ethischen Richtlinie' (18 November 2020) <https://www.parlament.ch/de/ratsbetrieb/suche-curia-vista/geschaeft?AffairId=20204082>

UNITED STATES

Lance Gable[591*] and Marie Carp[592**]and Allison Tuohy[**]
Wayne State University Law School

Introduction

The United States has had one of the largest and most severe outbreaks of COVID-19 in the world, both in terms of per capita infections and deaths and in terms of overall numbers of cases and deaths. The immense size of the COVID-19 outbreak in the United States has stretched health care and public health institutions nearly to the breaking point. In the early stages of the outbreak in the United States, between April and June 2020, New York City faced an unprecedented number of patients that resulted in 'widespread shortages of critical equipment and supplies' as well as staff at New York City hospitals.[593] Detroit and several other US cities also faced large patient surges in hospital settings during this time.[594] COVID-19 patient surges occurred in late 2020 in several different locations in the United States as well, including North Dakota, South Dakota, and Los Angeles.[595] Renewed outbreaks, fueled by the Delta variant of the disease have created new patient surges across the southern United States in August 2021.

Numerous resource shortages occurred during these patient surges. Medical supplies such as medication, ventilators, and personal protective equipment (PPE) became scarce; suitable space for treating patients was limited, necessitating hospitals and other facilities to repurpose areas to treat COVID-19 patients and expand

---

591 * Professor of Law, Wayne State University Law School, Detroit, MI, USA.

592 ** Juris Doctor Candidate, Wayne State University Law School, Detroit, MI, USA.

593 Eric Toner, et al., 'Crisis Standards of Care: Lessons from New York City Hospitals' (2020) COVID-19 Experience. <https://repository.netecweb.org/items/show/1476> accessed 1 August 2021

594 Miranda Bryant, 'Detroit: America's next COVID-19 hotspot battles to prepare for coming surge' (The Guardian, 31 March 2020) <https://www.theguardian.com/us-news/2020/mar/31/detroit-coronavirus-america-michigan-poverty> accessed 3 August 2021

595 Melanie Evans et al., '"It's a Desperate Time": Crush of Covid-19 Patients Strains U.S. Hospitals' (*The Wall Street Journal*, 3 January 2021) <https://www.wsj.com/articles/its-a-desperate-time-crush-of-covid-19-patients-strains-u-s-hospitals-11609721551> accessed 1 August 2021; Melanie Evans and Christine Mai-Duc, 'Covid-19 Crisis Forces California Hospitals to Plan Who Gets Life-Saving Care' (*The Wall Street Journal*, 8 January 2021) <https://www.wsj.com/articles/covid-19-crisis-forces-california-hospitals-to-plan-who-gets-life-saving-care-11610115894> accessed 1 August 2021

to alternative care sites; and staff with appropriate expertise became harder to find, as overwhelmed health care workers, especially those with critical and specialized skills struggled to respond to the influx of patients.

Shortages in health care resources certainly affected health outcomes related to COVID-19 in the United States, although it is difficult to quantify with specificity the extent of harm that these shortages caused across the population. Similarly, it is likely that people were deterred from seeking needed medical care due to shortages or perceived shortages of health care resources. This deterrent effect had short-term consequences in the form of sick people staying home longer before seeking treatment, either out of fear of infection or concern about the level of treatment they would receive, or the unfortunate prospect of being cut off from family and others who could not accompany them to a hospital. In addition, the deferral of needed health care services and screening will likely have longer-term consequences as illnesses that would have been detected earlier are left undiagnosed and untreated.

The health care resource shortages that occurred in the United States should have been predictable and avoided. Many preparedness plans developed in the years before the COVID-19 pandemic cautioned about the potential for resource scarcity during a pandemic caused by a novel infectious disease. States and health care institutions had engaged in years of planning, largely guided by series of influential national reports from the Institute of Medicine (IOM) and the National Academies of Science, Engineering, and Medicine (NASEM) that addressed the ethical, legal, and practical challenges of allocating scarce health care resources during emergencies that involved crisis standards of care (CSC), which comprise 'a substantial change in the usual health care operations and the level of care it is possible to deliver.'[596] By the time the influx of COVID-19 cases arrived in the United States in the spring of 2020, leaders were aware that hospitals in Bergamo, Italy and Wuhan, China already had been overwhelmed with COVID-19 patients. Moreover, the shortages that occurred in the United States in April 2020 should have provided a strong incentive to prepare for and avoid later shortages, yet that didn't prevent subsequent shortages from occurring when the second large surge of COVID-19 patients emerged in December 2020.

As the sections that follow demonstrate, the fractured system of scarce resource allocation in the United States leads to variations in approach and legal implications when allocation decisions are made. These inconsistencies result in ongoing legal uncertainty when scarce resource allocation occurs.

[596] Institute of Medicine, 'Guidance for Establishing Crisis Standards of Care for Use in Disaster Situations' (National Academies Press, 2009)

A. Questionnaire

1. What are the criteria for the allocation of scarce health care resources in your country?

The United States does not have national legislation or formal national guidelines that outline allocation of scarce health care resources during emergencies. The federalist governmental system in place in the United States, which apportions power between federal and state governments, shapes how law applies to scarce resource allocation criteria in the United States. The federal government has the authority to directly enact legally-binding allocation criteria for scarce health care resources, but it has not done so for political and practical reasons. Rather, the responsibility for developing criteria and preparing for allocation of scarce resources has been left to state governments or in some cases even to private health care entities. Many, but not all, state governments have developed allocation criteria for scarce health care resources. Most state-level criteria are not legally-binding, but these criteria nevertheless may influence how the standard of care will be interpreted during situations of resource scarcity. While many states have adopted CSC plans based on allocation criteria from reports developed by the IOM and NASEM,[597] the details of allocation criteria vary state-to-state, leading to a diversity of approaches and application across the country. For example, some states at greater risk of natural disasters or proclivities for other types of emergencies may focus their CSC plans toward those circumstances. Further, institutional actors such as private hospitals or long-term care facilities will often develop allocation criteria that apply specifically to their institutional settings. These institutional plans often follow state criteria, if available.

Most of the state and institutional CSC plans focus on allocating scarce resources according to several overarching goals: maximizing good health outcomes, such as trying to save as many lives as possible; conserving and targeting medical resources to where they will be most effective; and minimizing suffering when possible. Other commonly-included considerations include pursing equity in access to resources or health outcomes and prioritizing access to scarce resources for certain essential personnel.

CSC plans apply a number of different allocation criteria to pursue these goals. In the hospital setting, an assessment of a patient's immediate medical prognosis may comprise an important factor in allocating scarce health care resources. Many state and institutional CSC plans recommend the use of algorithms like the

[597] Institute of Medicine, 'Crisis Standards of Care: A Systems Framework For Catastrophic Disaster Response' (National Academies Press, 21 March 2012); Institute of Medicine, 'Crisis Standards of Care: A Toolkit for Indicators and Triggers' (National Academies Press, 2013); National Academies of Sciences, Engineering, and Medicine, 'Crisis Standards of Care: Successes and Challenges from the Past Ten Years — A Workshop' (21–22 November 2019) <https://www.nationalacademies.org/our-work/crisis-standards-of-care-successes-and-challenges-from-the-past-ten-years--a-workshop> accessed 1 August 2021

Sequential Organ Failure Assessment (SOFA) scoring system to take into account a patient's clinical frailty and likelihood of survival to release from hospital. But even where these algorithms are used, it is rare that they are used as sole factors in determining a patient's prognosis, especially since the SOFA by itself has limited accuracy in predicting clinical outcomes and could exacerbate racial and ethnic disparities in access to scarce resources.[598] While some allocation protocols would permit weighing patients' prognoses against each other to make prioritization decisions and would even permit reallocation of a scarce resource to a patient more likely to benefit from that resource (the state of New York's ventilator guidelines, for example), this application is far from universal.[599]

CSC plans often allow other criteria to be used as factors to prioritize between individuals that have equivalent medical prognoses, including age-related, lottery, and first-come, first-served approaches. States such as New Jersey and New York specifically utilize the lottery system, while other states like Rhode Island call for lifecycle considerations to be used as a tiebreaker with priority going to younger patients.[600]

Health care resource shortages during emergencies apply in non-hospital settings as well, and may impact the operations of emergency medical services (EMS), public health departments, and long-term care facilities. Most state CSC plans discuss criteria for emergency medical services (triage policies), acute care facilities (allocation of life-saving treatments such as ventilators, criteria for hospital admission, code situations, bed management and transfers, healthcare personnel policies), out-of-hospital care, and alternative care sites. Many states, like Michigan and Utah, have separate CSC plans for EMS and public health departments that provide legal, ethical, and practical guidance for allocating scarce resources in these settings.[601]

598 Emily Cleveland Manchanda, et al., 'Inequity in Crisis Standards of Care' (2020) 383(4) N Engl J Med 16 <https://www.nejm.org/doi/full/10.1056/NEJMp2011359> accessed 1 August 2021; Eamon P. Raith, et al., 'Prognostic Accuracy of the SOFA Score, SIRS Criteria, and qSOFA Score for In-Hospital Mortality Among Adults With Suspected Infection Admitted to the Intensive Care Unit'(2017) 317(3) JAMA 290–300 <https://pubmed.ncbi.nlm.nih.gov/28114553/> accessed 1 August 2021; Robert A. Raschke, et al., 'Discriminant Accuracy of the SOFA Score for Determining the Probable Mortality of Patients with COVID-19 Pneumonia Requiring Mechanical Ventilation' (2021) 325(14) JAMA 1469–70 <https://jamanetwork.com/journals/jama/fullarticle/2776737> accessed 1 August 2021

599 New York State Department of Health, 'Ventilator Allocation Guidelines' (*New York State Task Force on Life and the Law*, November 2015) <https://www.health.ny.gov/regulations/task_force/reports_publications/docs/ventilator_guidelines.pdf> accessed 1 August 2021

600 New Jersey Commission on Rationalizing Health Care Resources, 'Final Report' (24 January 2008), <https://www.nj.gov/health/rhc/documents/entire_finalreport.pdf> accessed 1 August 2021; New York State Department of Health, 'Ventilator Allocation Guidelines' (*New York State Task Force on Life and the Law*, November 2015) <https://www.health.ny.gov/regulations/task_force/reports_publications/docs/ventilator_guidelines.pdf> accessed 1 August 2021; Rhode Island Department of Health 'Crisis Standards of Care Guidelines' (27 April 2020), <https://health.ri.gov/publications/guidelines/crisis-standards-of-care.pdf?mc_cid=386ff10c1f&mc_eid=39d213ba26> accessed 1 August 2021

601 Utah Department of Health, 'Utah Bureau of EMS and Preparedness EMA Pandemic Coronavirus Plan' (30 March 2020) <https://health.utah.gov/wp-content/uploads/Final_Utah_Crisis_Standards_

Michigan's EMS CSC plan, for example, explains how EMS can implement a triage system that prioritizes care based on the severity of the shortage, capacity for treatment, handling incoming rescue calls, and alternate transport options, among other factors.

Many state and institutional CSC plans include oversight and decision-making infrastructure of some kind (such as statewide, regional, or institutional advisory committees). These structural mechanisms can serve multiple goals. Statewide and regional advisory committee can ensure that different decision makers across the state implement scarce resource allocation guidelines fairly, equitably, and consistently, while maintaining transparency. Institutional advisory committees provide perspective and allow allocation decisions to be made by decision-makers who are removed from the clinical context, insulating bedside clinicians from having to make difficult decisions regarding their own patients. For example, the CSC plan in the state of Washington recommends that a CSC hospital clinical triage team be formed at every hospital, that every health system maintain good communication between individual hospitals for situational awareness, and that there be a CSC regional clinical triage team to manage prioritization.[602]

2. What values are the allocation criteria based on?

The lack of coordinated and consistently-applicable scarce resource allocation guidance across the United States makes it challenging to generalize about the content of allocation criteria or the values that these criteria are based on. However, many state and institutional scarce resource allocation plans are based on ethical theories that combine utilitarian approaches with theories that value distributive justice, equity, and solidarity. Many of these plans draw from the key ethical values highlighted in the IOM and NASEM CSC guidance reports: fairness, duty to care, duty to steward resources, transparency, consistency, proportionality, and accountability.[603]

The COVID-19 pandemic has prompted a proliferation of new and updated CSC plans as states and private institutions rushed to ensure that plans were in

of_Care_011719-1.pdf> accessed 1 August 2021; State of Michigan Department of Community Health, Office of Public Health Preparedness, 'Guidelines for Ethical Allocation of Scarce Medical Resources and Services During Public Health Emergencies in Michigan' (16 November 2012) <http://www.mimedicalethics.org/Documentation/Michigan%20DCH%20Ethical%20Scarce%20Resources%20Guidelines%20v2%20rev%20Nov%202012.0.pdf> accessed 1 August 2021

602 Washington State Department of Health, Northwest Healthcare Response Network, 'Scarce Resource Management & Crisis Standards of Care' (2020) <https://int.nyt.com/data/documenthelper/6853-washington-state-triage-guidel/02cb4c58460e57ea9f05/optimized/full.pdf#page=1> accessed 22 June 2021

603 Emily C. Manchanda, et al., 'Crisis Standards of Care in the USA: A Systematic Review and Implications for Equity Amidst COVID-19' (13 August 2020) J Racial & Ethnic Health Disparities <https://www.ncbi.nlm.nih.gov/pmc/articles/PMC7425256/#:~:text=Key%20principles%20on%20which%20this,%2C%20and%20accountability%20%5B7%5D> accessed 1 August 2021

place to deal with scarcity as COVID-19 case numbers ballooned. The social and political dynamics surrounding the pandemic undoubtedly affected the ethical values underlying these plans. Indeed, in some states it is clear that CSC plans have been revised over time from approaches that were primarily focused on utilitarian goals and formal procedural equality to approaches that more explicitly focus on equity, anti-discrimination, and distributive justice. The CSC guidelines for the state of Michigan provide a good example of this trend. An older version of Michigan's guidelines highlighted utilitarian strategies that granted priority to patients with a positive medical prognosis and to essential personnel. The guidelines also permitted use of first-come, first-served and lottery approaches in some circumstances. The updated version of these guidelines from 2021 introduced a much stronger focus on equity; prognosis is still important and essential worker priority is still acceptable to achieve stability in health care systems, but the new guidance cautions about the inequity in using first-come, first-served approaches and champions the use of tools — like the CDC Social Vulnerability Index — that promote equity in access and outcomes.[604]

Prominent efforts to challenge potentially discriminatory provisions in CSC plans provide another example of the increasing attention to values of equity and anti-discrimination in these state-level plans. CSC plans may contain provisions that create or permit discriminatory outcomes, whether intended or unintended. For example, state-level prioritization and allocation schemas may put people from racial and ethnic minority groups, people with disabilities, and older people at a great disadvantage in accessing scarce resources and exacerbate already challenging structural inequities. In health care settings, members of these communities often face disproportionate and negative biases and assumptions about their quality of life, value, capacity to make decisions, and likelihood of survival.[605] Research has shown that among those younger than 65 years of age, Black and Indigenous adults were at higher risk of severe COVID-19 than white adults.[606] This presents a problem for allocation of scarce resources under CSC protocols, as Black, Indigenous, and other People of Color may receive lower priority in accessing scarce resources based on SOFA scores and other measures of prognosis, further penalizing members of minority groups that already face greater social and health vulnerability.

Age is also a factor that often is overlooked when activating CSC. According to the Centers for Disease Control and Prevention (CDC), over 80% of COVID-19

604 CDC, 'Social Vulnerability Index' (28 April 2021) <https://www.atsdr.cdc.gov/placeandhealth/svi/index.html> accessed 1 August 2021; Gopal K. Singh, 'Area Deprivation and Widening Inequalities in US Mortality, 1969–1998' (1 July 2003) 93(7) Am J Pub Health 1137–43 <https://ajph.aphapublications.org/doi/pdf/10.2105/AJPH.93.7.1137> accessed 1 August 2021

605 Center for Public Representation, 'Examining How Crisis Standards of Care May Lead to Intersectional Medical Discrimination Against COVID-19 Patients'<https://www.centerforpublicrep.org/wp-content/uploads/FINAL-Intersectional-Guide-Crisis-Care-PDF.pdf> accessed 1August 2021

606 Matthew A. Raiman and Julia R. Raifman, 'Disparities in the Population at Risk of Severe Illness from COVID-19 by Race/Ethnicity and Income' (27 April 2020) Am J Prev Med <https://www.ncbi.nlm.nih.gov/pmc/articles/PMC7183932/> accessed 1 August 2021

deaths have been among older adults.[607] Nursing homes and long-term care facilities became settings where concentrated outbreaks of coronavirus were likely to occur, since residents of these facilities face especially high risk because they are older, living in congregate settings, and often suffering from chronic illness or other ailments associated with older age.[608] In some CSC plans, these individuals receive lower priority since their long-term survival is shorter in duration, they are more likely to require scarce resources such as ventilators, and they often have preexisting health conditions.[609]

During the COVID-19 pandemic, various stakeholders and advocacy groups filed complaints to protect individuals who would face lower priority under CSC plans.[610] Some of these complaints were premised on legal theories of race, disability, and age discrimination. For example, Pennsylvania rapidly released an Interim CSC for Pandemic Guidelines in March 2020 to serve as a starting point if CSC needed to be activated due to the COVID-19 outbreak in the state.[611] However, around a month later, Disability Rights Pennsylvania filed a legal complaint alleging that the interim guidelines violated anti-discrimination laws, claiming that the plan automatically deprioritized persons based on particular disabilities, whether or not those disabilities actually impacted survivability.[612]

States need to ensure that CSC plans comply with federal civil rights laws and do not discriminate. As a response to complaints from individuals and disability rights organizations, the Office of Civil Rights within the federal Department of Health and Human Services required at least 8 jurisdictions, including Alabama, Connecticut, Pennsylvania, Tennessee, Massachusetts, and Delaware to revise their

---

607 CDC COVID-19 Response Team, 'Severe outcomes among patients with coronavirus disease 2019 (COVID-19) - United States' (12 February–16 March 2020) 69(12) MMWR Morb Mortality Wkly Rep 343–46 <https://www.cdc.gov/mmwr/volumes/69/wr/mm6912e2.htm> accessed 1 August 2021

608 Timothy W. Farrell et al., 'Rationing Limited Healthcare Resources in the COVID-19 Era and Beyond: Ethical Considerations Regarding Older Adults'(6 May 2020) J Am Geriatrics Soc <https://onlinelibrary.wiley.com/doi/full/10.1111/jgs.16539> 1 August 2021

609 Andrew Pulrang, 'The Disability Community Fights Deadly Discrimination Amid the COVID-19 Pandemic' (*Forbes* 14 April 2020) <https://www.forbes.com/sites/andrewpulrang/2020/04/14/the-disability-community-fights-deadly-discrimination-amid-the-covid-19-pandemic/?sh=797ac373309c> accessed 1 August 2021

610 American Association of People with Disabilities, 'Over 400 Organizations Urge Department of Health and Human Services to Issue Guidance to Prohibit Discrimination during Medical Rationing' (17 April 2020) <https://www.aapd.com/press-releases/civil-rights-letter-covid-medical-rationing/?fbclid=IwAR0uKHogSaq8zknb--gVKL9-oplHXyX1a1lGpyx306WHpr0ZQWoxSk2C1oM> accessed 1 August 2021

611 Pennsylvania Department of Health, The Hospital and Healthsystem Association of Pennsylvania, 'Interim Pennsylvania Crisis Standards of Care for Pandemic Guidelines' (22 March 2020) <https://int.nyt.com/data/documenthelper/6850-pennsylvania-triage-guidelines/02cb4c58460e57ea9f05/optimized/full.pdf>

612 Disability Rights Pennsylvania, 'Letter from Disability Rights Pennsylvania, to Roger Severino, Director of Office of Civil Rights' (3 April 2020) <https://www.disabilityrightspa.org/wp-content/uploads/2020/04/s04.03.2020-DRP-OCR-Complaint-with-Exhibit-A-1.pdf> accessed 1 August 2021

CSC plans to eliminate possibly discriminatory provisions and to comply with federal disability and civil rights protections found in three federal laws: Section 1557 of the Affordable Care Act (ACA), Section 504 in the Rehabilitation Act, and the Americans with Disabilities Act.[613] The modifications to these CSC plans removed problematic language that would have deprioritized people with disabilities in accessing scarce health care resources. Pursuant to these changes, allocation of treatment and life-saving resources must be made according to individualized determinations, which will prohibit treatment allocation decisions based on misguided assumptions that people with disabilities experience a lower quality of life, have a lower prospect of survival, or will require the use of greater treatment resources.[614] The federal Department of Health and Human Services reiterated this point through guidance reminding health care providers to uphold 'their obligations under laws and regulations that prohibit discrimination on the basis of race, color, national origin, disability, age, sex, and exercise of conscience and religion.'[615]

3. In what type(s) of document(s) are the allocation criteria set? Is it in binding or non-binding guidelines, in the law, or in another type of document?

As described briefly above, the United States does not have a consistent set of national allocation criteria for scarce health care resources. The federal government has the authority to codify such criteria under law through legislation, but has not done so. Many state governments have developed allocation criteria, but state-level efforts have largely resulted in non-binding guidance that is not required by legislation. In addition, many non-government actors have developed non-binding guidance for their organizations and institutions to inform allocation decisions.

After the 2009 H1N1 influenza outbreak, the Institute of Medicine — a division of the non-profit National Academies of Science, Engineering, and Medicine — began to develop a series of influential reports that have since been widely used by policymakers who are developing allocation criteria for scarce health care resources during emergencies.[616] These reports defined the concept of crisis standards of care

613 Ari Ne'eman, 'I Will Not Apologize for My Needs,' (NY Times, 23 March 2020) <https://www.nytimes.com/2020/03/23/opinion/coronavirus-ventilators-triage-disability.html> accessed 1 August 2021; U.S. Department of Health and Human Services, Office for Civil Rights, 'HHS-OCR Complaints Re COVID-19 Medical Discrimination' (The Arc, 23 March 2020), <https://thearc.org/resource/hhs-ocr-complaint-of-disability-rights-washington-self-advocates-in-leadership-the-arc-of-the-united-states-and-ivanova-smith/> accessed 1 August 2021

614 Ari Ne'eman (n 21)

615 HHS Office for Civil Rights in Action, 'BULLETIN: Civil Rights, HIPAA, and the Coronavirus Disease 2019 (COVID-19)' (28 March 2020) <https://www.hhs.gov/sites/default/files/ocr-bulletin-3-28-20.pdf> accessed 1 August 2021

616 Institute of Medicine, 'Crisis Standards of Care: A Systems Framework For Catastrophic Disaster Response' (n 5); Institute of Medicine, 'Crisis Standards of Care: A Toolkit for Indicators and

(CSC), which occur when there is a 'substantial change in the usual health care operations and the level of care it is possible to deliver'[617] and outlined ethical, legal, and practical criteria for scarce resource allocation in health care, public health, pre-hospital, and long-term care settings.

Many state governments have adapted the guidance from these expert reports to develop non-binding crisis standards of care plans applicable to their states and have worked with private sector entities like hospitals, nursing homes, and EMS providers to develop guidelines for their own operations that are consistent with state guidance.[618] Each state has the power to create their own CSC guidance and to date more than 30 states have drawn up their own individual state scarce resource allocation guidance and CSC plans.[619] Additionally, many states published pandemic plans specific to COVID-19 that include criteria for the allocation of scarce health care resources. Some examples include California's 'COVID-19 Health Care System Mitigation Playbook'[620] and Montana's 'COVID-19 Surge and Crisis Care Guide for Emergency Medical Services.'[621]

In the CSC plans, states often differentiate between different types of resource scarcity. For example, the state of Utah organizes their allocation protocols and plans according to various types of resource scarcity that may occur.[622] Utah has released a CSC Plan, a CSC Guidelines Annex for COVID-19, a document for Pediatric Disaster Surge Planning CSC, an appendix CSC for a burn crisis, an appendix for pandemics, and a COVID-specific EMS plan.[623] Each plan has a distinct strategy based on the unique circumstances presented by a public health issue at hand. Other states, such as Minnesota, have a more cohesive CSC plan supplemented by specific attachments that address each possible scarcity setting or scenario.[624]

Triggers' (n 5); National Academies of Sciences, Engineering, and Medicine, 'Crisis Standards of Care: Successes and Challenges from the Past Ten Years — A Workshop' (n 5)

[617] Institute of Medicine, 'Guidance for Establishing Crisis Standards of Care for Use in Disaster Situations' (n 4)

[618] Minnesota Department of Health, 'Crisis Standards of Care: Minnesota COVID Ethics Collaborative (MCEC)' (2 July 2021) <https://www.health.state.mn.us/communities/ep/surge/crisis/index.html> accessed 7 December 2020

[619] ASPR TRACIE HHS, 'Topic Collection: Crisis Standards of Care' < https://asprtracie.hhs.gov/technical-resources/63/crisis-standards-of-care/0> accessed August 3 2021

[620] California Department of Public Health, 'COVID-19 Health Care System Mitigation Playbook' (March 2020), <https://www.cdph.ca.gov/Programs/CHCQ/LCP/CDPH%20Document%20Library/AFL-20-23-Mitigation-Playbook.pdf> accessed 1 August 2021

[621] Montana Department of Public Health and Human Services, Montana EMS & Trauma System Program, 'Montana COVID-19 Surge and Crisis Care Guide for Emergency Medical Services' (3 April 2020) <https://nasemso.org/wp-content/uploads/Surge-and-Crisis-Care-Guide-EMS-MT.pdf> accessed 1 August 2021

[622] Utah Department of Health (n 9)

[623] Utah Department of Health (n 9)

[624] Minnesota Department of Health Concept of Operations, 'Minnesota Crisis Standards of Care Framework' (25 February 2020) < https://www.health.state.mn.us/communities/ep/surge/crisis/conops.pdf> accessed 1 August 2021

State-level CSC plans are largely non-binding guidelines, and therefore function as more of a framework for state government departments and private institutions like hospitals and nursing homes to use in the event of a scarce resource situation. Nevertheless, a few states have enacted statutory provisions that grant state officials explicit authority to alter the legal standards of care during a declared emergency. The states of Maryland and Virgina, for example, set out a clear process outlined in state statutes for the state governor to declare that crisis standards of care are in effect.[625] Other states permit their governors to broadly enact measures to respond to emergencies and disasters that impact public health, and such authority can be used to enact crisis standards of care via executive order, as both Arizona and New Mexico did during 2020.[626]

A formal declaration by a state that crisis standards of care are in effect changes the legal landscape in the state, potentially affecting legal requirements and the threshold for applying civil liability to individuals and institutions providing health care and related services. Even absent a formal government recognition that crisis standards of care are in force, the existence of these standards, definitions, criteria, and protocols to ensure ethical allocation may influence how courts will interpret the legal standard of care that individuals or institutions need to provide in exigent circumstances where health care resources are limited. It still remains to be seen to what extent courts will grant deference to these plans and protocols, since few have needed to be implemented and legal challenges have been rare. However, as described further below, institutions and individuals that follow the guidance outlined in these plans and guidelines will likely be considered to have provided a reasonable standard of care and are likely to prevail if challenged through civil litigation.

4. Are providers of health care obliged by the law to provide (urgent) care to all patients? If the answer is yes, are there any legally recognised exceptions from this duty?

Whether a health care provider needs to provide health care to all patients depends on whether federal or state law applies to the situation at hand. Federal law requires that some health care providers provide health care to all patients. The Emergency Medical Treatment & Labor Act (EMTALA), a federal statute, requires hospitals that have an emergency department to examine any patient suffering from an emergency

625 Virginia Code s. 8.01-225.01, 8.01-225.02; Maryland Code, Public Safety, s. 14-3A-06.

626 Lance Gable, 'Allocation of Scarce Medical Resources and Crisis Standards of Care' (COVID Policy Playbook, August 2020) <https://papers.ssrn.com/sol3/papers.cfm?abstract_id=3675837> accessed 2 August 2021 ; Lance Gable, 'Allocating Medical Resources During Times of Scarcity' (COVID-19 Policy Playbook, Volume II, March 2021) <https://static1.squarespace.com/static/5956e16e6b8f5b8c45f1c216/t/6058f349b45e443eaef035e0/1616442186083/Chp25-Gable_COVIDPolicyPlaybook-March2021.pdf> accessed 2 August 2021

medical condition[627] and to subsequently provide stabilizing treatment within that hospital's capability.[628] This stabilizing treatment must be provided regardless of a patient's ability to pay,[629] but additional treatment beyond stabilization is not mandated.[630] Crisis Standards of Care (CSC) are not required to provoke EMTALA protections; all that is required is that the patient must be suffering from an emergency medical condition.[631] However, CSC conditions may affect a hospital's capabilities to respond to a patient's emergency needs, and they may be unable to provide the necessary stabilizing treatment due to resource shortages. Additionally, EMTALA does not apply to non-emergency treatment or to facilities that do not have a dedicated emergency department — therefore, many settings and circumstances are not covered by this requirement.[632]

A hospital may transfer a patient to another facility who has not yet been stabilized if the necessary stabilizing treatment cannot be provided by the initial hospital where the patient presents for treatment.[633] If a patients refuses transfer under these circumstances, the hospital would not face liability under EMTALA if it did not provide stabilizing treatment as long as the hospital informs the patient, or a person acting on the patient's behalf, of the risks and benefits that a patient may face if not transferred and takes reasonable steps to secure the patient's written informed consent to refuse transfer.[634] Additionally, hospitals that are required under EMTALA to accept transfer patients cannot refuse a transfer if the hospital has the capacity to treat the individual.[635] It is unclear whether a hospital would be in compliance with EMTALA if it transferred a patient to a different hospital because it could not provide stabilizing treatment, but only because the hospital is conserving some supplies based on a CSC assessment.

Importantly, EMTALA does not establish a national standard of care for emergency treatment, and does not preempt state remedies for malpractice.[636] A hospital's

---

627 Emergency medical condition is defined as 'a medical condition manifesting itself by acute symptoms of sufficient severity (including severe pain) such that the absence of immediate medical attention could reasonably be expected to result in: (i) placing the health of the individual (or, with respect to a pregnant woman, the health of the woman or her unborn child) in serious jeopardy, (ii) serious impairment to bodily functions, or (iii) serious dysfunction of any bodily organ or part.' 42 USC s. 1395dd(e)(1)(A)(i)–(iii). Additionally, in the case of a pregnant woman having contractions, there is an emergency situation if '(i) [] there is inadequate time to effect a safe transfer to another hospital before delivery, or (ii) that transfer may pose a threat to the health or safety of the woman or the unborn child.' 42 USC s. 1395(e)(1)(B)(i)–(ii)

628 42 USC s. 1395dd(b)(1)(A)

629 42 USC. s. 1395dd(h)

630 42 USC s. 1395dd

631 ibid

632 42 USC s. 1395dd(a)

633 42 USC s. 1395dd(c)

634 42 USC s. 1395(b)(3)

635 42 USC s. 1395dd(a)

636 Construction and Application of Emergency Medical Treatment and Active Labor Act, 104 ALR Fed 166 (Originally published in 1991)

liability under EMTALA stems from whether the hospital treats an incoming patient the same way other patients with similar symptoms would be treated, and not based on whether the patient was correctly diagnosed or not or whether the health care providers adhered to the applicable standard of care.[637] Instead, the standard of care in emergency medical situations and applicable medical malpractice causes of actions are state-specific.[638] Some states, such as Georgia, have adopted laws that are analogous to EMTALA.[639] Georgia requires for there to be an actual medical emergency that *"could reasonably be expected to result in placing the patient's health in serious jeopardy, serious impairment to bodily functions, or serious dysfunction of any bodily organ or part[]"* in order for the requirement to treat to be applicable to the situation at hand.[640] This requires the healthcare provider to make a subjective opinion about the patient's condition.[641] This sort of law protects healthcare providers and institutions from civil liability by requiring a high burden of proof ('clear and convincing evidence')[642] while also reducing the applicable standard of care required in a medical emergency to gross negligence.[643]

All fifty states and the District of Columbia have 'Good Samaritan' laws, which provide immunity from civil liability in situations where individuals voluntarily care for and rescue others in emergency situations.[644] These laws can apply to physicians under certain conditions.[645] In the United States, there is no duty placed on individuals to treat or rescue in emergency situations, but this exception does not typically apply to on-call physicians or physicians that have a pre-existing relationship with the patient.[646] For example, in the state of Michigan, a medical provider does not have a duty to treat a patient in an emergency situation, unless professional relationship, such as a physician-patient, physician assistant-patient, or nurse-patient relationship, existed prior to the emergency. However, if a medical provider who does not have this pre-existing duty responds in good faith to provide care during a life-threatening emergency, they are not liable for civil damages 'as a result of an act of omission in the rendering of emergency care, except an act of omission amounting to gross negligence or willful and wanton misconduct.'[647] Additionally, in most states, health care providers cannot receive compensation for the care they provide, or else the Good Samaritan liability protections do not apply.[648]

637 Construction and Application of Emergency Medical Treatment and Active Labor Act (n 42)
638 ibid
639 OCGA s. 31-1-29.5 (2010)
640 OCGA s. 51-1-29.5(a)(5)
641 ibid
642 OGCA 51-1-29.5(c) (2010)
643 ibid
644 Brian West and Matthew Varacallo, 'Good Samaritan Laws' (2021) StatPearls <https://www.ncbi.nlm.nih.gov/books/NBK542176/> accessed 1 August 2021
645 ibid
646 ibid
647 MCL s. 691.1502
648 ibid

5. On what legal basis is it possible to apply the allocation criteria in practice?

Emergency declarations and orders can assist in figuring out how care is delivered and how resources are allocated. Governors can declare state emergencies, disasters, or public health emergencies, which often change the legal landscape and authorize state government and its partners to respond rapidly to an emerging crisis. Many states' statutory emergency laws recognize out-of-state health care licenses for the limited duration of a declared emergency.[649] Through memoranda of understanding, mutual aid agreements, compacts, and other agreements, states and health systems can share resources or health care equipment during scarce resource situations where some areas are better equipped than others.[650] Every state has its own specific powers during a declared emergency, and many of these emergency powers grant broad authority to state executive branch officials. Kansas, for example, affords 'authority to issue orders and proclamations with the force of law and to suspend or modify the provisions of any state law or regulation.'[651]

There is a wide variety of mechanisms through which the state can formally and legally authorize CSC. The implementation of CSC plans varies state by state, with most states establishing a process that envisions shared decision-making and collaborative efforts between state health department officials and the governor's office in responding to the triggers, indicators, and health system requests. Many CSC plans outline possible legal triggers that may activate CSC protocols during public health emergencies and also describe when a public health emergency may be considered ended. Many CSC plans list non-exhaustive lists of indicators and triggers to guide decision-making, such as changes in demand, resources, or other critical functions in health care settings. State health departments will evaluate these indicators and triggers, and consult with the Governor's office to then make the decision whether to activate CSC.

Some, but not all, state CSC plans allude to an associated executive order from the state governor or other designated official. In New Mexico's plan, the state health department plays a prominent role in activating CSC. If indicators point to insufficient health care resources, negative impacts to multiple healthcare access points, and other related factors, the New Mexico state department of health may

649 Institute of Medicine, 'Crisis Standards of Care: A Systems Framework for Catastrophic Disaster Response, Committee on Guidance for Establishing Crisis Standards of Care for Use in Disaster Situations' (National Academies Press, 21 March 2012)

650 Institute of Medicine, 'Crisis Standards of Care: A Systems Framework for Catastrophic Disaster Response, Committee on Guidance for Establishing Crisis Standards of Care for Use in Disaster Situations' (n 57)

651 Gianfranco Pezzino, 'Guidelines for the Use of Modified Health Care Protocols in Acute Care Hospitals During Public Health Emergencies,' (*Kansas Health Institute*, August 2010) <http://media.khi.org/news/documents/2010/08/11/Scarce_resources_technical_FINAL.pdf> accessed 1 August 2021

lead the New Mexico Department of Health to consider CSC activation.[652] From there, the state department of health can activate and notify state, local, tribal, and federal partners of activation.[653] In other states such as New Hampshire, the state health department commissioner can consult with stakeholders and initiate the CSC plan based on key indicators, triggers, and situational factors. In situations where local conditions may point to activation, hospital systems are expected to reach out to state officials and the state health department to alert them of such necessity.[654] In Minnesota, the governor approves any state disaster declaration requests and issues emergency declarations, while the lead health official consults with others to approve activation of CSC.[655] In Colorado, by contrast, the governor plays a more prominent role. The CSC plan can only be activated after the Governor's Declaration of a Public Health Emergency and may be accompanied by associated Executive Orders.[656]

State orders that authorize the use of CSC protocols often leave the actual decision-making to individual institutions or providers, so the authorization of CSC at the state level doesn't necessarily mean that CSC will actually be implemented in practice. The states of Arizona and New Mexico, for example, both authorized the use of CSC during the COVID-19 pandemic through state-level orders, but no health care providers or institutions ever implemented CSC protocols in their facilities. Furthermore, providers and institutions can claim that the implementation of CSC guidelines was necessary even without a declared emergency or specific authorization from the government, but their position will be legally stronger if the declaration/authorization has been made by government officials.

6. What level of legal certainty do the health professionals and the health care providers have when applying the allocation criteria?

In the United States, individual states are largely responsible for regulating health care professionals and institutions. This means that legal liability protections can vary from state to state. Even when CSC guidelines are activated, 'no uniform legal protection exists for the provision of care under disaster circumstances or pursuant

652 New Mexico Department of Health, 'New Mexico Crisis Standards of Care Plan' (*New Mexico Department of Health*, 27 June 2018) <https://www.nmhealth.org/publication/view/plan/4877/> accessed 1 August 2021

653 New Mexico Department of Health (n 60)

654 New Hampshire Department of Health and Human Services, 'New Hampshire Crisis Standards of Care Plan' <https://www.dhhs.nh.gov/documents/nh-csc-plan.pdf accessed> 7 December 2020

655 Minnesota Department of Health Concept of Operations, 'Minnesota Crisis Standards of Care Framework' (n 33)

656 Colorado Department of Public Health & Environment, 'Colorado Crisis Standards of Care' (5 April 2020) <https://cdphe.colorado.gov/colorado-crisis-standards-care> accessed 1 August 2021

to state resource allocation guidance.'[657] Therefore, health care providers must become familiar with their applicable state's laws in order to fully understand what liability protections are available.

Even though liability protections are mainly state-specific, there are a few, limited federal liability shields that apply in specific scenarios, including the National Childhood Vaccine Injury Act of 1986 (providing liability protection for vaccine manufacturers), the Volunteer Protection Act of 1997 (providing liability protection for volunteers, including medical volunteers), and the Public Readiness and Emergency Preparedness (PREP) Act of 2005.[658] The PREP Act[659] is most applicable to public health emergencies such as the COVID-19 pandemic, as its liability shields apply to countermeasures such as drugs, devices, and vaccines that are used to combat national emergencies which result in death or serious injury.[660]The PREP Act also shields manufacturers and other actors in the supply chain.[661] Notably, during the COVID-19 pandemic, the PREP Act was amended by the Families First Coronavirus Response Act to also cover personal respiratory protection devices as a covered countermeasure.[662] However, immunity does not apply in cases of willful misconduct. It is unclear whether these liability protections would apply to a decision not to administer a countermeasure.

State laws also provide liability shields during public health emergencies.[663] Prior to the COVID-19 pandemic, many states had legal rules or guidance that applied health care malpractice liability protections for care provided during a public health emergency.[664] Some states provide protection against civil liability claims, others against both criminal and civil liability claims, and some states provide no liability protections.[665] As of the beginning of 2021, about a third of states had enacted some form of additional health care provider immunity during the COVID-19 pandemic either through executive order or legislation.[666] It is important to note that liability shields put in place through executive orders are often time-limited and may only apply temporarily during the COVID-19 pandemic. There may be an actual end-date written into the order, or the order may cease to apply when emergency situations are terminated. While most of the liability shields initially put in place during

[657] Valeria Gutmann Koch, 'Crisis Standards of Care and State Liability Shields' (2020) 57 San Diego L Rev 973, 979

[658] Nicolas P. Terry, 'Liability, Liability Shields, and Waivers' (*COVID-19 Policy Playbook: Legal Recommendations for a Safer, More Equitable Future*, March 2021) <https://papers.ssrn.com/sol3/papers.cfm?abstract_id=3809455> accessed 1 August 2021

[659] Public Readiness and Emergency Preparedness Act, 42 USC s. 247-6d, 247-6e

[660] Nicolas P. Terry (n 66) 185

[661] ibid

[662] ibid

[663] ibid 186

[664] Sharona Hoffman, 'Responder's Responsibility: Liability and Immunity in Public Health Emergencies' (2008) 96 Geo LJ 1913, 1937–1950

[665] ibid 1947-49

[666] Valeria Gutmann Koch (n 65) 982

the COVID-19 pandemic were promulgated through gubernatorial emergency declarations, later shields were typically put in place through statutes and may continue to apply after pandemic-related legal orders have been revoked.[667]

Legislatively-created shields usually provide statutory protection from civil liability when care is provided pursuant to state directives or CSC, unless the actions alleged are intentional, willful, wanton, or constitute gross negligence; therefore, civil immunity in these scenarios is conditional.[668] Maryland, New York, and New Jersey additionally provide protections to physicians from criminal liability that may result during a public health emergency.[669] During the early months of the pandemic, many states enacted COVID-specific shields to immunize health care providers from negligence liability, prompted by concerns that many health care providers were providing services and care beyond what they were licensed, and therefore authorized, to provide, meaning they operated outside of their scope of practice.[670] These liability shields allowed health care workers to act outside of their scope of practice to meet the needs of the pandemic without fearing legal liability. These protections can be considered a type of 'Good Samaritan' law, and like many Good Samaritan laws the applicable immunity does not extend to cases that involve willful, reckless, or criminal conduct.[671]

Health care provider actions that are protected under state civil liability shields may vary from state to state. Liability shields may immunize health care providers and institutions from liability for injury or death only when providers are complying with federal, state, local, or institutional plans, guidelines, or CSC criteria.[672] Other shields may provide immunity if the provider acted negligently while 'acting consistent with emergency plans,' as is the case in Minnesota.[673] Protections may be limited to negligent care of patients that specifically have COVID-19, 'for whom the standard of care may be modified due to scarce resources.'[674] This is a more narrow and targeted version of the type of protection that liability shields may provide. Some states, such as Michigan and Ohio, have enacted limited civil liability for health care providers and communities.[675] In Georgia, health care providers can use assumption of liability waiver signs at points of entry to their businesses.[676] Broader liability statutes may provide 'civil liability protections for injury or death law

667 Nicolas P. Terry (n 66) 186
668 Valeria Gutmann Koch (n 65) 982
669 ibid 1947–49.
670 Nicolas P. Terry (n 66) 186
671 ibid
672 Valeria Gutmann Koch (n 65) 982
673 ibid
674 ibid 983. The language of this sort of protection is similar to what is in place in Pennsylvania. ibid
675 Nicolas P. Terry (n 66) 187
676 An example of what an assumption of liability waiver sign may say is: 'Warning: Under Georgia law, there is no liability for an injury or death of an individual entering these premises if such injury or death results from the inherent risks of contracting COVID-19. You are assuming this risk by entering these premises.' Nicolas P. Terry (n. 66) 188

occurs due to medical services that are provided in support of the state's response to the COVID-19 pandemic,' as is the case in a number of states.[677] A patient does not need to have COVID-19 for this type of immunity to apply, and the health care provider does not have to act in accordance with specific CSC or guidance in order to be protected from liability.[678]

7. What are the civil and criminal liability implications of allocation of scarce health care resources? Have there already been any related legal suits and/or criminal proceedings?

As explained in the response to question six, there are a variety of liability protections that may apply to health care providers at both the state and federal level. Many of these liability protections guard health care providers who act negligently while rendering care under CSC scenarios.[679] However, these liability protections cease to exist when willful or wanton misconduct is involved while rendering care.[680] In these scenarios, patients may pursue their medical malpractice or other related civil claims against the health care provider, and possibly the institution, as governed by state law. The applicable standard of care may vary depending on the issues involved in a specific case. The core issue is whether a health care provider will be held to a professional standard or basic negligence.[681] There are no strict liability, or 'no fault,' provisions in statutes relating to health care provider liability. Instead, the statutes may require various options for the required standard of care or intent level. The professional standard of care presents a higher threshold than plain negligence, which therefore typically makes these cases harder for plaintiffs to win.

Some cases brought against a health care provider can be categorized as medical malpractice claims under state law.[682] In those cases, the standard of care depends on 'expert testimony as to whether there was compliance with the professional standard of care.'[683] The professional standard of care may vary depending on what region of the country the care is provided in and what resources are available, and importantly, hinges on what care a reasonable professional would have provided under the same or similar circumstances. Consequently, even when CSC are not formally in place, liability claims based on the failure to provide appropriate care will be evaluated in light of the circumstances at hand when the treatment decisions were made.

---

677 ibid 985. This sort of broad protection can be found in Arizona, Arkansas, Connecticut, Iowa, Maryland, Massachusetts, Michigan, New Jersey, New York, Oklahoma, Vermont, and Virginia. Ibid

678 ibid

679 Nicolas P. Terry (n 66) 186

680 ibid

681 ibid 185

682 ibid

683 ibid

Health care providers who are following a carefully developed allocation protocol will have a strong case that their treatment and allocation decisions were reasonable, even without an official declaration that CSC apply.

In some scenarios, non-medical negligence may be alleged.[684] This may occur if there is a lack of necessary supplies or improper infection control.[685] These non-medical negligence cases would only require an ordinary showing of negligence, and liability waivers may protect providers or institutions from liability for this sort of negligence.[686] Additionally, public health crises may foster conditions for possible intentional torts. One example of an intentional tort that made headlines during the COVID-19 pandemic was deliberately coughing on another individual, where the victim did not know whether the cougher was infected with COVID-19.[687] Nursing homes may also find themselves under legal scrutiny during a public health emergency, as they may be subject to specific statutory claims such as elder abuse or qui tam Medicaid fraud suits.[688] However, many laws and executive orders promulgated directly in response to the COVID-19 pandemic additionally provide liability protections to a broad array of health care facilities, including long-term care facilities and nursing homes. These protections will not apply to situations that involve 'willful or intentional misconduct, gross negligence, recklessness, or the provision of care in the absence of good faith.'[689] As described above, liability protections vary significantly in different states. In New York and New Jersey, for example, criminal immunity is extended to health care facilities that provide care during the pandemic.[690] Each state will differ as to what criminal ramifications may be applied to healthcare providers[691] and institutions. Further, liability protections may only apply in specific scenarios, depending on the state laws available.

Under EMTALA, described in detail above in response to question four, both civil monetary penalties and civil enforcement may apply to hospitals and health care providers that violate the Act.[692] Participating hospitals that negligently violate EMTALA requirements are subject to a civil monetary penalty of not more than fifty thousand U.S. dollars (or twenty-five thousand U.S. dollars for hospitals with less than one hundred beds) for *each* violation.[693] Physicians subject to EMTALA requirements that negligently violate the law are subject to a civil monetary penalty of not more than fifty thousand U.S. dollars.[694] If the violation 'is gross and flagrant or

684 ibid
685 ibid
686 ibid
687 ibid
688 ibid
689 Valeria Gutmann Koch (n 63) 988
690 ibid
691 Criminal immunity is provided to health care providers for liability that may result from a public health emergency in New York, New Jersey, and Maryland. ibid 982
692 42 USC s. 1395dd(d)(1)–(2)
693 42 USC s. 1395dd(d)(1)(A)
694 42 USC s. 1395dd(d)(1)(B)

is repeated,' the physician is subject to exclusion from state health care programs.[695] If an individual suffers personal harm that is a direct result of the participating hospital's violation of EMTALA, they may bring a civil action against the participating hospital for damages available for personal injury under state in the state in which the hospital is located, as well as any other appropriate equitable relief.[696] If another medical facility suffers a financial loss as a direct result of a participating hospital's violation of EMTALA, the medical facility can bring a civil action against the participating hospital.[697] The facility can bring the action to obtain damages for financial loss under state law in the state in which the hospital is located, and any appropriate equitable relief.[698]

Hundreds of thousands of complaints have been filed in relation to the COVID-19 pandemic.[699] Complaints based in tort have been made regarding wrongful death and/or personal injury in healthcare settings, as well as medical malpractice claims.[700] Other lawsuits, including class action lawsuits, have been targeted specifically at long-term care facilities, where individuals are making complaints regarding deaths of residents, inability to visit their relatives, and other injuries or deaths that long-term care facility staff members may have suffered.[701] Secondary damages may be available to complainants depending on each state's specific causes of action and whether liability protections apply in specific scenarios. However, very few, if any, lawsuits have been filed that allege civil liability based on resource allocation decisions.[702]

B. Case studies

Case 1

As a result of a rapid worsening of the epidemiological situation, the material and personal capacities have been drastically overloaded in all the hospitals in the country. Within just a few minutes, ambulances transport ten patients to one particular hospital's emergency unit. The patients all need admission to the hospital, preferably to the intensive care unit (ICU). However, only two beds are available there. Other hospitals are overwhelmed too, so it is not possible to transport patients to any of them. All of the ten newly coming patients suffer from COVID-19;

695 ibid

696 42 USC s. 1395dd(d)(1)(C)(2)(A)

697 42 USC s. 1395dd(d)(1)(C)(2)(B)

698 ibid

699 Hunton Andrews Kurth, 'Covid-19 Complaint Tracker' (*HuntonAndrewsKurth*, 2021) < https://www.huntonak.com/en/covid-19-tracker.html > accessed 1 August 2021

700 ibid

701 Nicolas P. Terry (n 66) at 184

702 Hunton Andrews Kurth (n 107)

they have breathing difficulties, fast-rising fever, and decreasing oxygen saturation. Nevertheless, they differ in age, comorbidities, clinical fragility, and other factors.

Theoretically, the eight patients who cannot be admitted to beds can be placed in improvised settings in the hospital corridors, laying on gurneys or mattresses on the floor. Nevertheless, it will be impossible to provide them with the care they need.

Evaluation of the case

- What criteria can be used to choose the patients who will be admitted to the beds (i.e. what are the possible allocation criteria)?
  Some combination of medical prognosis assessment will be applied first in most states. If any of the patients are essential personnel they may receive priority. Lottery, first-come first-serve, and age could also be used as tie-breakers in some jurisdictions. Each tie-breaker comes with its own set of problems and ethical questions. Some state and institutional criteria consider equity issues and will seek to allocate the beds to avoid discrimination. In addition, many state or institutional allocation criteria would require alternative treatment and palliative care to be provided for anyone not receiving a scarce resource or treatment.
- What legal consequences can this decision have for the health professionals and the hospital? How strong is their legal certainty that there will be no adverse legal consequences if they follow the above-mentioned criteria?
  Since state laws implementing liability protections vary in scope and coverage, health professionals and hospitals may not have clear guidance or parameters to follow that would allow them to avoid all potential adverse legal consequences from resource allocation decisions. However, if health professionals and hospitals follow plans and guidance set out by their facility and under state law, act in good faith, consult with ethics experts, and use their best reasonable judgment to provide the best care possible under the circumstances, they are likely to avoid civil and criminal liability.
- What legal defences could the health professionals and the hospital use against a civil lawsuit and/or criminal prosecution for the allocation decision?
  Health professionals and hospitals may be able to invoke applicable liability shields that have be implemented under state law or federal law. In the absence of applicable liability shields, health professional and hospitals could argue that the standard of care provided was reasonable under the circumstances. If health professionals and hospitals can demonstrate that they followed ethical guidance, articulated plans, best practices, and used reasonable judgment under the circumstances, courts are unlikely to impose civil liability.

Additional questions

- Would it be legally permissible to lower the standard of care provided to all patients in order to provide at least basic decent care to the newly admitted patients who are placed in the hospital corridors? To what extent?
  This may be legally permissible. It is possible to make the case that this would be an acceptable alternative. For example, stopping the provision of a high-resource

treatment like ECMO to disperse personnel to help a greater number of patients might be ethically appropriate and could be legally justifiable. This may also depend on what is said in the ethical guidelines and what other states and physicians are doing in similar situations. There is no clear standard of care to give a definitive answer, and guidance is only clear if governmental bodies implement CSC plans. To ensure that this is legally permissible, one would have to be able to convince the court that the reallocation of resources across the facility was reasonable even though it would have negative effects on the health of specific individuals. The outcome of a case challenging this reallocation of care would depend largely on how the judge and jury where the case is heard evaluate the professional standard of care relevant to this situation.

Case 2

Two patients in an ICU are suffering from COVID-19. After admission to the hospital, they were provided with the high-flow nasal oxygen therapy (HFNO). During one night, the condition of both patients starts to worsen rapidly. At dawn, it is clear that neither of them will survive without artificial ventilation. However, there is just one ventilator available.

<u>Evaluation of the case</u>

- What criteria can be used to choose which of the two patients will be provided with artificial ventilation and which one will be left without it, possibly to die?
  Many jurisdictions would use defined prognosis algorithms like the SOFA score to assess which patient is more likely to survive, as described in detail in Question 1. While the SOFA algorithm is not ideal, it can be a helpful diagnostic tool to be used in collaboration with other tools and factors to reach an ethical allocation decision. Discrimination issues could also arise in deciding which criteria can be used in this situation, as detailed further in Question 2. Many jurisdictions have implemented criteria that attempt to reduce discrimination in resource allocation by ensuring that only immediate medical prognosis and likelihood of survival to discharge are considered, rather than measures of long-term capacity or longevity that may deprioritize patients with chronic health conditions or disabilities.[703]
- What legal consequences can this decision have for the health professionals and the hospital? How strong is their legal certainty that there will be no adverse legal consequences if they follow the above-mentioned criteria?
  Health professionals and hospitals will face the same types of legal uncertainty in this case as they do in the scenario described in Case 1. If the jurisdiction has implemented CSC plans and protocols that explicitly address the allocation of scarce ventilators, then following the criteria and protocols will reduce the potential for adverse legal consequences for health professionals and hospitals.

[703] Raschke et al. (n 5)

- What legal defences could the health professionals and the hospital use against a civil lawsuit and/or criminal prosecution for the allocation decision?
  The same legal defences would be available in this case as would be available in Case 1. Health professionals and hospitals may be protected from liability by immunity shield law that have to be implemented under state law or federal law, if these liability shield are deemed to cover ventilator allocation decisions. Furthermore, health professionals and hospitals may be able to make a strong legal case that they followed a reasonable professional standard of care under the circumstances, a case that will be even stronger if specific CSC guidance exists addressing the issue of ventilator allocation.

Additional question

- If the allocation criteria specified in your answer to the first question to this case consisted of the patients' clinical features (such as their age, clinical fragility, etc.), please identify what criteria could be used for the allocation decision if all the relevant clinical features of both patients were practically the same?
  Using a lottery to randomly select between the two patients would be deemed acceptable in some allocation plans. Since both patients are existing patients at the hospital, the ventilator will not be able to be allocated according to which patient needs it first. Some ethicists also argue that age unrelated to prognosis could be an acceptable factor to use in making this allocation decision, with priority being given to the younger patient.[704] Most allocation plans also make clear that many other demographic and social factors like race, gender, ethnicity, sexual orientation, gender identity, ability to pay, or other indicia of social worth or social standing are not acceptable criteria to use to differentiate between patients in making this type of allocation decision.

Case 3

There is a single extracorporeal membrane oxygenation (ECMO) device in the hospital. It is currently being used for an 84-year-old patient suffering from COVID-19, with diabetes as an underlying disease, clinical frailty score (CFS) 6–7 (moderate to severe frailty). It is possible that the patient will survive and will be discharged from the hospital if the ECMO treatment is continued. However, a younger COVID-19 patient is admitted to the hospital. This new patient is 51 years old, otherwise healthy, but her health condition has been rapidly deteriorating. Soon she will most likely need ECMO to survive.

Evaluation of the case

- Can it be legally permissible for the hospital staff to discontinue the ECMO treatment of the older patient and provide palliative care to her in order to save

704 Ezekiel J. Emanuel et al., 'Fair Allocation of Scarce Medical Resources in the Time of COVID-19' (21 May 2020) N Engl J Med. <https://www.nejm.org/doi/full/10.1056/nejmsb2005114> accessed 1 August 2021

the younger and healthier patient's life? Please keep in mind that the older patient could survive if the treatment continued, but her chances may be lower than those of the younger patient.

In many jurisdictions the answer would be no. Reallocation of an ECMO device would be either explicitly or implicitly prohibited and therefore would carry significant legal risk. In other states, like New York and Minnesota such reallocation could be authorized in some circumstances under existing state CSC guidance. However, even in these states, the legal and ethical case for reallocation of an ECMO device would be strongest if the patient currently receiving ECMO is unlikely to survive and the recipient patient is likely to survive if they receive it. Under the Case 3 scenario, the older patient may survive to discharge if the treatment is continued, which renders the removal of ECMO treatment less clear-cut and more legally and ethically fraught. In states that allow ventilator or ECMO reallocation, applicable criteria do not authorize a pure utilitarian calculus, where the scarce resource will be reallocated to the patient most likely to survive. Rather, these criteria envision that a ventilator or ECMO unit would only be reallocated if the current user is unlikely to survive to hospital discharge.

- If the answer to the first question is positive, what specific criteria can be used in clinical decision-making regarding replacing one patient with another with respect to a particular treatment unavailable for all?

  In jurisdictions that do allow resource reallocation, a patient's immediate medical prognosis will be the most relevant criterion. If a patient is unlikely to survive until discharge, the CSC criteria may allow reallocation of scarce treatment resources, like a ventilator or ECMO, if they are needed to treat other patients who are likely to survive with this treatment. Health professionals and hospitals who are taking this step will often try to do so with the consent of the patient from whom the resource is being withdrawn or that patient's family members or legal guardian. Additionally, CSC allocation criteria require that a patient who has had a treatment resource withdrawn should continue to receive alternative and palliative treatment as appropriate to their health condition.
- What legal consequences can this decision have for the health professionals and the hospital? How strong is their legal certainty that there will be no adverse legal consequences if they follow the above-mentioned criteria?

  Health professionals or hospitals that discontinued ECMO treatment of one patient and allocate it to another patient, could face legal consequences through criminal or civil liability. The risk of these legal consequence varies depending on applicable state law. In states that have broadly-worded immunity provisions applicable to civil liability claims related to COVID-19-related health care, health professionals or hospitals would likely be shielded from liability from a civil lawsuit based on reallocating a scarce resource. To decrease the risks of liability, clinicians and hospitals should follow approved CSC guidelines and strategies in their decision making and allocation.

Criminal liability present a more complex legal risk for health professionals. Most states that provide immunity from civil liability do not provide similar immunity from criminal prosecution. Since prosecutors have a great deal of discretion about bringing criminal charges, a health professional who removes a critical resource from a patient without consent and hastens that patient's death could face manslaughter or other serious criminal charges. While such charges have not been brought in the past and may not succeed if attempted, the potential legal risk exists unless state law specifically provides immunity from criminal prosecution. Maryland has such a statute stating 'a health care provider is immune from civil or criminal liability if the health care provider acts in good faith under a catastrophic health emergency proclamation.'[705] Finally, an older patient from whom ECMO is discontinued to allocate to a younger patient could also allege violations of federal age discrimination laws. Because of threats of age discrimination, many health professionals and hospitals are hesitant to remove ventilators and ECMO treatment from older patients.

– What legal defences could the health professionals and the hospital use against a civil lawsuit and/or criminal prosecution for the allocation decision?
  The same legal defence strategies apply to this case as the previous cases. Health professionals and hospitals can raise immunity defences if they apply, and may defend the decision to reallocate the ECMO treatment as reasonable under the circumstances, given the ethical obligation to save lives and consistent with their hospital protocols, state's CSC plan, or other promulgated guidance.

Additional question

– Suppose there are two different scenarios: a) the older patient was admitted to the hospital and provided with the ECMO treatment, and only later, after several days, the younger patient was admitted, and b) the younger patient was admitted before the older patient, however, the older patient required ECMO treatment soon after admission while the younger patient's health condition deteriorated only after a longer time when the ECMO was already occupied (i. e. at the time when the younger patient was admitted to the hospital, she did not yet need it). Would there be any difference in the allocation decision making between these two scenarios?
  In these two scenarios, the analysis described above would apply, and the allocation decisions would likely be the same. The relative timing of two patients' admissions to the hospital would not affect the analysis of each patient's prognosis or the other relevant factors that would go into making the decision at the time that reallocation would be considered.

[705] Glenn Cohen et al., 'Potential Legal Liability for Withdrawing or Withholding Ventilators During COVID-19: Assessing the Risks and Identifying Needed Reforms' (April 1, 2020) 19 JAMA 1901

The list of abbreviations

ACA	Affordable Care Act
CDC	Centers for Disease Control and Prevention
CFS	clinical frailty score
CSC	Crisis Standards of Care
ECMO	extracorporeal membrane oxygenation
EMS	emergency medical services
EMTALA	Emergency Medical Treatment & Labor Act
HFNO	high-flow nasal oxygen
ICU	intensive care unit
IOM	Institute of Medicine
NASEM	National Academies of Science, Engineering, and Medicine
PPE	personal protective equipment
PREP	Public Readiness and Emergency Preparedness
SOFA	Sequential Organ Failure Assessment

Bibliography

• Legislation

42 USC s. 1395dd

Construction and Application of Emergency Medical Treatment and Active Labor Act, 104 ALR Fed 166 (Originally published in 1991)

Maryland Code, Public Safety, s. 14-3A-06.

MCL s. 691.1502

OCGA s. 31-1-29.5 (2010)

Public Readiness and Emergency Preparedness Act, 42 USC s. 247-6d, 247-6e

Virginia Code s. 8.01-225.01, 8.01-225.02

• Case law

• Books

Institute of Medicine, 'Guidance for Establishing Crisis Standards of Care for Use in Disaster Situations' (National Academies Press, 2009)

Institute of Medicine, 'Crisis Standards of Care: A Systems Framework For Catastrophic Disaster Response' (National Academies Press, 21 March 2012)

Institute of Medicine, 'Crisis Standards of Care: A Toolkit for Indicators and Triggers' (National Academies Press, 2013)

Institute of Medicine, 'Crisis Standards of Care: A Systems Framework for Catastrophic Disaster Response, Committee on Guidance for Establishing Crisis Standards of Care for Use in Disaster Situations' (National Academies Press, 21 March 2012)

• Articles

CDC COVID-19 Response Team, 'Severe outcomes among patients with coronavirus disease 2019 (COVID-19) - United States' (12 February–16 March 2020) 69(12) MMWR Morb Mortality Wkly Rep 343–46 <https://www.cdc.gov/mmwr/volumes/69/wr/mm6912e2.htm> accessed 1 August 2021

Cleveland Manchanda E, et al., 'Crisis Standards of Care in the USA: A Systematic Review and Implications for Equity Amidst COVID-19' (13 August 2020) J Racial & Ethnic Health Disparities <https://www.ncbi.nlm.nih.gov/pmc/articles/PMC7425256/#:~:text=Key%20principles%20on%20which%20this,%2C%20and%20accountability%20%5B7%5D> accessed 1 August 2021

Cleveland Manchanda E, et al., 'Inequity in Crisis Standards of Care' (2020) 383(4) N Engl J Med 16 <https://www.nejm.org/doi/full/10.1056/NEJMp2011359> accessed 1 August 2021

Cohen G et al., 'Potential Legal Liability for Withdrawing or Withholding Ventilators During COVID-19: Assessing the Risks and Identifying Needed Reforms' (April 1, 2020) 19 JAMA 1901

Emanuel E J et al., 'Fair Allocation of Scarce Medical Resources in the Time of COVID-19' (21 May 2020) N Engl J Med. <https://www.nejm.org/doi/full/10.1056/nejmsb2005114> accessed 1 August 2021

Farrell T W, et al., 'Rationing Limited Healthcare Resources in the COVID-19 Era and Beyond: Ethical Considerations Regarding Older Adults'(6 May 2020) J Am Geriatrics Soc <https://onlinelibrary.wiley.com/doi/full/10.1111/jgs.16539> 1 August 2021

Gutmann Koch V, 'Crisis Standards of Care and State Liability Shields' (2020) 57 San Diego L Rev 973, 979

Hoffman S, 'Responder's Responsibility: Liability and Immunity in Public Health Emergencies' (2008) 96 Geo LJ 1913, 1937–1950

Raiman M A and Julia R. Raifman J R, 'Disparities in the Population at Risk of Severe Illness from COVID-19 by Race/Ethnicity and Income' (27 April 2020) Am J Prev Med <https://www.ncbi.nlm.nih.gov/pmc/articles/PMC7183932/> accessed 1 August 2021

Raith E P, et al., 'Prognostic Accuracy of the SOFA Score, SIRS Criteria, and qSOFA Score for In-Hospital Mortality Among Adults With Suspected Infection Admitted to the Intensive Care Unit'(2017) 317(3) JAMA 290–300 <https://pubmed.ncbi.nlm.nih.gov/28114553/> accessed 1 August 2021

Raschke R A, et al., 'Discriminant Accuracy of the SOFA Score for Determining the Probable Mortality of Patients with COVID-19 Pneumonia Requiring Mechanical Ventilation' (2021) 325(14) JAMA 1469–70 <https://jamanetwork.com/journals/jama/fullarticle/2776737> accessed 1 August 2021

Singh G K, 'Area Deprivation and Widening Inequalities in US Mortality, 1969–1998' (1 July 2003) 93(7) Am J Pub Health 1137–43 <https://ajph.aphapublications.org/doi/pdf/10.2105/AJPH.93.7.1137> accessed 1 August 2021

• Other secondary sources

American Association of People with Disabilities, 'Over 400 Organizations Urge Department of Health and Human Services to Issue Guidance to Prohibit Discrimination during Medical Rationing' (17

April 2020) <https://www.aapd.com/press-releases/civil-rights-letter-covid-medical-rationing/?fbclid=IwAR0uKHogSaq8zknb--gVKL9-oplHXyX1a1lGpyx306WHpr0ZQWox-Sk2C1oM> accessed 1 August 2021

ASPR TRACIE HHS, 'Topic Collection: Crisis Standards of Care' < https://asprtracie.hhs.gov/technical-resources/63/crisis-standards-of-care/0> accessed August 3 2021

Bryant M, 'Detroit: America's next COVID-19 hotspot battles to prepare for coming surge' (The Guardian, 31 March 2020) <https://www.theguardian.com/us-news/2020/mar/31/detroit-coronavirus-america-michigan-poverty> accessed 3 August 2021

California Department of Public Health, 'COVID-19 Health Care System Mitigation Playbook' (March 2020), <https://www.cdph.ca.gov/Programs/CHCQ/LCP/CDPH%20Document%20Library/AFL-20-23-Mitigation-Playbook.pdf> accessed 1 August 2021

CDC, 'Social Vulnerability Index' (28 April 2021) <https://www.atsdr.cdc.gov/placeandhealth/svi/index.html> accessed 1 August 2021

Center for Public Representation, 'Examining How Crisis Standards of Care May Lead to Intersectional Medical Discrimination Against COVID-19 Patients'<https://www.centerforpublicrep.org/wp-content/uploads/FINAL-Intersectional-Guide-Crisis-Care-PDF.pdf> accessed 1August 2021

Colorado Department of Public Health & Environment, 'Colorado Crisis Standards of Care' (5 April 2020) <https://cdphe.colorado.gov/colorado-crisis-standards-care> accessed 1 August 2021

Disability Rights Pennsylvania, 'Letter from Disability Rights Pennsylvania, to Roger Severino, Director of Office of Civil Rights' (3 April 2020) <https://www.disabilityrightspa.org/wp-content/uploads/2020/04/s04.03.2020-DRP-OCR-Complaint-with-Exhibit-A-1.pdf> accessed 1 August 2021

Evans M and Mai-Duc C, 'Covid-19 Crisis Forces California Hospitals to Plan Who Gets Life-Saving Care' (*The Wall Street Journal*, 8 January 2021) <https://www.wsj.com/articles/covid-19-crisis-forces-california-hospitals-to-plan-who-gets-life-saving-care-11610115894> accessed 1 August 2021

Evans M et al., '"It's a Desperate Time": Crush of Covid-19 Patients Strains U.S. Hospitals' (*The Wall Street Journal*, 3 January 2021) <https://www.wsj.com/articles/its-a-desperate-time-crush-of-covid-19-patients-strains-u-s-hospitals-11609721551> accessed 1 August 2021

Gable L, 'Allocating Medical Resources During Times of Scarcity' (COVID-19 Policy Playbook, Volume II, March 2021) <https://static1.squarespace.com/static/5956e16e6b8f5b8c45f1c216/t/6058f349b45e443eaef035e0/1616442186083/Chp25-Gable_COVIDPolicyPlaybook-March2021.pdf> accessed 2 August 2021

Gable L, 'Allocation of Scarce Medical Resources and Crisis Standards of Care' (COVID Policy Playbook, August 2020) <https://papers.ssrn.com/sol3/papers.cfm?abstract_id=3675837> accessed 2 August 2021

HHS Office for Civil Rights in Action, 'BULLETIN: Civil Rights, HIPAA, and the Coronavirus Disease 2019 (COVID-19)' (28 March 2020) <https://www.hhs.gov/sites/default/files/ocr-bulletin-3-28-20.pdf> accessed 1 August 2021

Hunton Andrews Kurth, 'Covid-19 Complaint Tracker' (*HuntonAndrewsKurth*, 2021) <https://www.huntonak.com/en/covid-19-tracker.html > accessed 1 August 2021

Minnesota Department of Health Concept of Operations, 'Minnesota Crisis Standards of Care Framework' (25 February 2020) < https://www.health.state.mn.us/communities/ep/surge/crisis/conops.pdf> accessed 1 August 2021

Minnesota Department of Health, 'Crisis Standards of Care: Minnesota COVID Ethics Collaborative (MCEC)' (2 July 2021) <https://www.health.state.mn.us/communities/ep/surge/crisis/index.html> accessed 7 December 2020

Montana Department of Public Health and Human Services, Montana EMS & Trauma System Program, 'Montana COVID-19 Surge and Crisis Care Guide for Emergency Medical Services' (3 April 2020) <https://nasemso.org/wp-content/uploads/Surge-and-Crisis-Care-Guide-EMS-MT.pdf> accessed 1 August 2021

National Academies of Sciences, Engineering, and Medicine, 'Crisis Standards of Care: Successes and Challenges from the Past Ten Years — A Workshop' (21–22 November 2019) <https://www.nationalacademies.org/our-work/crisis-standards-of-care-successes-and-challenges-from-the-past-ten-years--a-workshop> accessed 1 August 2021

Ne'eman A, 'I Will Not Apologize for My Needs,' (NY Times, 23 March 2020) <https://www.nytimes.com/2020/03/23/opinion/coronavirus-ventilators-triage-disability.html> accessed 1 August 2021; U.S. Department of Health and Human Services, Office for Civil Rights, 'HHS-OCR Complaints Re COVID-19 Medical Discrimination' (The Arc, 23 March 2020), <https://thearc.org/resource/hhs-ocr-complaint-of-disability-rights-washington-self-advocates-in-leadership-the-arc-of-the-united-states-and-ivanova-smith/> accessed 1 August 2021

New Hampshire Department of Health and Human Services, 'New Hampshire Crisis Standards of Care Plan' <https://www.dhhs.nh.gov/documents/nh-csc-plan.pdf accessed> 7 December 2020

New Jersey Commission on Rationalizing Health Care Resources, 'Final Report' (24 January 2008), <https://www.nj.gov/health/rhc/documents/entire_finalreport.pdf> accessed 1 August 2021

New Mexico Department of Health (n 57)

New Mexico Department of Health, 'New Mexico Crisis Standards of Care Plan' (*New Mexico Department of Health*, 27 June 2018) <https://www.nmhealth.org/publication/view/plan/4877/> accessed 1 August 2021

New York State Department of Health, 'Ventilator Allocation Guidelines' (*New York State Task Force on Life and the Law*, November 2015) <https://www.health.ny.gov/regulations/task_force/reports_publications/docs/ventilator_guidelines.pdf> accessed 1 August 2021

New York State Department of Health, 'Ventilator Allocation Guidelines' (*New York State Task Force on Life and the Law*, November 2015) <https://www.health.ny.gov/regulations/task_force/reports_publications/docs/ventilator_guidelines.pdf> accessed 1 August 2021

Pennsylvania Department of Health, The Hospital and Healthsystem Association of Pennsylvania, 'Interim Pennsylvania Crisis Standards of Care for Pandemic Guidelines' (22 March 2020) <https://int.nyt.com/data/documenthelper/6850-pennsylvania-triage-guidelines/02cb4c58460e57ea9f05/optimized/full.pdf>

Pezzino G, 'Guidelines for the Use of Modified Health Care Protocols in Acute Care Hospitals During Public Health Emergencies,' (*Kansas Health Institute*, August 2010) <http://media.khi.org/news/documents/2010/08/11/Scarce_resources_technical_FINAL.pdf> accessed 1 August 2021

Pulrang A, 'The Disability Community Fights Deadly Discrimination Amid the COVID-19 Pandemic' (*Forbes* 14 April 2020) <https://www.forbes.com/sites/andrewpulrang/2020/04/14/the-disability-community-fights-deadly-discrimination-amid-the-covid-19-pandemic/?sh=797ac373309c> accessed 1 August 2021

Rhode Island Department of Health 'Crisis Standards of Care Guidelines' (27 April 2020), <https://health.ri.gov/publications/guidelines/crisis-standards-of-care.pdf?mc_cid=386ff10c1f&mc_eid=39d213ba26> accessed 1 August 2021

State of Michigan Department of Community Health, Office of Public Health Preparedness, 'Guidelines for Ethical Allocation of Scarce Medical Resources and Services During Public Health Emergencies in Michigan' (16 November 2012) <http://www.mimedicalethics.org/Documentation/Michigan%20DCH%20Ethical%20Scarce%20Resources%20Guidelines%20v2%20rev%20Nov%202012.0.pdf> accessed 1 August 2021

Terry N P, 'Liability, Liability Shields, and Waivers' (*COVID-19 Policy Playbook: Legal Recommendations for a Safer, More Equitable Future*, March 2021) <https://papers.ssrn.com/sol3/papers.cfm?abstract_id=3809455> accessed 1 August 2021

Toner E et al., 'Crisis Standards of Care: Lessons from New York City Hospitals' (2020) COVID-19 Experience. <https://repository.netecweb.org/items/show/1476> accessed 1 August 2021

Utah Department of Health, 'Utah Bureau of EMS and Preparedness EMA Pandemic Coronavirus Plan' (30 March 2020) <https://health.utah.gov/wp-content/uploads/Final_Utah_Crisis_Standards_of_Care_011719-1.pdf> accessed 1 August 2021

Washington State Department of Health, Northwest Healthcare Response Network, 'Scarce Resource Management & Crisis Standards of Care' (2020) <https://int.nyt.com/data/documenthelper/6853-washington-state-triage-guidel/02cb4c58460e57ea9f05/optimized/full.pdf#page=1> accessed 22 June 2021

West B and Matthew Varacallo M, 'Good Samaritan Laws' (2021) StatPearls <https://www.ncbi.nlm.nih.gov/books/NBK542176/> accessed 1 August 2021

CONCLUDING REMARKS

Petr Šustek
Charles University

If you fail to prepare you are preparing to fail.[706]

H. K. Williams

On 5 May 2023, the World Health Organization issued a statement declaring that Covid-19 no longer constituted a public health emergency of international concern.[707] It had this status for more than three years.[708] According to official statistics, the disease caused about seven million deaths in the whole world during that period.[709] Due to under-reporting of Covid-19 deaths in many countries, the true death toll is estimated to be up to several times higher.[710]

Even though it is not possible to objectively ascertain their number, many of these deaths were preventable. Many of them could have been averted with better access to vaccination[711] or more effective and better-enforced public health measures.[712] Nevertheless, a lot of lives in some of the hard-hit areas were also lost be-

[706] As cited in Wolfgang Mieder, Fred R. Shapiro, Charles Clay Doyle, *The Dictionary of Modern Proverbs* (Yale University Press 2012) 73.

[707] World Health Organization, 'Statement of the fifteenth meeting of the International Health Regulations (2005) Emergency Committee regarding the coronavirus disease (COVID-19 pandemic' (5 May 2023) <https://www.who.int/news/item/05-05-2023-statement-on-the-fifteenth-meeting-of-the-international-health-regulations-(2005)-emergency-committee-regarding-the-coronavirus-disease-(covid-19)-pandemic> accessed 5 May 2023.

[708] Covid-19 was declared a public health emergency of international concern on 30 January 2020. World Health Organization, 'COVID-19 Public Health Emergency of International Concern (PHEIC) Global research and Innovation forum' (12 February 2020) <https://www.who.int/publications/m/item/covid-19-public-health-emergency-of-international-concern-(pheic)-global-research-and-innovation-forum> accessed 5 May 2023.

[709] See World Health Organization, 'WHO Coronavirus (COVID-19) Dashboard' (5 May 2023) <https://covid19.who.int/> accessed 5 May 2023.

[710] See Luke Taylor, 'Covid-19: True global death toll from pandemic is almost 15 million, says WHO' (2022) The BMJ doi: https://doi.org/10.1136/bmj.o1144.

[711] See for example Selena Simmons-Duffin, Koko Nakajima, 'This is how many lives could have been saved with COVID vaccination in each state' (*NPR,* 13 May 2022) <https://www.npr.org/sections/health-shots/2022/05/13/1098071284/this-is-how-many-lives-could-have-been-saved-with-covid-vaccinations-in-each-sta> accessed 5 May 2023.

[712] See for example Howard Schneider, 'U. S. COVID response could have avoided hundreds of thousands of deaths: research' (*Reuters,* 25 March 2021) <https://www.reuters.com/article/us-health-coronavirus-usa-economy-idUSKBN2BH1DK> accessed 5 May 2023.

cause of the depletion of resources in health facilities, especially in intensive care. Health professionals were in many places all over the world forced to make the tragic choices[713] of patient triage, inevitably leading to the death of some patients who might have survived in better circumstances. The approach to this crisis patient prioritisation in various countries is the topic of this book.

We gathered eleven national reports from Europe, North and South America, and Africa. The broad scope of involved countries enables the reader to compare legal and practical approaches from very different parts of the world. As this comparison reveals, regulations of patients' crisis prioritisation are not as clearly differentiated and coherent as in many other areas of law. The approaches converge across countries to a certain degree. The differences do not follow universal patterns and sometimes reflect the countries' legal or cultural peculiarities.

Nevertheless, the common theme is the dominance of extra-legal norms. Even though they are applied on the legal background, their nature is predominantly medical and ethical. The law itself is not directly involved in their formulation, but usually makes them legally relevant by using them as an important substantive source of the standard of care the providers and health professionals are legally obliged to comply with.

Almost all national reports claim that ethical values behind patient prioritisation are in principle utilitarian, sometimes mentioned as consequentialist (Serbia) or described as an effort to save as many lives as possible (Austria, Spain). Only in some countries the principles of medical ethics including beneficence, non-maleficence, respect for autonomy, and justice were cited as the primary concern (France, Portugal, and Switzerland). Nevertheless, practical solutions adopted by these countries were usually very close to utilitarian approach — we may recall the example of the very detailed and strict exclusion criteria for intensive care in Switzerland. On the other hand, the preference for saving the greatest number of lives is also meant to be subjected to certain proportional limits in all countries (as we discuss in more detail in the chapter on legal-ethical grounds of crisis patient prioritisation).[714]

Another almost universal theme is the absence of legal regulation directly focusing on patient prioritisation in a crisis on the level of the whole society. Among the countries involved in this publication, only some US states — and to a certain extent Switzerland — are reported to have had directly applicable legal regulation as of spring 2021. It is understandable that in the chaotic first phases of the pandemic, most countries were not able to enact special legislation on the very specific and sensitive topic of health rationing, however helpful such legislation might have been. Nevertheless, the almost universal absence of more general rules on crisis rationing reveals systematic unpreparedness for calamities whose occurrence cannot be anticipated in specific details, but which are generally foreseeable to strike from time to time.

[713] See Guido Calabresi, *Tragic Choices* (W. W. Norton & Company 1978).

[714] See Martin Šolc, 'Legal-Ethical Grounds of Crisis Patient Prioritisation' in this book.

In this context, it is not surprising that every national report mentions low legal certainty the health professionals and health services providers must face in the rationing of intensive care. It is a direct consequence of missing comprehensive binding regulations on the matter. Only the US report suggests that in some states, the situation is better as specific state executive orders or statutes might apply.

In most countries, health services providers are obliged to provide urgent care to all patients who come to their facilities and need it. On the other hand, their legal systems also allow providers and health professionals to invoke legal defences in case of a legal action or criminal proceedings. Mostly in Germanic legal systems including the Austrian one (but also in Portugal in criminal cases), the defendant may prove that they acted in a conflict of duties, in which it was only possible to fulfil one of these colliding obligations. In various countries, the legal defence would consist in the absence of unlawfulness (Portugal, Serbia, Switzerland) or fault (Portugal, South Africa). A defence of a state of necessity is also cited relatively frequently (Austria, Brazil, Serbia, Spain, South Africa). However, its applicability might be problematic in cases where the doctors need to make a choice between two lives.

A pressing question in a situation of depleted resources may be whether it is legal to lower the standard of care if the normal standard cannot be met in caring for all the additional patients. Most national reports respond to this question in the affirmative. For example, lowering the standard of care is permissible in Italy if it enables better rationing, and in France the standard might be lowered to ensure the continuity of care. The amount of decrease in the standard is, of course, limited, but these limits are defined in rather vague terms: various reports state that the lowering has to be proportional (South Africa), rational (USA), or is permissible if *"a hypothetical reasonable and very diligent professional of the relevant specialization would act the same under the same circumstances"* (Serbia). Nevertheless, in Austria, the lowering of the standard of care that could negatively affect the health or life of a patient is not admissible, even though legal defences might apply. In Switzerland, the lowering of the standard is not regulated. Some reports do not specify the answer (Portugal, Spain), while the Brazilian report is the only one that suggests a rather negative answer.

In many countries the criteria for patient prioritisation are uncertain in a hypothetical case where intensive care can only be provided to one of two patients but all the relevant clinical characteristics of both patients are practically the same. If the clinical criteria cannot be used since both patients are comparable in this respect, what can the allocation decision be based on? Some countries would use random allocation (Austria), chance (Brazil), or lottery (some allocation plans in the USA). Such a decision might be considered ethical as it is purely non-discriminatory. In some other countries, however, lottery (Italy) or even other additional criteria such as the first come, first served rule (Switzerland) are not permitted. Nevertheless, even ethical principles that are sometimes understood as obsolete might still apply in other countries, such as the first come, first served rule in the Czech Republic. The Serbian report interestingly states that in the outlined situation, the decision-making would be left to the health professionals, and it is hard to say what criteria they would use — which might also be the case in many other countries from the practical perspective. French, Portuguese, and Spanish reports admit no specific rules for such cases.

A very controversial question is whether it is permissible to discontinue life-saving treatment so it can be provided to another patient, perhaps with a better chance of survival. This model issue presumes that such care is still appropriate and beneficial for the former patient, but the latter patient's case may seem more promising to the involved health professionals. The Brazilian, Czech, Italian, Portuguese, Serbian, and Spanish reports respond with a decisive rejection — such an action would not be legal. The French report cautiously states that it is *"not ruled as out as a matter of principle"*, while in Austria, the withdrawal of life-saving treatment might be excusable but would be connected with low legal certainty. On the other hand, it would be possible in Switzerland (we may once again recall their detailed and strict utilitarian exclusion guidelines) and some US states (e.g. in New York or Minnesota). Among all the outlined questions, the one of withdrawal of life support seems to create the clearest divide, with answers rather straightforwardly categorised in two opposite groups. Nevertheless, the countries where withdrawal is not permissible — or at least where it would be legally unsafe to do so — seem to form a large majority.

During the Covid-19 pandemic, health systems across the globe faced very similar challenges. A steep increase in the number of patients needing intensive care, arduous hygienic measures and inaccessibility of some materials and equipment forced the health service providers to apply sometimes harsh rationing measures, often without the necessary legal certainty. The crisis revealed that legal systems, whether pertaining to continental or common law legal culture, are as a rule not very well prepared to deal with sudden crisis scenarios. Nothing less was at stake than human lives. Even though there is no universally recognised hierarchy of human rights, the right to life is often understood as the highest value protected by the law, as it is a necessary condition to exercise any other right.[715] Taking into account how extremely sensitive the issue is, it is not surprising that legal systems struggle with addressing it systematically and rationally.

It would be very difficult to suggest any recommendations with an ambition for their universal validity and applicability. However, the endeavour towards clear and specific allocation rules is vitally needed.

There is a consensus, one that only requires basic historical and biological knowledge, that there will be future pandemics.[716] The question is not whether they will come, but when. It may be that the next global contagion will take the form of a new influenza strain, perhaps similar to the Spanish flu which killed tens of

[715] See e.g. Cees Van Dam, *European Tort Law* (Oxford University Press 2006) 143 or *Streletz, Kessler and Krenz v. Germany* App nos 34044/96, 35532/97 and 44801/98 (ECtHR, 22 March 2001) § 87.

[716] See for example Richard Hodson, 'How Can the World Prepare for the Next Pandemic' (*Scientific American,* 15 November 2022) <https://www.scientificamerican.com/article/how-can-the-world-prepare-for-the-next-pandemic/> accessed 4 May 2023.

millions of people a century years ago.[717] However, the number of infectious agents that may potentially cause a pandemic is almost endless. And while attempts are already ongoing to develop artificial intelligence-powered tools to identify the viruses that are likely to spread from animals to humans with pandemic potential,[718] the next contagion might strike at any time.

If the disastrous Covid-19 pandemic brought about anything positive, it was the opportunity to fully realise the danger of epidemics. It reminded the industrially developed world with a painful urgency that infectious diseases continue to be a potent threat to the whole society, just like they have been for the whole human history. No event in the modern history could serve as a better opportunity to initiate the public debate on sensitive, uncomfortable and hard questions related to these issues, to gather political will to make a change, and to take systemic measures to increase preparedness. All the relevant agents could have been involved in commencing this process, including governments, public health bodies, scientific institutions, the media, individual experts and citizens.

However, a short time after the end of the worst phase of the pandemic, it seems that nothing of the above-mentioned is going to happen. Engaging in a meaningful discussion on future pandemics would mean to open wounds from the contemporary one. Instead, many societies seem to take the opposite approach, trying to turn time back before 2020 as if all the horrors of the pandemic can be comfortably contained in a clearly defined part of history.

One of the issues that so desperately need to be addressed is patient prioritisation in a crisis. A lot of experience had been gathered in this regard during the most tragic months of 2020 and 2021. However, as our book clearly shows, the response on the society level was largely chaotic, disunited or even arbitrary. To prevent a similar failure in the future, it will not suffice to have professional medical societies formulate better guidelines. Many crucial questions involved in prioritisation decision-making are not medical in their nature. Is it permissible to weight the value of one life against another, and is it even feasible? Should it be possible to discontinue life-saving treatment even in cases where there still is hope? Who should make the prioritisation decisions and how? By whom and how often should they be revised? These and other similar questions cannot be answered solely by means of science. They rather pertain to the spheres of ethics and philosophy, and if they are to navigate practical decision-making with legal certainty, they need to be reflected by the law.

We do not have to engage here in the eternal discussion on the role of judiciary in the creation of legal norms. Nevertheless, if the rules are meant to provide legal certainty, they must be defined in advance. One of the recurring themes of patient

717 See Niall P. A. S. Johnson, Juergen Mueller, 'Updating the accounts: global mortality of the 1918–1920 'Spanish' influenza pandemic' (2002) 1 Bulletin of the History of Medicine 105–115 doi: https://doi.org/10.1353/bhm.2002.0022.

718 See Simon Makin 'Could an algorithm predict the next pandemic?' (*Nature,* 26 October 2022) <https://www.nature.com/articles/d41586-022-03358-4> accessed 4 May 2023.

prioritisation during the Covid-19 crisis was the cautious approach of health providers who were, for very good reasons, afraid to rely on rules that could potentially be accepted or rejected by the courts in their future case law. For this reason, it is highly commendable when the legislator takes over and enacts the relevant norms.

The content of these norms would ideally concern two basic areas of improvement: measures to increase the robustness of the health care system (which would, however, require a very complex long-term endeavour),[719] and crisis preparedness[720] consisting in pre-definition of crisis decision-making and other necessary processes and creation of suitable institutional framework for their realisation. Considering the topic of this book, we may now focus on the latter issue, particularly on the problem of crisis patient prioritisation.

In the current state of affairs, crisis patient prioritisation has been mostly governed by extra-legal norms, medical and ethical. While some authors question the fundamental distinction between legal and other norms,[721] they crucially differ at least in their relevance for legal certainty. Nevertheless, even in the ideal scenario of an active legislative approach, extra-legal norms would not be simply replaced. Even now, they are to a certain extent incorporated in the legal system: most prominently, professional guidelines often serve as crucial evidence for assessing an alleged breach of a health care provider's duty.[722] Enacting more concrete criteria would ensure that clinicians and providers know which conduct recommended by any guidelines is legal and which conduct might likely be contested in court. An even greater difference would be made by any specific legislation in the realm of ethical norms,[723] most of which can only be understood as broad recommendations in the absence of their explicit legal reflection.

In a manner similar to extra-legal norms, general legal principles can too be applied to clinical decision-making in the absence of specific legislation. The principle according to which nobody can be obliged to do what is impossible *(ad impossibilia nemo tenetur)*[724] *excludes legal liability for not providing intensive care to everyone*

719 See World Health Organization, Health systems resilience toolkit (2022). For a further discussion on the concept of health systems robustness, for example Seye Abimbola, Stephanie M. Topp, 'Adaptation with robustness: the case for clarity on the use of 'resilience' in health systems and global health' (2018) 1 BMJ Global Health doi:https://dx.doi.org/10.1136/bmjgh-2018-000758.

720 See World Health Organization, Toolkit for assessing health-system capacity for crisis management (2012).

721 See the analysis in a classical Joseph Raz's paper: Joseph Raz, 'Legal Principles and the Limits of Law' (1972) 5 The Yale Law Journal 823–854.

722 See Brian Hurwitz, 'How does evidence based guidance influence determinations of medical negligence?' (2004) 7473 The BMJ 1024–1028 doi: https://doi.org10.1136/bmj.329.7473.1024 or Jaako Taipale, Lotta Hautamäki, 'Clinical practice guidelines in courts' representation of medical evidence and testimony' (2011) Social Science & Medicine doi: https://doi.org/10.1016/j.socscimed.2011.113805.

723 For an analysis of ethical aspects of crisis patient prioritisation, see Martin Šolc, 'Legal-Ethical Grounds of Crisis Patient Prioritisation' in this book.

724 See Petr Šustek, Tomáš Holčapek, Martin Šolc, 'Příloha 1: Právní rozbor situace nedostatku vzácných zdrojů v systému zdravotní péče [Appendix 1: Legal Analysis of the Situation of the Lack

who needs it if it is objectively impossible. This principle is not always explicitly mentioned (such as in the Italian report or in the Czech doctrinal discussion of late 2020[725]*), probably because it seems so intuitive and self-evident that it is often automatically assumed. Other legal principles are in line with the principles of applied ethics and may be understood as upholding them from within the legal system: for example, the maxim "do no harm to anyone" (neminem laedere)* can translate to the principle of nonmaleficence as we know it from Beauchamp's and Childress' principles of biomedical ethics.[726]

For health professionals and providers, legal defences as they are generally applied in law have often represented one of very few assurances that they may overcome potential legal actions or prosecution. Among the most cited of these defences in our book is the state of necessity (as mentioned above, it is explicitly mentioned in the Austrian, Brazilian, Serbian, Spanish and South African reports). However, the scope of application of this defence may differ from country to country. One of the most pressing questions in the context of patient prioritisation is whether the state of necessity can be applied to a situation when one human life is exchanged for another.

While this question needs to be addressed in each jurisdiction *de novo*, we may assume that the state of necessity cannot generally be used if it caused more harm that would have otherwise been occurred. For example, this is an explicit part of Czech law, which clearly states that the state of necessity can only be applied if the consequence caused by the agent's action is neither as serious nor more serious than the one which had threatened.[727]

It is interesting that more than forty years ago, the then-Czechoslovak case law[728] came to a conclusion that the state of necessity might apply to cases when one human life was sacrificed to save a greater number of lives. The source case of this principle was, however, very unique with its utterly tragic and reprehensible circumstances. It arose from an unhappy marriage in which an aggressive man terrorised his family. Amidst the ongoing conflicts, the wife left for another part of the country. Since the husband did not have enough money to travel after her, he asked his mother-in-law, but she refused to help him. The man then forced his children

of Scarce Resources in the Health System]' (2020) 5 *Anesteziologie a intenzivní medicína* 254.

[725] See Tomáš Doležal, 'Konflikt povinností jako okolnost vylučující protiprávnost – východisko pro úvahy o možné prioritizaci pacientů v případě nedostatku zdrojů [Conflict of Duties as a Legal Defence — A Starting Point for Consideration of Possible Patient Prioritisation in the Event of the Lack of Resources]' (*Zdravotnické právo a bioetika,* 2 November 2020) <https://zdravotnickepravo.info/konflikt-povinnosti-jako-okolnost-vylucujici-protipravnost-vychodisko-pro-uvahy-o-mozne-prioritizaci-pacientu-v-pripade-nedostatku-zdroju/> accessed 4 May 2023.

[726] See Tom L. Beauchamp, James F. Childress, *Principles of Biomedical Ethics* (7th edn, Oxford University Press 2013), or Martin Šolc, 'Legal-Ethical Grounds of Crisis Patient Prioritisation' in this book.

[727] Section 2906 of Act No. 89/2012 Coll., the Civil Code, and Section 28 of Act No. 40/2009 Coll., the Criminal Code.

[728] The Supreme Court of the Slovak Socialist Republic judgment 3 To 72/80 (R 20/1982 tr.).

to strangle the woman (their grandmother) to death under the threat that he would kill them all. At the time of the murder, the oldest daughter was already criminally liable. The court, however, applied the state of necessity to the case. As the court explained, the loss of one life is a less serious consequence than the death of several persons.

The said conclusion is controversial on its own and it is not difficult to imagine situations where it would be in collision with constitutional limits. For example, a physician cannot legally hasten the death of a patient only to harvest organs that can save the lives of several transplant recipients. Such an action might be tempting to some. A Czech doctor who would kill a patient in this hypothetical situation might try to invoke the above-mentioned court decision as a defence in court. However, it would be extremely controversial for the court to apply the state of necessity to such a case, diminishing the right to life and circumventing all the special legislation on transplantation medicine and provision of health services. Remembering the uniquely terrifying circumstances of the said murder case, we may legitimately ask whether it is not an example of those very specific cases that are famously difficult to use for defining general rules, a principle that common law lawyers aptly summarise in a saying that *hard cases make bad law*.[729]

In the context of intensive care rationing, the explained legal defence can only hardly work. While we may construct a possible model situation in which the physicians would reasonably presume that a patient's death would free resources for saving more lives, it is very unlikely for such a case to happen in practice. As a rule, withdrawal of life sustaining treatment simply enables health professionals to use the resources for one other patient. The uncertainty of how long the latter patient will use these resources means that one life is exchanged for one life. The consequence — the death of a patient who would otherwise still have some (albeit low) chance of survival — is therefore as serious as the imminent threat (the death of another patient). In countries that define it in a way similar to Czech law, the state of necessity does not apply to such cases.

The more general legal principles, such as the above-mentioned maxim that nobody is obliged to the impossible or the conflict of duties (so widely used in Germanic jurisdictions), can uphold the legality of the rationing decisions just to a certain extent. While they explicitly justify the inevitable conclusion that when resources are depleted, some patients will not be given the otherwise adequate care, they still do not add anything to answering the crucial question: what rules can be used to make a decision which particular patient will receive suboptimal care?

However important the legal principles and relevant extra-legal norms are, they are simply not able to functionally replace specific legal regulation. When the next health crisis comes — be it caused by a pandemic, climate change or any other event — we will fall into the same chaos and preventable loss of lives as in early 2020 unless we do find enough courage to discuss the most painful questions even

[729] See Bryan A. Garner (eds) *Black's Law Dictionary.* 11th ed (Thomson Reuters 2019) 860–861.

when times are better. By failing to enhance our preparedness, we are failing to use a unique opportunity provided by the pandemic. We are failing to make the tragedy of 2020 and 2021 be at least a bit meaningful. We are preparing to fail again.

INDEX

A

allocation criteria

–, age AU[730]: 18, 32; BR: 44, 49, 51; FR: 76, 82, 83, 85–87; IT: 92, 93, *98*[731], 101; PT: 110, 122–124; SE: 131–133, 135, 136, 141, *147*–150; SA: 156, *165*, 168; SP: 174, 175, 178, 181, 183, 188; SW: 197–200, *208*, 210, 211, 213; US:222–224, 236, 238, 240

–, chances / likelihood / probability of survival / prognosis AU: 20–24, 27–30, 32–36; BR: 44, 45, 49, 51, 53, 54; FR: 76, 85, 87; IT: 92, 101; PT: 108, 109, 121, 123, 125; SE: 132–136, 141, 142, 148–151; SA: 157, 169; SP: 178, 179, 181, 185; SW: 198, 199, 210, 212, 213; US: 219, 220, 222–224, 236–240

–, comorbidities BR: 45, 51, 54; FR: 76, 83, 85, 87; IT: 92, 98, 101; SE: 132, 134–136, 148–150; SA: 157, 169; SP: 182, 183; SW: 198, 199, 210, 211

–, equity AU: 28, 30–33, 36; BR: 44, 45, 49, 52; FR: 76; PT: 124; SE: 145; SP: 180, 181; SW: 197, 199, 200; US: 219, 221, 222, 236

–, frailty / (clinical) fragility / clinical frailty score / CFS AU: 23, 32, 34, 35; BR: *49*, 52, *53*; FR: 76, *82*, 83, 85–87; IT: *98*, *101*; PT: *122*, 124, *125*; SE: 132, 147–150; SA: 156, *165*, 168, *169*; SP: 188; SW: 198, 199, *208*, 209, *213*; US: 220, *236*, 238

–, order of arrival / precedence AU: 21, 32; IT: 93; PT: 110, 123, 125; SE: 129, 134, 135; SA: 168; SW: 201

–, random / drawing lots / raffle / lottery AU: 21, 29, 32, 34; BR: 44, 49, 52; IT: 92; SW: 206; US: 220, 222, 236, 238

–, social role BR: 44; FR: 86; IT: 92, 93, 101; SA: 158; SP: 179, 187, 190

–, state of health / urgency of treatment AU: 17, 18, 21, 22, 25, 32, 33; FR: 78; IT: 93; PT: 110, 113, 123; SA: 160, 162; SW: 202

artificial ventilation (see ventilation)

B

burden of proof

IT: 96, 99; PT: 119; SE: 143, 144; SA: 164, 166; US: 228

C

care / treatment / surgery

–, discontinuation / stopping / withdrawal of AU: 22, 24, *35*, 36; BR: 53; FR: 82, *87*; IT: 101, 102; PT: *125*; SE: *150*, 151; SA: *169*; SW: 199, 212, 213; US: 236, *238*, 239

–, elective AU: 18, 25, 33; BR: 43; SW: 200, 203

–, emergency BR: 46; SE: 131, 133, 136, 137, 141; SA: 162; SW: 204; US: 220, 226–228

–, intensive AU: 20, 22–24, 27, 28, 34, 35; BR: 43, 44; IT: 91, 95; PT: 108, 110, 123, 124; SE: 130, 132, 133, 141; SW: 197, 198, 200–203, 206, 210, 212, 213

730 AU = Austria, BR = Brazil, FR = France, IT = Italy, PT = Portugal, SA = South Africa, SE = Serbia, SP = Spain, SW = Switzerland, US = USA.

731 Vyznačení stránky kurzívou znamená, že je termín obsažen pouze v textu případu či v otázce dle formuláře.

– –, care unit / ICU AU: 17, 18, 20, 22, 23, 25, 27, 28, *32*, 34–36; BR: 43, 45, 49, *51*; FR: 76, 81, *82, 85*; IT: 92, 93, 96, *98, 100*; PT: *122, 124;* SE: 132, 142, *147*, 148–150; SA: 155–157, *165, 167,* 169; SP: 178–183, 185, 186, 188, 191; SW: 197–204, 206, *208*, 209–213; US: *235, 237*
–, life-saving AU: 24; IT: 102; SA: 162; US: 220, 224
–, minimum AU: 26; FR: 78
–, palliative AU: 18, *35*; BR: *53*; FR: 76, 86, *87*; IT: *101*; PT: *125*; SE: 134, *150*; SA: *169*; SP: 186; SW: 197, 213; US: 236, *238*, 239
–, planned / scheduled AU: 18, 25, 26; IT: 99; PT: 108, 111
–, postponement / suspension of AU: 20, 26, 33; BR: 43; PT: 106, 125; SW: 203
–, standard of care (see separate term)
case-law AU: 18, 30, 31, 33, 36; FR: 82, 84; IT: 103; SE: 153; SA: 170; SP: 188, 193; SW: 205, 208, 215
–, Constitutional Court IT: 95; SA: 161, 162; SP: 174, 175, 177
–, Council of State / Highest Administrative Court FR 79–81, 83, 84, 88
–, Court of Appeal FR: 82
– current IT: 98
–, European Court of Human Rights AU: 18
–, Federal Court SW: 201
–, Supreme Court / Court of Cassation / Supreme Court of Cassation AU: 19, 27, 38; BR: 41, 47; FR: 82, 88; SE: 143; SP 190, 193
causal link / criterion / causation AU: 31, 36; IT: 96; PT: 117, 119; SA: 164; SE: 141, 144
close / dependent persons AU: 32; SA: (see also family members); SP: 188; SW: 199
compensation AU: 31, 32; FR: 81; IT: 96; SE: 144, 145; SP: 176, 191
–, equitable (for reasons of equity / on the grounds of equity) AU: 32; SE: 144, 145, 147
–, for breach of contract AU: 31
–, for loss of profits BR: 49
–, for loss of support and maintenance BR: 49; SE: 145; SA: 164;
–, for provided health care US: 228
–, for psychological pain / suffering AU: 32; SE: 137
–, reduction of SE: 145
consent AU: 18; IT: 95, 96; SE: 132, 140; SA: 156; US: 227, 239, 240

D

damages AU: 28, 30, 32, 33, 36; BR: 49, 50; IT: 96, 99, 100; PT: 114, 117–119; SE: 143, 145, 147 (see also compensation); SW: 208; US: 228, 235
–, action for SE: 143, 146
–, civil US: 228
–, emerging BR: 49
–, moral BR: 49
–, property BR: 49
–, secondary US: 235
death AU: 27, 31–33, 36; BR: 51, 53; FR 77; IT: 93, 97, 98, 102; PT: 105, 106, 109, 120; SE: 132, 134, 140, 141, 144, 151; SA: 156, 164; SP: 188; SW: 209; US: 217, 223, 231, 232, 235, 240
–, probability of BR: 51, 53
defence (see legal defence)
defensive medicine IT: 96
discrimination / non-discrimination / discriminatory AU: 22, 35; BR: 46; FR: 75, 79, 82, 85, 87; SE 132, 151; SP: 174, 175, 180, 181, 188; SW: 197, 200, 208; US: 222–224, 236, 237, 240

E

emergency situation / state of emergency AU: 19, 24, 33; BR: 42; FR: 76, 78; IT: 91, 95, 97, 98; PT: 110, 113, 115, 131; SE: 135–137, 141, 147; SA: 162, 166, 167; SP: 182, 184, 188, 190; US: 226–228, 231
exceptional circumstance FR: 76, 77, 80, 84, 85; IT: 92; SP: 182

European Convention on Human Rights AU: 18, 22
euthanasia IT: 102; SW: 201

F

failure
– to act AU: 31, 33; SE: 144
– to continue treatment AU: 31
– to help / to provide assistance / to save life / to rescue BR: 48, 52; FR: 82; PT: 120; SE: 140, 145; US: 233
– to perform IT: 94
– to treat SP: 189
family members / relatives AU: 28, 29; BR: 45, 52; IT: 94, 96; PT: 110; SE: 143, 144; SW: 209; US: 218, 235, 239

H

homicide BR: 52; PT: 120; SA: 163, 164; SP: 189
hospital
–, private / profit-orientated AU: 17, 18, 25, 26, 28, 32, 33; IT: 94; PT: 107, 116; SE: 143; SA: 159, 162; SP: 191; US: 219, 225, 226
–, public / non-profit AU: 17–26, 28, 32, 33; FR: 78; IT: 94; PT: 107, 116; SA: 159, 161, 162; SP: 187, 188, 191; US: 217
–, transfer between (see transfer)

I

improvised beds / settings AU: 26, *32*; BR: *49*; FR: *82*; IT: *98*; PT: *122*; SE: 133, *147*; SA: *166*; SW: *208*; US: *236*
informed consent (see consent)
injunction AU: 30
insurance
–, health SE: 137, 143
–, liability AU: 28, 31, 32; SE: 145
–, overexposure IT: 96
–, private SE: 130; SP: 188
–, social AU: 19; PT: 106
intent AU: 29, 32, 36; BR: 47, 48, 50; FR: 82; IT: 99; PT: 113, 117, 119; SE: 139, 141, 143, 144; SA: 164; US: 232–234

L

law
–, administrative PT: 117
–, civil AU: 23, 27, 28, 30, 31, 33, 36; BR: 48, 52; PT: 113; SE: 138, 148; SA: 163, 164, 166; SW: 208; US: 223
–, constitutional SA: 159
–, criminal AU: 21, 23, 27, 28, 30, 31, 33, 34, 36; BR : 47, 48, 50, 52; FR: 82, 84; PT: 113–115, 120, 122, 126; SE: 140, 142, 151; SA: 164, 166; SP: 189; SW: 206, 208
–, medical FR: 81
–, soft FR: 80, 81, 85; PT: 113
–, tort AU: 27, 31; SA: 164; SE: 145; SP: 188
legal defence AU: *33, 34, 36;* BR: *50, 52*; FR: *86, 87;* IT: *99, 101;* PT: *123, 124, 125;* SE: *148, 149, 151;* SA: *166, 168, 170;* SW: *211, 213, 214;* US: *236, 238, 240*
–, conflict of duties AU: 27–29, 33; PT: 120–123; SE: 141; SW: 204, 207
–, impossibility of performance IT: 94, 96, 100; SE: 146
–, necessity (state of) AU: 27, 28, 30, 33, 34, 36; BR: 50, 52; FR: 81; IT: 94, 99; PT: 111, 114, 115, 121; SE: 147; SA: 166, 167; SP: 189
–, self-defence AU: 28, 29
–, technical problems of special difficulty IT: 99
lege artis (see standard of care)
liability
–, administrative FR: 77, 80
–, civil AU: 30–32, 36; BR: 47, 48, 50; FR: 77, 80; IT: 92, 94, 96; PT: 111, 116, 118, 120, 123, 126; SE: 132, 137, 139, 143, 151; SA: 163–166; SW: 206–208; US: 226, 228, 231–233, 235, 236, 239, 240
–, contractual AU: 27, 31; IT: 95, 96; SE: 146
–, criminal AU: 31; BR: 47, 48; FR: 77, 80, 81, 83; IT: 92, 94, 96, 97, 99; PT: 116, 117, 120, 122, 123; SE: 132, 137–142,

151; SA: 163–166; SW: 206–208; US: 232, 233, 236, 239, 240
–, disciplinary FR: 80; SE: 137, 139
–, joint PT: 117; SE: 143
–, negligent SP: 190
–, objective / strict BR: 50; IT: 100; PT: 118; SE: 145; US: 233
–, professional / medical FR: 80, 81, 83, 84; IT: 97, 99; SE: 137; SP: 188
–, release from (see legal defence)
–, subjective / fault-based BR: 47, 48; FR: 80, 84; IT: 94; PT: 118, 123; SE: 145
–, tortious / delict / non-contractual AU: 27, 31; BR: 47; IT: 96; PT: 116; SE: 143, 145, 146; SA: 164; SW: 207
–, vicarious SE: 143, 144; SA: 164

M

medical students BR: 43; SE: 134, 135
Ministry / Department of Health BR: 42, 43, 46; PT: 108–110; SA: 158, 159; SP: 184; US: 223, 224, 229, 230
murder AU: 31, 36; BR: 48; IT: 102; SE: 141

N

negligence AU: 31, 32; BR: 47, 48; IT: 96, 97, 99; PT: 117; SE: 137, 139–148; SA: 164–166; SP: 190; US: 228, 232–234
–, gross AU: 32; BR: 47; IT: 99; PT: 117; SE: 143; US: 228, 232, 234, 278

P

pharmaceutical / medical products / drugs FR: 80, 84; IT: 100; PT: 112; SW: 202; US: 231
physical / bodily integrity AU: 27; IT: 102; PT: 115, 120, 121; SE: 141, 145; SA: 166, 167; SP: 175
proportionality FR: 79, 82; PT: 110, 123; SA: 167; SP: 180; US: 221
prioritisation AU: 18, 22, 25; FR: 76, 85; PT: 107, 108, 113; SE: 129, 130, 134; SA: 161; SW: 205, 206; US: 219–222

R

recommendations / guidelines
–, of medical academy SW: 197–201, 205–213
–, of medical association BR: 44; PT: 109, 110, 122, 124; SE: 132, 133, 136
–, of medical commission / board AU: 20, 22, 24, 25, 35, 36; BR: 46, 47, 51; SP: 178, 181
–, of medical council BR: 43, 45, 46; FR: 77; SE: 133
–, of medical society AU: 20–25, 30, 32, 35–37; FR: 77, 80; IT: 92, 93, 95, 98, 99; SA: 155–169; SP: 178, 179, 182; SW: 201
–, of state PT: 108, 110; US: 219, 220, 222, 223, 225
right
–, economic, social and cultural PT: 112; SA: 159, 161
–, suspension of PT: 115
–, to dignity FR: 78; PT: 120, 121, 124; SA: 160, 166; SE 131
–, to equal treatment SP: 174, 185; SW: 197
–, to freedom PT: 115
–, to health (protection) / treatment BR: 41, 46, 48; FR: 78, 81, 84; IT: 91, 99, 100; PT: 112, 116; SE: 135, 136; SA: 159, 160, 162, 167; SP: 174, 175, 187
–, to life AU: 18, 22; BR: 48; PT: 120; SA: 162
–, to physical integrity PT: 115, 120, 121; SA: 166, 167
–, to respect for private and family life AU: 18

S

standard of care / (medical) state of the art AU: 18, 24, 26; IT: 94; PT: 118; SE: 130, 131, 133, 134, 136, 138, 139, 142; SA: 165; US: 219, 226–228, 232, 233, 236–238
–, lowering AU: 33; BR: *51*; FR: *84*; IT: *100*; PT: *123*; SE: *148*, 149; SA: 167; SW: *211*; US: *236*

T

transfer
–, between hospitals AU: 19, 25, 26; BR: 46; FR: 76, 85; SP: 183; SW: 203, 212, 213; US: 220, 227
–, of resources AU: 21, 23, 27; PT: 122
triage AU: 18–37; BR: 44, 53; FR: 75, 79–81, 83, 84; IT: 92, 93; PT: 125; SE: 130, 132, 133, 138, 142, 148–150; SA: 155–158; SP: 173–175, 178, 181–185, 187, 189, 191; SW: 197–201, 205–208, 211–213; US: 220, 221
–, criteria (see allocation criteria)
–, ex-ante / on admission AU: 23–25, 27, 28, 30, 31, 33–36; SE: 132, 148, 149; SP: 189; SW: 203
–, ex-post AU: 21, 23–25, 27–31, 35–37 (see also discontinuation of care); SP: 189
–, team SA 155–157, 169; SW: 206; US: 221

U

utilitarianism AU: 15, 22; BR: 44; FR: 75; IT: 92, 93, 98, 101; SP: 181; SA: 158; SP: 180–182, 186, 191; US: 221, 222, 239

V

ventilation AU: 22, 26, 34; BR: 43, 44, 46, 51; FR: 85; IT: 96, 100, 105; PT: 121, 122, 123–125; SE: 130, 132, 142, 146, 148–151; SA: 156, 168; SP: 179, 187, 189, 191; SW: 200, 209, 210, 212; US: 217, 220, 223, 237, 238–240

www.ingramcontent.com/pod-product-compliance
Lightning Source LLC
Chambersburg PA
CBHW071242230926
51849CB00001B/198
9789403529486